A History of the
East Lancashire Royal Engineers

A HISTORY OF THE
EAST LANCASHIRE
ROYAL ENGINEERS

COMPILED BY
MEMBERS OF THE CORPS

PRINTED FOR PRIVATE CIRCULATION

PREFACE

IN producing this volume so long after the Great War terminated, the editors feel that some explanation of the delay is due. Work on this history was begun immediately after the Armistice in November 1918. Official war diaries and individual memories were ransacked for material, but long before the results could be collected and collated those who had undertaken the work were dispersed, and involved afresh in the duties of civil life. The editors, no less busy than others, were thus compelled to correspond by post with the several authors, to get their narratives criticized by others, dates checked and conflicting versions reconciled—operations more tedious even than they sound.

Almost every reader will call to mind unrecorded incidents worthy of inclusion here. Full use has been made of all matter actually contributed, and the omissions are therefore unavoidable. It will be seen, moreover, that certain facts are on record in more than one part of the book, but this is due to the arrangement of the history, which surveys separately the careers of the two Divisional R.E. groups, and, in the case of that of the 42nd Division, of each of the component units also. The continual variation in the style of writing throughout the book serves to illustrate the number of authors who assisted. It is to them and to those who have given their spare time in reading manuscripts, correcting errors and suggesting anecdotes—a body of helpers too many to quote by name—that the editors' thanks are offered.

Publishing costs to-day are high, and at the sale price fixed this work will hardly pay for itself. Should it do so, any profit will be handed to the East Lancs. R.E. Association, but if—as is more likely—there is a loss on the production, Colonel W. J. Galloway, the Honorary Colonel of the East Lancs. R.E., has very generously offered to make it good. Our best thanks are due to him for this proposal, but it behoves every past or present member of the Corps to help in selling the whole of the copies published, and thus make the venture as nearly as possible self-supporting.

It is only right that memories of the part played by the East Lancs. R.E. in the war should be kept alive. If this history helps to do this; if, moreover, it brings pleasure to those who served in that Corps and to their friends, and especially if it brings some little comfort to the relatives of those who served but did not return, it has not been written in vain.

Manchester, 1920.

CONTENTS

BEFORE THE WAR

THE 3RD EAST LANCASHIRE ROYAL ENGINEERS (VOLUNTEERS), AND THE EAST LANCASHIRE ROYAL ENGINEERS PRIOR TO AUGUST, 1914. BY COL. H. T. CROOK, V.D. . . xi

WAR HISTORY

PART I

DIARY OF MOVEMENTS, 42ND DIVISIONAL ROYAL ENGINEERS . . 1

PART II

A SUMMARY OF THE WAR HISTORY OF THE 42ND DIVISIONAL ROYAL ENGINEERS (1914–1919) 21

PART III

THE 427TH FIELD COMPANY, ROYAL ENGINEERS (1914–1919) 47

CHAP.
I. EGYPT AND GALLIPOLI 49
II. EGYPT AND SINAI 62
III. FRANCE (MARCH 1917–MARCH 1918) 68
IV. FRANCE (MARCH 1918–APRIL 1919) 77

PART IV

THE 428TH FIELD COMPANY, ROYAL ENGINEERS (1914–1919) 91

CHAP.
I. EGYPT AND GALLIPOLI 93
II. EGYPT AND SINAI 114
III. FRANCE (MARCH 1917–MARCH 1918) 118
IV. FRANCE (MARCH 1918–APRIL 1919) 133

CONTENTS

PART V

THE 429TH FIELD COMPANY, ROYAL ENGINEERS (1915–1919)   151

CHAP.
   I. EGYPT AND SINAI 153
  II. FRANCE (MARCH 1917–MARCH 1918) 166
 III. FRANCE (MARCH 1918–APRIL 1919) 182

PART VI

THE 42ND DIVISIONAL SIGNAL COMPANY (1914–1919) . . 197

PART VII

DIARY OF MOVEMENTS, 66TH DIVISIONAL ROYAL ENGINEERS (1917–1919) 221

PART VIII

THE 66TH DIVISIONAL ROYAL ENGINEERS (1914–1919) . . 227

PART IX

A BRIEF NOTE ON THE 3RD LINE EAST LANCS. ROYAL ENGINEERS 257

ROLL OF HONOUR 263

HONOURS AND AWARDS 266

LIST OF ILLUSTRATIONS

	Facing page
ACHI BABA	26
GULLY RAVINE	27
SAILLY AU BOIS CHURCH	44
HAUTMONT	44
LA BASSÉE SECTOR	232
NIEUPORT	232
NIEUPORT BAINS AND RIVER YSER	233
YPRES	234
ZONNEBEKE CHURCH	234

BEFORE THE WAR

INTRODUCTORY

THE Territorial Force has now been tested in the greatest war the world has known. Throughout the long and devastating struggle it has worthily borne its part. In the widespread conflict there is scarce an arena in which it has not been represented. Its soldiers have fought and bled on the desert sands of Asia and Africa, amidst the tepes and gullies of Gallipoli, in the marshes of Flanders, on the rolling lands of Picardy and Artois, by the mountains of Judæa, of Macedonia and the Alps, or stood guard by the waters of Indus and Ganges.

The time being come to set forth the story of its valour and endurance, of its trials and sufferings, of its heroic dead, of its honours and awards, it has been thought fitting that the section of the great story which details the doings of the 42nd and 66th Divisional R.E. should have as preface some notice of the pre-war history of the parent Corps and its progenitor the 3rd Lancashire R.E. (Vols.). Though the tale of peace-time may appear but tame beside that of the episodes of war which follow, yet it may be of some interest to trace the origin and development of the Royal Engineer forces of those divisions which have earned so great renown.

The Territorial Force Act of 1907 brought into being but few new units. Its practical effect was the reconstitution and reorganization, under a new name, of the existing Volunteer Force. The scheme for the Territorial Force could hardly have succeeded but for that sense of patriotic duty kept alive for so many years by the Volunteers. The willing acceptation of the full duty of citizenship when none was bound to such service was, and is now as much as ever, necessary to its existence. Certainly it would never have shown that cohesion, that *esprit de corps*, and that will to succeed, had not the soul of the old force passed into the new.

THE 3RD LANCASHIRE ROYAL ENGINEERS (VOLS.)

The 3rd Lancashire R.E. (Vols.) had not so long a history as the other units from which the East Lancashire Territorial Division was built up. Its creation was due primarily to that crisis in the South African War, early in the year 1900, when the Government asked for active service contingents from the Volunteers, and at the same time made a considerable increase in the establishment of the force. Manchester being so great a centre of engineering and kindred industries, it was at once suggested that locally the increase, or a large part of it, should take the form of an Engineer Corps, as that would give to numbers of its citizens the opportunity of bringing to the service of the State their special knowledge and skill. The idea met with so much favour, especially amongst the students of the Municipal School of Technology, that Mr. Reynolds, the Principal, convened a public meeting to consider what steps should be taken to found a Corps.

This meeting, held on the 31st March, 1900, resulted in the establishment of a Formation Committee, of which Mr. Thos. Craven was Chairman and Mr. F. C. Forth the Hon. Secretary. The Committee was thoroughly representative of the engineering profession and employers in the engineering, building, and allied trades of the district, as well as of the technical departments of the municipalities of Manchester and Salford.

The work of the Committee was so successful, that by the beginning of May, more than 900 applications to join the proposed Corps had been received. On the 16th of May, 1900, the offer of service was submitted to the then Secretary of State for War, Lord Lansdowne.

There seemed every reason to expect that the offer would be at once accepted, coming as it did at a time when the Government had determined upon an increase in the Volunteer Force, and from a region so favourably circumstanced for the raising of an Engineer Corps, and where, also, it would complete the representation of the different branches of the service. But it was far otherwise. The promoters had to struggle through a long and dreary period of negotiation, of reports, minutes, and interviews; first, to convince the authorities that the proposed Corps would be composed of officers and men qualified by their vocations for the engineer service, and secondly, after it had been intimated that the offer might be accepted, to obtain an establishment large enough to give the new Corps the chance of earning by its efficiency, sufficient grants to maintain it after the formation and first year's expenses had been met from privately subscribed funds.

It was not until November that the War Office notified that a Corps of eight companies would be sanctioned. The illness and death of Queen Victoria caused further delay, but the first military gazette of King Edward's reign, 15th February, 1901, contained the following announcement—

"The King has approved the formation of a Corps of Volunteer Engineers designated the 3rd Lancashire Royal Engineers (Volunteers)."

And in a subsequent issue—

"Major H. T. Crook from the 1st Lancashire R.E. (Vols.) to be Lieut.-Colonel and to command under para. 55a Vol. Regs., dated 28th February, 1901."

BEFORE THE WAR xiii

The long period of uncertainty was at last at an end, but it had not been without effect upon the list of applicants for enrolment, some of whom, tired of waiting, had joined other units, though fortunately most of the best qualified had awaited the issue.

On the 23rd April, Captain R. A. McNab was appointed Acting Adjutant, and 2nd Corporal Sizer, R.E., joined for duty as Instructor.

The Commanding Officer having now obtained a staff of two, all those who had applied to be enrolled and others interested were invited to a meeting at the Memorial Hall on the 29th of April. At the conclusion of the meeting enrolment was commenced. By the end of May, twelve officers had been appointed, and the total strength had attained to 252. During the month the house at Seymour Grove was taken for the Headquarters, and the first general assembly of the Corps took place there on the 24th, though drills had previously commenced at the Albert Street Police Yard. From that time progress was rapid, the strength at the conclusion of the Volunteer year being 402, of whom 351 were returned as efficient; a creditable record after only six months' existence, signifying frequent attendance and close application by recruits almost all new to military work. In those early days there was no drill hall, and other accommodation was very inferior to that of the older established units. But working mainly in the open and at high pressure was a necessity if the Corps was to succeed. The system on which the State supplied the funds to the Volunteers was peculiar in its operation in the case of a new formation. The capitation grant was said to be paid in advance on the 1st of April in each year, with the proviso that no part of it was to be expended in meeting any obligations incurred before that date. The amount of the grant was based upon the number of efficients at the conclusion of the Volunteer year on the 31st of the preceding October. Now as the Corps was not in existence in 1900 it is obvious that it could not show any efficients for that year. The Treasury would not listen to the appeal that the grants for 1901 should be allowed on the basis of the figures for that year, consequently the cost of the first year's work had to be found from private sources. The Formation Committee and its friends amongst the Engineers and kindred professions and industries raised a fund of some £8000 towards the cost of establishing the Corps and of providing it with quarters. Without the public spirit thus displayed success could hardly have been attained. How productive that initial success was to be in its subsequent developments none could foresee, but to which the pages of the history of the 42nd and 66th Divisional R.E. now bear witness.

In the spring of 1902, the visit of King George, then Prince of Wales, to Manchester (12th March) gave the Corps its first opportunity of participating in the ceremonial of a royal event. On this occasion it furnished the Guard of Honour at Victoria Station, and lined the route in Cross Street and Albert Square.

Three years later it was to enjoy a similar privilege, when on the 13th July, 1905, King Edward, accompanied by Queen Alexandra, came to Manchester to open the new Docks, the Corps had the distinction of furnishing the Guard of Honour at the Docks and of lining the route on the Broadway approach. At the conclusion of his inspection of the Guard, His Majesty was pleased to express his gratification upon viewing this representation of the first military body created in his reign.

In the early months of 1902 close attention was required to the preparation for Camp. The training took place at Ilkley from the 17th to the 25th May, when eighty per cent. of the strength, at that time 517, attended. The arrangements for and programme of the camp training of Engineers was always an onerous task for those responsible, for they were beset by difficulties—difficulties most of which remained even after the Territorial conversion, being more or less special to the particular service.

The first was that of finding a suitable site, one which would give opportunities for the practice of military engineering in its various forms. To find a site by a river or other obstacle for bridging exercise was perhaps the easiest part, as to obtain the use of land for "digging" was the hardest. The mere mention of the latter sometimes led to the abrupt termination of negotiations with landlord or tenant; it was "taboo" even on Salisbury Plain.

Time and distance were involved in the second difficulty. The greater the work accomplished in the early days of the training the greater the time required for dismantling. For the Volunteer Camps allowances could only be drawn for eight days, and the amount admissible towards the cost of conveyance of stores limited the choice of sites to a radius of seventy miles. A curious effect of the operation of the regulations applying to travelling allowances, was that the nearer the approximation to this distance the more favourable the result.

An eight days' Camp, after deducting the Sunday, the days of arrival and departure and the time for dismantling, left but four days for the essential part of the training. By deferring the departure of the troops to the second Sunday the duration of that part could be increased by twenty-five per cent. It was for this reason that the 3rd Lancs. R.E. in its seven camps under the Vol. Regs., always went out for nine days. It had, however, to do the nine days on eight days' grants and allowances. True, on one occasion, when Mr. Arnold Forster was Secretary for War, it drew the grants for the nine days, but in the following year, under his successor, it was refused, and after a long fight with the Treasury the extra grant for the year before had to be refunded.

The third difficulty was that of the provision of sufficient technical equipment and stores for instructional purposes. The quantity of material of this nature provided by Government was quite inadequate, especially in bridging requirements, and not only inadequate in quantity, but in strength and suitability for use in the structures in which they were intended to be employed. This difficulty was to a great extent overcome by the purchase from time to time from private funds of a quantity of extra stores, so that by the end of its career as a Volunteer Corps the 3rd Lancs. was probably better equipped in this respect than any other. " How do you come to be possessed of all these stores ? " was the query put at more than one Annual Inspection by the officer appointed for that duty.

With this better equipment works of military engineering, even of the larger size, could be carried out, completed and fit for practical use, thus adding greatly to the interest and value of the instruction.

What could be done in this way, and done well in quick time, was demonstrated in the early days of the Corps' existence by the construction of a composite bridge, 150 feet in length, across the Irwell at Peel Park one Saturday afternoon, 11th October, 1902.

The following table shows the locality of and the attendance at the subsequent training camps of the Volunteer period—

1903, Ilkley, 30th May to 7th June, 496 = 84 per cent. of strength.
1904, Ruthin, 21st to 29th May, 469 = 83½ per cent of strength.
1905, Ilkley, 10th to 18th June, 455 = 82½ per cent. of strength.
1906, Denton (Ilkley), 2nd to 10th June, 446 = 81 per cent. of strength.
1907, Ballahot (I.O.M.), 18th to 26th May, 524 = 82 per cent. of strength.

The proportion of attendance shown by these figures is high even for East Lancashire, which in comparison with other parts of the kingdom has always held a distinguished position. It will be seen that all these Trainings were held at Whitsuntide. It has been and is still urged that this time is too early in the year, for the reason that the recruits of the new year being required to attend a certain number of drills to qualify for Camp, the later the Training be deferred the better the chances for a good attendance. But the experience of later years, when camps were held in August, scarcely supports this view, for there are other circumstances, local and general, to be taken into account in determining the best date for Training.

The Camp of 1907 was the largest of any of the Volunteer Camps, for the reason that the Corps was then approaching the greatest strength to which it ever attained; this, the last completed year of its Volunteer constitution, closed with a membership of 682. The highest figure previously reached was 642 at the end of 1903. The next year (1904) showed a fall to 582, due to the considerable exodus of men who had completed their three years' engagement, whilst the number of recruits was about normal. In theory, or according to law, the Volunteer could resign at any time upon giving a fortnight's notice to his Commanding Officer, but in practice the absurdity of this relation was circumvented by making it one of the rules of the Corps, and the rules of the Corps were sanctioned by authority, that every man joining must undertake to serve for three years, or pay a fine sufficient to recoup the cost incurred in clothing and equipping him.

The records of 1905 show that the loss and gain in numbers about balanced. During 1906 the rise towards the culminating point began; the main factor contributing to this result was undoubtedly the large extensions to the Headquarters. Although the house and land in Seymour Grove were suitable and convenient, for certain purposes the accommodation was very limited, and that essential adjunct, a drill hall, was wanting.

From the start the promoters of the Corps had realized that it must be provided with quarters of a character at least equal to that of other units in the district. The necessary expenditure, however, could not be faced without the assistance of a Government loan. In the circumstances of the comparative youth of the Corps to obtain a loan from the Treasury was not a matter so easy to arrange as might be suggested by reference to the financial part of the Volunteer Regulations. The Treasury had to be satisfied that the Corps was firmly established, and would continue to progress in a manner which would enable it to bear out of its capitation grants the annual charges of principal and interest. Consequently there ensued another period of negotiation and discussion before a loan was granted and authority obtained for taking additional land and for the erection of the new buildings. The scheme was designed by and carried out under the superintendence of Captain (now Lieut.-Colonel) S. L. Tennant. The old house was adapted for use as Officers' Quarters, Lecture Room, Orderly Room and Caretaker's Quarters; the new buildings included the Drill Hall, Sergeants' Mess, Members' Room, Clothing Stores, Armoury, Magazine, etc. Building operations were commenced in the winter of 1905-6, and completed late in the autumn of the latter year. On the 15th January, 1907, they were officially opened by Mr., now Lord, Haldane, the Secretary of State for War. The event gave the Corps some public distinction, for at the time Mr. Haldane had completed the reorganization of the Regular Army, had formed the Expeditionary Force, and was cogitating upon a plan for creating a Home Defence Army. Anticipating that he would give some indication of the results of that process, representatives of the Press from all parts gathered in great force. These, with the rest of the great audience which crowded the Drill Hall that night, were on the tiptoe of expectation. Their disappointment was complete when after declaring the new buildings open Mr. Haldane spoke for but a few minutes, mainly in praise of the ancillary service, as he called it, of the Engineers, and then proceeded to the distribution of prizes.

It was a fortunate circumstance for the East Lancashire Royal Engineers that these extensions of Headquarters were carried out before the Territorial regime, for there was issued soon after the new force was constituted an official schedule laying down the maximum dimensions which would be authorized for the various departments in any new buildings; dimensions which allow only extremely niggardly accommodation.

THE EAST LANCASHIRE ROYAL ENGINEERS

1908 was to see the end of the Volunteers, or their conversion to Territorials. The authorized establishment of the 3rd Lancashire R.E. (Vols.) was eight companies of Fortress Engineers, of which six had been formed, and the seventh, of telegraphists and electricians, was in process of formation. The new organization consisted of two Field Companies and a Telegraph Company, making a total establishment, including the C.R.E. and Staff, of 501.

The general scheme for the conversion was to enlist as far as possible from "A," "B," and "C" Companies for the 1st Field Company, from "D," "E," and "F" for the 2nd Field Company, and "G" to be the nucleus for the Telegraph Company.

The Commanding Officers appointed to the new units were: for the 1st Field Company, Major C. E. Newton; for the 2nd Field Company, Major H. A. Fielding; and for the Telegraph Company, Captain E. C. Holden.

On the 1st of April, the day on which the new force came into existence, the total of the roll of the 3rd Lancs. R.E. (Vols.) inclusive of all ranks, was 580, which by the end of the month had fallen to 145, whilst the Territorial appointments and enlistments were but 236. In this latter number were included almost the whole of the officers and the greater part of the N.C.O.s.

The recruiting for the Territorial Force was at the outset slow, owing to the rather ridiculous scare which was raised about the form of attestation. To allow time for the agitation to subside the Volunteer was given three months in which to make up his mind whether or not he would transfer. A further concession was made to him in the length of the engagement, originally fixed at a minimum of four years. The efficient Volunteer could elect to serve for any less number of years at his option; the full term only being enforced in the case of men joining with no previous service to their account. As the Camp Training was to take place at Whitsuntide it was important that the organization of the new units should proceed as quickly as might be, consistently with the exercise of proper care in their composition.

The concession in regard to the duration of engagement was the more effective of the two, in fact it revealed the other—the extension of the time of choice—to have been hardly necessary, for after the expiration of the first month but few came over. The remnant of the Volunteers gradually petered out to its end on the 30th June.

The general extension of the period of Training for the new force to fourteen days did not have, in this district, the deterrent effect which it had in other parts of the kingdom. In the case of the E. Lancs. R.E. it was practically inappreciable, and as we shall see the percentage of attendance at the Territorial Camps was considerably higher than the previous good record of the 3rd Lancs. R.E.

BEFORE THE WAR

To the various causes militating against recruiting the complement required, must be added, in the case of the Engineers, the effects of the reduction in the establishment. It was not possible to find for all places in the new force commensurate with the position and rank held in the old; as a consequence there were some "hard cases," especially amongst the officers and N.C.O.s. Then, too, there were the difficulties in connection with the numbers of particular trades, of which in the old Corps there was sometimes a redundance and in others a shortage, for the requirements of the new organization.

Whilst the transition from the old order to the new involved for the Engineers greater changes than it did for other branches of the service, both in organization and equipment, there was one fundamental alteration which affected all—namely, the coming of the County Association, into whose hands was committed the general administration of the public grants in the upkeep of quarters, the supply of clothing and other requisites. By this the position and relation of the Commanding Officer to his unit were greatly altered. The Volunteer C.O. had great responsibilities. Within the four corners of the regulations his powers were all but absolute. It might be said that he was in the position of a chief of a tribe of "friendlies" in receipt of a subsidy. He with the approval of his Finance Committee disposed of the Government grants, and if private funds were available decided in what way they could make up for the inadequacy of those grants in any department, or the best manner in which they could be devoted to provide any of those amenities which promote the success of a Corps.

The system of separate subsidies to individual units was, however, unduly favourable to the larger bodies, as must almost necessarily be any subsidy paid on a head-money basis; for the reason that the working expenses, as they may be called, do not rise in proportion to the numbers dealt with. Thus the larger Corps were better off than the smaller and were able to provide better quarters with greater amenities, and in some cases had a surplus sufficient to enable allowances to be made to their members for attendance in Camp. Now and henceforward the County Association was to be the authority charged with the raising, maintenance and personal equipment of the Force. All buildings and other property acquired from public funds passed to it, and it received the grants *en bloc*. The Secretary of State for War declared that the Commanding Officers, being now relieved from financial cares and responsibilities, would have more time to attend to their proper military duties: the education and training of their commands. But this desirable state of things for the C.O.s did not come about, at least not during the first few years after the change-over. Certainly there was some relief from the anxieties of finance, but the transition brought no relief in administrative work, but on the contrary added to it. Instead of being their own masters in the ordering of all supplies they had now to indent on an intermediary—the Association; a new

BEFORE THE WAR xix

system which only time and experience could get to work smoothly and methodically, and, as members of the Association, they had to assist in devising a scheme to replace the former direct individual administration.

Beyond adapting themselves to the alteration in administration, those responsible for the Engineers had to tackle many tough jobs more or less special, consequent upon the change in organization. First there was that of obtaining from ordnance stores the field equipment. They were lacking in most things required for the mobility of the new units: the pontoons, wagons, tool-carts, etc., the whole of the telegraph equipment, and the harness and saddlery. Then additional buildings were necessary in the shape of wagon sheds and harness rooms, for which plans had to be made and approved before the construction of the urgently required accommodation could be begun. There was also the question of the provision of a Riding School, concerning which there was prolonged discussion, the authorities contending that one Riding School—that agreed to be provided at the Artillery Headquarters—was sufficient for the whole of the mounted units of Manchester. Ultimately a joint School for the Engineers and the R.A.M.C. was sanctioned. Until that building was opened the Engineers had to have recourse to a private School, with all the inconveniences of distance, limited occasions and hours. The field equipment was very gradually supplied, the tool carts last of all. The correspondence about the latter would alone make a handsome volume.

Notwithstanding all the dispiriting delay and disappointments in connection with these matters the first Training at Abergavenny was successfully carried out, the mounted branches getting preliminary instruction, the bridges and other field work being executed on the lines of former years with the materials and stores of the old Corps. The period of Training was from the 6th to the 20th June. The total strength at that time had only attained to 814, but the percentage of attendance was remarkably good, being $95\frac{1}{4}$ per cent. for the first week and 71 per cent. for the second, and adding the small number who joined for the second week only, made the percentage of qualifying attendance 96·2 per cent.

A few days before this first Territorial Training, Captain P. H. French, R.E., was appointed Adjutant, and continued in that office until after the Training of 1912. Many and great were the services he rendered during those years. Especially valuable was his assistance in the prolonged period of building up the new organization, and contending with the various difficulties of the nature just mentioned. To his labours must be attributed in large measure the success to which the East Lancashire R.E. attained. No one, however, would be more ready than he to admit that much was due to the work of his predecessors of the old Corps. For all the seven years of its existence, except for a part of 1903, when Captain A. C. Scott, R.E., was Adjutant, the post had been filled by officers of the Corps. These officers were—

BEFORE THE WAR

Captain (afterwards Major) R. A. McNab. April to July 1901.
Captain (now Lieut.-Colonel and D.S.O.) P. F. Story. July 1901 to February 1903.
Captain (now Lieut.-Colonel and T.D.) S. L. Tennant. November 1903 to June 1908.

The summer of 1908 found the East Lancashire Division still some way off the attainment of its proper strength. The Association endeavoured by various expedients to encourage recruiting, which had lagged rather markedly after the expiration of the three months during which choice of the length of term of service was open to the Volunteers. The situation of the Engineers was particularly trying. Despite much urgent correspondence, little of the field equipment had materialized. There were some field sketching implements, compasses and drawing pins, some demolition apparatus, a portion of the Telegraph Company's lighter equipment, but the wagons, pontoons, trestles, tool carts and most of the requisites for the mobility of the units were still lacking. It was felt that something special must be done to rouse interest in the work of the Engineers. To this end, after an application to the Association for the cost of transport of materials, a bridging display was decided upon. On Saturday afternoon, the 3rd October, in little more than three hours' time, the Irwell was again bridged at Peel Park in the presence of General Fry, G.O.C. the Division, Colonel Shute, Chief Engineer N.W. Command, and a large crowd of spectators. The results were in every way satisfactory, again showing the utility of giving in public practical demonstrations of Military Engineering.

Musketry training, which in the Volunteer days was not always an absolute condition of efficiency, very properly became so under the Territorial regime. Owing to the deficiency in range accommodation in East Lancashire the Corps had in its early days to go so far afield as Altcar for rifle practice. Later the E. Lancs. R.E. were allotted certain days in the season on the Diggle Ranges, but the accommodation was inadequate. The war broke out before the new large ranges which the Association have constructed at Holcombe were completed, so the Units R.E. throughout their history have never enjoyed proper facilities for rifle shooting. They therefore deserve credit for what they did accomplish under disadvantageous circumstances.

From the dawn of history, from the tom-tom and bones to the full band, from the chant of the savage to "Tipperary," martial music has played no insignificant part in the life of the soldier; as much in peace as in time of war. It has sometimes been said that a band is an expensive luxury, but although it was oft-times a source of worry to the Volunteer C.O., yet it was by most deemed indispensable. In the 3rd Lancs. R.E., besides the difficulty that no bandsmen as such were allowed on the establishment, there was that of finance; the Corps had not reached a position strong enough to bear the cost of a full band; though during the latter years of its

BEFORE THE WAR

career a drum-and-fife band under the direction of Q.M.S. Nolan had been brought to a very creditable state of efficiency. Under the new regime the conditions were more favourable. The Association, " moved with the concord of sweet sounds," had resolved to make grants in aid of their maintenance but not as yet to supply the wherewithal to produce them. This remaining difficulty was removed by the very handsome presentation by Captain Tennant of a complete set of instruments. The formation of a full military band was at once undertaken, and Mr. W. H. Ellwood appointed Bandmaster 28th January 1909.

During the winter and spring months of 1909 recruits came in more rapidly; by Camp time the strength had reached 488, nearly the full establishment. The Training this year was at Ben Rhydding (Ilkley) from 29th May to 12th June, when the attendance was over 97 per cent., the highest ever recorded; the first week showing 95½ per cent. and the second 83 per cent.

The weeks preceding had been full of anxiety for the Staff, for neither Woolwich nor Weedon had signalled the supply of wagons or carts. One tool cart had adventitiously come into possession. The West Lancashire R.E. had a fully equipped Field Company in Volunteer days; they had now to make that equipment serve for their two Territorial Companies, nevertheless they were directed to divest themselves of one double tool cart in order to aid their starving brothers of the East.

Just after the departure for Camp notice was received at Headquarters that the pontoon and trestle wagons had been dispatched and were on the way to Manchester. By telegraphic orders these were diverted to Ilkley, where they arrived in the early days of the training.

This Camp was perhaps, in respect of all-round instruction and practical work, the best ever held by the East Lancs. R.E. They never again, so far as the Field Companies were concerned, had so varied an assortment of stores, the best part of the new equipment and the stores of the old Corps being available. Above all the whole fourteen days were at disposal for training in their own particular duties, conditions which were not to prevail in future years, when they went to train in Divisional Camps, where special instruction was much interfered with by field days and manœuvres. General Heath, then I.G.R.E., inspected the Camp and expressed his approval of the scheme of instruction and his satisfaction with the results.

The event of the summer was the Royal Review in Worsley Park on the 6th July when King Edward, after presenting colours to each unit entitled to carry them, inspected the assembled Division, the ceremony concluding with a March Past in which 403 officers and 9223 other ranks took part. The E. Lancs. R.E. parade-state showed 18 officers and 382 other ranks. The Review was in every way a brilliant success; it was a great day in the history of the Division.

To ensure the success of the Review carefully organized preparations had been made. This preparatory work brought home in emphatic manner to those behind the scenes that much remained to be done before the Territorial Force could as a whole be made ready for mobilization; the most serious question being that of the supply of horses. The West Lancashire Division had been reviewed by King Edward at Knowsley Park the day before. Most of the 1100 horses, of which some 400 were borrowed from the Regular Artillery, and some of the vehicles, had done duty there, being afterwards trained to Manchester to pass before His Majesty once more. Up to this period the problem of horsing the Force had not been systematically treated. The major portion of the newly created mobile units each made its own arrangements for the hire of horses for Camp, often with unsatisfactory results. Ultimately and by slow degrees some approach to a proper system was devised, the authorities developing the registration scheme and also authorizing the Association to buy a limited number of horses for permanent service in the Territorial Riding and Driving Schools. In the furtherance of the work of registration in this district Captain French had much extra duty thrown upon him, in the performance of which he rendered material service not only to his own units but to the Division.

By the opening of the year 1910 the new organization of the Engineers may be said to have become set. Wagon sheds and harness rooms had been erected at Headquarters, and except for the proper complement of tool carts the units were possessed of the full equipment of peace times. From this date onwards to the outbreak of the war there were only minor fluctuations in numbers, which remained during the intervening years at or near the authorized establishment.

For the Training of 1910 the Engineers with nearly all the other units of the Division went to Salisbury Plain, where they were encamped on West Down, from the 14th to the 28th of May. The week before its commencement the nation was plunged into mourning by the death of King Edward. On the day and at the hour of his burial at Windsor the Division assembled on the Downs for a memorial service, a solemnity the remembrance of which remains with all who participated.

The Plain is far from being an ideal locality for engineering training. The conditions at Whitsuntide were in any case awkward, even for the infantry, for at that season the battery training of the regular R.A. is in full swing, so that any manœuvre is hampered by the necessity of getting across the ranges, which cut up the Plain, before gun practice commences. The time therefore is very shortened for the development of any scheme of operations, and if it should reach that stage where by any possibility the Engineers could be brought into play the day is so far spent that scheme No. 1 has to be dropped and No. 2 scheme taken up; that is one which will bring the troops home again. Thus so far as the Engineers are concerned they will have had little more than a route march.

In pre-war days scarcely anywhere on the Plain was it permissible

BEFORE THE WAR xxiii

to turn a sod, and any suggestion involving the use of wire, in the practice of which the East Lancs. R.E. rather prided themselves, would have given the authorities fits. There was also the further disadvantage that the usual complement of stores could not be taken on account of the distance and cost of transport. To sum up the matter : fourteen days on the Plain as part of the Division was not equal for practical instruction to four or five days of a Regimental Camp. The total attendance at West Down was 91 per cent. of the strength, 89 per cent. for the first week and 68 per cent. for the second.

The next year's Training (4th to 18th June, 1911), was again with the Division at Garstang. Here the conditions were for the Engineers more favourable than on the Plain, and by arrangement they were allowed to devote more of the training time to exercise and instruction in their special work, though the principal bridging site was rather distant from Camp. The attendance on this occasion equalled 95 per cent. of the strength, $92\frac{1}{4}$ per cent. for the first period and 66 per cent. for the second. The rather low percentage for the second week was probably attributable to the shortening of the Whitsuntide holidays in favour of other days for the forthcoming Coronation celebrations in the following week.

Colonel Crook having been appointed to the command for the Coronation ceremonies of the combined representative contingents of the Territorial Royal Engineers, had consequentially the appointments of Adjutant and M.O. in addition to the two officers and twenty-five other ranks to represent the East Lancashire R.E. contingent.

The provisional battalion T.R.E. about 700 strong was composed of thirty-seven units, representative of the Divisional, the Army Troops (Telegraph), the Fortress, Railway, and Electrical, which had to be organized in eight companies with as far as possible due regard to precedence, seniority and other conditions. The bulk of the work of arranging the preliminaries in correspondence with the thirty-six other units fell upon Captain French. How well this was done was made manifest by the facility with which the actual organization was carried out after the arrival of the troops in the Kensington Gardens Camp.

Captain S. L. Tennant and Lieutenant J. G. Riddick were the officers who accompanied the East Lancashire contingent.

On the day of the Coronation (22nd June), the R.E. (T.) lined the upper portion of Constitution Hill, and on the next, the day of the Royal Progress, they were stationed in the same locality but to the north of the Archway.

In October of this year Captain Holden, who was leaving for British Columbia, resigned the command of the Telegraph Company and was succeeded by Captain A. N. Lawford.

The debatable question of the best season of the year for the Territorial encampments arose again in 1912. Were service obligatory there would be no doubt about it ; the Camp or Field Training would be late on in summer or in the autumn, for it is, or should be, the culmination of the annual course of instruction; but for a voluntarily enlisted force it is a very different matter; it must be at a time when it will cause the minimum of interference with trade and industry, which is to say that it should coincide with some holiday season. In the Manchester district Whitsuntide has generally been the longest of these, consequently during the Volunteer period and, as we have seen, for the first four years of the Territorial, it has been the time of Field Training. If Whitsuntide were not a movable feast, but was fixed for mid-June, it has been forcibly contended that it would be as good a season as any. One of the reasons advanced is that it would cause the qualifying drills before Camp to be compressed into a short period, which, in view of the limited number required, would make them more effective than when distributed over one of longer extent.

The Whitsuntide holiday is not always the longest holiday throughout East Lancashire. Some of the towns have their special or Wakes holidays at different times of the summer and autumn, so that it is not possible to hit upon a period which shall be equally convenient for all the units of the Division.

After much consideration it was determined to try the August bank-holiday time for the East Lancashire Divisional Training of 1912. The locality selected was the Craven district, the Camps being distributed from around Skipton to beyond Gargrave. The Craven district has some advantages for tactical instruction; being of a varied character and intersected by the Rivers Ribble and Aire, it had long been the scene of War Game practices. Unfortunately this August month was of unusual inclemency. During the Training the district was visited by thunderstorms, causing flooding in the rivers and streams, squalls, snowfall, and even frosts at night, uncomfortable incidents which may have affected the total attendance. This was in the case of the Engineers the lowest recorded of any of their Territorial Camps, namely, a total attendance of 88 per cent. of the strength—80 per cent. for the first week and 71 per cent. for the second. The figure for the second week is relatively good, and might tend to show that, after all, the influence of weather is not of material importance. But on this occasion there was another element which may have influenced the attendance for the second week. The days of training, 28th July to 11th August, were selected so that the principal bank-holiday days should fall within the latter, with the idea that this would tend towards a nearer equality of numbers throughout the period.

The camp attendances have been noted in some detail, because the time of Territorial training being so short it is worth while that the factors which contribute to or militate against a full attendance should be sought for and their value ascertained. It may be useful to supplement the figures of the percentage of strength attending Camp by those showing what proportion of the attendance trained for fifteen or only eight days.

BEFORE THE WAR

Locality.	Type of Camp.	Date.	Per cent. of strength trained.	Proportion trained for	
				15 Days.	8 Days.
1908. Abergavenny	Regimental	Whit-week	96·2	73·2	26·8
1909. Ben Rhydding (Ilkley)	,,	,,	97·3	83·0	17·0
1910. Salisbury Plain	Divisional	,,	91·5	71·7	28·3
1911. Garstang	,,	,,	95·3	66·0	34·0
1912. Gargrave	,,	August	88·0	71·7	28·3
1913. Denton (Ilkley)	Regimental	,,	93·6	81·2	18·8

The Telegraph Company did not train with the Division in 1912, but was quartered in the neighbourhood of Newmarket from 7th to 21st September, being one of the Territorial Units selected to take part in the Autumn Manœuvres with the Regular Army. In August of the same year Captain French's term of service, which had been extended to cover the Training period, came to an end, and on the 17th of that month Captain G. W. Denison, R.E., took up the duties.

In the spring-time of 1913 the second extension of time in command which had been given to Colonel Crook expired. The consequent changes are thus recorded in the *Gazette*—

" East Lancs. Divisional Engineers, R.E. : Lieut.-Colonel and Hon. Colonel Henry T. Crook, M.Inst.C.E., C.R.E., East Lancs. Territorial Division, on completion of his period of service in command is retired, and is granted permission to retain his rank and wear the prescribed uniform. Dated 12th March, 1913.

" Major C. E. Newton, M.Inst.C.E., from the 1st Field Company, to be Lieut.-Colonel. Dated 12th March, 1913.

" 1st East Lancs. Field Company : Captain S. L. Tennant from the 2nd East Lancs. Field Company to be Major. Dated 12th March, 1913."

For the training of 1913 Ilkley (Denton) was again selected, where a Regimental Camp was formed from 27th July to 10th August, the attendance on this occasion being 93·6 per cent. of the strength.

For the seventh Territorial Training, that of 1914, all preparations had been made for a Regimental Camp at Carnarvon, to which the 2nd Field Company had already departed, and the 1st Field Company was about to follow, when the order cancelling the arrangements and recalling the 2nd Field Company arrived. This episode, however, belongs more properly to the war than to the peace history.

The chief events in the latter have now been reviewed. There are many other incidents and activities both in the instructional and social sides of that history, such as the week-end camps, tactical tours, field days, competitions and the doings of the various sports' and pastimes' clubs, which it is unnecessary to detail, important though they be in the life of a vigorous Corps.

We have seen that after the East Lancs. R.E. Units were once recruited to full strength there was no falling off. The Association Return for the 1st August shows that at the outbreak of war they were amongst the few of the East Lancs. Division which were at the full establishment. We may then conclude their pre-war history with this evidence that those responsible had done what lay within their power to prepare for the evil day. Though ostensibly a Home Defence Army, there were amongst the Territorials some who never disguised their conviction that the Force would certainly be called upon to volunteer for active service abroad whenever the crisis came. They believed, with Lord Roberts, that "Germany would strike when Germany's hour had come," and that the whole manpower of the nation would be required to withstand the blow.

PART I

DIARY OF MOVEMENTS
OF THE 42ND DIVISIONAL ROYAL ENGINEERS
1914–1919

EAST LANCS. R.E. HISTORY

DIARY OF MOVEMENTS, 1914–1919

1914
- 4th Aug. Mobilized at OLD TRAFFORD. C.R.E.: Lieut.-Col. C. E. NEWTON.
- 18th Aug. Left OLD TRAFFORD for DOFFCOCKER CAMP, BOLTON.
- 31st Aug. Lieut.-Col. S. L. TENNANT appointed C.R.E.
- 9th Sept. Left BOLTON by train, 6.80 p.m.
- 10th Sept. Arrived SOUTHAMPTON DOCKS, 5.0 a.m. Embarked. Sailed 11.0 p.m.
- 25th Sept. Arrived ALEXANDRIA HARBOUR.
- 26th Sept. Moved to quay-side.
- 27th Sept. Disembarked. Left by rail for CAIRO.
- 28th Sept. Field Cos. arrived KASR-EL-NIL BARRACKS, CAIRO, 2.30 a.m. Signal Co. arrived ABBASSIA BARRACKS.
- 27th Oct. 1/2nd Field Co. moved to KANTARA and EL KUBRI on the SUEZ CANAL.
- 29th Oct. 1/1st Field Co. moved to ISMAILIA. Transport of both field companies remained at GEZIREH ISLAND, CAIRO.

1915
- 6th Jan. 1/1st Field Co. moved from ISMAILIA to CAIRO. 1/2nd Field Co. moved from KANTARA and EL KUBRI to CAIRO.
- 25th Jan. 1/1st Field Co. moved to ISMAILIA. Two sections 1/1st Field Co. moved on to SERAPEUM.
- 6th Feb. 1/2nd Field Co. moved to ISMAILIA. Remainder of 1/1st Field Co. moved from ISMAILIA to SERAPEUM.
- — Feb. Two sections 1/2nd Field Co. moved to EL FERDAN.
- 29th Apr. 1/1st Field Co. concentrated at ISMAILIA.
- 2nd May. 1/1st Field Co. moved to ALEXANDRIA and started embarking.
- 3rd May. 1/1st Field Co. sailed from ALEXANDRIA.
- 4th May. H.Q. R.E. and 1/2nd Field Co. left ISMAILIA and CAIRO for ALEXANDRIA.
- 5th May. H.Q. R.E. and 1/2nd Field Co. sailed from ALEXANDRIA.
- 6th May. 1/1st Field Co. arrived CAPE HELLES.
- 8th May. H.Q. R.E. and 1/2nd Field Co. arrived off CAPE HELLES.
- 10th May. 1/2nd Field Co. commenced disembarking.

EAST LANCS. R.E. HISTORY

1915.

11th May.	H.Q. R.E. and 1/2nd Field Co. completed disembarkation.
12th May.	1/1st Field Co. disembarked; their horses and some of 2nd Field Co.'s returned to ALEXANDRIA.
13th May.	1/1st Field Co. moved forward to neighbourhood of MORTO BAY. 1/2nd Field Co. moved forward to PINK FARM.
4th June.	The British and French troops attacked along the whole front. 42nd Div. attacked at KRITHIA NULLAH. The two field companies sent over R.E. parties to consolidate.
7th Aug.	42nd Div. attacked.
19th Aug. 20th Aug.	42nd Div. relieved the 29th Div. on the left of the CAPE HELLES front. 1/1st Field Co. moved to quarters in GULLY RAVINE. 1/2nd Field Co. took up forward billets in the GULLY near GEOGHEGAN'S BLUFF, keeping rear billets at PINK FARM. C.R.E. with Divisional H.Q. at GULLY BEACH.
12th Sept.	1/1st Field Co. took up forward billets in BRUCE'S RAVINE.
— Sept.	1/2nd West Lancs. Field Co. R.E. joined the Div.
13th Oct.	Half of 1/2nd West Lancs. Field Co. took over from the 1/1st Field Co.
14th Oct.	The other half of the West Lancs. Field Co. took over from the 1/2nd Field Co. 1/1st Field Co. concentrated at previous rear billets in GULLY RAVINE. 1/2nd Field Co. moved to GULLY BEACH. West Lancs. Field Co. had half their company in BRUCE'S RAVINE, and the other half in the previous forward billets of the 1/2nd Field Co., Company H.Q. being at the latter place.
28th Dec.	The relief of the 42nd Div. by the 13th Div. was started. The two East Lancs. Field Cos., less small rear parties, left with 13th Div. until the evacuation on night of Jan. 8/9th, embarked from LANCASHIRE LANDING at 23.30 hours on s.s. *Redbreast*.
29th Dec.	The two East Lancs. Field Cos. disembarked at MUDROS at 13.00 hours, and went under canvas at SARPI CAMP.

1916

3rd Jan.	H.Q. R.E. left CAPE HELLES.
4th Jan.	H.Q. R.E. arrived at MUDROS.
8th Jan.	1/2nd West Lancs. Field Co. left CAPE HELLES for MUDROS.
12th Jan.	Advance party left MUDROS for EGYPT.
14th Jan.	Field Cos. embarked on s.s. *Egra* for EGYPT.
15th Jan.	Left MUDROS.
17th Jan.	Arrived at ALEXANDRIA.

42ND DIVL. R.E.

1916.

18th Jan.	Field Cos. disembarked and entrained immediately for CAIRO, proceeding to MENA CAMP.
19th Jan.	H.Q. R.E. left MUDROS.
22nd Jan.	H.Q. R.E. arrived ALEXANDRIA.
24th Jan.	Advance parties left for TEL-EL-KEBIR.
26th Jan.	The three field companies moved to TEL-EL-KEBIR.
29th Jan.	Advance parties left for SHALLUFA.
31st Jan.	The three field companies moved to SHALLUFA.
7th Feb.	One section 1/2nd Field Co. moved to GENEFFE.
13th Feb.	Another section 1/2nd Field Co. moved to GENEFFE to relieve the section already there, which then moved on to ASHTON POST.
17th Feb.	One section 1/1st Field Co. moved to BURY POST.
21st Feb.	One section 1/1st Field Co. moved to SALFORD POST. The section at BURY POST moved to WIGAN POST.
17th Mar.	1/2nd Field Co. moved from SHALLUFA to GENEFFE.
31st Mar.	1/2nd Field Co. concentrated at GENEFFE, and 1/1st Field Co. at SHALLUFA. The Division commenced to hand over to the 54th Div.
1st Apr.	1/2nd Field Co. marched from GENEFFE to SUEZ.
3rd Apr.	1/1st Field Co. marched from SHALLUFA to SUEZ.
13th Apr.	Lieut.-Col. S. L. TENNANT left for England.
16th Apr.	Lieut.-Col. E. N. MOZLEY was appointed C.R.E. 42nd Div.
10th May.	1/2nd West Lancs. Field Co. R.E. left the Division and proceeded to MUDROS.
1st June.	Situation of the units : H.Q. R.E. and the three field companies under canvas at SUEZ.
21st June.	1/2nd Field Co. moved to EL FERDAN.
24th June.	H.Q. R.E. moved to EL FERDAN.
30th June.	The 1/3rd East Lancs. Field Co. joined the Division from ALEXANDRIA, having left England on 1st June.
1st July.	Situation of the units : 1/1st Field Co. divided between BALLAH and BALLYBUNNION ; 1/2nd Field Co. at EL FERDAN railhead ; 1/3rd Field Co. at EL FERDAN bridgehead.
25th July.	Divisional R.E. (less 1/2nd Field Co.), proceeded with the Division by march route to KANTARA. H.Q. R.E. camped close to the quarantine buildings there. 1/1st Field Co. went to HILL 70. 1/2nd Field Co. at EL FERDAN ; 1/3rd to GILBAN.
27th July.	1/2nd Field Co. moved from EL FERDAN to KANTARA.
28th July.	1/2nd Field Co. moved from KANTARA to HILL 40.
4th Aug.	H.Q. R.E. moved to PELUSIUM ; 1/1st Field Co. and 1/3rd Field Co. also to PELUSIUM.
5th Aug.	1/2nd Field Co. moved to GILBAN. H.Q. R.E., 1/1st and 1/3rd Field Cos. left for KATIA, and reached HOD ES SEIFANIYA.
6th Aug.	H.Q. R.E., 1/1st and 1/3rd Field Cos. reached KATIA.

1916.

8th Aug. — 1/2nd Field Co. moved to PELUSIUM.
11th Aug. — H.Q. R.E. returned to PELUSIUM. 1/1st and 1/3rd Field Cos. moved back to ROMANI.
9th Sept. — 1/2nd Field Co. moved from PELUSIUM to ROMANI on Mobile Column Equipment.
10th Sept. — H.Q. R.E. left PELUSIUM, and 1/3rd Field Co. left ROMANI for OGHRATINA. 1/2nd Field Co. left ROMANI for EL RABAH.
11th Sept. — H.Q. R.E., 1/2nd and 1/3rd Field Cos. arrived in the neighbourhood of OGHRATINA.
20th Sept. — H.Q. R.E. and 1/2nd Field Co. moved from OGHRATINA to NEGILIAT.
2nd Oct. — A water reconnaissance party composed of detachments of all three field companies started from RABAH as base to report on the water supply in a specified area. Detailed moves of this party were as follows :

2.10.16.	To RABAH.	20.10.16.	To MARAIEH.
5.10.16.	To MEZAHMI.	24.10.16.	To NUSS.
7.10.16.	To MBYAD.	28.10.16.	To ROMANI and
15.10.16.	To BIR WASET.		awaited orders to return to companies.

10th Oct. — H.Q. R.E. and 1/3rd Field Co. returned to ROMANI.
11th Oct. — H.Q. R.E. moved to MAHAMDIYA.
13th Oct. — 1/2nd Field Co. moved to Kilo 60 on broad-gauge railway from KANTARA.
25th Oct. — 1/2nd Field Co. moved bivouac a short distance but remained near Kilo 60. A second water reconnaissance party from 1/2nd Field Co. left NEGILIAT, working S.E. towards BAYUD.
27th Oct. — Another section 1/2nd Field Co. started on water reconnaissance and bivouacked at HOD ABU SHARAB.
30th Oct. — 1/3rd Field Co. marched to RABAH, and then to NEGILIAT, and there relieved the 1/2nd Field Co.
Both water reconnaissance parties of 1/2nd Field Co. returned, and their work was taken over by the 1/3rd Field Co.
31st Oct. — One section 1/2nd Field Co. moved to SALMANA on water reconnaissance.
1st Nov. — Remainder of 1/2nd Field Co. less rear party moved to BIR EL ABD, having handed over at Kilo 60 and NEGILIAT. Situation of the units : H.Q. R.E. at MAHAMDIYA ; 1/1st Field Co. at ROMANI ; 1/2nd at BIR EL ABD, less one section at SALMANA and rear party at Kilo 60 ; 1/3rd Field Co. at NEGILIAT, less one section at BAYUD.
3rd Nov. — Rear party 1/2nd Field Co. rejoined. One officer and eleven other ranks to BIR EL ABD ; ten other ranks to party at SALMANA.

1916.
5th Nov. Water reconnaissance party of one section 1/1st Field Co. moved to BIR EL ABD, and commenced working in a southerly direction towards BAYUD.
7th Nov. 1/2nd Field Co. sent a water reconnaissance party to ABU TILUL from SALMANA, and a party to SALMANA from ABD.
8th Nov. 1/2nd Field Co. moved from BIR EL ABD to ABU TILUL.
9th Nov. 1/2nd Field Co. concentrated at ABU TILUL.
11th Nov. One section 1/2nd Field Co. moved to south of the position; about two miles distant.
15th Nov. 1/3rd Field Co. moved from NEGILIAT to KHIRBA.
16th Nov. The water reconnaissance party of the 1/3rd Field Co. returned from BAYUD.
18th Nov. The water reconnaissance party of the 1/1st Field Co. returned from BAYUD.
20th Nov. 1/1st Field Co. moved to RABAH, less one section sent on water reconnaissance to DUEIDAR on 19th Nov., and one officer and a half-section left at ROMANI to complete work there.
21st Nov. 1/3rd Field Co. concentrated at BIR EL ABD, and 1/1st at KHIRBA.
22nd Nov. 1/1st Field Co. moved to BIR EL ABD, one section of 1/2nd to MAZAR, and 1/3rd Field Co. to SALMANA.
23rd Nov. 1/1st Field Co. moved to SALMANA, 1/3rd to ABU TILUL, two sections 1/2nd Field Co. moved from TILUL to MAZAR.
24th Nov. 1/1st Field Co. moved to ABU TILUL, remainder of 1/2nd and all 1/3rd Field Co. to MAZAR.
25th Nov. H.Q. R.E. and 1/1st Field Co. moved to MAZAR. Co. H.Q. and two sections 1/2nd Field Co. moved to new bivouac two miles east of MAZAR station.
26th Nov. Remaining two sections 1/2nd Field Co. moved to new bivouac three-quarters of a mile east of MAZAR station.
1st Dec. Situation of the units : All in neighbourhood of MAZAR.
2nd Dec. 1/3rd Field Co., less one officer and forty other ranks, proceeded on water reconnaissance to Kilo 128.
5th Dec. Two detached sections of 1/2nd Field Co. rejoined Co. H.Q. two miles east of MAZAR station.
7th Dec. 1/2nd Field Co., less one section, moved to Kilo $125\frac{1}{4}$. Co. H.Q. and two sections moved from there to BIR EL GERERAT, leaving one section at Kilo $125\frac{1}{4}$. 1/3rd Field Co. moved to GERERAT.
8th Dec. 1/2nd Field Co. H.Q. and two sections at GERERAT moved bivouac to a new site near by.
9th Dec. Remaining section of 1/2nd Field Co. from MAZAR moved to Kilo $125\frac{1}{4}$, thus making two sections at the latter place.

EAST LANCS. R.E. HISTORY

1916.

11th Dec. Water reconnaissance party of 1/1st Field Co. returned from work near DUEIDAR. H.Q. R.E. moved from MAZAR to Kilo 125½ (MAADAN).

12th Dec. H.Q. R.E. and two sections 1/2nd Field Co. moved to Kilo 127. One section 1/1st Field Co. joined 1/2nd Field Co. here.

14th Dec. 1/2nd Field Co. concentrated at Kilo 128.

15th Dec. 1/2nd Field Co. moved three-quarters of a mile further east and commenced developing the water supply of GHURFAN EL GIMMEL.

16th Dec. One section 1/3rd Field Co. left GERERAT for Kilo 126.

17th Dec. One section 1/3rd Field Co. went to assist 1/2nd Field Co. at Kilo 129½.

18th Dec. 1/3rd Field Co. H.Q. and one section left GERERAT for Kilo 129½.

20th Dec. 1/1st Field Co. left MAZAR (with the Division) and bivouacked near Kilo 128. 1/2nd Field Co. moved back one mile to join 126th Infantry Brigade. 1/3rd Field Co. concentrated at Kilo 128.

21st Dec. H.Q. R.E. and the three field companies marched back to MAZAR.

1917

1st Jan. Situation of the units : All at MAZAR.

2nd Jan. 1/1st and 1/3rd Field Cos. left for EL ARISH and bivouacked at night near Kilo 128.

3rd Jan. 1/1st and 1/3rd Field Cos. arrived at Kilo 138. 1/2nd Field Co. moved bivouacs west to a point a quarter of a mile south of MAZAR station.

7th Jan. 1/1st and 1/3rd Field Cos. arrived at EL ARISH, and bivouacked at Kilo 153.

13th Jan. 1/3rd Field Co., less one section, left EL ARISH for Kilo 142.

14th Jan. H.Q. R.E. moved to Kilo 128.

15th Jan. 1/2nd Field Co., less one section, marched to Kilo 128.

16th Jan. H.Q. R.E. and 1/2nd Field Co. marched to Kilos 139 and 142 respectively, the latter bivouacking east of EL BITTIA wells.

17th Jan. H.Q. R.E. moved up to EL ARISH. Remainder of 1/2nd Field Co. moved from MAZAR to Kilo 139 by rail.

18th Jan. Details East Lancs. R.E. moved from KANTARA to ROMANI with all transport.

21st Jan. 1/2nd Field Co. moved to EL ARISH with 126th Infantry Brigade.

22nd Jan. 1/3rd Field Co. left EL ARISH for EL BURJ.

42ND DIVL. R.E.

1917

24th Jan.	1/3rd Field Co. arrived at EL BURJ and commenced to develop the water supply.
29th Jan.	1/3rd Field Co. left EL BURJ and returned to EL ARISH.
31st Jan.	Details left ROMANI for MOASCAR, on outskirts of ISMAILIA. Advance parties left the field companies for KANTARA and PORT SAID.
1st Feb.	Situation. Whole of 42nd Div. R.E. at EL ARISH.
2nd Feb.	1/3rd Field Co. left EL ARISH for KANTARA. H.Q. R.E. left EL ARISH for KANTARA.
3rd Feb.	1/1st, 1/2nd and 1/3rd East Lancs. Field Cos. became respectively the 427, 428 and 429 Field Cos. R.E.
5th Feb.	427 Field Co. moved from EL ARISH to KANTARA. 428 Field Co. moved from EL ARISH to KANTARA. 429 Field Co. marched to EL FERDAN.
6th Feb.	427 Field Co. marched to EL FERDAN. 429 Field Co. marched to MOASCAR. H.Q. R.E. moved by train to MOASCAR.
7th Feb.	427 Field Co. marched to MOASCAR.
12th Feb.	H.Q. R.E., 427 and 429 Field Cos. moved by train from MOASCAR to ALEXANDRIA. 428 Field Co. moved from KANTARA to ALEXANDRIA. Whole Div. R.E. camped at GABBARI Camp.
22nd Feb.	The C.R.E. and the 427 Field Co., also eight other ranks from the 428 Field Co., embarked on H.M.T. *Manitou* for France.
23rd Feb.	Remainder of H.Q. R.E., and two officers and eighty other ranks of 428 Field Co., embarked with Div. H.Q. on H.M.T. *Transylvania* for France.
26th Feb.	Remainder of 428 Field Co. (3 officers, 120 other ranks) embarked on H.M.T. *Huntspill* for France.
1st Mar.	427 Field Co. arrived at MARSEILLES.
2nd Mar.	427 Field Co. left MARSEILLES by train. H.Q. R.E. and portion of 428 Field Co. arrived at MARSEILLES, and entrained.
3rd Mar.	429 Field Co. embarked at ALEXANDRIA on H.M.T. *Menominee*.
4th Mar.	427 Field Co. detrained at PONT REMY, and marched to LIMEUX.
5th Mar.	H.Q. R.E. detrained at PONT REMY, and proceeded to billets at HOCQUINCOURT.
6th Mar.	Main body of 428 Field Co. disembarked at MARSEILLES, and entrained.
8th Mar.	After an eight hours' halt at JUVISY, main body of 428 Field Co. arrived at PONT REMY, and marched to billets at LIMEUX, arriving there at 2.30 a.m. on 9th.
10th Mar.	428 Field Co. drew all horses except riders from ABBEVILLE.

EAST LANCS. R.E. HISTORY

1917

12th Mar.	429 Field Co. disembarked at MARSEILLES, and entrained.
14th Mar.	429 Field Co. detrained at PONT REMY, and marched to billets at HOCQUINCOURT. Advance party of 427 Field Co. proceeded to HAMEL.
15th Mar.	427 Field Co., less mounted section, marched to LONGPRÉ station, entrained for CORBIE, and from there marched four miles to HAMEL.
18th Mar.	Advance parties, which had been sent on ahead from EGYPT in January, rejoined the companies, after having been attached to the 1st Div. One section 428 and one section 429 to FLIXECOURT to 4th Army School.
23rd Mar.	427 Field Co., under orders from 3rd Corps, were attached to the 1st Div. for duty, and marched to ESTRÉES, where they bivouacked for the night. Two sections 427 proceeded to BELLOY to work for the 2nd Infantry Brigade on roads.
26th Mar.	Two sections 428 and two sections 429 Field Cos. proceeded to billets at ERONDELLE to practise bridging in the RIVER SOMME.
24th Mar.	H.Q. and two sections 427 Field Co. proceeded to BRIE, to erect an " A "-class bridge over the SOMME.
27th Mar.	H.Q. and one section 429 moved to MERELESSART.
29th Mar.	429 Field Co., less one section at FLIXECOURT, entrained at PONT REMY, detrained at CHUIGNES, and marched to CHUIGNOLLES. H.Q. R.E. moved to HERBECOURT.
30th Mar.	H.Q. and one section 428 Field Co. joined the two sections at ERONDELLE.
31st Mar.	Two sections 429 Field Co. moved to HERBECOURT.
1st Apr.	Situation of the units: H.Q. R.E. at HERBECOURT; 427 Field Co. at BRIE and BELLOY; 428 Field Co. at ERONDELLE, less one section at FLIXECOURT; 429 Field Co. H.Q. and one section at CHUIGNOLLES; two sections at HERBECOURT; one section at FLIXECOURT. Each company had 100 infantry from the respective Brigades of the 42nd Div. attached with four officers as a permanent pioneer working party.
4th Apr.	428 Field Co., less one section, marched from ERONDELLE to PONT REMY, entrained for CHUIGNES, and marched from there to BECQUINCOURT, where they bivouacked for the night.
5th Apr.	428 Field Co., less one section, marched to LE CATELET, near PÉRONNE.
6th Apr.	H.Q. R.E. moved from HERBECOURT to PÉRONNE.
7th Apr.	One section 429 Field Co. rejoined the company at CHUIGNOLLES from FLIXECOURT.

42ND DIVL. R.E.

1917

8th Apr.	429 Field Co., less one section, and 427 Field Co. moved to PÉRONNE, and were billeted in the FAUBOURG DE PARIS.
10th Apr.	Remaining section of 428 Field Co. rejoined the company from 4th Army School at FLIXECOURT.
11th Apr.	Two sections of 427 Field Co. were attached to 428 Field Co. at LE CATELET to help in the erection of 3rd Corps H.Q. Camp.
17th Apr.	H.Q. and the two other sections of 427 Field Co. moved back to BRIE.
19th Apr.	Two sections of 427 Field Co. left 428 and moved to ESTRÉES-EN-CHAUSSÉE. One of these two sections later moved to TINCOURT.
21st Apr.	429 Field Co. moved their billets to GRANDE PLACE PÉRONNE.
30th Apr.	428 Field Co. with attached infantry moved by march route to VILLERS FAUCON, and bivouacked there for the night.
1st May.	427 Field Co. moved to RONSSOY. 429 Field Co. moved to EPÉHY. H.Q. R.E. still at PÉRONNE. 428 Field Co. at VILLERS FAUCON.
4th May.	Two sections of 428 Field Co. moved to RONSSOY.
3rd May.	H.Q. R.E. moved to near VILLERS FAUCON and took over from 48th Div. R.E.
12th May.	427 Field Co. moved back to bivouacs near VILLERS FAUCON. 428 concentrated in RONSSOY, and took over 427's old billets.
15th May.	429 Field Co. moved from EPÉHY to VILLERS FAUCON.
17th May.	42nd Div. was relieved by the 2nd Cavalry Div. 428 Field Co. moved to bivouacs near VILLERS FAUCON. 427 proceeded by march route to NEUVILLE BOURJONVAL.
19th May.	H.Q. R.E. moved to BRUSLE. 428 Field Co. moved by march route to FINS, and bivouacked there for the night. 427 Co. H.Q. and two sections moved to RUYAULCOURT; remaining two sections to HAVRINCOURT WOOD.
20th May.	428 Field Co. moved to METZ-EN-COUTURE. 429 Field Co. moved to FINS. 42nd Div. relieved 20th Div.
22nd May.	429 Field Co. moved to DESSART WOOD. Two sections moved on to GOUZEAUCOURT WOOD.
23rd May.	H.Q. R.E. moved to LITTLE WOOD, YTRES, and took over from C.R.E., 20th Div.
24th May.	Two sections 429 Field Co. from DESSART WOOD moved, one to BERTINCOURT, and the other to YTRES.
26th May.	One section 429 Field Co. moved from GOUZEAUCOURT WOOD to YTRES.
27th May.	429 Field Co. H.Q. and one section from GOUZEAUCOURT WOOD, moved to BUS.

1917

30th May.	428 Field Co. handed over their section of the front to a field company of the 59th Div.; also their billets in METZ-EN-COUTURE, and moved into a camp in HAVRINCOURT WOOD.
1st June.	Situation of the units: H.Q. R.E. in LITTLE WOOD, YTRES; 427 Field Co. at RUYAULCOURT with two sections forward in HAVRINCOURT WOOD; 428 Field Co. in HAVRINCOURT WOOD; 429 Field Co. at BUS and YTRES.
3rd June.	Lieut.-Col. D. S. MacInnes, C.M.G., D.S.O., R.E., took over the duties of C.R.E., 42nd Div. 429 Field Co. (less one section remaining at YTRES) concentrated in HAVRINCOURT WOOD.
15th June.	428 Field Co. handed over their work to 429 Field Co. (who remained in the same camp), and moved back into the divisional back area, being distributed as follows: one section to YTRES, one to BERTINCOURT, two to RUYAULCOURT.
19th June.	427 Co. H.Q. and one section moved up to HAVRINCOURT WOOD. Remaining section stayed at RUYAULCOURT.
1st July.	Situation of the units: H.Q. R.E. in LITTLE WOOD, YTRES; 427 Field Co. at RUYAULCOURT and HAVRINCOURT WOOD; 428 Field Co. at RUYAULCOURT, BERTINCOURT and YTRES; 429 Field Co. in HAVRINCOURT WOOD.
4th July.	42nd Div. started to hand over to 58th Div.
5th July.	428 Field Co. concentrated at YTRES and were inspected by Brig.-Gen. SCHREIBER, C.B., D.S.O., C.E. 3rd Corps.
6th July.	428 Field Co. marched to the rest area; half company to BIHUCOURT, and the other half to GOMIECOURT, near BAPAUME.
7th July.	427 and 429 Field Cos. were inspected by Brig.-Gen. SCHREIBER in HAVRINCOURT WOOD.
9th July.	H.Q. R.E. and 429 Field Co. moved to ACHIET-LE-PETIT.
10th July.	427 Field Co. moved to GOMIECOURT; two sections of 428 Field Co. from GOMIECOURT to BIHUCOURT to rejoin their company.
11th July.	428 Field Co. moved to COURCELLES-LE-COMTE.
12th July.	Field companies commenced training.
20th July.	429 Field Co. moved to BEAUCOURT-SUR-ANCRE to practise bridging.
23rd July.	429 Field Co. returned to ACHIET-LE-PETIT.
24th July.	427 Field Co. moved to BEAUCOURT-SUR-ANCRE to practise bridging.
27th July.	427 Field Co. returned to GOMIECOURT.
25th, 26th 27th, 28th	428 sent parties daily to MIRAUMONT for bridging.

42ND DIVL. R.E.

1917.

1st Aug. — Situation of the units : H.Q. R.E. and 429 Field Co. at ACHIET-LE-PETIT; 427 Field Co. at GOMIECOURT; 428 Field Co. at COURCELLES-LE-COMTE.

20th Aug. — 427 Field Co. marched from GOMIECOURT to BOUZINCOURT.

21st Aug. — 429 Field Co. marched to neighbourhood of BOUZINCOURT. 428 Field Co. marched to a camp near MAILLY MAILLET. H.Q. R.E. to ACHEUX.

22nd Aug. — H.Q. R.E. to AVELUY.

23rd Aug. — 427 Field Co. entrained at Albert, detrained at GODWAERSVELDE, and were billeted for the night near WATOU. 428 Field Co. entrained at BEAUCOURT, detrained at PROVEN. 429 Field Co. entrained at AVELUY, detrained at POPERINGHE, and were billeted there. H.Q. R.E. left camp 1.30 a.m., entrained AVELUY, detrained HOPOUTRE near POPERINGHE, 7.0 p.m. marched to WATOU.

24th Aug. — 427 Field Co. marched to VLAMERTINGHE. 428 Field Co. to WATOU.

29th Aug. — 427 Field Co. marched to YPRES, and were billeted in the Ramparts. 429 Field Co. marched to VLAMERTINGHE.

30th Aug. — 428 Field Co. marched to POPERINGHE, where they entrained for YPRES.

31st Aug. — 429 Field Co. marched to YPRES. H.Q. R.E. WATOU to BRANDHOEK.

1st Sept. — Situation : H.Q. R.E. at BRANDHOEK; the three field companies in YPRES, 427 and 428 being in the Ramparts; 16th Batt. Royal Irish Rifles (Pioneers) were working under C.R.E., 42nd Div.; two companies of this battalion were in YPRES, and two in BRANDHOEK; 267 Field Co. R.E. were also attached to the Division and billeted in YPRES.

5th Sept. — Heavy gas shell attack on YPRES. Twenty-eight other ranks casualties in the three field companies.

6th Sept. — 125th Infantry Brigade attacked BORRY FARM, BECK HOUSE, and IBERIAN FARM. 427 and 428 Field Cos. sent out parties which were to wire in front of the concrete pill-boxes when these were captured. Attack unsuccessful.

16th Sept. — 428 and 429 Field Cos. moved from YPRES to their transport lines at BRANDHOEK.

17th Sept. — 427 Field Co. moved from YPRES to BRANDHOEK. 429 Field Co. moved to BUSSEBOOM. Late at night the 428 Field Co. were called out to repair the road screening along the YPRES–MENIN Road. This was done early morning on 18th.

1917.

18th Sept.	H.Q. R.E. moved to POPERINGHE. 42nd Div. was relieved by the 9th Div.
19th Sept.	427 Field Co. moved to ST. JAN TER BEZEN. 428 Field Co. moved to WINNEZEELE.
20th Sept.	429 Field Co. moved to the WINNEZEELE Area.
21st Sept.	428 Field Co. moved to WORMHOUDT.
22nd Sept.	H.Q. R.E. moved to LA PANNE. 427 Field Co. moved by train to ARNEKE. 428 Field Co. continued their march to the TETEGHEM Area. 429 Field Co. moved by bus to COXYDE.
23rd Sept.	428 Field Co. continued their march, and arrived at LA PANNE.
24th Sept.	427 Field Co. moved by train to GHYVELDE. 428 Field Co. marched to OOST DUNKERQUE BAINS. 429 Field Co. marched to NIEUPORT BAINS. H.Q. R.E. moved to ST. IDESBALDE. 42nd Div. took over from the 66th Div.
25th Sept.	427 Field Co. moved to OOST DUNKERQUE BAINS.
1st Oct.	Situation of the units : H.Q. R.E. at ST. IDESBALDE ; 427 Field Co. and 428 Field Co. at OOST DUNKERQUE BAINS ; 429 Field Co. at NIEUPORT BAINS.
5th Oct.	42nd Div. handed over to the 41st Div. and began to take over from the 32nd Div. in NIEUPORT.
5th Oct.	427 Field Co. moved to NIEUPORT.
6th Oct.	428 Field Co. moved two sections to NIEUPORT, and two to near WULPEN. 429 Field Co. moved to NIEUPORT.
7th Oct.	H.Q. R.E. moved from ST. IDESBALDE to COXYDE BAINS.
19th Oct.	One section 428 Field Co. moved back to run an R.E. Dump near COXYDE.
1st Nov.	Situation of the units : H.Q. R.E. at COXYDE BAINS ; 427 Field Co. at NIEUPORT ; 428 Field Co. at NIEUPORT and WULPEN ; 429 Field Co. at NIEUPORT.
18th Nov.	42nd Div. was relieved by a French division. All three field companies were relieved by companies of the 28th Régiment du Génie.
19th Nov.	All three field companies commenced the march to new area, moving via WORMHOUDT.
20th Nov.	H.Q. R.E. arrived at AIRE.
22nd Nov.	428 Field Co. arrived at GLOMENGHEM.
23rd Nov.	427 Field Co. arrived at STEENBECQ. 429 Field Co. arrived at LA ROUPIE.
26th Nov.	H.Q. R.E. and three field companies commenced the march to the BÉTHUNE sector to relieve the 25th Div. R.E.
29th Nov.	H.Q. R.E. moved to LOCON.
30th Nov.	427 Field Co. relieved the 106th Field Co. at LE PREOL. 428 Field Co. billeted at ESSARS. 429 Field Co. relieved the 130th Field Co. at GORRE.

42ND DIVL. R.E.

1917.

1st Dec. — Situation of the units : H.Q. R.E. at LOCON; 427 Field Co. at LE PREOL; 428 Field Co. at LE QUESNOY; 429 Field Co. at GORRE.

4th Dec. — 428 Field Co. moved to LE QUESNOY near GORRE.

22nd Dec. — Lieut.-Col. D. S. MacInnes, C.M.G., D.S.O., R.E., left the 42nd Div. to assume the appointment of Deputy E.-in-C. and Inspector of Mines at G.H.Q. Lieut.-Col. R. E. B. Pratt, D.S.O., R.E. took over command of the R.E. of the 42nd Div.

29th Dec. — 422 Field Co. R.E. (55th Div.) and 1/4th (Pioneer) Batt. South Lancs. Regt. were attached to the 42nd Div. for work.

1918

1st Jan. — Situation of the units : As on 1st Dec., 1917.

24th Jan. — 422 (West Lancs.) Field Co. was relieved by the 423 Field Co. R.E.

1st Feb. — Situation of the units : As on 1st Jan.

11th Feb. — 429 Field Co. assisted in a raid carried out at GIVENCHY by the 1/9th Batt. Manchester Regt.

13th Feb. — Relief of the 42nd Div. by the 55th Div. started. 429 Field Co. were relieved by the 419 Field Co., and after relief moved to LES HARISOIRS. H.Q. R.E. moved to HINGES.

14th Feb. — 427 Field Co. handed over to the 422 (West Lancs.) Field Co. and moved to BUSNES. 428 Field Co. remained at LE QUESNOY, and handed over their work to 423 Field Co., but continued work in the same sector under 55th Div. R.E.

12th Feb. — 1/7th Batt. Northumberland Fusiliers arrived and became the Pioneer Battalion of the 42nd Div.

17th Feb. — 427 Field Co. moved from BUSNES to BEUVRY to work under C.R.E. 55th Div. 428 Field Co. came under orders of C.E. 1st Corps for work.

20th Feb. — 429 Field Co. moved from LES HARISOIRS to HINGES.

1st Mar. — Situation of the units : H.Q. R.E. at HINGES; 427 Field Co. at BEUVRY; 428 Field Co. at LE QUESNOY; 429 Field Co. at HINGES.

4th Mar. — 427 Field Co. moved to BUSNES for training. G.O.C. 42nd Div. addressed the officers and N.C.O.'s of the divisional R.E. on the situation in France, and the necessity for strenuous training, introducing at the same time the divisional motto: " Go one better."

5th Mar. — H.Q. R.E. moved to LABEUVRIÈRE.

14th Mar. — 429 Field Co. moved from HINGES to OBLINGHEM.

23rd Mar. — Orders to move to 3rd Army front. 427 and 428 Field Cos. embussed on the BUSNES–LILLERS Road. H.Q. R.E. and 429 Field Co. embussed on the

EAST LANCS. R.E. HISTORY

1918.

HESDIGNEUL–LABUISSIÈRE Road. The transport of the three field companies moved by road to MONCHY BRETON. H.Q. R.E., 427 and 428 Field Cos. debussed and bivouacked for the night at ADINFER. 429 Field Co. debussed at ADINFER, and marched to AYETTE, where they bivouacked for the night.

24th Mar. H.Q. R.E. moved to MONCHY-AU-BOIS. Late in the day the field companies moved forward to hold if necessary the old German line BEHAGNIES–ERVILLERS, and to take over from the 40th Div. Owing to a misunderstanding in the orders regarding guides, the 40th Div. guides were not met, and the above line was not reached, and the 40th Div. were not relieved that night. 428 Field Co. were ordered late at night to act as infantry escort to the artillery.

25th Mar. 427 and 429 Field Cos. took up a position in the railway cutting N. of ACHIET-LE-GRAND and W. of GOMIECOURT. H.Q. R.E. moved to FONQUEVILLERS. The field companies retired into LOGEAST WOOD. Transport arrived at DOUCHY-LEZ-AYETTE.

26th Mar. Early in the morning the 427 and 429 Field Cos. moved to ESSARTS-LEZ-BUCQUOY, transport going further back to BIENVILLERS.

28th Mar. H.Q. R.E. moved to ST. AMAND. 428 Field Co., no longer required as artillery escort, moved to ESSARTS. 427 Field Co. took over part of the front line under O.C. 1/7th N.F., in front of BUCQUOY Cemetery.

29th Mar. 42nd Div. was relieved by the 41st Div. Late at night all three field companies moved to GOMMECOURT WOOD and were accommodated in old German dug-outs.

1st Apr. 428 and 429 Field Cos. took over part of the front line in rear of ABLAINZEVELLE. 427 Field Co. took up a reserve position near BUCQUOY. 42nd Div. relieved the 41st Div.

2nd Apr. All three field companies came out of the line and moved into old trenches in rear of the support line, 429th going to the neighbourhood of GOMMECOURT WOOD.

2nd Apr. The transport of all three field companies moved to SOUASTRE.

3rd Apr. At night, the 427 Field Co. reported to the 125th Brigade for engineer work, and were accommodated in an old German trench W. of BUCQUOY. H.Q. R.E. moved to HÉNU.

7th Apr. 42nd Div. were relieved by the 62nd Div. H.Q. R.E. moved to PAS. 427 Field Co. moved to HÉNU.

8th Apr. 427 Field Co. moved by 'bus to VAUCHELLES. 428 Field Co. moved by 'bus to PAS. 429 Field Co. marched to HÉNU.

42ND DIVL. R.E.

1918.

11th Apr. G.O.C. 42nd Div. addressed 428 and 429 Field Cos. assembled at PAS with 126th Infantry Brigade, and 427 Field Co. with the Pioneer Battalion at AUTHIE.

12th Apr. All three field companies and the Pioneer Battalion moved to the COIGNEUX valley for work on the defence line known as the CHÂTEAU DE LA HAIE Switch. All were bivouacked under canvas sheets on the slopes of a hill between COIGNEUX and SAILLY-AU-BOIS.

15th Apr. 428 Field Co. relieved the 154 Field Co. (37th Div.) in GOMMECOURT WOOD, one section remaining on the transport lines, which were situated near COIGNEUX. 42nd Div. commenced the relief of the 37th Div.

16th Apr. H.Q. R.E. took over from the 37th Divl. R.E. at COUIN. 427 Field Co. relieved the 153 Field Co. in GOMMECOURT WOOD. 429 Field Co. relieved the 152 Co. in SAILLY-AU-BOIS.

1st May. Situation of the units: H.Q. R.E. at COUIN; 427 Field Co. in GOMMECOURT WOOD; 428 Field Co. in GOMMECOURT WOOD; 429 Field Co. at SAILLY-AU-BOIS.

6th May. Relief of 42nd Div. by 57th Div. was commenced. 427 Field Co. were relieved by 505 Field Co., and moved to billets in HÉNU. 428 Field Co. were relieved by 421 Field Co., and moved to BOIS DE ST. PIERRE near PAS. 429 Field Co. were relieved by 502 Field Co., and moved to COUIN, where they were encamped in the woods near the Château. H.Q. R.E. moved to PAS.

14th May. The Pioneer section of the 307th Infantry Regiment, U.S.A. Army was attached to the 427 Field Co. for training. The 307th Infantry Regiment was attached to the 42nd Div.

1st June. Situation of the units: H.Q. R.E. at PAS; 427 Field Co. at HÉNU; 428 Field Co. near PAS; 429 Field Co. at COUIN.

7th June. 42nd Div. commenced the relief of the N.Z. Div. in the COLINCAMPS Sector. 427 Field Co. relieved the 3rd N.Z.E. Co., billeted near BERTRANCOURT. 428 Field Co. moved into reserve in BUS Woods. 429 Field Co. took over from 1st N.Z.E. Co. and moved into shelters W. of SAILLY-AU-BOIS.

The transport of all three field companies moved into a camp beside the BUS–LOUVENCOURT Road. H.Q. R.E. moved into the village of BUS-LES-ARTOIS and took over from C.R.E., N.Z. Div.

21st June. Lieut.-Col. R. E. B. PRATT, D.S.O., R.E., proceeded to England on sick leave.

EAST LANCS. R.E. HISTORY

1918.

1st July. — Situation of the units : H.Q. R.E. at BUS-LES-ARTOIS; 427 Field Co. at BERTRANCOURT; 428 Field Co. in BUS WOODS; 429 Field Co. near SAILLY-AU-BOIS.

8th July. — Major A. T. SHAKESPEAR, D.S.O., M.C., Staff Officer to C.E., 5th Army was appointed C.R.E., 42nd Div. and arrived.

12th July. — Major SHAKESPEAR appointed C.R.E. 12th Div. Major J. G. RIDDICK appointed C.R.E., 42nd Div. with the acting rank of Lieut.-Col.

16th July. — H.Q. R.E. moved back with Div. H.Q. to AUTHIE.

1st Aug. — Situation of the units : H.Q. R.E. at AUTHIE; Field Cos. as on 1st July.

15th Aug. — The enemy commenced a retirement in the SERRE Sector. H.Q. R.E. moved forward again into BUS-LES-ARTOIS.

21st Aug. — A successful attack was carried out on the front of the Third Army.

23rd Aug. — 428 Field Co. moved to COURCELLES-AU-BOIS.

24th Aug. — 429 Field Co. moved to LUKE COPSE.

25th Aug. — H.Q. R.E. moved with 42nd Div. H.Q. to COLINCAMPS. 427 and 429 Field Cos. moved to MIRAUMONT.

27th Aug. — H.Q. R.E. with Div. H.Q. moved to ACHIET-LE-PETIT.

29th Aug. — 429 Field Co. moved to the neighbourhood of PYS.

30th Aug. — 427 and 428 Field Cos. moved to PYS. H.Q. R.E. moved to GREVILLERS. 429 Field Co. moved to the R.E. Dump near LA BARQUE.

1st Sept. — Situation of the units : As on 30th Aug.

3rd Sept. — 429 Field Co. moved to BARASTRE. Two sections 427 Field Co. moved to VILLERS-AU-FLOS.

4th Sept. — H.Q. R.E. moved to RIENCOURT-LEZ-BAPAUME. Remainder of 427 Field Co. moved to VILLERS-AU-FLOS. 428 Field Co. also moved to VILLERS-AU-FLOS.

5th Sept. — 42nd Div. handed over to N.Z. Div.

6th Sept. — 42nd Div. moved into rest. H.Q. R.E. remained at RIENCOURT. 427 Field Co. moved to THILLOY. 428 to old camp between PYS and WARLENCOURT. 429 to PYS.

21st Sept. — 42nd Div. took over from the 37th Div. H.Q. R.E. moved to a small wood S.W. of VELU; 427 Field Co. to a sunken road between BERTINCOURT and HERMIES; 428 Field Co. to HAVRINCOURT WOOD, 429 to a camp just west of LEBUCQUIÈRE.

27th Sept. — 42nd Div. attacked successfully in front of TRESCAULT.

29th Sept. — 42nd Div. was relieved by the N.Z. Div. 427 and 429 Field Cos. moved to BERTINCOURT. 428 remained in HAVRINCOURT WOOD.

1st Oct. — Situation of the units : H.Q. R.E. near VELU; 427 Field Co. moved to HAVRINCOURT WOOD; 428 Field Co.

42ND DIVL. R.E.

1918.

	also in HAVRINCOURT WOOD; 429 Field Co. at BERTINCOURT.
2nd Oct.	429 Field Co. moved to the neighbourhood of TRESCAULT.
4th Oct.	428 Field Co. moved to the neighbourhood of TRESCAULT.
8th Oct.	H.Q. R.E. moved with Div. H.Q. to TRESCAULT.
9th Oct.	H.Q. R.E. with Div. H.Q. moved to ESNES. All three Field Cos. moved to LESDAIN.
11th Oct.	427 Field Co. moved to FONTAINE-AU-PIERRE.
12th Oct.	H.Q. R.E. moved to BEAUVOIS. 427 Field Co. to PRAYELLE. 428 and 429 Field Cos. to JEUNE BOIS.
20th Oct.	42nd Div. attacked successfully, across the River SELLE.
23rd Oct.	42nd Div. continued their advance in front of SOLESMES.
24th Oct.	427 and 429 Field Cos. moved into SOLESMES. Situation of the units: H.Q. R.E. at BEAUVOIS; 427 and 429 Field Cos. at SOLESMES; 428 Field Co. at JEUNE BOIS.
1st Nov.	42nd Div. R.E. Sports held at PRAYELLE.
5th Nov.	H.Q. R.E. moved to BEAUDIGNIES and then on to POTELLE. 427 Field Co. moved to LE CARNOY. 428 and 429 Field Cos. moved to LE QUESNOY.
6th Nov.	428 and 429 Field Cos. moved to LE CARNOY.
7th Nov.	All three field companies moved to PETIT BAYAY, at the Eastern edge of the FORÊT DE MORMAL.
8th Nov.	H.Q. R.E. moved to PETIT BAYAY. Portion of 428 Field Co. moved to HAUTMONT, and portion of 429 moved to BOUSSIÈRES.
9th Nov.	H.Q. R.E. moved to HAUTMONT. 427 and 428 concentrated in HAUTMONT.
10th Nov.	Two sections of 429 Field Co. moved to FERRIÈRE-LA-GRANDE; remainder of 429 to LOUVROIL.
11th Nov.	Official intimation received that an armistice had been signed; hostilities ceased 11.00 hrs.
13th Nov.	Main portion of 429 Field Co. (from LOUVROIL) moved into HAUTMONT.
17th Nov.	429 Field Co. concentrated in HAUTMONT.
1st Dec.	Situation of the units: All in HAUTMONT.
6th Dec.	Advance party consisting of one section from each field company and 1 platoon 1/7th Northumberland Fusiliers left HAUTMONT for CHARLEROI, taking three days on the journey. First day to BINCHE; second day to FONTAINE L'EVÊQUE; third day to CHARLEROI. One section 428 Field Co. and three sections 429 Field Co. moved to VIEUX RENG.
10th Dec.	Another section 428 Field Co. moved to CHARLEROI.
12th Dec.	One section 428 Field Co., and three sections 429 Field Co. moved from VIEUX RENG to CHARLEROI. One section 428 Field Co. moved from CHARLEROI to FLEURUS.

EAST LANCS. R.E. HISTORY

1918.

13th Dec. — Two sections 427 Field Co. moved to MARPENT. H.Q. R.E. moved to CHARLEROI.

14th Dec. to 18th Dec. — Remainder of the field companies at HAUTMONT moved by march route to CHARLEROI, marching on the 14th, 15th, 16th and 18th, and resting on the 17th.

1919.

2nd April. — 428 Field Co. cadre left CHARLEROI.
3rd April. — 427 Field Co. cadre left CHARLEROI.
4th April. — 427 Field Co. cadre arrived at ANTWERP; embarked and sailed.
5th April. — 428 Field Co. cadre sailed from ANTWERP.
6th April. — 428 Field Co. cadre arrived TILBURY.
6th April. — 427 Field Co. cadre disembarked at TILBURY and entrained.
7th April. — 427 and 428 Field Co. cadre arrived at OSWESTRY.
10th April. — The cadres were dispersed.

PART II

A SUMMARY OF THE WAR HISTORY
OF THE 42ND DIVISIONAL ROYAL ENGINEERS
1914–1919

At the end of July 1914 the East Lancs. R.E. had despatched advance parties to prepare the camp for the annual training, which was to have been at Carnarvon. Rumours of war were in the air, but all proceeded as usual until the camp was ready and the 2nd Field Company had left Old Trafford by train for Carnarvon, and the 1st Field Company had entrained but had not left. The preparations having reached this stage, orders were received cancelling the camp. This was on Sunday, August 1. The 1st Field Company returned to Headquarters at Seymour Grove at once, and the 2nd Field Company returned the following day. At 6.0 p.m. on August 4 mobilization orders came, and all ranks were ordered to report at Headquarters, Seymour Grove, forthwith. The units had for some time previously been at full strength, so that, although many former members wished to join up again, the only vacancies for them were those caused by a few of the serving members failing to pass the doctor's examination.

At Old Trafford, the men were billeted in the hard, cold schools next door to Headquarters, and the officers in the mess and in empty houses. The succeeding days were busy ones; requisitioned horses came in, a few at a time, and were placed on lines in the playground; civilian carts were obtained according to Lord Haldane's scheme to make up the full number of vehicles; tools in job lots were supplied by Messrs. Baxendale according to arrangements previously made. The men were drilled, and inspected much and often as regards kit and equipment. Bounties were paid, forms were filled up for the payment of separation allowances, and a hundred-and-one details of real and previously unpractised mobilization were attended to. On the night of August 10 a telephone message came from Divisional Headquarters to the effect that Lord Kitchener required to know who would volunteer to serve immediately abroad. This was announced in the crowded hall of the schools amidst the cheers of all ranks, and during the remainder of the time before embarkation, the number of volunteers was made up as nearly as possible to full strength.

After about a fortnight at Old Trafford, the two field companies, with the C.R.E.s Headquarters, moved to Doffcocker, near Bolton, and were quartered in a bleak and damp, and later unspeakably muddy, camp on a hillside, close to a camp occupied by the D.L.O. Yeomanry. Some days were spent here, chiefly in early morning exercise, and horse exercise, and in clearing up the mud; later there were several practice moves. After billeting parties had spent some days at Wellingborough arranging billets, it became known that the Division was detailed for foreign service, and units were hastily made up to full strength, a few vacancies having occurred through some members being unable to volunteer for foreign service.

At the time of entraining at Bolton Station on the evening of September 9, many people were still sceptical as to the destination being Egypt, but 5.0 a.m. on the 10th saw the units at Southampton Docks. The embarkation arrangements were a model of what should be. Two Staff Officers met the train with complete details of the allotment of accommodation on board, and the men marched straight aboard by messes. The 1st and 2nd Field Companies embarked on the *Neuralia* and *Aragon* respectively, and the Signal Company on the *Saturnia*. The horses of both field companies, with an altogether inadequate detachment of drivers, embarked on the *Messaba*.

Passing down Southampton Water in the evening, the convoy of about fourteen ships foregathered the next day off the Eddystone, and were picked up by an escort. Moving off past Ushant and into the Bay of Biscay, the majority soon found the motion of the ocean too much for them, and had a rather stuffy time in their quarters, which at the time seemed cramped and uncomfortable, until past Finisterre. After this, life took on a more pleasant aspect; and after a lovely voyage along the coast of Portugal, accompanied by a rumour of a German cruiser in the neighbourhood, Gibraltar was reached. The stop here only lasted half a day, so there was no going ashore. A few days later Malta was passed in the night, and the following day, in lovely hot weather, the great fleet of transports carrying Indian troops for France was met, and escorts were exchanged. And so the voyage went on, the monotony being varied by drills and exercises, and last, but not least, by inoculation. Alexandria was reached after three weeks at sea, and after a wait in the harbour the units were landed and proceeded by train to Cairo. The field companies went to the old but centrally situated barracks at Kasr-el-Nil, overlooking the Nile; the Signal Company to more modern barracks out at Abbassia; the horses, which had sustained some losses on the voyage, to the Agricultural Exhibition grounds on Gezireh Island, conveniently near Kasr-el-Nil barracks.

Drill clothing and helmets were now issued to all three units, which were very busy getting really smart. The necessity for this latter was particularly impressed on all ranks.

The days passed quickly in hard training, spare time being spent in looking round Cairo and neighbourhood, many going to the Pyramids on Sundays. As is usual with the R.E., this sort of life was of short duration, and in the third week of October, both field companies, and later some signallers, were sent to the Suez Canal. An Indian Expeditionary Force had arrived to defend the eastern frontier of Egypt, but had no sappers. The 1st Field Company went into camp at Ismailia, and the 2nd in two portions at Kantara and Kubri; and for the first time since the outbreak of the war, they started to do some real sapper work.

Three bridges were thrown across the Canal, defences were made, searchlights erected, water supply arranged, and many other works were carried out. It was an interesting and a hard-working time with the Indians, from whom, and from the Canal Company, every kindness and help was invariably received. The transport lines remained in Cairo during this period, as did the Signal Company.

At Christmas each camp had a holiday and a great meal, and few of those who survive will forget that first Christmas away on the edge of the desert by the side of the Canal. They will also remember the enemy prize ships going home, and how they were cheered as they passed; the liners whose passengers threw out cigarettes; the Indian mule lines; the trenches at Kantara; the cinema at Ismailia; the washing at Suez.

Soon after Christmas the Divisional Commander arranged for the R.E. to be withdrawn from the Canal, and to return to Kasr-el-Nil Barracks to take part in divisional training. This meant large and elaborate field days on the Suez road east of Abbassia, and on these occasions the field companies had an extra march each way to and from Abbassia, and a night out on the desert. The intervals between field days were filled in with other forms of training.

Rumours of a Turkish advance were now heard, culminating in the despatch of the field companies to Ismailia and Toussoum. At the latter place two sections of the 1st Field Company were involved in the Turkish attack of February 3 and 4, and did very well. After the repulse of this attack the field companies settled down to another period of defence works with the Indians, and much good work was done. The 1st Field Company were now at Serapeum, and the 2nd at Ismailia and El Ferdan.

The C.R.E. decided to attach Captain English, the Regimental M.O., to the 1st Field Company, as that unit was remote from Ismailia. In a very few days the doctor returned, ostensibly to buy one or two things in the town, but he was heard to appeal to his commanding officer thus: " Shure now, Colonel, you wouldn't be after ordherin' me to return to Serapeum. It's an awful place entirely. Mosquitoes in the air and scorpions in the ground, the flies driving ye dotty by day and the fleas feeding on ye by night, 'tis no place for y'r own midical adviser to be!"

The sappers all fired a musketry course on a range near Ismailia, and Colonel Earle of the Divisional Staff paid frequent visits to see how this was progressing. Meanwhile the 1st Field Company sent an officer and ten sappers to Cairo to act as instructors for a class in field engineering, or pioneer work. The course was attended for one week by the pioneers of each infantry battalion of the Division, and the model trenches dug near Abbassia reproduced many of the problems which were to arise on Gallipoli; here the use of stick bombs was practised with great keenness.

In April more rumours of war were in circulation, this time in connection with Gallipoli, and at the beginning of May the field companies hastily packed up, said good-bye to the Indians, and to their equally good friends the Canal Company, and moved to Alexandria, where the mounted sections joined them.

They were embarked with all speed; the C.R.E. and the 2nd Field Company on the *Toronto*, the 1st Field Company on the *Nessian*, and the Signal Company with Divisional Headquarters on the *Crispin*. This time there was no convoy. All ships made their way as quickly as possible to the entrance to the Dardanelles, where the landing at Cape Helles on the Peninsula of Gallipoli had taken place some few days earlier. The Signal Company landed the first of the R.E. units, the 2nd Field Company and their horses next, and the 1st Field Company without horses last. The C.R.E. rapidly received his orders, and the field companies moved forward—the 1st Field Company to a point near some water towers near the east coast of the peninsula, and the 2nd to " Pink Farm."

In a few days the Division was placed definitely in the front line, although the infantry had been used by brigades for fighting as soon as they went ashore. On the left of the divisional front was the 29th Division, and on the right the Royal Naval Division. On the right of the latter the line was held by the French.

Each company established two sections forward with the battalions in the line. This first period till the middle of August was one of the finest of the whole war. The conditions were harder, the casualties higher, the danger greater than at any later period. But all believed that we were winning; casualties, hard work, lack of drafts, absence of good food and of comforts did not matter. Every one thought that it was only a matter of days before we should be beyond Achi Baba, that evil hill which the navy shelled at intervals and from which the Turk watched all our movements. It appeared that we were just on the point of breaking through, as, indeed, we were, though we never actually did it.

May passed with a great deal of digging and advancing the line bit by bit. On the 4th of June, the sappers of both field companies attacked with the infantry, and succeeded in doing a great deal of useful work, but also at a great price. Like all the battles in Gallipoli, the day was ours, but there were not enough men to push through and win. So the 4th of June added much greater work to the task of the R.E.

June and July passed in increasing heat, and with an increasing number of flies, and the next great attack came on August 8. Both field companies had a very hard time in their respective sectors; the 1st Field Company's unremitting efforts consolidated the " Vineyard," while the 2nd Field Company did well in the Krithia Nullah. After this the Division was withdrawn from the line, and the sappers moved back to their respective company headquarters. It may be mentioned here that going back from the line for a rest in Gallipoli was not the same thing as going back from the line for a rest in France. No part of the ground we held on the peninsula was out of range of field guns, and the headquarters of the field companies were just within range of rifle fire. Although shell fire was com-

ACHI BABA FROM HIGH GROUND ABOVE "LANCASHIRE LANDING."

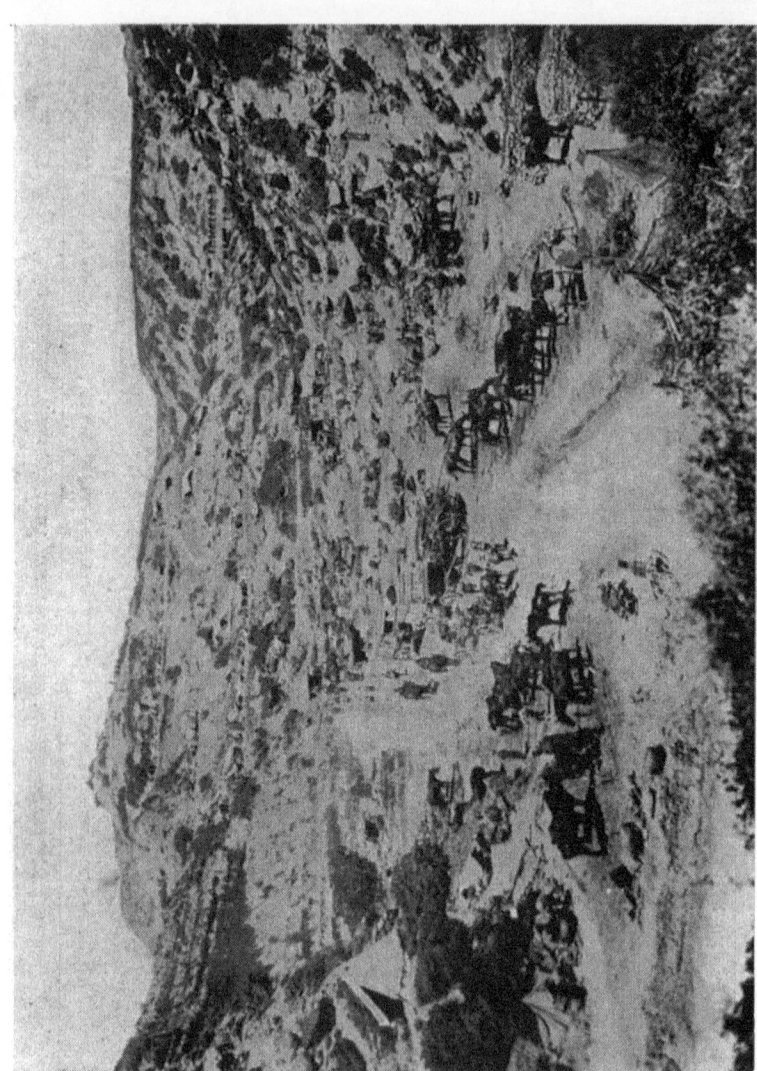
GULLY RAVINE. HEADQUARTERS OF SIGNAL CO. AND 2ND FIELD CO. R.E.

paratively light, rifle fire went on every day and every night to an extent unheard of during normal trench warfare in France; and at night quite a number of more or less "spent" bullets used to fall in and around the companies' headquarters. The result was that one could never get away from the war for a real rest, except by going off the peninsula altogether. Certain units were at one time and another taken off to the islands of Imbros or Lemnos for a few days, but the field companies never left the peninsula at all, till the end of the occupation.

The so-called rest in August only lasted two days, as the 29th Division had to be sent to Suvla Bay, and the 42nd Division were called upon to take over the left of the front vacated by the 29th. This was sometimes called the Gully Ravine sector, and the 2nd Field Company took over work in the right half across the Gully itself, while the 1st Field Company went to the left near Fusilier Bluff and Inniskilling Inch. The Gully was the largest of the many gullies or nullahs, of which the Krithia Nullah and the Achi Baba Nullah were other examples.

The trenches here were in a very bad state, so the R.E. had all their men in the line, doing what they could by day and the balance by night. It was found that the Turk, not having been checked in this sector by counter-mining, had an extensive minefield under our lines at the "Gridiron." The mining company therefore made strenuous efforts to get in some protective galleries, but in spite of this a succession of mines were fired by the enemy during the last days of September, and each of them caused large damage to our line and heavy casualties. In each case, also, the trenches had to be repaired or patched up in some way. At Fusilier Bluff the mining company managed to get ahead of the Turk, and so this most important position was not endangered. The field companies were now so depleted in numbers by casualties and sickness that in spite of the arrival of a small draft of reinforcements in August, each company could only turn out about thirty men for work. The War Office had meanwhile decided that each division was to have three field companies instead of two, and for this reason the 1/2nd West Lancs. Field Company R.E. (T.F.) was sent out to join the 42nd Division, and arrived during September. At first the C.R.E. kept this company at the mouth of the Gully and used it for working on roads there. Its baptism of fire came when a detachment was sent to assist the 2nd Field Company with a more than usually large crater.

By the middle of October it had become clear that more defence works in rear of the main position were a necessity if we were to remain on the peninsula without pushing forward. The C.R.E. therefore ordered the West Lancs. Company to take over the whole of the work in the front and support lines, and withdrew the two East Lancs. Companies to work on the reserve lines. This meant in practice that they were still working every night within 500 to 700 yards of the enemy.

Winter quarters were much talked of, but lack of material and labour made them illusory. However, more settled conditions and worse weather, culminating in a storm and a flood, frost, snow and a blizzard, made us make our bivouacs as warm as we could. Thus with many a minor incident November and December passed. The shelling increased after the evacuation of Suvla, but the flies and dust of earlier months had gone. The companies did their best to celebrate Christmas, and then came sudden orders to leave, to destroy tool carts, and pack the tools in boxes, and to be relieved by the 13th Division; though there was still no news of a real evacuation. Sappers guided the infantry of the 13th Division up to relieve our own battalions. Then one by one the units, in their mixture of summer and winter kit, assembled at Lancashire Landing or " V " Beach, and so on board the "beetles," and away on a sweeper to Mudros. The two East Lancs. Field Companies left first, the West Lancs. Company, with a few East Lancs. officers attached, remaining with the 13th Division until the final evacuation on the night of January 8, 1916.

At Mudros the companies were placed under canvas at Sarpi Camp, and tried to sleep in the unusual silence. The next few days were spent in runs, games, and a little drill; the luxury of tents was enjoyed, as also was the undreamed-of existence of canteens, which provided the first real delicacies since leaving Egypt eight months previously. The weather was cold and boisterous, and every one was glad to make a move for Egypt. It was disappointing to find, however, that it was raining at Alexandria on arrival there, whilst at Cairo it tried to drizzle as we ate buns and drank tea at the buffet, prior to being conveyed in trams to Mena Camp; tools, etc., following in native donkey carts. On the day after arrival there the horses and drivers of the 1st Field Company and of the West Lancs. Company came from Alexandria and rejoined, and the sight of their comparatively smart appearance suddenly reminded those from the peninsula that their clothing was not fit to be seen. They were literally in rags, but had not noticed it before. Scarcely any new clothing had reached the peninsula; the climate had varied from a hot spring to a really hot, dusty, flybitten summer, and back to a cold winter; and the kit was very much the worse for it. It was now understood why the units had been taken out to Mena by tram; they were not sufficiently respectable to be seen marching.

After three or four days with the Ordnance Department and the tailors, they looked themselves again, although small in numbers, and could once more venture into Cairo.

With the West Lancs. Field Company arrived the last remnants of the Division. The evacuation had been lucky; there still was a 42nd Division, although small. So the 31st and 46th Divisions, parts of which had arrived to defend the Suez Canal, were sent back, and the 42nd Division Field Companies proceeded via Tel-el-Kebir to Shallufa, near Kubri, where Major Wells' swing bridge of October 1914 still swung. At Shallufa horses were received to make up losses, and some of the wounded and sick rejoined.

In March and April various defence works, hutted camps and a water pipe line were proceeded with; this was a real good rest after Gallipoli, and in May all three companies marched to a camp near Suez.

Lieut.-Colonel S. L. Tennant, who had come out with the Division as C.R.E., now left, to the great regret of all. He had been with us all through our early difficulties, and had with great ability and courage carried us successfully through the many trials and triumphs of Gallipoli. His devotion to duty on the peninsula, when he declined to leave even for a few days' rest, had told on him, and he had more than earned a period of rest and change. It was with great regret that we said good-bye and wished him good luck. Lieut.-Colonel E. N. Mozley, D.S.O., R.E., a Regular officer, was then appointed C.R.E.

At Suez a large hutted camp, with roads and water, for the whole Division, plus some other units, was quickly put in hand, and was finished in early July. Drafts arrived for all units, and although they found the heat and dust of Suez trying, they soon settled down to new conditions. In July the 11th Division, in which Major Denison, our late adjutant, had the command of a field company, proceeded to France, and the 42nd Division moved to El Ferdan to relieve them. In this sector the East Lancs. R.E. received their own 3rd Field Company from home; the West Lancs. Field Company left us at Suez, before this move northwards. The new field company was put on to camp duties at El Ferdan whilst the 1st Field Company went to Ballah and Ballybunion, and the 2nd to Ferdan Railhead and Abu Urûk. The work was interesting, consisting of defences, water supply, roads, etc., and the camps, although dusty, were cooler than Suez.

Three weeks here, and rumours of more war caused a hurried move to Kantara, and out again towards Gilban. A railway now existed to Romani, the outpost position held by the 52nd Division. In the next couple of days the units were issued with camels, and left their heavy gear and horses and vehicles behind at Kantara; and, taking with them certain well-sinking tackle, etc., sallied forth along the railway line to Pelusium. Meanwhile the enemy had advanced very rapidly, and was endeavouring to attack the 52nd Division in the flank and rear, being held off by the Australian and New Zealand Mounted Division. Two brigades of the 42nd Division, therefore, with the 1st and 3rd Field Companies, proceeded across the desert over very bad country and in scorching heat, in the direction of Katia, in support of the cavalry. The infantry took some prisoners, and after two days' very hard going the Katia oasis was occupied, the enemy being then in full retreat, pursued by the cavalry. The R.E. spent the ensuing days in developing the water supply in the palm groves, and after about a week the Division was withdrawn; the 1st and 3rd Field Companies settling down in camps at Romani, and the C.R.E. and Divisional Headquarters going back to Pelusium, where the 2nd Field Company had remained. The mobile equipment was overhauled, and the table below gives it in the form it held with slight additions during the next few months.

Establishment of Divisional R.E. with Camel Transport.

UNIT.	PERSONNEL.			TRANSPORT.			
	Officers.	Other ranks.	Total.	Riding horses.	Camels.	Native drivers.	Fanatis.*
H.Q. R.E.	3	9	12	6	3	1	2
Field Co. R.E.	6	152	158	8	55	25	18
Total for Divnl. R.E.	21	465	486	30	168	76	56

Summary of Stores carried by a Field Company, R.E.—

Nature of Load.	Camels.
Water supply Norton Tube Well	1 †
" " Canvas Tank	1
Well Units (12), Pumps, Troughs, Corrugated Iron, and Timber.	24
Explosives	1
Wire; barbed and plain; Sandbags	6
Tools and Lashings	8
Blankets and Baggage	5
Water	9
Total camels	55 ‡

Establishment of a Division and attached (for Water Supply purposes).

FANATIS.	HORSES.	CAMELS.
1526	1530	2552

The Turks having retreated, the British Army was ordered to advance, and so the 52nd and 42nd Divisions took it in turns until the following December to advance with the railway head, and when relieved, to rest at the last main camp behind. The water supply arrangements were as follows: all water for human drinking was transported in tanks on trucks to railhead, there placed in canvas tanks, and thence distributed in fanatis on camels to the troops. The water for horses and camels had to be found and developed as

* Ten gallon zinc water tanks, of which a camel carried two.
† Later increased to 5 Norton Tube Pumps per Field Company.
‡ Later increased to 69 camels per Field Company.

we went. This proved a heavy but very interesting duty, and whilst the main body of each field company was developing wells and watering places, sections were out continuously reconnoitring the desert ahead and reporting on samples and quantities of water found. Thus the line of advance was determined, and the R.E. preceded the main body, whose advance was dependent on the water development. A rest camp was formed at Mahamdiya, where the C.R.E. resided for some little time, and later some men received a holiday at Alexandria. The advance culminated in a great concentration of the 42nd and 52nd Infantry Divisions and the Anzac Mounted Division at Maadan on December 20 for a night march and attack on El Arish.

But the Turks were only bluffing, and they abandoned their positions at Masaid. Thereupon, much to their disappointment, the 42nd Division went back along the wire road to Mazar, and spent a sandy but cheerful Christmas, whilst the 52nd Division, to which we had lost Major Wells as C.R.E., went on to El Arish. As soon as the rumours of really fresh water had been proved at El Arish, the 42nd Division went on again, and the 1st and 3rd Field Companies did some excellent work on the wonderful fresh-water wells on the beach.

El Arish appeared, indeed, as the promised land; in the Wadi, the first green fields since the Delta; in the village, the first houses since the Canal; it was quite like a picture from the Old Testament. After a few days of work the great news came that we were going to France. We packed up hastily, handed in our camels and special gear, and at last went by train on our wonderful desert railway back to Kantara, now a vast camp with sidings and a swing railway bridge under construction, wharves and parks of material. There we gathered up our vehicles, horses, and tools, and were trained away to Gabbari, Alexandria. On the 3rd of February, 1917, the Field Companies were re-numbered 427, 428 and 429 Field Companies respectively. At Alexandria the companies had a welcome few days in a large town, whilst the equipment was made up, and the few horses allowed to be taken to France were picked out. The transports had meanwhile arrived, and in a few days the 427 Field Company with the C.R.E. sailed, followed by the 428 and later by the 429.

The voyage was made in pleasant weather, and, although risky, as could be seen by the amount of wreckage passed, it did not produce any exciting incidents. It was particularly interesting to pass through the Straits of Messina, and to go close in up the coast of Italy, and around the Riviera, and so into Marseilles, where it was freezing.

The 427 Field Company landed at Marseilles on the 1st March, while the 429 Field Company, the last of the three, did not land until the 12th March. By the 14th March, the whole of the divisional R.E. were billeted in the neighbourhood of Abbeville.

The climatic conditions were, of course, very different from those of Egypt, and as the weather was particularly wintry, many felt the cold severely.

It was a new experience to find civilians who, whilst they did not speak English, took a genuine interest in one's movements, and gladly offered coffee and similar refreshments on all possible occasions.

As soon as horses and certain other additional items, such as bicycles, had been drawn, the 42nd Division started to move further forward. The 427 Field Company went ahead on the 15th March, and a week later was attached to the 1st Division for work. The enemy had just lately retreated, and this forward move involved going into the evacuated area, where, of course, all villages were destroyed. There was necessarily a great deal of work to be done, including some road repairing, and some bridging, and during the first half of April, the remainder of the divisional R.E. followed the 427 Field Company and went to the Péronne area.

During the first few days of May, the 42nd Division took over a part of the line in front of Ronssoy and Epéhy from the 48th Division. The weather was now fine and warm, and the trials of life in the front line in France were therefore gradually learnt, cold and mud being at first avoided; those who had been in Gallipoli soon got back their trench habits. The 427 and 429 Field Companies went to live in cellars in Ronssoy and Epéhy respectively, while the 428 Field Company, though at first having their headquarters further back near Villers Faucon, also worked in the line.

The work of the field companies here consisted mainly of making and wiring a new front line, as at the beginning of May no such thing existed, the front being held in this sector by a series of disconnected posts. A good deal of work was also done on a reserve line, further back, for that also was non-existent. There was nothing strikingly new in this work, and the companies soon reaccustomed themselves to working at fairly close quarters with the enemy. Cellar-life in ruined villages was rather more of a novelty, but nobody takes long to grow accustomed to these " cave-man " habits.

Though this was by no means a bad part of the line, compared to others, it was not a very pleasant place in which to start one's career in France after a long spell in Egypt, and the 429 Field Company in particular had a very nasty experience in Epéhy. On May 13 a shell landed in a cellar occupied by one of their sections, and they had fifteen men killed.

On May 17, however, the 2nd Cavalry Division took over this part of the line, and the 42nd Division moved further north to the neighbourhood of Havrincourt Wood. At the time of this move Lieut.-Colonel E. N. Mozley, D.S.O., R.E., left the Division and went to hospital, and shortly after arrival in the Havrincourt Wood sector, Lieut.-Colonel D. S. MacInnes, C.M.G., D.S.O., R.E., came from the 20th Division and was appointed C.R.E.

Colonel Mozley's departure was a great loss to the R.E., whom by his exertions and example he had tuned up to a high pitch of organization. He was an exacting commanding officer, but he worked no one as hard as he worked himself.

It was on the 3rd June that Lieut.-Colonel MacInnes took over the duties of C.R.E., and the R.E. units soon found that in the appointment of so distinguished an officer they had again been fortunate.

The 42nd Division remained in the Havrincourt Wood sector for seven weeks, and the field companies had more varied and more interesting work than they had had near Ronssoy. This sector had the additional advantage that it was quieter from the point of view of hostile shelling, and none of the R.E. units ever had their camps shelled. Havrincourt Wood made a quite useful screen, and it was possible to approach the front line in comfort and security. The weather was good, and those who lived in the wood itself found conditions quite delightful. The front part of the wood near Havrincourt village had been felled by the enemy during his retirement, and across all the " rides " trees had been " dropped " so as to make them impassable as roads. The greater part of the wood, however, remained standing, and at this time of the year was very attractive and very different to what we found on our return fifteen months later.

Just before leaving Havrincourt Wood to move back to rest early in July, the field companies were each inspected by Brigadier-General Schreiber, C.B., D.S.O., C.E., 3rd Corps, and complimented on good work done in 3rd Corps area. They then went to the area round Achiet-le-Petit, Courcelles-le-Comte, and Gomiecourt, where vigorous training was carried out. Having had about two months in comparatively quiet sectors of the line, the units had had time to realize what were the main difficulties to be contended with in warfare in France, and were able to arrange their training accordingly. The C.R.E., being a man of wide experience, was able to give a great deal of valuable help and advice, and when the Division moved to the Ypres sector at the end of August, there is no doubt that the field companies were remarkably efficient, and were prepared for anything that might turn up, from a grand offensive to a long period of monotonous line work. It was generally understood that the Division would shortly be called upon to take part in a big attack, and keeping this in view, the C.R.E. himself addressed each field company to give them as clear an idea as possible of all that this would mean. In addition, he asked the C.R.E. of the 3rd Division to come and address the officers and N.C.O.s on the same subject. This officer, Lieut.-Colonel Walker, gave a most interesting account of the various attacks in which the R.E. of his own Division had taken part, describing the tasks which had been allotted to field companies, and how they had been carried out.

Colonel MacInnes arranged for the companies to have some practice in bridging, and sent them each in turn for a few days to the River Ancre for this purpose. He also did a very generous thing, of which few people would have thought, by offering a fine silver cup to the winning field company in competitions in Musketry,

D

Rapid Wiring and Football. This was won by the 429 Field Company.

After this period of training, the Division had three weeks in the line in front of Ypres, which included a somewhat unsuccessful attack on a restricted front on the 6th September. The 427 and 428 Field Companies took part in this attack, as they each had wiring parties whose duties were to get the new front line wired as soon as possible after capture. Unfortunately the front line did not reach the appointed place, and the R.E. parties were not called upon to work as had been expected.

On the night of the 5th September, there was a heavy gas-shell bombardment of Ypres, the greater part of these shells falling on and around the ramparts, near the Menin Gate. As the 427 and 428 Field Companies both had their quarters in dug-outs in the ramparts just at this point, they found themselves in the thick of it. This was their first experience of mustard gas in any quantity, and it was found that it had its most serious effect the following day, as it did not disperse for a very long time afterwards. The dug-outs were fitted with gas-proof curtains, and there were no ill-effects noticed due to gas getting inside the dug-outs. Men who had to go out during the bombardment or immediately after it did not suffer due to that cause alone, since they wore respirators, but those whose duties kept them in and around their quarters the following day suffered severely. Thus cooks, orderly room staff, and similar people, were employed round about these dug-outs during the whole day, and none of them noticed sufficient gas about to make it necessary to wear respirators; nevertheless, it was there in sufficient quantity to affect them, and many of them had to be sent to hospital, whilst men whose work took them away from their billet into areas which had not been affected in this manner, were all right.

There was an impression that the 42nd Division had been sent to Ypres to take part in a big attack, and it is possible that this had been at one time the intention. Whether the losses of the 125th Brigade on September 6 caused a change of plans is not known, but the 42nd Division never did take part in any big attack in this sector. They were relieved by the 9th Division on September 18, and moved back behind Poperinghe, whence they moved up to the coast, taking over the coastal sector of the line on September 24 from the 66th Division, the East Lancs. 2nd Line Division.

The stay here was short, however, and on the 5th and 6th October the R.E. units moved to the right into the Nieuport sector, where the line was taken over from the 32nd Division. Nieuport, though interesting, was what was generally known as a "sticky" place, and one went about with the impression that one was going to meet a shell round the next corner. The R.E. work here was strenuous and exacting, and involved a great deal of bridge maintenance. Bridge work, however amusing it may be in the summer under peace conditions, when one can afford to laugh at some one else falling into the water, is no fun at all in October and November, carried on under all sorts of weather, and with an unpleasant amount of hostile shell fire going on. The 428 and 429 Field Companies each had over thirty bridges of different kinds under their charge.

The reason for this enormous number of bridges will easily be understood by a reference to the map of Nieuport and district, when it will be seen that Nieuport is almost surrounded by canals, while at the N.E. corner of the town no fewer than six canals meet and run through sluice gates into the Yser Maritime, which is tidal. The main road from Nieuport to Ostend crosses these six canals at the point where they join the Yser Maritime, and for some mysterious reason this place is known as the " Five Bridges "; as there are really six of them, the reason for the number five is not clear.

The six canals meeting here are : (1) the Dunkerque Canal, which is a traffic waterway; (2) the Noord Vaart, or Groote Beverdyk Vaart, which is for drainage purposes; (3) the Yser River, which is canalized for traffic; (4) the Crique de Nieuwendamme, which is for drainage purposes; (5) the Plasschendaele Canal, and (6) the Evacuation Canal. Round the south and west of the town there was also the Koolhof Canal, which was for drainage of the low-lying country, and discharged into the Yser Maritime at low tide through automatic lock-gates to the north-west of the town. To get into the town at all from the rear, it was necessary to cross the Koolhof, and to get from the town forward to the front line, it was necessary to cross the Yser Maritime, or to go round by the " Five Bridges." The left brigade in the line held the front to the north of the town, and used three floating bridges across the Yser Maritime as their main communication route, occasionally going round by the " Five Bridges."

The right brigade held the line to the north-east and east of the town, and they had rather more choice of routes by which to get forward to the line.

The drainage of the forward area on the north side of the town was a problem of considerable magnitude, which is mentioned in detail in the portion of this book dealing with the 427 Field Company, R.E. A work of great importance in this connection was " Dam 66," which was notoriously the worst job which the R.E. had to tackle in this sector. Work was at times carried on under the greatest possible difficulties, and although there were several casualties on this job, it was perhaps surprising that there were not more. The 429 Field Company had the matter in hand at one time, but later, as they were fully occupied with the repair of the three floating bridges, and sundry other jobs which could be best undertaken by them, they had to hand it over to the 427 Field Company.

A familiar figure in Nieuport at this time was the C.R.E., Colonel MacInnes. How or when he rested no one ever knew, but he was very often walking round the works early in the morning, having set out from his headquarters at Coxyde Bains in the very small hours. Sometimes he spent the night in Nieuport, and on one occasion when there was a good deal of anxiety about Dam 66, he spent the whole night on the Dam with the working party, to see whether he could give any assistance or suggest any steps that might be taken to make things easier. The reason for his early morning appearances in Nieuport was that most of the R.E. work was done either by night, or between 5.0. a.m. and 11.0 a.m., this being the quietest time of the day; and he always wanted to be there when the work was going on. As a result of this untiring energy, he was able to give a great deal of valuable assistance and advice.

Each of the three field companies had a certain amount of concrete work to do, and each of them required a big supply of stores for bridge maintenance. Consequently, the volume of transport sent up to Nieuport each night was enormous. Quite apart from R.E. stores and materials, there were of course ration wagons for all the units in or near the front line, and the main road from Coxyde to Nieuport was a mass of transport from dusk till about midnight, when most of it had returned empty. Although this road came in for a good deal of shelling both by day and night, there was never any great disaster to the column of transport coming up in the evening. Those who tried riding a bicycle along this main road in pitch darkness, when the road was crowded with transport, found that it was one of the nightmares of the war.

Most of the main streets in the town of Nieuport had covered "boyaux," made by the French, running along the greater part of their length, and these were used instead of walking along the street, the latter not being very safe. Certain streets had no trenches or boyaux, the one leading down to Crowder Bridge being a case in point. Walking along that particular street gave one an uncomfortable sensation of being stared at, as it faced the enemy lines. As a matter of fact, they probably could not see along it, as they were a considerable distance away, but one was apt to get that nasty sensation which one might expect a sleepwalker to experience if he were to awake and find himself walking naked along a public thoroughfare.

Fortunately many of the houses in Nieuport were of very strong construction, and life in their cellars was reasonably safe. The billet occupied by the 427 Field Company was an old powder factory, and the thickness of the walls and roof was tremendous, with the result that the whole building was absolutely shell-proof, and they could live in it in security, without worrying about cellars. Another similar building was the one known as "Indiarubber House," which was on the forward side of the Yser Maritime, and earned its name from the fact that shells were said to bounce off it. This was used as the headquarters of one of the battalions in the line on the left brigade front.

On the 18th November, the 42nd Division were relieved by a French division, the three field companies being relieved by the 28th Régiment du Génie. A long march then followed, ending in the La Bassée sector, where the 42nd Division took over from the 25th Division.

Working in this sector for periods varying from two and a half months in the case of the 429 Field Company, to three and a half months in the case of the 428 Field Company, the field companies put in some of the most satisfactory and useful work they ever did in France. At Nieuport, much of the work done had been merely maintenance, which may be interesting for a time, but soon becomes dull, even under good conditions, whilst under conditions such as those prevailing at Nieuport, it was really objectionable. In the La Bassée sector, however, there was not nearly so much shelling as there had been at Nieuport, and there was a great deal of entirely new work to be done, so that there was something to show for one's activities.

At the time of the 42nd Division's arrival in this sector, at the end of November 1917, it was already realized by those in a position to judge, that there would be a big enemy offensive before many months had passed; and as there was remarkably little shell-proof cover in that sector, it was necessary to put in hand at once the provision of something of this sort on an extensive scale. Shell-proof cover had to be provided in or near the front line, at the headquarters of battalions in the line, and along what was known as the " village line," for the accommodation of the support battalions; the gunners also had to be considered. Added to this there was a certain amount of maintenance work on communication trenches, and on drains in the flat part of the sector, so that the programme of work was a very formidable one.

At the end of December, it was found necessary to attach one field company and the pioneer battalion of the 55th Division to work under the C.R.E., 42nd Division. The work was pushed ahead so well, however, that when the 55th Division were attacked in this sector in April 1918 (after the departure of the 42nd Division), they were able to hold out, and the concrete shelters which the 42nd Division had put in were found to be invaluable. To indicate the amount of concreting done there is included in the account of the 428 Field Company a table which refers to one brigade sector only. If this is doubled, it gives a rough idea of the amount of concrete work put in, exclusive of work for the artillery.

The Division remained in the line in this sector from the end of November until the middle of February 1918, and during the whole of that period, the 429 Field Company remained at work in the left brigade sector forward, whilst the 428 Field Company did most of the work in the right brigade sector, with the 427 Field Company working in the reserve area. At first the 427 Field Company had the front line work on the right, and the 428 were in the reserve area, but their positions were reversed after quite a short time.

Just before Christmas 1917, Lieut.-Colonel D. S. MacInnes left the Division to proceed to G.H.Q. as Deputy Engineer in Chief. Every one in the Division realized what a great loss this was; but perhaps no one quite so much as the Divisional R.E., and more especially the field company commanders. No one on the Divisional

Staff knew the front line better than he did, and if there was dangerous work going on, his great idea was to visit such work regularly and encourage all engaged on it. His frequent visits to that famous Dam 66 at Nieuport provide a case in point. His great abilities, sound judgment and insistence on good organization were reflected in the work of the field companies, and the unsparing way in which he worked himself ensured the best efforts of every officer, N.C.O. and man under his command. As one of his officers put it : "No one so well exemplified the 'will to victory.'" He was succeeded by Lieut.-Colonel R. E. B. Pratt, D.S.O., R.E., who came to us from the 11th Division.

There was a very severe frost during the latter part of December and early January, and when the thaw came, there was a great deal of trouble with the trenches. They were mostly old, and the revetting materials were not as good as they had been, and consequently many of the trenches caved in and became in places absolutely impassable. This added a lot to the work to be done, and naturally had the effect of impeding to some extent the concreting and similar work. Another trouble then cropped up in the form of a shortage of cement. However, in spite of these difficulties, plenty of useful work was done.

When the 42nd Division was relieved in the middle of February 1918, the 428 Field Company remained behind to work in the same area under the direct orders of the C.E. 1st Corps. The 427 Field Company, who were at first relieved and sent to Busnes, were recalled after a few days, and went back to live in Beuvry, and to work under the 55th Division, until early in March, when they were finally relieved, and went back to Busnes for training. The 429 Field Company, after relief in the middle of February, moved back to Les Harisoirs, and later to Hinges, and still later to Oblinghem, where they remained until the enemy offensive began in March.

In February the 1/7th Battalion Northumberland Fusiliers (Lieut.-Colonel H. Liddell, D.S.O., M.C., commanding) came from the 50th Division to be the pioneer battalion of the 42nd Division. They supplied a long-felt want, and after their arrival it was no longer necessary to attach permanent infantry working parties to the field companies. In the 50th Division the 1/7th Northumberland Fusiliers had made a great name as a fine fighting battalion and had seen a great deal of hard service; and there is no doubt that they left their old division to take up their new rôle with feelings of regret. But they quickly settled down among us, and although strange to some of their new work and duties, it did not take them long to find out what was wanted and how to do it.

It so happened that soon after their arrival they had to be used as infantry for fighting purposes, and very well they did it. After that, when they settled down to pioneer work, the enterprise of all ranks in the battalion made them of the very greatest assistance to the Division, and in particular, to the R.E.

In February and March there was an outbreak of mange in the

42ND DIVL. R.E.

Division, and the 428 Field Company's horses suffered severely, and a great many were evacuated. The other field companies also had the same trouble, but did not lose so many horses.

The Division, now in G.H.Q. reserve, had been at eight hours' notice to move for some days, when on the night of 22nd March, orders were received for the move southward. The whole Division moved the following morning by lorries to the neighbourhood of Adinfer, south of the Doullens–Arras road. On the evening of the 24th March, the Division went forward to relieve the 40th Division, and for the next three days the field companies, with the exception of the 428 Field Company, who were detailed as escort for the R.F.A., did not get a chance to do much useful R.E. work. They were mostly held in reserve, and moved back from near Gomiecourt to Logeast Wood, and thence to Essarts-lez-Bucquoy. After the enemy advance had been stopped on 26th March, all three field companies had a little time in the line as infantry, although they were not all in the line at the same time. With the exception of an interval of forty-eight hours, during which the line was held by the 41st Division, the 42nd Division remained in the line until the night of the 7th April. This was one of the most exhausting periods the field companies ever experienced. There were not many officers or men who had their boots off except for a hasty change of socks during those seventeen days. The weather was cold and very wet. The companies bivouacked in any old shell holes or trenches they could find, close up to the front line. There was a great deal of work to be done in digging new trenches and putting up wire entanglements, and there were little or no R.E. materials. The roads were atrocious, and there was no material for their repair. Rations had a long way to come and there could be no cooking in the line, but thanks to the organization and determination of the company quartermaster sergeants, the sappers never went short.

During the latter part of the period a certain amount of useful R.E. work was done, partly in and near the front line between Bucquoy and Ablainzevelle, and partly on a defensive line further back near Gommecourt and Essarts. Few will forget the delight of a rest and more especially a wash in Pas and Hénu, two quite attractive French villages, well back from the line.

The Division was out of the line from 7th to 15th April, and again from the 6th May to 7th June. The field companies were working during practically the whole of this time. They had a few days complete rest from the 8th to 12th April, and were then sent to work on a new defence line called the "Château de la Haie" Switch. Going back to the line with the Division on 15th and 16th April, they did more work on defences round Hébuterne, and on 7th May went back to Hénu, Pas, and Couin, and continued on defence works for the next month.

Relieving the New Zealand Division on 7th June, the 42nd Division went back to the line to the right of, and including, Hébuterne.

Meanwhile, at the end of April, there had been changes in the commands of the field companies. Lieut.-Colonel A. N. Lawford left the 429 Field Company, and Major Riddick took his place, whilst Captain Entwistle was appointed to command the 428 Field Company, and was made acting Major. Lieutenant Bateman was made Captain and Adjutant, and Captain Walker went to the 428 Field Company as second in command. Lieutenant Mackenzie, of the pioneer battalion, was attached to H.Q. R.E. as stores officer. Early in July the departure of Colonel Pratt necessitated further changes, Major Riddick being appointed C.R.E. with the acting rank of Lieut.-Colonel. Major M. S. Hanmer, coming from the 5th Division, took over command of 429 Field Company. Later still, Major Mousley left the 427 Field Company to become C.R.E. 4th Corps Troops, and Major Forsyth from a Field Squadron of the 2nd Cavalry Division replaced him as O.C. 427 Field Company.

In noting the departure of Colonel Pratt, it should be mentioned that one of his very strong points was transport, and the outbreak of mange shortly after he came to the Division made him even more than usually keen on the supervision of the field companies' horse lines. He missed nothing, and kept the companies very well up to the mark, with the result that the smartness of turnout and general efficiency of the R.E. transport improved greatly under his administration. It is true that he was once heard to admit that the transport officer of one company completely baffled him. Every time he found something amiss on that company's lines, the transport officer had a plausible and apparently flawless excuse for it. It was only after he had thought the matter over for a few hours, the Colonel said, that the flaw (for there always was one) in the answer occurred to him; it was then too late to say much about it, and the next time he visited those lines, that particular fault had always been put right. He declared that he would defy even the Divisional Commander to trip up such a master of ready answers. Notwithstanding regret at Lieut.-Colonel Pratt's departure, every one was pleased at the appointment of Major Riddick as C.R.E., and all realized that they could not be in better hands.

During June, July, and August, the field companies were very busy in the sector south of Hébuterne, still mostly on new defensive works, and the weeks passed uneventfully. It was a very pleasant sector to work in, and became fairly quiet. Our own artillery fire, which had reached an enormous volume about the middle of April, was gradually reduced as the summer wore on, presumably because it had been discovered that the enemy had cancelled his offensive programme in this neighbourhood. There was still enough left, however, to keep him quiet, and whenever he attempted to have a noisy "hate," he got about double the quantity back.

The divisional system of defence was based on the now well-known maxim of "defence in depth and chequer-wise." A very elaborate system of strong points or localities, usually with a platoon as garrison, was gradually constructed, work commencing on the rear defence lines first, work nearer the line following later. In addition to construction of fire trenches, communication trenches and wire entanglements, each strong point was provided with a deep tunnelled dug-out with at least two entrances to shelter the garrison. From eight to ten tunnelled dug-outs were always in course of construction, and in addition to the field companies, sections of 179 and 252 Tunnelling Companies, R.E. and the 1/7th Northumberland Fusiliers (Pioneers) were employed on the work. Similar provision was also made for machine guns and their teams, and for many of the divisional artillery gun positions, and the divisional sector rapidly became exceedingly strong.

Plans were being made to provide for the winter, but this, fortunately, turned out to be unnecessary. In the middle of August, the enemy evacuated Serre, and retired about a mile on the divisional front, and on August 21, the great British offensive opened along the Third Army front.

Although they had been continuously in the line since the 7th June, the 42nd Division were used to start the offensive on their bit of the front, and remained in the line in pursuit until September 5. Between August 21 and September 5, they had to carry out several attacks, and carried the line east of Ytres, near the Canal du Nord. During this period, and also during later advances, it was found best to allot work to companies in the following way : One company on front-line work and reconnaissance for water supply and smaller jobs, such as searching for mines and obstacles, and gas-proofing dug-outs, etc. The second company on more thorough development of water supply, and assisting the pioneers on road work. The third company in reserve, and on " Q " work. If possible, portions of the other two companies were kept in reserve also. Otherwise, it was impossible to cope with emergency work which could not be foreseen.

Captain Dean's section of 252 Tunnelling Company, R.E. worked with the forward field company, and rendered invaluable assistance in reconnaissance work close up behind the advancing infantry, not only in searching dug-outs and roads and tracks for booby traps and mines, but in the immediate investigation of all wells in the villages, as the enemy evacuated the latter. He usually attempted to blow all the wells in, but fortunately his retreat was hurried and his demolitions suffered in consequence.

With the exception of the River Ancre at Miraumont, and the Canal du Nord at Ytres and Ruyaulcourt, until the River Escaut at Crèvecoeur was reached, the line of advance for the Division was through a waterless country. Consequently, until the village wells could be re-opened and lift-and-force pumps replaced by power-driven chain Helice or belt pumps, water had to be carried forward by Garford lorries and emptied into 2300 or 9000 gallon canvas tanks erected as near the firing-line as possible.

The provision of pumps (hand and power driven), canvas tanks and horse troughs, with all the necessary fittings in the right places, and at the right time, was often a tricky proceeding, as sapper parties on three-ton lorries had to be sent back to areas now being left behind, to dismantle and bring forward R.E. stores. Apart from the splendid work of all three field companies, the rapid development of new water points owed much to Lieutenant Mortimer (of the 1/7th Northumberland Fusiliers and temporarily attached to R.E. Headquarters), and to Sergeant-Major F. J. Sowray, D.C.M., R.E. They, in conjunction with the stores officer and his N.C.O.s, brought the resources and organization of the Divisional R.E. dump to a very high standard.

After the first few days of the advance, the 429 Field Company were given the forward work to do, tackling the preliminary work on water supply, and carrying out reconnaissances of roads, and searching for mines and booby traps.

They continued to do the forward work until the relief of the Division on the 5th September. During a part of this advance also, they had a section attached to one of the battalions of the leading brigade, but as this arrangement was not satisfactory, it was discontinued.

When the New Zealand Division took over the line on September 5, the field companies moved back into what had then become a back area, the 427 Field Company going to Thilloy, while the 428 and 429 were close together near Pys, and all three companies got a fortnight's training.

Tents and various kinds of shelters sprang up all over the desolate country over which the advance had recently taken place, and to return from leave at this time was one long succession of surprises. The leave train came up from Boulogne by Candas, Colincamps, Puisieux, Achiet-le-Grand, and so on to Bapaume, and for any one who had gone away before the advance started, it was quite a novelty to find Colincamps perfectly quiet, with a Casualty Clearing Station in course of erection, whereas formerly the Sucrerie there had been an unhealthy spot.

After the fortnight's rest and training, the 42nd Division relieved the 87th Division on the left of the 4th Corps sector. The line by this time had been carried forward to Havrincourt and Trescault, and the 428 Field Company, who took over the forward work, found themselves back in old haunts in Havrincourt Wood; they also found that the enemy's bombing 'planes were rather unpleasantly active at night time in this locality.

After a week spent in more or less normal line work, the Division attacked on the morning of September 27 in front of Trescault, and in spite of considerable resistance, succeeding in capturing the Hindenburg Line, which lay between Trescault and Ribécourt. This was one of the stiffest bits of fighting which the Division ever had. They were at one time in danger of being badly held up on the right, as the 5th Division had great difficulty in taking Beaucamp, and as long as this place remained in the hands of the enemy, it was a serious menace to the right flank of the 42nd Division. However, it was finally captured in the afternoon, and the line was carried forward to Welsh Ridge, which was not far short of the Escaut Canal.

The 42nd Division was then relieved by the New Zealand Division, who continued the pursuit up to, and in places across, the Escaut Canal. There was then another pause lasting rather over a week, during which the three field companies moved up to the forward side of Havrincourt Wood. The R.E. work at this time was mainly on water supply and the erection of camps for such things as a divisional reception camp and Divisional H.Q. The New Zealand Division led off the next advance, and the 42nd Division followed up on the 9th October and following days, finally taking over the line again on the River Selle on the 12th October. The 427 Field Company then became the forward company, and went to live at Le Prayelle, whilst the other two companies were billeted at a large farm at Jeune Bois, near Beauvois. By this time it had become evident that the advance was to be a more or less continuous affair, and when people settled down at places like Jeune Bois, no one supposed that they were going to be there long. All the work undertaken was in the nature of preparation for a continuance of the advance at an early date, and included road repairs, the filling in of big road craters, and of course, water supply as usual. The 427 Field Company had to erect some foot-bridges over the River Selle, and preparations were made for the erection of two pontoon bridges, and of a bridge to carry tanks, as soon as the advance was resumed. On the night of 19th/20th October, the 42nd Division attacked again, crossed the River Selle by pontoon bridges and other bridges erected by 427 Field Company, and carried the line forward beyond Solesmes. The bridging operations of the 427 Field Company at the River Selle were most successful, and a complete account of this work is given in Chapter IV of the 427 Field Company. On 23rd October, the Division made another attack, and immediately handed over to the New Zealand Division, who took the line forward almost to Le Quesnoy. Between the 20th and the 23rd October, two railway bridges had to be cleared from the road leading into Solesmes. The demolitions carried out by the enemy in his retirement were very thorough, and the railways in particular suffered. The railway between Cambrai and Caudry was badly smashed up, and in addition to the damage which had been done before our arrival, there were a number of delay-action mines, which exploded some considerable time afterwards, with the result that railway traffic was interrupted several times after the line had been re-opened.

During the Division's rest in the neighbourhood of Caudry the Divisional Engineers held an inter-field-company transport competition, and in addition athletic sports for the companies and the pioneer battalion. Lunch was provided on the ground, and the Divisional Commander kindly joined us, judging some events and distributing the prizes.

The final advance on the 4th Corps front was started by the New Zealand Division on the 4th November, and the 42nd Division followed up and took over on the night of 5th November at the east end of Mormal Forest. The 427 Field Company were again the forward company, the 429 following up to take over any big jobs which the 427 might be unable to tackle owing to the speed of their advance, while the 428 Field Company were detailed to look after water supply. The first jobs of any magnitude which were encountered were the passage of some large craters in the roads through Mormal Forest. One of these was far too big to bridge, and a deviation had to be made. This of course took time, and some delay was caused through the traffic having to be diverted by another road. There was a good deal of rain at the time, which made the conditions of work difficult, and as the companies had to keep on moving and working more or less simultaneously, they had a pretty hard time. After getting through Mormal Forest, the next obstacle was the River Sambre, and as this had been foreseen, pontoons were kept close up. In addition to the pontoons of the 42nd Division, the bridging equipment of the New Zealand Division was held available for use on the Sambre, and this meant that when our own companies had moved, on any day, they generally had to send back teams to bring up the New Zealand pontoons. The drivers and horses therefore got very little rest. Early on the morning of the 8th November, the pontoons were got up to the Sambre, and the 427 Field Company put across a light bridge in the early hours of the morning. Another bridge was erected by the 429 Field Company later in the same day, and as this one was required to get guns, etc., forward, proper road approaches had to be made to it at once. The approaches to this bridge, which was at Boussières, were made passable on the 9th November.

Hautmont had been taken on the 8th about midday, and all bridges having been demolished by the enemy, a bridge to carry tanks was now required over the River Sambre in the centre of the town. Meantime a pontoon bridge was commenced at noon on the 9th and completed by 8 p.m. The 427 and 428 Field Companies reached Hautmont on the morning of the 9th, and concentrated on the completion of this work. On the 10th November the 429th Field Company, having finished all necessary work at Boussières, and having also removed some road mines near Petit Bayay, were sent forward to Louvroil, half their company going further forward still to Ferrière-la-Grande, where some more bridges had to be thrown across the River Solre.

On this date, word was received that the advance of the 42nd Division would cease, and the further advance would be carried on by the cavalry and cyclists. The difficulties in the way of any further advance of the Division were, in fact, very great, as supplies had to come up a very long way by road, owing to the trouble with the Cambrai-Caudry railway. Also, the roads through Mormal Forest were unfit for motor transport of any kind, so that horse transport had to be used for a very long distance in rear. It was found that at this time we had apparently advanced too fast for the enemy's demolitions

SAILLY AU BOIS CHURCH. THE CATACOMBS IN THE VICINITY WERE USED BY THE RESERVE BATTALION.

HAUTMONT, CAPTURED BY 126TH BRIGADE ON NOV. 8, 1918. THE BRIDGES WERE ERECTED BY THE DIVISIONAL ENGINEERS.

42ND DIVL. R.E.

LIST OF BRIDGES CONSTRUCTED DURING OCTOBER, NOVEMBER AND DECEMBER, 1918, BY THE 42ND DIVISIONAL ROYAL ENGINEERS.

	River.	Road on which situated.	Spans. No.	Spans. Width.	Nature of Bridge.
1	Selle	Open country near Briastre	10		footbridges having an average length of 35'
2	Selle	Briastre–Solesmes : at Briastre	4	15'	Medium pontoon
3	Selle	Briastre–Solesmes : diversion at Briastre	4	15'	Medium pontoon
4	Selle	Ditto, to replace No. 3	4	15'	Timber trestle
5	Small stream in Mormal Forest	Gommegnies–Pont sur Sambre : N.W. of Forester's House	2	15'	Service trestle over blown culvert
6	Small stream in Mormal Forest	Le Quesnoy–Hargnies : W. of Forester's House	2	15'	Ditto
7	Ruisseau de la Fontaine	Petit Bayay–Boussières : 1 mile W. of Boussières	2	15'	Service trestle
8	Sambre	Open country south of Boussières	5	15'	Light pontoon 4 ½-pontoons
9	Sambre	Boussières–St. Rémy-du-Nord : at Boussières	5	15'	Medium pontoon
10	Sambre	Bavai–Ferrière : in Hautmont	5	15'	Medium pontoon
11	Sambre	Ditto	1	18' 6"	Girder bridge : 10-ton axle load
12	Sambre	Ditto			Footbridge on debris of demolished bridges
13	Sambre	Ditto, to replace No. 10	7	Various : longest 30'	To carry tanks
14	Sambre	Ditto, to replace No. 11	1	18' 6"	To carry tanks
15	Sambre	Sous-le-Bois–Louvroil : at Louvroil	3	30', 32' & 30'	Trestles & steel joists : 30-ton axle load
16	Solre	Ferrière-la-Grande to les Trieux railway station	3	17'	Trestles & joists : 8-ton axle load
17	Solre	Ferrière-la-Grande to Ferrière-la-Petite : at Ferrière-la-Petite	2 single-span bridges	14' & 15'	Rails and sleepers : 4-ton axle load
18	Solre	Maubeuge–Colleret : at Ferrière-la-Grande	4	18'	Trestles & joists : 17-ton axle load
19	Ruisseau de l'Hôpital	Maubeuge–Vieux Reng to main Mons–Beaumont road : N. of Elesmes	Culvert		17-ton axle load
20	La Trouille	Ditto, S.W. of Vieux Reng	3	15', 16' & 17'	Trestles & joists : 17-ton axle load
21	Sambre	Vieux Reng–Marpent : at Marpent	5	15'	Medium pontoon (German pontoons)
22	Sambre	Ditto, to replace No. 21 after breakage by lorry	5	15'	Medium pontoon (British pontoon)

to be properly carried out. Thus, although at Hautmont all the factories had been completely stripped, all bridges blown, and so forth, at Ferrière-la-Grande there were factories which had not been damaged at all; and although the bridges at Ferrière had been blown, all road craters which had been made in this neighbourhood had evidently been done very hastily, and were easily repaired. In the railway station at Ferrière there was enemy rolling stock, and the railway itself had not been damaged at all. It appeared, therefore, that the enemy was being badly hustled, and although every one was tired out and very glad of a rest, it was in one way disappointing that we were not to be able to follow up any further.

One felt curious to see what would happen next, but this was soon settled, for on the morning of the 11th November, as all the world knows, word was received that hostilities would cease at 11.0 a.m. It remained then to finish off the bridges in hand, and settle down to a quieter life.

Bridging was by no means finished, as another bridge at Ferrière had to be taken over from the 62nd Division, who had been working to the north of us; a new heavy bridge had to be put up across the Sambre between Louvroil and Sous-le-Bois; and, later, early in December, more were required at Vieux Reng, to enable the Division to move on to Charleroi.

The amount of bridge work carried out by the three field companies during November was quite abnormal, and the table on p. 45 shows all the bridges constructed during the month with various details as to dimensions.

The move to Charleroi took place in December, an advance party of R.E. and pioneers going on ahead under Major Hanmer on 6th December, taking three days to reach Charleroi, and the remainder of the Division moved at the middle of the month, the move being completed on 18th December. For the first month in Charleroi, the R.E. were very busy, as a great deal of work was required on the infantry accommodation; but during February, 1919, work began to slacken off. The first men for demobilization were sent home just before Christmas, and in January and February demobilization proceeded fairly quickly.

Lieut.-Colonel J. G. Riddick carried on as C.R.E. until about the middle of March, when he left for home; H.Q. R.E. then remained in charge of Captain J. P. Echlin, acting as adjutant, Captain Bateman having been demobilized previously. It was a fitting conclusion to the active service of the Divisional R.E., that an East Lancs. R.E. officer should have held the post of C.R.E. during the later stages of the war, more especially as he filled the post with success.

When the field companies had been reduced by demobilization to cadre strength, they were not kept long in Belgium. They left at the end of March, and were dispersed from Oswestry.

PART III
THE 427TH FIELD COMPANY, ROYAL ENGINEERS
1914–1919

CHAPTER I

EGYPT AND GALLIPOLI

THE annual training for the East Lancs. Divisional R.E. was to have taken place at Carnarvon during August of 1914. The 1/2nd Field Company had already started off, and the 1/1st, with H.Q. R.E., were due to go off from Old Trafford Station, when the stationmaster was told to cancel the train. In due course instructions came through to the C.R.E. that mobilization was to commence at once, and that the 1/2nd Field Company, R.E., were on their way back from Carnarvon.

In fourteen days' time the units completed their mobilization, which speaks well for the arrangements which had been made by the Permanent Staff. All the horses, entire vehicles, stores, etc., had been purchased and the men's kit inspected. In these days each man had to provide his own boots, small kit and under-clothes. All ranks were medically examined and vaccinated where necessary. Owing to shortage of proper instruments, a jack-knife was used in this operation, with the result that the O.C.s arm did not heal for six months.

The Divisional R.E. then proceeded by march route to the neighbourhood of Bolton, where it was under canvas for about three weeks previous to embarking at Southampton on September 9, 1914, for Egypt on H.M.T.s *Neuralia* and *Deseado*.

The 1st Field Company travelled in the s.s. *Neuralia*, and disembarked at Alexandria on September 26, 1914, after a very pleasant voyage, passing *en route* near Malta the large convoy of about twenty-six transports conveying the first consignment of Indian troops to France.

The company was then sent by train to Kasr-el-Nil Barracks, Cairo, where the Divisional R.E. relieved the 2nd Field Company R.E., who soon afterwards departed for the Western Front.

The following month was devoted to training on the square and simple field engineering. The company was then sent to Ismailia, arriving there about October 29, 1914. The first job of any note was the construction of a floating bridge over the Suez Canal at Ismailia Ferry to carry camels loaded and infantry in fours. The gap was ninety-seven yards wide. Red Sea fishing boats were obtained, the average size being 24 feet long by 7 feet beam. The road-bearers consisted of 7-inch by 4-inch seasoned timber about 16 feet 6 inches long, each fitted with half-inch round irons at each end to clip over the saddle-beams. The saddle-beams were built up from the keel, supported by a strut under the position of each road-bearer. The distance between centre of each boat was 15 feet, five road-bearers being used. The bridge was constructed by "booming out," two small boats being used to place the upstream and downstream anchors respectively. The time taken to make the bridge with seventy men was about one hour. Afterwards rafts were kept moored to the west bank and floated down into position in accordance with the way the tide was running; this method, of course, was considerably quicker. The time to dismantle was twenty minutes.

Bridge- or ferry-head positions were prepared at Ismailia Ferry, Toussoum, Serapeum and Deversoir, varying in size from battalion to company posts. The trenches had to be dug in either sand or the spoil heaps from the Suez Canal excavation, and considerable difficulty was experienced in obtaining good revetting material, as there were scarcely any R.E. stores available. The most successful was the stiff clay which could be got from the salt lakes or ponds on the east bank. Overhead cover was provided in the more important parts of the works, made out of 4-inch by 4-inch timber and scrap-iron sheets; amongst the latter were station sign-boards which had been dismantled from stations in the Soudan. Barbed wire entanglements were put out in front of the posts and were arranged so that they could be enfiladed. Petroleum flares were extensively used, and arranged with ignition devices from trip wires or wires that could be pulled off from the trenches. A false alarm was caused at Deversoir post by a "prairie" dog pulling off the trip wire of a large flare, which burnt for about half an hour and caused a certain amount of ammunition to be wasted by the Indian troops holding the post. Christmas 1914 was spent by the company at Ismailia; the turkey purchased for the officers' mess about a fortnight beforehand disappeared several times from the camp, but was always recovered from the neighbouring Indian Brigade camps. About this time the 42nd Division Sports were held in Cairo, and the Divisional R.E. tug-of-war team (all except two were found from the 1/1st Field Company) beat all comers, each member of the team, including the coach, receiving a wrist watch for the prize. On New Year's Eve a company dance was got up by Lieutenant Mackenzie, very ably assisted by the wives of some of the officers of the Indian Brigade, and held at the Suez Canal Company's Hall at Ismailia; the fair sex were unfortunately conspicuous by their absence, but it turned out to be a very jolly evening, and finished up with "Auld Lang Syne" as the New Year came in.

On January 6th the company struck camp at Ismailia and returned to Kasr-el-Nil Barracks, Cairo, to take part in brigade and divisional route marches and field days. One field day took place along the Suez Road between Towers No. 1 and No. 2, in which the field company had to site near "Large Rock" a rallying-point to which a brigade could withdraw. Another field day was spent on

427TH FIELD COY. R.E.

Heliopolis "Ocean," which, although it was not realized at the time, was intended to prepare the Division for a possible landing on the Gallipoli Peninsula, at Alexandretta, or elsewhere in the Turkish Empire. On each of these field days the company had to bivouac the previous night in the open at Abbassia, so as to be able to reach the starting-point in time; this was rather a cold proceeding, but it was useful training. On January 23rd the G.O.C. 42nd Division held a conference at Abbassia on the previous field days, and at 1 p.m. we received orders to return on the 25th to the Suez Canal, as the Turks were reported to be advancing across the Sinai Peninsula. Lieutenant Mackenzie was sent on in advance to make preparations for the arrival of the company, and also to take charge of the distribution of drinking water to all the posts on the Suez Canal. This was done by steam water-boats drawing from the filtering stations at Suez and Ismailia. Sapper Andrews was chosen to assist in this work. On arrival at Ismailia one section, under Lieutenant Taunton, was employed on renewing and providing additional flares at the various Canal posts.

Captain Riddick and Lieutenant Ainley, with Nos. 1 and 2 Sections, were sent to Serapeum and worked under Lieut.-Colonel Geoghegan, who commanded the 22nd Indian Infantry Brigade.

Orders were received to construct a barrel pier bridge over the Sweet Water Canal at Ain Ghosein, which was the nearest railway station to the Serapeum post. This bridge was completed within twenty-four hours by No. 3 and part of No. 4 Section under Lieutenant Gough, assisted by Lieutenant Scott, who had only just joined the company. The span was 36 feet, and consisted of three bays each 12 feet long. Twenty-four forty-gallon casks were used for each of the two piers. The bridge was used by the reinforcements which were sent from Ismailia when the Turks attacked the Canal between Toussoum and Serapeum posts a few days later.

On February 1st the Turks were sighted from the "Bench Mark" position, which was about one and a half miles north of Ismailia Ferry up the Canal; a small action took place the following day in front of the Ferry Post, and on the 3rd the post was shelled intermittently all day. No. 3 Section came under shell fire on Lake Timsah as they were proceeding to work at Bench Mark post, but no casualties were sustained.

Nos. 1 and 2 Sections on the days of 3rd and 4th came in for all the fighting at the point where the Turks tried to cross the Canal, and the company had its first list of casualties: Sapper Mottram killed, Sapper Austin wounded in the chest, and Sapper Collins slightly wounded. On February 5th some of the prisoners were brought to Ismailia and bivouacked on the football ground in the gardens. The scene was rather an impressive one, and when night came on the ground was lighted up with the crude petroleum used for the flares.

The following day the 1/2nd Field Company came down from

Cairo to Ismailia, and the next day Headquarters and Section Nos. 3 and 4 joined Nos. 1 and 2 Sections at Serapeum.

Between February 7 and March 30, 1915, nothing of any particular note occurred. The scheme for defence of the Canal was not changed, as with the few troops at the disposal of the G.O.C. it was only possible to defend the Suez Canal by using it as an obstacle, which method had already proved so successful at the beginning of the month. Captain Riddick with Corporal Sprosson and twelve picked N.C.O.s and sappers left for Cairo on April 5, 1915, to form a class of instruction for the pioneers of the infantry battalions; the excellent work done on this short course proved of infinite value to the Division on arrival at Gallipoli, especially for those battalions who had taken the trouble to choose sound men for their pioneers.

The 1/2nd Field Company constructed a classification musketry range near Ismailia. This enabled all sections to fire a course during the last two weeks of April; previous to this course the company received very helpful instruction in musketry from Lieutenant Battye of the 1/10th Ghurka Regiment, who were encamped next to us at Serapeum. On April 29, 1915, orders were received to concentrate the company at Ismailia, and during the following two or three days much-needed articles of clothing, boots, etc., were issued. On May 2, 1915, the company entrained at 1.10 p.m. and arrived at Alexandria at 8.30 p.m. We immediately commenced to embark on s.s. *Nessian*, of the Leyland Line, and spent most of the night getting all the vehicles and equipment on board. Anchor was weighed at 5.45 p.m. the next day, and we started off in company with the G.O.C. R.A. and one of the East Lancashire Artillery Brigades on board. The entrance to the Dardanelles was sighted first at 5 a.m. on May 6, 1915, and we anchored opposite Gaba Tepe. At 9 a.m. anchor was weighed and we came to Cape Helles, where fighting, apparently near the village of Krithia, was taking place. The following day we came nearer in to Cape Helles with a view to landing, which, however, was cancelled at the last moment. The 8th May was spent on board watching the fighting, and on the 9th, after the O.C. had gone on shore personally to report of the existence of the unit, anchor was weighed and we went to Lemnos. On arrival there orders were received for our immediate return to Cape Helles. This time the Ammunition Column and some men of the 6th East Lancashire Battery, R.A., disembarked, and we again returned to Lemnos in the evening. At 1.30 p.m. on the 11th we started back to Cape Helles, and on the following day (12th) disembarked the company with two double tool carts complete with teams and one mounted N.C.O. (Corporal Lee), leaving remaining horses, pontoons, and civilian four-wheeled wagons on board to return to Egypt under Lieutenant Walker of the 1/2nd Field Company. The first two nights we bivouacked on the top of the cliffs above " W " Beach, and during the day collected our stores and dug a well for D.H.Q.,

427TH FIELD COY. R.E.

also a small dug-out with overhead cover. On the 14th the company moved up to bivouac at a point 17 W 6 on 1/20,000 Dardanelles map overlooking Morto Bay; this remained the rear headquarters of the unit until the middle of August. The Division took over part of the line held by the Royal Naval Division, the company relieving the 2nd R.N.D. Engineers. The chief work was the construction of the mule track which ran up the Achi Baba Nullah and then branched off to the left just before the Australian trench crossed the Nullah, and became the chief means of communication to the front line on the right flank of the divisional sector. Our first Peninsula casualties were on May 16th, when Lance-Corporal Haynes and Driver McMasters were both hit in camp by so-called spent bullets, and on 20th May the camp was rather heavily shelled, killing Sapper Hulme and five horses. Sapper Broady was badly wounded in the head, and eventually died of his wounds at sea; also Sapper Ogden was wounded and Driver Frederichson was slightly wounded by a spent bullet. Whilst going to the 127th Brigade H.Q. on the evening of the 21st Lieutenant Mackenzie was slightly wounded in the leg by a dropping bullet. About this time preparations were commenced for the offensive action which was timed to take place early in June; the roads from Cape Helles were improved, properly drained, and No. 1 Section constructed a small bridge of about 7 feet span by 18 feet wide over a small nullah. The mule track communication trench mentioned above was widened out to five feet, and passing places about every seventy-five yards were made large enough to take a stretcher. Small wheel track bridges were prepared for all the trenches which crossed the Krithia road, so as to enable the armoured cars to come up and support the attack. Nos. 2 and 3 Sections, under Captain Riddick and Lieutenant Gough, went to bivouac in the front-line system of trenches, and assisted the infantry in improving the parapets, traverses, etc., of the trenches, which were in a very bad state. The infantry made two advances of about fifty to eighty yards each in front of the old firing-line, and were greatly assisted by the R.E. in taking up a proper alignment, making proper trenches and laying out the communication trenches back to the old line. Most of this work was done at night, as sapping forward was found to be far too slow. The two sections working in the front line were relieved every eight days; those in the rear H.Q. camp were occupied in making good the mule track communication trench, also constructing *chevaux de frises*, cross-pieces, artillery signs, red on one side and khaki on the other, to be used by the infantry in case of an advance to show their position, and torpedoes made of guncotton slabs cut in half placed between 4-inch by 3-inch boards and about 6 feet long for demolishing barbed wire entanglements. On June 4, 1915, a general advance was made, preceded by a heavy artillery bombardment. The assault was arranged in four waves with two objectives, No. 1 being the " Turkish Trench " immediately in front of our front firing-line, and No. 2 being the

Turkish support line about 400 yards in advance. The third and fourth waves consisted of two sections R.E. each and both with working parties of sixty infantry, who were to consolidate the first and second objectives respectively. The company was responsible for 600 yards of the front on the right flank of the Division, and the working party consisted of 240 1/6th Lancs. Fusiliers under Major Joyce. A small party of sappers in addition were detailed to carry the torpedoes to destroy the barbed wire in front of the Turkish trenches, but these were found to be unnecessary, as the artillery bombardment had made sufficient gaps for the infantry to get through without any delay. After the second wave had reached the first objective the third wave, under Captain Riddick, with Section No. 1 on the left under Lieutenant Ainley, and No. 4 Section on the right under Lieutenant Taunton, each with their attached infantry, immediately advanced over the parapet and set about converting the Turkish front-line trenches into fire trenches for us. At the same time a strong party of infantry under Captain Leach, 6th L.F., commenced to work on the sap which had been carried some forty yards towards our lines by the Turks just east of the Krithia main road to meet the sap already commenced by 2nd Lieutenant Evans, R.E., from our first-line trench; at night a large party of infantry and R.E. were put on, and by daylight had connected up the Turkish trench with our old system sufficiently deep to enable ammunition, stores, water, etc., being carried through under cover. The first objective in the left sector, held by the 5th Battalion, Manchester Regiment, was soon converted with the assistance of the sappers into a fairly good fire trench, with the exception of the traverses, which were of little use, and there were only sufficient sandbags available to reconstruct two traverses.

In the right sector the trenches were much less secure, owing to the traverses being poor and the trench shallow, while there was exposure to enfilade fire from our extreme right flank, where the R.N. Division had been unable to make good their advance. For this reason the Turks were able to enter the trench from the nullah on our right flank, and commenced to bomb us out of the further portions of the trench. Lieutenant Taunton, who was in charge of the R.E. section on this flank, assisted by Lieutenant James, scout officer of the 5th Battalion, Manchester Regiment, took this promptly in hand; and though they had hardly any bombs or grenades to start with, they were able to hold the Turks in check by throwing back their bombs just before they exploded. They carried on this defence for nearly two hours until a sandbag barricade with loophole was erected to enfilade the trench, and this saved a further retirement on this flank. Lieutenant Taunton was awarded the Military Cross for the above gallantry, thus gaining the first honour awarded to a member of the company; unfortunately he was mortally wounded a few days later. During the night 4th/5th June the raising and thickening of the traverses in this sector was carried on to the limit of the supply of sandbags.

427TH FIELD COY. R.E.

By reason of the failure, already mentioned, of the advance on the extreme right, those of the 5th Battalion, Manchester Regiment, who were holding the left of the second objective, had their right flank exposed. Captain Riddick, therefore, and the infantry officer in command of the first objective, together tried to find some position at the end of the vineyard between the two objectives which would afford some protection to this exposed flank; but it was later ordered that all troops should retire to the first objective (afterwards known as G 12).

The fourth wave consisted of 2nd Lieutenant Scott with No. 2 Section, R.E., and sixty infantry on the left, and Lieutenant Gough with No. 3 Section and sixty infantry on the right. The left group advanced up to the line of the second objective, held by the 5th Battalion, Manchester Regiment, and were about to commence to dig themselves in, when the retirement to the first objective was ordered. Lieutenant Scott's party then helped to consolidate the line under Captain Riddick.

Lieutenant Gough's group sustained heavy losses in their advance up the Achi Baba Nullah from machine-gun fire to their right front across the Nullah. On reaching our front firing-line, they waited until the second wave advanced towards their objective. This, however, never took place in this part of the sector, as the right flank was by that time exposed.

As soon as darkness fell Lieutenant Gough organized a working party of the Nelson Battalion, R.N. Division, of about 250 men, and dug a switch trench from near Taunton's barricade in the first objective to join across into our old front firing-line at the point where it crossed the nullah on our extreme right flank. This trench was deep enough at daylight to get communication through to the old Turkish front line. The following day, 5th June, was spent in consolidating the latter and widening and deepening the main communication trench. Lieutenant Ainley was killed whilst running outside this communication trench; there was a block in the traffic and he wanted to get to the cause of the delay; by his death the company lost one of its most capable and energetic officers. The casualties from May 22 to June 5, 1915, inclusive, were as follows—

22 May, 1915.		Sapper F. Dixon, bullet in the leg in camp.
22 ,,	,,	Sapper Maginess, bullet wound in leg.
23 ,,	,,	Sapper Vear, bullet wound in the neck.
24 ,,	,,	Sapper Greatbatch, bullet wounds in arm and side whilst assisting the infantry to dig new trenches.
27 ,,	,,	Sapper Catterall, bullet wound in thigh.
29 ,,	,,	Sergeant Blamey, bullet wound in the chest.
29 ,,	,,	Lance-Corporal Horne, bullet wound in the face.
29 ,,	,,	Sapper Hallas, bullet wound in the neck.
30 ,,	,,	Lance-Corporal Toole, shrapnel wound in the hand in camp.

EAST LANCS. R.E. HISTORY

1 June, 1915.		Lance-Corporal Smith, bullet wound in the head, from which he died in hospital.
3	,, ,,	Lance-Corporal (now Sergeant) Templeton, bullet wound in arm.
4	,, ,,	Captain J. G. Riddick, slight wound in head.
4	,, ,,	Lieutenant W. N. Malcolm (attached to 1/2nd Field Company), wounded, and afterwards died from his wounds.
4	,, ,,	Sapper T. Bishop, killed.
4	,, ,,	Sapper J. Farnworth, killed.
4	,, ,,	Sapper T. Melville, killed.
4	,, ,,	Sapper E. Loxley, killed.
4	,, ,,	Corporal E. Abrahams, died of wounds.
4	,, ,,	Sapper Rothwell, wounded.
4	,, ,,	Sapper Dubberley, wounded in foot.
4	,, ,,	Sapper Hitchmough, wound in shoulder.
4	,, ,,	Sapper F. Francis, head wound.
4	,, ,,	Sapper J. Morgans, foot wound.
4	,, ,,	Sapper A. Lyson, wrist wound.
4	,, ,,	Sapper B. Jeffrey, wound.
4	,, ,,	Sapper C. Rushton, wound.
4	,, ,,	Sapper J. Toole, wound.
5	,, ,,	2nd Lieutenant K. E. D. Ainley, killed.
5	,, ,,	Corporal G. Sprosson, killed.
5	,, ,,	Sapper W. Cottrill, wounded.
5	,, ,,	Sapper E. R. Wilson, wounded.
5	,, ,,	Sapper A. Welsby, seriously wounded.
5	,, ,,	Sapper W. Hall, wounded.

The company was fully occupied for the next two or three weeks in improving the front-line system of trenches, providing sleeping recesses and cutting new communication trenches. About the middle of June we received very large working parties from the 52nd Division, which had just landed. These were employed in constructing the second line of defence, named the Eski Line, which ran right across the Peninsula about 2000-2500 yards behind our front line. The company was responsible for laying out the portion of this trench which ran from West Water Tree in the main Krithia Road to a point 120 yards west of the nullah on our left flank; in addition three long communication trenches were started to connect this trench up with our front-line system and also right back to the rear. Owing to shortage of labour only one of these communication trenches was really completed. On the 12th and 13th July the 52nd Division on our right attacked and made a considerable advance, and captured the nest of machine-guns on our right which had caused so much trouble in the nullah on June 4th. This advance necessitated our cutting two new trenches on our right flank to link up with the 52nd new front-line system. In view of a possible attack on our part, an accommodation trench,

427TH FIELD COY. R.E.

4 feet 6 inches deep by 2 feet 6 inches wide, was dug about twenty yards back along the whole length of our front line, with forward communication trenches every fifty yards or so. It was whilst siting this trench that Sergeant Garstang was killed on July 9, 1915, and the following night Lieutenant Evans, who had joined the company about May 31, was wounded in the arm almost in the same spot; it was thought the Turks had a rifle set to fire in one place at intervals during the night. By the death of Sergeant Garstang the company lost one of its best N.C.O.s; he was looked upon by No. 3 Section more as a father than an N.C.O., and in his work he was the exact type of man a sapper sergeant should be, with a keen sense of duty, a strong character and thorough appreciation for detail. About this time great strides were made in the siting of machine-gun positions; formerly they were distributed in the front line, and little attempt at concealment was aimed at. Positions were now made off communication trenches about 100 yards or so behind the front line by tunnelling under the parapet and making an emplacement 4 feet 6 inches long by 2 feet 6 inches wide, and a platform for the tripod about 3 feet square just at the foot of the communication trench parapet. On August 7, 1915, a general advance along the front of the 42nd Division was planned to cover the landing at Suvla Bay; in this object it was entirely successful, as Turkish reinforcements were sent to Cape Helles and so were not available on the Suvla Bay front. As far as the right sub-sector was concerned the first objective was F12 on the right, G12 on the left, and the second objective F13 and G13 and G13*a*. The first wave of attack carried the first objective, and ten minutes later were joined by the second wave, which, however, except in a few isolated cases, did not go forward to their objective. The first line went over about one man per yard strong, including a working party of 120 infantry and twenty-six sappers. The working parties of each wave were divided into four, each party in the first wave being under an infantry sergeant, and in the second wave under an infantry officer. The orders given to these parties were to search for mine wires, reverse the Turkish trenches, construct traverses where necessary, erect barricades about twenty-five to thirty yards up all communication trenches to our front. On the right flank the first objective was in a bad piece of ground from our point of view, and proved to be untenable; most of the infantry officers were killed, and a retirement took place about 4 p.m., leaving only the vineyard (G12) in our possession. This position had only one communication trench, which ran along the north-west side of the vineyard, and the north-east end was held by a bombing station alone; it was therefore decided to push through a communication trench joining up the north-east end with our old firing-line; this work was carried out by Lieutenant Scott that night with a party of 200 infantry and six sappers, during which there were only twelve casualties. Of the sappers who advanced with the two lines three were killed, eight wounded and

four missing, afterwards reported killed, and two were delirious through shell-shock. In the vineyard position, under supervision of Lieutenants Mackenzie and Gough and Sergeant-Major Sowray, temporary barricades were erected at three bombing stations, and the communication trench along the edge of the vineyard improved. The following day the barricades were made good with loopholes, but unfortunately were lost during the night of 8th–9th August. At 6 p.m. the same evening orders were received to construct a new fire trench to connect the centre of the right flank of the vineyard position with trench F12; this new trench was roughly about 100 yards in front of the old front line and from 120 to 150 yards from the Turkish lines. Only 128 men were available for the total length of (from the aeroplane photo) 320 yards; these were divided into pairs, equipped with rations for twenty-four hours and two sandbags apiece. These two men were posted at five-yard intervals to dig themselves in and then sap each way towards their neighbours. Sufficient notice was not given to the field company to see the lie of the country by daylight, but the working party was put out half from the right flank and half from the centre by means of the prismatic compass. It was found that the total length was 400 yards, so a gap occurred near the centre. The next night the above working party were relieved by a second, and a trench 2 feet 6 inches deep and 2 feet wide was made right through from the vineyard to F12 by the morning of the 10th. A little wiring was done around the vineyard position, consisting of *chevaux de frises* and the French concertina wire; owing to the proximity of the Turkish trenches the latter type was put out by a party of four men, all creeping or rolling; two moved the coil forward from one end which had been firmly stapled down, and the remaining two arranged and stapled down the coil at intervals. On August 13, 1915, the company was relieved by the 2/2nd Lowland Field Company of the 52nd Division. Owing to casualties and sickness the strength had dwindled down to twenty-five fit N.C.O.s and sappers. After five days' rest in the base camp near Morto Bay the company took over the work of two field companies of the 29th Division which had been urgently sent for to strengthen our position at Suvla Bay. Owing to lack of transport it took two days to move our headquarters to the new bivouac in the Gully Ravine just below the farm at the point where the Eski Line crossed the ravine. The new front for the left sector of the Division extended from the sea along Fusilier Bluff and Inniskilling Inch towards the Gully Ravine, and could be enfiladed from the right sector of the Division nearly all the way along. At Fusilier Bluff the Turkish trenches were only about thirty to forty yards away, which necessitated the provision of head cover; various types of loopholes were tried: ammunition boxes filled with sand and gravel; these failed, as if the box was hit, the sand used to leak out and so make the box useless; four-inch pipes and boxes with tapering sides were also tried, but owing to the sandy nature of the parapet

427TH FIELD COY. R.E.

the ends used to become exposed to view, so these proved useless. The steel plate loopholes were proved to be the best, especially if draped with stuffed canvas to give the resemblance of sandbags on the outside; these were set obliquely on the parapet and sloped back at the top so as to cause bullets to ricochet upwards; they were also fitted with a hood at the back, like that of a large camera, so that the enemy could not observe if the loophole was open or not. There were about three bombing stations in the left subsector; they were usually known as the "Western Birdcage" and "Eastern Birdcage," because they were protected by wire-netting screens fixed at an angle of 55° in the parapet, held in position by a strut from the parados and a wire stay from the bottom edge; an overhead covered shelter was made for the bombing party near by, as only twelve to fifteen feet separated our own and the enemy's trench. About this time Lieutenant Wilson and twenty-five O.R. reinforcements joined the unit from our third line at home. On the 1st of September a scheme was prepared with a view to meeting winter conditions; this comprised drainage of all trenches, revetting of the firing and support lines, winter quarters for the reserve, and protection of all wells from pollution of surface water. This scheme was eventually approved and work was commenced. On October 10, 1915, whilst setting out a short length of trench in the third line of defence, Lieutenant Mackenzie was wounded in the groin; at the time the wound was not considered serious, and he was in the best of spirits when he left to join the hospital ship; it was therefore a great shock to all when the news came a month later that he had died at sea.

On the 13th of October the company was relieved from frontline work by the 1/2nd Field Company, West Lancs. R.E., which had been sent out to act as the third company for the Division. The company were now chiefly employed on making winter quarters for the infantry brigade in reserve; these consisted of shelters to hold about ten men, each made 15 feet long by 8 feet wide, sunk 3 feet in the ground, and the sides built up of sandbags for another 3 feet, covered with corrugated iron supported along the centre by 9-inch by 2-inch timber on edge, with one 4-inch by 4-inch support in the middle, the ends of the roof joist resting on the two outside sandbag walls. A layer of earth 4 inches thick was spread over the top to make the roof shrapnel-bullet proof. The positions for these shelters were sited on the sides of the Gully Ravine, but the progress of construction was extremely slow, due to lack of labour and proper materials. A pumping plant was installed in Bruce Ravine which drew water from the wells into three treating tanks, and also pumped the water from the treating tanks up to the delivery tanks against a head of 180 feet and a distance of about 1000 feet. A five B.H.P. petrol engine was used, mounted on a concrete foundation, but it had only been in operation for about two days when orders were received for it to be dismantled, owing—as it turned out afterwards—to the evacuation.

EAST LANCS. R.E. HISTORY

Christmas Day was observed as a holiday. The divisional band played selections in the Gully Ravine, and a football match was played against the 1/2nd Field Company, which, of course, resulted in a win for the 1/1st Company. On 28th December the company was relieved by a field company of the 13th Division, all stores were packed up and removed from the tool carts, which were to be left empty; owing to the bad state of the Gully Road and lack of transport only some orderly room papers, officers' baggage and cooks' stores were got to Lancashire Landing. The company, after marching down, eventually embarked on s.s. *Redbreast* at 11.30 p.m., and disembarked at Mudros West in the Isle of Lemnos at 1.0 p.m. the following day. Lieutenant Watkinson and eleven men were left behind to assist in the final preparations for the evacuation and to bring off the company stores if transport was available. After a fortnight in Sarpi Camp the company embarked on board H.M.T. *Egra* for Egypt on January 15th, an advance party under Lieutenant Scott having gone ahead a couple of days before on H.M.S. *Mars*.

The casualties from June 6, 1915, to December 31, 1915, were as follows—

6 June, 1915.		Sapper O. Thomas, wounded in the back.
6 ,,	,,	Sapper W. Straw, slight head wound.
6 ,,	,,	Sapper R. Dixon, serious head wound; afterwards died and buried at Mudros East.
8 ,,	,,	Captain J. G. Riddick to hospital on account of acute sciatica.
13 ,,	,,	Lieutenant O. H. Taunton, M.C., serious bullet wound in the head; died 14/6/15, and was buried at Mudros East.
17 ,,	,,	Sapper Newton, bullet wound right shoulder.
21 ,,	,,	Sapper Greenhalgh, slight shell wound on hand from a splinter.
30 ,,	,,	Sapper L. Burton, bullet wound in the back.
1 July	,,	Sapper E. Bailey, bullet wound in the back; afterwards died.
9 ,,	,,	Sergeant J. E. Garstang, killed by bullet in the head.
10 ,,	,,	Lieutenant G. F. Evans, bullet wound in left arm.
10 ,,	,,	Sapper A. Dwyer, killed by shell in the rest camp.
12 ,,	,,	Sapper Worthington, bullet wound in chest.
12 ,,	,,	Private A. Massey, R.A.M.C., wounded.
26 ,,	,,	Corporal T. Lee, bullet wound.
30 ,,	,,	Sapper F. Francis, bullet in thigh; afterwards died of his wounds.
6 Aug.	,,	Sapper G. N. Halliwell, killed by bullet in the mouth.
7 ,,	,,	Sapper T. Conway, killed.
7 ,,	,,	Sapper R. Maher, killed.
7 ,,	,,	Sapper E. A. Greenhalgh, missing (known to have been wounded, afterwards reported killed).

427TH FIELD COY. R.E.

7 Aug. 1915.		Sapper Burkinshaw, missing; afterwards reported as killed.
7 ,,	,,	Sapper G. Coglan, missing; afterwards reported as killed.
7 ,,	,,	Sapper A. Jennings, missing; afterwards reported as killed.
7 ,,	,,	Lance-Corporal F. Perkins, missing; afterwards found to have been killed.
7 ,,	,,	Corporal G. Stevenson, wounded.
7 ,,	,,	Lance-Corporal D. Law, wounded.
7 ,,	,,	Lance-Corporal W. Horne, wounded.
7 ,,	,,	Sapper R. Lister, wounded.
7 ,,	,,	Sapper J. Hallas, wounded.
7 ,,	,,	Sapper R. Dewhurst, wounded.
7 ,,	,,	Sapper T. Stevenson, wounded.
7 ,,	,,	Sapper A. Hughes, wounded.
12 ,,	,,	2nd Corporal R. S. Tolson, killed whilst wiring in No Man's Land.
27 Sept.	,,	Lieutenant D. E. Gough, to hospital and operated upon for acute appendicitis.
9 Oct.	,,	Lieutenant L. A. Mackenzie, wounded by rifle bullet in the groin; afterwards died from his wounds.
3 Nov.	,,	Private Fawcett, R.A.M.C., killed by shell fire.

CHAPTER II

EGYPT AND SINAI

H.M.T. *Egra* arrived in Alexandria harbour 17th January, 1916. The accommodation and feeding for the men on board were abominable. No hammocks were available, and the rations consisted of bully and biscuits with no cooking facilities and hot water alone provided by the ship. The following day we disembarked and entrained for Cairo, and on arrival tea and refreshments at one piastre per head were very kindly provided by some English ladies at the station. After a week's stay at Mena Camp, which was beside the famous Pyramids, the company moved to Tel-el-Kebir camp, where we stayed four days before going on to El Shallufa on the Suez Canal. We took over the defences of this section of the Canal from the 46th Division, who after a fortnight's stay or so in Egypt went back to France. Lieutenant Hunter arrived on 5th February, 1916, with a draft of 70 reinforcements from England, and for one week the company devoted all its energies to company training, including physical drill, rifle exercises and section drill. Every one came in for a share of " ginger," the officers receiving an extra large dose one day from the C.R.E., because they were all on parade but each in a different turnout.

Works were started again on the bridgehead defence of Shallufa, which consisted of thirteen lunettes capable of holding about twenty men each; barbed wire entanglements were erected round with enfilading fire from the posts. Hurdle revetments were used which had been made to a set design allowing about twenty-one feet in between traverses, the length of the traverse being made the same as the length of the parados of the fire trench. Cocoanut matting was used behind the hurdles, which were well anchored back with wire and about seven rows of sandbag revetting was built on the top of the hurdles. In order to carry out Lord Kitchener's scheme of defence, three posts were commenced about seven miles east from the Canal. They were christened by the Division " Manchester," " Wigan " and " Salford," and a section of R.E. was sent to each and attached to each battalion responsible for the work. Each post was laid out to hold a garrison of one battalion, all trench work being revetted with hurdles and matting and the wire entanglements being laid so as to be enfiladed between the lunettes. On 31st August, 1916, all works were handed over to the 54th Division, and the company moved to Suez. A course of training in infantry drill and musketry then took place, lasting about two and a half weeks, and during this time several reinforcements arrived. For the following seven weeks the company was employed on the erection of huts for the 125th and 127th Infantry Brigades, which were just completed when the Division was ordered to return to the Suez Canal defences and take over from the 11th Division, which was going to France. The company replaced the 86th Field Company, R.E. (which was commanded by Major Denison, our late adjutant) at Ballah. Two sections under Captain Riddick went to Bally Bunion, which was about six miles due east of Ballah, and completed the hutting for the 125th Brigade, a squadron of Warwickshire Yeomanry, and also stabling for one regiment of Australian Light Horse. At Ballah the work consisted of the upkeep of the bridgehead defences, and provision of shelters for all animals. During this period all sections, with the exception of No. 2, underwent a week's training at Ballah in pontoon and trestle bridging, barrel piers, demolitions, wire-rope making, etc. On 30th July, 1916, the company moved to Kantara by march route, and the following day to Hill 70, having left behind all the first-line transport. The following four days were employed in preparing all the stores required to meet the scale of the Desert Mobile Establishment and practising the loading of same on camels; special wooden racks were made for this purpose, with a view to rapid loading and off-loading and also to keep the stores together.

On 4th August, 1916, the company moved to Pelusium: the personnel by train and the baggage and stores by camel transport; after bivouacking for the night, we pushed on the next morning with the 125th Brigade via Mount Royston to a point about one mile south of Katib Gannit hill, making a total march of eight miles, accomplished in heavy sand and mostly during the heat of the day. Near Mount Royston we passed through some outposts of the Turks which had fallen into our hands on the previous day, also a captured Turkish Ambulance, and were much surprised to see the completeness of their arrangements for camel transport. Before bivouacking for the night we erected a 600-gallon trough, also a 30′ × 30′ tank to hold our supply of water for that and the following day, and our water camels were then sent back to Pelusium to fetch a further supply. The following morning, 6th August, 1916, we moved off again at 4.0 a.m., and eventually reached Katia at 10.30 a.m., after about seven miles march. Captain Riddick was left behind with ten sappers to bring in all water and other equipment stores as soon as our transport camels returned from Pelusium. He eventually rode back to Pelusium, and after great difficulty, owing to some misunderstanding, got together all the first-line transport camels of the 125th Brigade and brought them through to Katia, arriving about 8.30 p.m. on the 7th August. Luckily, water was found in Katia, and wells were allotted for men's and animals' drinking. For the following week the water supply of Katia was developed by sinking three wells (the average depth being 13 feet), with the stores carried in our first-line transport, also a storage tank 30' × 30' was erected to hold the water supply for the whole Brigade, which was brought up by the water camels. During all this period the ration of water was one gallon per day per man for all purposes, which only allowed one water-bottle full for each of the long marches. On 14th August, 1916, the Brigade marched back to Romani; an advance party of two sections set out at 6 a.m. to prepare the camp sites and arrange water supply for the Brigade. The company stayed three months in Romani; the first two weeks were devoted to training with the Infantry Brigade and in well-sinking, and laying down of storage tanks and water supply generally. It was during this training that Lieutenant Hunter of No. 1 Section lost a spearpoint of a Norton tube well. With dogged determination No. 1 Section dug down about 18 feet and eventually found the missing tube, which, of course, necessitated the excavation of an inverted cone with a base diameter of nearly 36 feet at ground surface level, as sand will not stand at a steeper slope than 1/1 for any length of time. This incident provided a most useful lesson, as the Norton tube well played a very prominent part in our work later on. The construction of a road was commenced from Romani to El Rabah, employing about ten R.E. and one hundred of the Egyptian Labour Corps. Several methods were tried, but palm-leaf fascines (four leaves wired together) covered with 3 or 4 inches of sand well damped with salt water from the marshes and "tupped" down proved the most successful. At the end of August the Division was ordered to take up a position just north of Oghratina. This necessitated the development of the water supply for all the animals of the Division in the area behind the line, and each company sent one section complete with its mobile column equipment to carry out this work. Lieutenant Watkinson and twenty-two sappers of No. 3 Section went from the 1/1st Field Company. This party made sixteen Norton tube well "prickings," all of which were tested, and the position marked with a notice board showing the No. of well, salinity, and approximate output in gallons per hour. Ten wells were selected for development, four of these being done by Lieutenant Watkinson's party; the total output from the ten wells amounted to about 2900 gallons per hour. Each well was fitted with a lift- and force-pump and 600-gallon trough. The wells varied in depth to water level from 7 feet 6 inches to 16 feet, and 3 feet of water was aimed at in each well. A large crater was first dug out nearly to water level; then a 4-feet square case made of corrugated iron and 4" × 4" timber frames was put down and the crater filled in all round it. A smaller case 3 feet square was then sunk inside to 3 feet below water level. Storage tanks for the men's drinking water were always erected alongside the railway, as railhead moved forward, so that they could be filled from the water trucks; ten 30' × 30' sheet tanks, twenty-five 2300 gallon tanks and two 6000 gallon tanks were put up in four days. Four hundred of the Egyptian Labour Corps (E.L.C.) were employed in addition to Lieutenant Watkinson's

427TH FIELD COY. R.E. 65

section, as a great deal of levelling had to be done. During this time Lieutenant Hunter and No. 1 Section were working on the outer defences of Romani with about 1300 E.L.C.; these were completed to about 85 per cent. and then abandoned, as it was thought that there would not be sufficient number of troops to hold them if a general advance was made. So an inner defence scheme was started upon which about one section of R.E. and 600 E.L.C. were employed for three weeks. These consisted of about fourteen lunettes designed to hold about one platoon of infantry, all wired in and arranged so that the wire could be enfiladed between each post. The G.O.C. Eastern Force, General Sir Charles Dobell, personally complimented the company on its work upon these defences. A further water reconnaissance was at this time made in the country about ten miles wide, south of a line through Romani and Negiliat, the detachment sent from the company being No. 2 Section under Lieutenant Bogle. Norton tube well prickings were made and all likely wells marked, tested and recorded on a large-scale map. This section afterwards made a similar reconnaissance of the country between Abd and Bayud. On 20th November, 1916, Lieutenant Eastwood and No. 4 Section were sent to make a reconnaissance of the country between Dueidar–Bir-el-Nuss–Hod-Abu-Simara–Hod-el-Aras.

On 20th November, 1916, the great advance commenced. The Headquarters of the company and Sections 2 and 3 were attached to the 125th Brigade, and after six days marching, halting for the night at Rabah, Khirba, Abd, Salmana, Tilul, we eventually arrived at Mazar, a total distance of about forty-five miles from Romani. Captain Riddick, who had been attached to Divisional Headquarters for some time, took over the command of the 1/2nd Field Company, R.E., about this time, Major L. F. Wells having been appointed C.R.E. 52nd Division. The whole Division collected in this area, and all animals had to be watered from two groups of wells, called the Southern Group and the Stone House Group; borings were tried all round, but the salinity of the water found was too high. The company took over the upkeep of the Southern Group, which consisted of six wells each with 30 feet or so of troughs, which were made of wood lined with canvas, and so arranged that the ends would take out so that the troughs could be flushed out daily. A party of four R.E. and seven infantry were necessary for upkeep and filling the troughs full just before watering times commenced; about 2000 horses watered daily at this group of wells.

On 20th December, 1916, the whole Division marched to Maadan and bivouacked for the night, prior to making with the 52nd Division a forced march on El Arish. However, news came through that the Turks were evacuating El Arish, so that it was decided that the 52nd Division only should push forward. Few who were present on the night of 20th December, 1916, will forget the weird effect of all the camp fires glowing and the lights of the various unit headquarters. There was also an undercurrent of intense excitement, as most people

F

realized that the transport of food and water during the coming forced march was a complex problem, and unless everything turned out exactly to programme, was bound to break down. There was bitter disappointment when the news came through that the 52nd Division were to go forward alone, as it was their turn to go forward first. The following day we returned to Mazar and devoted our time to a short course of training.

On Christmas Day some company sports were arranged, to which General Frith and the Staff of the 125th Brigade came and took part in a tug-of-war: officers versus O.R.s. This event is not entered in the war diary, but it is believed that the officers' team was badly beaten by the " jockeys " (drivers). The men had their Christmas dinner at midday, but the officers' mess arranged theirs, unfortunately, in the evening; rain came on just as the turkey arrived, so instead of being placed on the table it was thrust underneath until a tarpaulin roof had been fixed over the mess!

On 1st January, 1917, the company received orders to proceed to El Arish to develop sufficient water supply for the whole Division. The first night was spent at Maadan, the second at Bardawil and the third at Masaid; the march between Maadan and Bardawil was most unpleasant, as it rained hard on arrival and was very cold. At Masaid we stayed for three days, and came in contact with a brigade of the Australian Light Horse. Three wells were put down, and the salinity of the water was found to be as low as 12 parts in 100,000, quite the best that had so far been found. On 7th January, 1917, we received orders to push on to El Arish, where we bivouacked at Kilo 153, and immediately started to make a reconnaissance of the water supply in the neighbourhood. Within about 100 yards of the sea and close to the railway a group of wells was sunk, which were called No. 1 Railway Group; this group consisted of one 4 feet square, four $8' \times 4'$ and one $12' \times 4'$, wells with a depth of water in each of 2 feet 6 inches and an average yield of 3100 gallons per hour. This water level was within 6 feet of the surface. About 250 feet run of troughs were put down, which proved capable of watering 1500 horses per day; in order to facilitate the control of the troughs the whole group was wired in, and " in " and " out " points notice-boarded. An excellent supply of water was found about one mile inland at Abu Ebeid; this supply was developed at three points by Nos. 2, 3, and 4 Sections by sinking three wells at each, the average depth being 12 feet; these were revetted with corrugated iron and finished off with sandbags. The water was reached by driving down $2\frac{1}{2}$-inch spear points about 4 feet 6 inches below water level and drawing the water by the service lift-and-force pump; the yield per well proved to be about 600 gallons per hour. The water at each group was led into four 11 feet square storage tanks, which each held 1500 gallons, so that each group was sufficient to supply water for one brigade of infantry, or about 4000 men.

On February 1, 1917, all work in hand, plans of the El Arish defence scheme and upkeep of water-supply arrangements were

427TH FIELD COY. R.E.

handed over to the 53rd Divisional R.E. All the technical equipment other than the company stores were handed in to the R.E. Park, which was being formed at El Arish railhead, and on February 3 the company entrained for Kantara, the first stage of our long journey to the Western Front. An advance party under Lieutenant Watkinson had proceeded a few days before direct to France, and were attached to the 26th Field Company, R.E., belonging to the 1st Division, where they had an insight into the type of warfare in which we were destined soon to be engaged. The company stayed a couple of days at Kantara to transfer the company stores from the Mobile Column back to the standard tool-cart method of transport, and then marched via El Ferdan, where one night was spent, to Moascar camp, near Ismailia. Five days were spent here, chiefly in re-equipping for service in France, and in reviving old memories of Ismailia as we found it in 1914 and the early part of 1915. Ten days at Alexandria completed us with everything except anti-gas apparatus, steel helmets, and, what we perhaps felt most. of all, our transport horses, most of which had been kept right through since we had left England; rumour has it that the gunners, who were always envious of our horses, somehow got the authorities to transfer the field company animals to them, but the real reason was lack of seasoned animals in Egypt, which would eventually be and of course were used in the Palestine Expedition as it developed. Captain Gracey was posted as second in command to the company on February 15, 1917, from the 428 Field Company.

CHAPTER III

FRANCE

(*March* 1917—*March* 1918)

On February 22, 1917, the company embarked on H.M.T. *Manitou* for France, and after an uneventful voyage arrived at Marseilles on March 1, 1917, where we had to unload the ship, and eventually entrained at 8 a.m. for the north of France.

After a very cold journey, lasting two days, with discomfort, owing to delays in getting proper meals at the various *halte repas* stations, which all seemed timed to supply us with food between 10 p.m. and 5 a.m. instead of during the day, we detrained at Pont Rémy, a few miles from Abbeville. We then had to march five miles to the village of Limeux, where billets had been allotted to the unit. The first morning we were welcomed with two or three inches of snow, but the unit suffered very little sickness which could be traced to the great change in climatic conditions. In a few days' time we received our new horses, which were a very sorry lot and in poor condition compared to those we had left behind in Egypt; most of them were heavily marked with old, and a few with recent, skin diseases. However, with the characteristic pluck of " the jockeys," teams were paired off and soon knocked into shape for marching. About the middle of March the company moved to Hamel, near Corbie, the transport by march route and the sappers by train from Longpré Station. Here we were attached to the 125th Infantry Brigade, and at once commenced to provide baths, ablution benches, etc., for the battalions. The three bridging vehicles, less stores, were sent to La Flaque to assist in carrying up bridging material to the Somme, and on the 23rd March orders were received from 3rd Corps H.Q. for the unit to be attached to the 1st Divisional R.E. at Brie-sur-Somme, where we arrived on March 24, 1917. Our accommodation consisted of ten tents only for H.Q. and Nos. 3 and 4 Sections, and the officers' sleeping room and mess was made from an old German gun position covered with the G.S. wagon sheet; to make matters worse the weather was bitterly cold and wet, a great contrast to the climatic conditions of the East. The bridging of the Somme at this place required two bridges of 60 feet span each, one of about 30 feet span, one of 24 feet span, and one of about 15 feet span. Temporary wooden bridges for horse traffic were first of all constructed, to be followed by bridges to take heavy guns and ordinary lorry traffic. The two sections were given the footings of one of

427TH FIELD COY. R.E.

the 60 feet Class A girder bridges to prepare; this was done in seventeen working hours, each section doing eight hours per day. After the girders had been launched, the roadway took about twelve hours to complete; these times were considered good, as none of the men had had any practice in erecting this type of bridge. Nos. 1 and 2 Sections during this time were billeted in the cellars of Belloy, and were employed on the repair of the Estrees-Villers-Carbonnel road under the 2nd Infantry Brigade.

On 8th April the company marched to Péronne, and was billeted for about ten days in the Faubourg de Paris, the least damaged portion of the town. The upkeep of all bridges was taken over from the 48th Divisional R.E., and a small bridge on the Péronne-Flamicourt road was built to carry lorry traffic. The span was 21 feet 6 inches, and five 18" × 12" timber baulks 25 feet long were laid across and 2½-inch wood chesses used on top of them, the old brickwork of the abutments being utilized for the footings.

For the last fortnight of the month the company H.Q. and Nos. 1 and 2 Sections moved back to Brie and took over the repair and maintenance of roads. On May 1, 1917, the whole company moved up into the front line at Ronssoy, and took over from the 48th Divisional R.E. Here it was found that a trench system had barely been commenced; three strong points about 800 yards apart were immediately dug to hold about two platoons each, and the whole of the brigade front, some 2500 yards long, was wired with two single apron fences 10 yards apart. Also a communication trench was dug back to Quechettes Wood from the left strong point. After a fortnight the company went to billets near Villers-Faucon, being relieved by the 428 Field Company, and shortly afterwards the Division was relieved by the 2nd Cavalry Division. The company then marched to Ruyaulcourt, staying at Neuville Bourjonval one day, where the transport lines were left, but afterwards sent to Ytres, near the Division H.Q. For the first three weeks or so, the company carried out work on the left sector of the divisional front; then, owing to the large amount of work to be done in preparation for important offensive operations, the company concentrated its efforts on front-line work, all back area jobs being handed over to the reserve field company. During all this period the company was attached to the 127th Infantry Brigade, although the new C.R.E., Lieut.-Colonel MacInnes, never lost touch with the work in hand. On the whole, this front was regarded as a fairly quiet sector, although occasionally the German gunners used to barrage the trenches; on one particular occasion they put down a fifteen minutes' barrage on the front-line system about 10.30 p.m., heralded by a display of golden rain and red rockets, which gave the Brigadier and battalion commanders and a few others who happened to be going round a very uncomfortable time, as the trenches had only been recently dug, and were narrow and shallow in several places.

The left flank of the Brigade front rested on a spoil heap of the Canal du Nord, called Yorkshire Bank, the top of which consisted entirely of chalk. At the end of the first week in June it was decided to push our front line forward some 300–350 yards, the R.E. being made responsible for the direction and setting out of the new line. A reconnaissance of Yorkshire Bank was made two nights before the advance took place, and the trench was taped out, including the traverses; just as the tracing out had been completed a German patrol of two men came up on to the far end of the Bank, but luckily did not come along to where we had taped out the new trenches; the Bank could easily be swept by machine-gun fire from the left flank, and could have been made untenable for our troops two nights later whilst they were digging in. The following night the two section officers and O.R.s who were to give the direction to the infantry, made a careful reconnaissance of the whole front, and noted the bearings of certain landmarks.

In the meantime sufficient wiring materials had been prepared and put into dumps to enable the whole front to be wired with two rows of concertina barbed wire. The new line was taped out with flashes of tape put where each traverse should be made, and guides of the various digging parties (detailed by companies) were shown exactly where their particular part of the line commenced. The whole line was dug six inches deep, so as to show a continuous trench to the enemy, and posts for sections were made at twelve points in the line, these being of course dug deep enough to give cover to their garrisons. The operation was most successful, and along nearly the whole front the wiring was completed according to schedule. An attack on a large scale was mooted about this time; light railways were laid parallel with the reserve line, stores were collected into brigade dumps, communication trenches were constructed and provided with trench boards, also a trench tramway was laid from Broken House to Yorkshire Bank by Lieutenant Eastwood and No. 4 Section. A tunnelling company was kept busy constructing deep dug-outs for Battalion and Brigade Headquarters, which had to be furnished and provided with partitions, stoves, etc., by the nearest field company. On June 8, 1917, all work was handed over to the 48th Division R.E., and on the 10th the company marched to Gomiecourt, a distance of over twelve miles. After doing a certain amount of work for the 125th Brigade, to whom we were attached, the six weeks' rest was devoted to training, including three days bridging over the River Ancre near Beaucourt. The C.R.E., Lieut.-Colonel MacInnes, about this time presented a challenge cup to the Divisional R.E. for the company obtaining the best number of points in field engineering, shooting and games; this was won by the 429 Field Company. About this time Captain Gracey left the company to take command of the 432 Field Company in the 66th Division, also Lieutenant Bogle was exchanged for Lieutenant Dart of 429 Field Company. The company also lost Lieutenant Watkinson to hospital.

On August 20th the company moved by march route to Bouzincourt, near Albert, where we entrained for the Ypres salient two

427TH FIELD COY. R.E.

days later. We detrained at Godeswaerswelde about 7 p.m. and marched five miles to our billet in a farm-house; the following day we moved on to Vlamertynghe and worked for three days in the repair of back billets and camps in the area. Lieutenant Jones came from 429 Field Company as second in command, soon followed by 2nd Lieutenants Field and Chapman from the R.E. base.

On August 29, 1917, H.Q. and three sections marched to Ypres and took up quarters in the Ramparts just south of the Menin Gate, leaving No. 4 Section and its attached infantry on the transport lines at Brandhoek. Work in hand was taken over from the 15th Division R.E. The left brigade sector ran from the Hanebeck stream to the Potijze–Zonnebeke road with the left Battalion Headquarters in Square Farm and the right Battalion Headquarters in Low Farm. Both of these places consisted of reinforced concrete, which had been built by the enemy inside the walls of the original farm buildings, of which only slight traces remained; these structures were given the name of " pill-boxes," and their contents were certainly as a rule difficult to take. A line of strong points were sited and partially dug, commencing with one on the left behind Frezenberg Ridge, overlooking what remained of Grey Farm on the left flank and the Six Trees on the Potijze–Zonnebeke road on the right. Two trench-board tracks were laid up to the front posts; these, however, at the places where they passed through the German barrage line, were blown to pieces every day. Square Farm was hit twice by a large calibre shell almost in the same spot; this shattered the concrete, which was nearly 3 feet thick, but only made two small holes right through. These holes were plugged up and an abutment concrete wall was built up inside about 2 feet 6 inches average thickness, and on the outside ten steel joists were erected to form a burster course. The R.A.M.C. had an Aid Post at Bavaria House just west of the Frezenberg Ridge; this was strengthened and a sandbag wall erected to prevent the back blast of shells entering the shelter. A splinter-proof Aid Post for walking wounded was erected near New Cot, made of three elephant shelters dug 3 feet into the ground and faced with sandbags, the entrances being also screened with an additional wall.

On September 6, 1917, a brigade attack was planned on Iberian, Beck, and Borry farms; the R.E. were made responsible for providing a wire entanglement in front of these farms as soon as they had been taken and reported held. The Fourth Army Standard Pattern of wiring was adopted, and dumps of material were formed at point D 19 C78 for Iberian (at the bend of the Hanebeck stream on the left flank), also at Low Farm for Beck. The forming of these dumps, 600 yards and 400 yards of materials respectively, was not a pleasant business, as the carrying parties had to be led over trackless country, consisting entirely of shell craters, at night and through the German barrage, which was put down at least two or three times during the night. For Iberian there were six wiring detachments, each consisting of one R.E., one infantry N.C.O. and nine O.R.s with a carrying party of two officers and sixty O.R.s made up of the attached infantry and one R.E. guide; two R.E.s were at the dump, the whole being under Lieutenant Hunter and two R.E. N.C.O.s; for Beck, Lieutenant Dart had a similar party, but only two wiring detachments and a smaller carrying party. The attack took place about dawn, and Beck farm was taken; the wiring party were ordered to go forward; but only one sapper reached the objective, the remainder of the party being held up by machine-gun fire from Iberian and Borry Farms, which had not been taken, and which shortly afterwards made Beck Farm untenable. Lieutenant Hunter and Sapper Smith were killed in their assembly trenches, and Sappers Probyn and Ritchie were killed out of Lieutenant Dart's party. The above attack proved to be the last of its kind to be ordered, as the casualties for each attempt by a brigade alone had been heavy and the success nil. Future attacks were on a larger scale, and on the next occasion two whole divisional fronts attacked at the same time and were quite successful, as the enemy were unable to concentrate their flank guns on a small line of attack, in the way they did when only one brigade tried to advance alone.

Our quarters in the Ramparts at Ypres were the most objectionable the company had ever occupied, and took nearly three-quarters of the company two whole days to clean out and make habitable. Rats abounded and were almost tame, and the only redeeming feature of our billets was their comparative security against shell fire. As a result of a bombardment of the town by gas-shell and H.E. mixed, mainly the former, the company sustained fifteen gas casualties. During this bombardment, two men of another unit were wounded by H.E., and were brought into one of the dug-out entrances to wait till they could be got away. During a lull in the shelling, Sergeant Turner, the orderly room sergeant, rang up the field ambulance on the telephone to ask for an ambulance to be sent for them. The telephonic code name of the unit at the time was "Jolly," and Sergeant Turner was heard explaining through the telephone: "This is JOLLY; in the Ramparts;—yes, JOLLY.—Can you send an ambulance? Two men have been wounded here.—Yes, in the Ramparts!—Yes, I say it's *Jolly* speaking."

As every one else was struggling to breathe through gas-masks, no doubt the Field Ambulance were pleased to hear that some one was apparently enjoying it.

About this time Captain Allard replaced Lieutenant Jones as second in command, the latter returning soon afterwards to the 429 Field Company.

On the 17th September, 1917, the Divisional R.E. were relieved by the 9th (Scotch) Division R.E. The company moved by march and train route to the Nieuport sector, staying at Brandhoek, St. Jan-ter-Biezen, Couthouf Farm, Arneke—a very pretty old place—and Ghyvelde, about a couple of nights at each, and eventually taking over from the 431 Field Company, R.E., our opposite number in the second-line Division of the East Lancs. R.E., namely the 66th Division, at Oost Dunkerke Bains on the 25th September, 1917.

427TH FIELD COY. R.E.

The billets reminded us of the East, as they were situated in the middle of the sand dunes, consisting of huts originally built by the French troops; although within range we were not often shelled, but we were subject to bombing by aeroplanes. The work consisted of an Advanced Divisional H.Q. made in the sand dunes with cut-and-cover offices connected up by a deep dug-out mined by a tunnelling company, horse shelters for one brigade of artillery and general upkeep of camps. On October 5 the company, less transport, moved to Nieuport and took over from the 206 Field Company of the 32nd Division. The company was billeted in the town, all in one building said to have been a powder factory; the walls built of brick 7 feet thick in parts, and able, as far as our experience went, to withstand any shell of ordinary calibre striking it. Although most of the work was done by night, the shifts were short ones, and every one was able to get proper sleep. Health generally was good, and there was no trouble due to damp and cold, except a few cases of rheumatism and trench fever. The attached infantry, three officers and about seventy O.R., were in separate billets, cellars mostly, in the town. Baths and a drying room were instituted after some delay. The horse-lines were about six miles back from the billet, between Coxyde and La Panne, situated on sand, necessitating special precautions to avoid sand colic. The work allotted to the company was almost entirely devoted either to the preservation and improvement of the system of surface drains on which the breastwork defences north of the River Yser relied to maintain them fit for their garrison, or to the protection works which guarded the same defences from inundation by the sea tides. The whole of the area held by our troops north of the River Yser fell into two sections divided by the Lombardtzyde–Nieuport road. The eastern portion, roughly rectangular in shape, drained into a channel in its southern side, called the Evacuation Canal. The northern and eastern sides of the rectangle were our front line, the latter looking over lower ground to the east, which could be flooded by us at will. The water escaped through a permeable dam, Bath Dam, formerly Bridge No. 66, into the tidal Yser at the west end of the Evacuation Canal. The western portion drained into the moat of the Redan, a large obsolete earthwork defence which proved, however, useful in many ways. From the moat the water ran through a non-return sluice in York Dam, and then, after twenty yards, through a sluice in the river levee, called Hull Dam. The outlet of a stream, named the Geleide, which ran into the Yser from along the front of our left flank, had been blocked by shell fire, and, intentionally or otherwise, its waters flowed through a gap in our front line breastwork along the foot of the river embankment on the far side from the river, and so back into the Redan past the Huiteries, a basin connected with the river by a sluice which was then blocked with rubbish. To hinder surface drainage, therefore, the enemy had only to damage the sluices and Bath Dam; to flood out the area he had to breach the river levee and Bath Dam, the most vulnerable point in the former being Hull and York Dams. He therefore shelled these works at the time of maximum high tide, which occurred about the middle and end of each month, and whenever aeroplane or balloon observation showed us to have been active in repairing damage. Concealed escapes for the drainage works were, therefore, projected, one out of the Redan and one from the Huiteries basin. Concealment was to be attained by tunnelling the sluice and screening its ends, all spoil being thrown into the water. One of these only, the former, was begun, the work being undertaken by a Tunnelling Company, R.E. Owing to failure to prevent water creeping along the outer surface of the sluice lining it proved more dangerous than valuable. During October Hull Dam was damaged twice by shell fire, each time blocking up the non-return sluice gate; this, however, was repaired, and the dam rebuilt with sandbags. York Dam, which had only just been commenced by the 206th Field Company, R.E., was completed, being entirely made of sandbags with a 2-feet 6-inch square non-return sluice. On the west side the dam was joined up to the levee by a sandbag wall; this was breached once during the month by shell fire, but was rapidly repaired, and only a small amount of the tidal Yser penetrated the Redan during one day of October.

On the 17th October the Bath Dam (No. 66) was taken over from the 429 Field Company, and a ferro-concrete cap was in the process of being made when about 31st October the dam was shelled with 8-inch shell, and a breach about 15 feet wide and 7 feet deep was made, causing the flooding of the country up to the third-line trench. This breach was, however, filled up with sandbags, making a dam with a base of about 12 feet and about 6 feet wide at the top; it was during the repair of this breach that the C.R.E., Lieut.-Colonel D. S. MacInnes, insisted on taking charge of one of the reliefs, and it was largely due to his example of coolness and encouragement that the breach was repaired before the rapidly rising tide had time to make any effect. Lieutenant Mellor was awarded the M.C. for his skilful organization of labour for this repair under shell fire, Corporal F. E. Taylor and Lance-Corporal J. Mullaney being awarded Military Medals. It was now decided to build Mellor Dam on the tidal side of Bath Dam, and therefore hidden from observation from the enemy, except by aeroplane, by Bath Dam and neighbouring banks. The design allowed a dam of sandbags resting on a grillage of rolled steel joists, the upper layer being parallel to the stream and allowing the passage of water, the spaces between the lower joists being filled with bags of brickbats.

Altogether about 22,000 sandbags were used in this dam, and the average amount of labour employed nightly was 15 R.E. and 150 infantry. Enemy shell fire caused many casualties to these parties, resulting in the loss, amongst others, of Sergeant Moss, a most invaluable N.C.O. On 15th November, a fine day afforded the enemy a chance for aerial observation, and both Bath and Mellor Dams were blown up by heavy concentrated shelling. An attempt

427TH FIELD COY. R.E.

was made the same night to repair the damage, but the work was greatly hindered by the height of the tide at the time, and so was handed over incomplete to the French who relieved us. On November 3 York Dam was shelled and damaged, but Lieutenant Eastwood, with a large working party, closed the gap the same night with 2000 sandbags, and managed to get the non-return sluice working again. However, on November 13 both York and Hull Dams were heavily shelled and wiped out, but the debris formed a new dam without a sluice in it, so the draining of the Redan now depended entirely on the tunnelled sluice. During this month Second Lieutenant Arkieson joined the company. A great deal of work was done in clearing the surface drains right up to the front line, which improved the conditions of the garrisons concerned. Water gauges were erected at various points and read regularly, which helped the clearing patrols to localize faults and clear channels damaged by shell fire. On 18th November all work was handed over to the French Engineers, and the company concentrated at the horse-lines camp situated near the Windmill between Coxyde and La Panne.

The company then moved with the 125th Brigade chiefly by march route to the Béthune area, eventually arriving at Le Préol on 29th November, and taking over work from the 106 Field Company, R.E., of the 25th Division. Halts were made at Teteghem, near Dunkirk, Ledringhem, Hardifort, Staple and Steen-Becke, where a rest was made for four days, preparatory to the long march of sixteen miles to Essars.

The billets at Le Préol were amongst the best the company had so far found in France, their only disadvantage being the long distance of two miles from the bulk of the work, but as it was winter time, and there was no suitable place further forward, it was decided to remain there.

For the first three weeks the company was responsible from an R.E. point of view for the right sub-sector of the divisional front-line system. This sector was 2200 yards long, and was split into a northern and southern section by the La Bassée Canal. To the north, the tactical feature on which our retention of the whole sector depended was Givenchy Ridge, and to the south the Brickstacks, some of the latter being in both our own and the enemy lines. A geological fault existed just south of, and parallel to, the Canal; north of this, subsoil water was close to the surface and forbade the construction of tunnelled dug-outs in the clay soil, but a well-developed system of surface drains did much to keep the trenches dry. To the south of the fault it was possible to tunnel in the clay and underlying chalk, and many dug-outs existed. The trench system in this sector was very elaborate and was too extensive to keep in proper repair, so that work was only concentrated on the parts used by the present garrison. A dug-out was commenced in a large spoil bank on the north side of the Canal, but was eventually abandoned, as sufficient overhead cover could not be obtained before water was reached. Lieutenant Eastwood and Sergeant Kennedy of the 1/8th L.F. were killed whilst supervising the working-party on this job on December 5. This was the only casualty sustained by the company whilst it was in this sector, and by it we lost a sound officer and very practical engineer, who had been continuously with the unit since the autumn of 1915.

On December 22 the company was relieved by the 428 Field Company of all front-line work, and concentrated on the provision of ferro-concrete shelters in the third-line defence known as the Village Line. These shelters were made by placing heavy corrugated iron sheets bent to the shape of part of a circle and bolted together, in the rooms of the houses, and building over them walls 3 feet thick and roof 4 feet thick of ferro-concrete. The scheme proved too ambitious for the amount of material, transport and labour available. However, the few that were completed were found to be 5·9-inch shell proof, and materially helped the 55th Division three months later to make their famous stand against the big German offensive. Lieutenant Robinson joined the company as a reinforcement about this time.

Christmas 1917 was spent fairly quietly; a general holiday was given and football matches were arranged for the afternoon, followed by a very excellent concert in the evening, which showed that the company possessed some very good talent. During the next six weeks the repair of the Village Line was completed, and good headway made with the ferro-concrete dug-outs. Lieutenant Mellor was made divisional tramways officer, and several large extensions were carried out to assist the work in the forward area, and also to bring the rails far enough back to enable stores to be transhipped from road vehicles during the daytime under cover from observation. A considerable amount of work was also done for the R.F.A., both in ferro-concrete shelters and wiring. On 14th February the company was relieved by the 422 Company, R.E., of the 55th Division, who took over the whole sector. The company marched twelve miles to the rest area and were billeted at Busnes, but on 17th February we had to march back again to assist the 55th Division, and we were then quartered in Beuvry. After a fortnight or so the company returned to Busnes, arriving 3rd March, and then underwent a thorough rest and three weeks' training in infantry drill, musketry, bayonet fighting, gas drill, etc. Since Christmas several changes had occurred in the Divisional R.E. Captain Allard went to G.H.Q. in the Transportation Branch, and was replaced by Captain Echlin of the 428 Field Company as second in command of the company.

CHAPTER IV

FRANCE

(*March* 1918—*April* 1919)

WHILST the Division was at rest it came into the G.H.Q. Reserve, and on March 22 units were warned to be ready to move at short notice. The following day the company embussed near Busnes for an unknown destination, together with the 127th Infantry Brigade, and in the early hours of the next morning debussed at Adinfer in the Doullens area. Our transport came independently by march route and arrived during the afternoon. In the evening (24th) orders came through for the company sappers to relieve a company of the 40th Division R.E. near Gomiecourt; a mistake arose in the meeting-place arranged for the guides, with the result we were not met, and, after failing to get in touch with the C.R.E. of the 40th Division, we went on towards Gomiecourt, together with the 429 Field Company. An artillery patrol officer informed us that the line in front of Gomiecourt had been broken, so we decided to take up a position on the railway embankment of the Achiet-le-Grand–Courcelles line. Early next morning (25th) we got into touch with the 125th Brigade H.Q., who were at Gomiecourt Château, and learnt that the R.A. patrol officer's information had been incorrect; however, our position in the railway embankment was confirmed, and we remained as a reserve to the brigade until the evening. From the embankment we watched the Lancashire Fusiliers and some of the Manchester battalions fighting on the line in front of Gomiecourt running through Ervillers–Behagnies and Sapignies, which line was retaken from the Germans. Towards the evening we were much surprised to receive orders to fall back on Logeast Wood, as our troops had been so successful all day, but apparently our right flank was almost in the air, as the Germans were reported to have reached nearly to Hébuterne. The report that our line had been broken mentioned above apparently bore fruit in the rear, as the O.C. 428 Field Company was ordered to take his company and almost all drivers from the transport lines of the 427 Field Company to escort the divisional artillery on the morning of the 25th, with the result that no rations came up the same evening for the sappers, although a messenger had gone back to give Captain Echlin our location. The O.C. therefore cycled back to find the C.R.E., believing Divisional H.Q. to be at Bucquoy; on arrival there, however, it was found they had gone to Foncquevillers, about eight miles from our front line. He then found out that the horse lines had been moved still further back to Pommier. The cook's cart was immediately turned out and filled with the rations for the 26th; on the way back the wrong turning was taken in Bucquoy, and the cart arrived on the outskirts of Achiet-le-Petit at 5 a.m., which at the time was supposed to be in the hands of the Germans. Luckily the mistake was realized early enough, and the cart eventually arrived at Ablainzevelle about 7 a.m., where the company were preparing to move back to Essarts. Breakfast was cooked and eaten outside Bucquoy, and we arrived in Essarts about 10 a.m. A small defence work was commenced to hold the cross roads at the bottom of the hill on the east side of Essarts, but before this could be completed we were put into the Divisional Reserve under direct orders of the C.R.E. At 12.30 p.m. on the 27th this order was cancelled, and we again came under the G.O.C. 125th Brigade. A reconnaissance of the wiring of the brigade front was made, and the material wired for, but before dark this order was cancelled, and we again came in the Divisional Reserve with orders to be prepared to stand to and take up a position east of Essarts. At 1 a.m. on the 28th the "stand to" order was cancelled, and we were told to reconnoitre three suitable "strong points" on a line running through Essarts to Gommecourt Wood, afterwards known as the Purple Line; this was done in the early hours of the morning, but before work was commenced this order was also cancelled. On the evening of the 28th we again came under the orders of the G.O.C. 125th Brigade, who immediately sent the company to act as infantry, together with the 1/7th Northumberland Fusiliers (Pioneer Battalion), to take over part of the front line immediately in front of Bucquoy cemetery. This was the first time in France that the company was used to replace infantry. All ranks thoroughly entered into the novelty of the situation, and were glad to be really doing something useful to make up for the waste of time owing to orders and counter-orders received during the previous few days. A patrol, under Corporal Jervis, was sent out, but unfortunately they found nothing more exciting than a dead Boche. After twenty-four hours' experience as infantry in the front line we were relieved by an infantry company of the 41st Division, as the whole of the 42nd Division was withdrawn into support. The company then marched to Gommecourt Wood, arriving in the early hours of the morning of the 30th. Later in the day some excellent old German dug-outs were found, which held the whole company.

On the 31st three "strong points" on the Purple Line in rear of Hébuterne were reconnoitred, and were practically completed by the company the same night.

The Division went into the line again on the night of the 1st/2nd April, taking over from the 41st Division. The company received orders that it would be attached to the 1/8th Manchester Battalion of the 126th Brigade, and would be again used as infantry. This battalion was in support to the front line on the road between Bucquoy

427TH FIELD COY. R.E.

and Ablainzevelle, and after waiting four hours for one guide we took up our position in a sunken road just west of the northern end of Bucquoy. There was no accommodation in the road, and only room for two sections to dig themselves in under cover; the remaining sections were eventually placed in a trench running in rear of the road. After laying out and commencing a new trench about 100 yards long at dusk, we had orders to move to an old trench about 1000 yards in rear, and a cold wet night was spent in this.

In the evening of the 3rd we joined the 125th Brigade, and were given billets in an old German trench running parallel to the Bucquoy-Essarts road, about 500 yards west of the south end of Bucquoy; sufficient material was found in this trench to accommodate most of the company, including a " boudoir " for the C.S.M. and a deep dug-out for the officers' mess. The 4th April was spent in resting, as the men had had no rest during the last fortnight, and had been in the open for the last three nights; the work proposed was to provide Company Headquarter shelters for the infantry from the ruins of Bucquoy, and during the night sites were selected with the idea of collecting material the following day and carrying out the work the night of the 5th. On the early morning of the 5th the Boche attacked Bucquoy very heavily, and drove our line in on to the west side of the village. However, a counter-attack shortly after midday gave us back the greater part of the village. Owing to heavy losses of the 8th L.F. we were called upon to supply a carrying party to bring up S.A.A. for another counter-attack; this job we completed by 4 p.m. with a party of thirty men, ten of whom were wounded by shell fire. In the evening we had to supply ration carrying parties for two out of the three battalions that were then in the line; these returned at 4 a.m. the following morning. The next night we again provided ration carrying parties, one of which was retained in the line, as a further German attack was anticipated, but, however, did not occur. The following day, the 7th April, we received orders to wire the Yellow Line which ran just west of Bucquoy; this was reconnoitred, and work commenced at dusk. At 9.30 p.m. we were ordered to hand over our billets to an infantry company of the 62nd Division, which that night was taking over from the 42nd Division. The wiring parties were hurriedly withdrawn, and the company moved out about 11 p.m. Just as we were being relieved our billets were heavily shelled, the infantry company sustaining twenty casualties and ourselves two, one of which, Corporal Horne, proved fatal. The company then marched back to Henu, arriving there about 4.30 a.m. very nearly dead beat; at 11 a.m. the following morning (8th April) we embussed for Vauchelles. After four days' rest, during which we were inspected by Major-General Solly-Flood, the G.O.C. of the 42nd Division, we moved to a wood just south-west of Sailly-au-Bois and commenced work on the Switch Line in front of Sailly-au-Bois, which ran towards Chateau-de-la-Haie. The system of defence in depth was adopted.

On April 16th we went back into the line, and took over from the 153 Company, R.E., in Gommecourt Wood. At this period all three brigades were in the front line, and we were attached to the centre brigade, occupying as billets some deep German dug-outs, which had been in their old front-line system in 1916. The company was employed in completing the second line of defence, known as the Purple Line. This was arranged in depth, utilizing old German trenches, which were cleaned out and made suitable for platoon posts, and where necessary were cleared for communication. Double apron fences were erected three deep along the front line of this system, and two deep along the support line, which was known as Rum Trench. All old German dug-outs in use by our troops were fitted with gas curtains. A 5·9-inch shell-proof shelter was erected in Fonquevillers to accommodate thirty stretcher cases for the Advanced Dressing Station there. On the 25th the front was changed to two instead of three brigades, which allowed the 429 Field Company, R.E., to come out of the line and do back-area work under the C.R.E. This relieved a section of the 427 Company, which had been attached to the C.R.E. for work for the R.F.A.

On 6th May the company was relieved by the 505 Company of the 57th West Lancs. Division, and we moved back to rest billets at Hénu. After four days' respite for cleaning up and making the billets habitable, work was commenced on the Red Line, which ran from Coigneux in front of Souastre towards Bienvillers. The trenches and wiring had more or less been completed, but deep dug-out headquarters for a Divisional H.Q., three Brigade H.Q.s and about nine Battalion H.Q.s had still to be done. Owing to the immense amount of tunnelling work in hand, these dug-outs could not be undertaken by the tunnelling companies. With the help of an officer and about three N.C.O.s from the 252 Tunnelling Company our sappers soon became acquainted with the work, and after a fortnight or so made good progress, and during the last week in the rest area were able to give instruction to a party of American Army pioneers, who were attached to the unit for experience in field works.

On June 7 the 42nd Division relieved the New Zealand Division in the line between Mailly-Maillet and Hébuterne. The company took over from the 3rd New Zealand Engineers, who were working on the right sector of the divisional front. The billets lay near Bertrancourt, and consisted of trench cut-and-cover dug-outs made by our predecessors, and well furnished from the debris of Colincamps and neighbouring villages which had suffered in the spring from shell fire. The sector was most comfortable to work in, as all ground behind the front-line system was hidden from direct observation by the enemy, and our front line was situated just on the forward slope of the ridge east of Colincamps overlooking the whole of the enemy positions in front of Serre. These conditions enabled the bulk of the work to be done by day, and also transport by day up to the forward battalion headquarters. An excellent trench

427TH FIELD COY. R.E.

system had been carried out by the New Zealanders, so that little work was required beyond upkeep and adaptation to the "defence in depth" system. The bulk of the work again resolved itself into the provision of deep dug-outs for Brigade, Battalion, and eventually Infantry Company Headquarters.

Nothing of note happened on this front beyond occasional gas attacks and aerial bombing on the enemy's part, and "nibbling tactics" on our part, until the 15th August, when the Boche commenced to retire.

On August 4 Major Mousley, who had commanded the company since 31st August, 1914, was appointed C.R.E., 4th Corps Troops, and was replaced by Major Forsyth.

There was a general feeling amongst officers and men that such a long unbroken command of the Field Company on arduous active service must be marked in some special way, and a silver salver was presented to Major Mousley on his promotion. His gallantry and imperturbable bearing during dangerous work, his consideration for those under his command and his hard work as a result of which he had such an efficient Field Company, had won him the affection and esteem of all.

On the morning of the 15th August the enemy commenced a retirement from his salient in front of the 4th Corps, and although he had previously given no indication of his intentions, but, on the contrary, had held his outpost line very stubbornly against raids made by our infantry in the few days previous, his withdrawal was followed up promptly, our patrols maintaining touch with his covering patrols throughout the day and advancing till he took up a position immediately in front of Miraumont, about two miles in rear of his old line.

The new ground occupied in following up was where the Ancre battles had been fought in 1916. It was very badly torn with shell fire; the roads were considerably damaged, all but the main ones being obliterated; of the villages nothing remained but a few stumps of trees which marked their site. The next few days found the company working hard to obtain communication forward as far as possible to our new front line. The opening up of old roads on the brigade front was not practicable owing to their bad condition, the shortage of labour, and the immediate need of forward communication, hence all the labour available was employed in levelling and making two dry weather tracks "over the open" to the front line, to take horse transport. Fortunately the weather was favourable during the next few days, and the tracks were of great help.

On the 21st August the 4th Corps attacked and advanced along its whole front, and the advance was maintained by further attacks on the days following till on the 25th August the Division held a line immediately in front of Warlencourt. On the same day the company, with all its transport, moved first to Beaumont Hamel and then later continued on to Miraumont, the transport arriving there after having marched the greater part of the night—a pitch-dark one—

G

in pouring rain over a bad road congested with traffic. Some of our teams on this day travelled with loaded wagons close on forty miles, and were in harness the greater part of the day, yet on the following morning there was only one horse on the lines unfit for a full day's work that day, a great tribute to the work of Lieutenant Arkieson, Sergeant Hahn and the drivers of the company.

During the early part of the advance a party consisting of about one N.C.O. and six other ranks was attached to each of the two battalions in the line; these parties were used solely to locate and render harmless all booby traps found in dug-outs and shelters used by the advancing infantry as billets. They were very successful in discovering and destroying many of these traps, and there is no record of a single instance in which these dug-out traps proved effective on the brigade line of advance. They were made usually with a gas or H.E. shell, or else a few slabs of gun cotton, to which a detonator and a convenient length of safety fuse were fixed. The trap was so placed that the open end of the fuse was liable to be lit by a fire or by any one moving about with a lighted candle in the dug-out.

At Miraumont and later as the advance progressed many road mines were found and removed by the company. These consisted usually of a heavy charge of guncotton—a few that were opened had about 7 to 8 lbs. of it each—with a detonator connected to a friction tube. Through the head of the friction tube there was a small metal rod about three inches long. Pressing on this rod on each side of the tube were two metal prongs attached to the lid of the box in which the mine was placed. The mine was laid usually on the line of the wheel tracks, with the lid about nine inches below the road surface and covered with road metal. When a wagon wheel passed over the box the prongs attached to the lid were pressed down and pushed out the bar on the head of the friction tube, which lit the fuse. The traps were badly designed, as they needed a too careful adjustment of prongs and metal bar to obtain any result from the pressing down of the lids, and in most cases were badly laid. One mine laid under a railway bridge in Miraumont had the lid of the box put on with the prongs on the upperside, and in many other instances the prongs missed the metal bar, the lid evidently having been put on hurriedly, and no care taken to see that the mine was properly laid. One of these mines laid in the Pys–Miraumont road exploded when the wheel of a gun limber passed over, and killed four horses of the team drawing it.

We were now winning back country that had been fought over twice previously, country where all the villages had been completely destroyed by shell fire or by the Germans in their systematic destruction of villages before they evacuated them during their retreat to the Hindenburg Line in March 1917. As a result all, or nearly all, the wells which the villages relied on solely for their water were damaged badly, in most cases so badly that it was useless to attempt to reopen them. The Ancre River had its source in springs at Mirau-

427TH FIELD COY. R.E.

mont, the water in the river was good and clear and its supply inexhaustible, so this village in the early stages of the advance was the main watering-point of almost the whole Corps. Numerous water-points were erected by all companies of the 42nd Division and engineers of the New Zealand Division at all favourable sites in the village. Very soon, however, Miraumont became a back area.

On the 30th August the company moved forward to Pys in order to help in the development of all available sources of water in the villages of Thilloy, Ligny Thilloy and La Barque. In these three villages four wells were opened out and deepened, sufficient water being developed from them to water a complete Brigade Group (less artillery), animals and personnel, but no sooner were these arrangements completed than all troughs and tanks had to be dismantled and new water-points erected further forward.

On the 3rd September two sections moved to Villers-au-Flos, finding billets for the nights in huts that had been part of a British Corps Headquarters before the March retreat. That night horse watering-troughs were erected alongside the village pond, which was situated at the main cross roads in the village. The water, however, as was found to be the case in most of the ponds of these villages, was muddy and dirty, and the horses drank very sparingly from it; this added still more to the difficulties of water supply. At this period, and for some time after, wells in the villages occupied could not be developed sufficiently to meet all the needs of the Division, and Garford lorries that were specially built for water carriage alone had to be used a great deal. The number of these lorries available was small, and the equipment we had for water supply in the way of pumps, tanks, troughs, etc., was limited, so that besides natural difficulties, those of equipment and transport also entered into the water supply problem. It speaks well for the careful organization of the Q. Staff of the Division and the C.R.E. and the hard work of the field companies that throughout the advance on no occasion did the lack of water ever hinder our operations in the least. At a lecture given by the B.G., Q. Staff, 4th Corps, the 42nd Division particularly were complimented on the way they had met the water difficulty.

The remainder of the company moved into Villers-au-Flos on the morning of the 4th, and on arrival there sent out well-reconnaissance parties to the neighbouring villages of Barastre, Bus, Haplincourt and Velu; only two wells considered worthy of development were found.

On the 6th inst. the Division moved out of the line, for the first time since the commencement of the advance, to a back area near Bapaume for a fortnight's rest. The company came under the 126th Brigade, and was billeted, or rather built bivouac shelters, for themselves near the village of Thilloy. A training scheme for the company was planned for this fortnight, but owing to the pressing demands for work made by the Brigade and Division, the only consistent training was done by a special Lewis-gun team, which was instructed in the use and handling of this weapon by instructors from the infantry. For the Brigade, baths were erected at Thilloy, and a recreation and concert-room in Ligny Thilloy was extended to provide double its previous accommodation; when completed it provided seating accommodation for almost a brigade. A great deal of maintenance work was found necessary on all the water-points in the Brigade area, whilst some of the wells were deepened and further developed, particularly one in Thilloy, which supplied the baths and therefore received much attention from the higher command of the Division. The well was about fifty feet deep; the pumping arrangement consisted of a battle-worn petrol engine driving an endless canvas belt which hung down the well and was in the water about five feet. The water was drawn up in the belt and collected from it at the top of its travel. The engine while working needed the constant attention of at least four of the most skilled fitters and enginemen in the company.

The company were the fortunate possessors of a cricket set, and, in spite of the work and training, time was found on four or five afternoons in the fortnight for cricket matches. The pitch used—the best that could be found—was a very uneven one, but this was as it should be, for it placed good and bad cricketers on the same level. The best batsmen failed badly against a ball which broke the wrong way, or refused to rise more than six inches on a very hard pitch. Two matches were played and won outright against battalions of the 126th Brigade. In one of them all the opponents were dismissed for a total of not more than eight runs. Sappers Bullet and Williamson, professional cricketers in the days of peace, helped as they were by the pitch, were the terror of all batsmen.

The Division moved into the line again on the 21st September, relieving the 87th Division in the Havrincourt Wood sector. At this time the three field companies were working one forward, one intermediate and one on rear work. The 427 Company took over the intermediate sector. In view of coming operations, one of our first tasks was to make an immediate and very detailed census of all dug-outs and surface shelters in our sector. Water-points were constructed at Clayton Cross—a cross-roads in Havrincourt Wood—and Trescault, both in the very forward area. Two old dug-outs, which were to be used as battle headquarters for battalions, were cleared and strengthened and made habitable.

On the 27th the Division attacked and met with considerable resistance. The enemy were now back on the Hindenburg Line for the greater part of their front, their last well-constructed defensive line in France. The infantry, aided by tanks, which were invaluable in locating and destroying enemy machine-gun nests, attained by evening most of their final objectives. The attack was further pressed on the following day, and the enemy again commenced to retreat. That night the Division was relieved by the New Zealand Division, and on the 28th inst. the company moved to Bertincourt, continuing work on the same water-points, concentrating principally on Trescault, which was now one of the main divisional wateringpoints.

On the 1st October the company moved from Bertincourt village to bivouacs in Havrincourt Wood. Work at the Trescault waterpoint was continued, and also two sections were employed on the repair and drainage of roads forward of Trescault. On the 9th the company went forward to Lesdain, a few miles east of the Escaut Canal, and on the following day repaired in this village two road bridges over the stream Torrent d'Esnes. One of these bridges was a main road bridge, and was completely repaired by the following afternoon to take motor traffic. The enemy attempt at the demolition of the bridge—a masonry one—had resulted in the blowing in of half the roadway and in damaging the abutments. These latter were well propped with heavy timber, the roadway was made good with timber road-bearers and timber decking covered with rubble. A heavy wooden trestle was put in at the centre of the bridge to support it at the crown, at which place it had been most damaged. Also a water-point was completed in the village alongside the stream. This water-point was dismantled on the 11th when the company marched to Fontaine-au-Pierre, and that evening sent out well reconnaissance parties to forward villages. In this area it was found that very few of the wells had been destroyed or even contaminated by the enemy in their retreat. The houses were in fairly good condition owing to the advance having been so rapid, that the villages had experienced very little shell fire. Most of the main cross-roads, however, had been mined and blown up by the enemy on their retirement, resulting in huge craters in many cases thirty to forty feet in width. Quite a large number of inhabitants were found in these villages. They were very pleased that they had decided to brave the chances of a battle over their villages, and welcomed the British troops very cordially.

On the 12th October the Division went into the line, relieving the New Zealand Division. Our front line was now in the valley of the Selle river, between the villages of Solesmes and Briastre, the outpost line being a few hundred yards east of the river and approximately parallel to it. The enemy held all the higher ground on the forward slope of the hill east of the river, and therefore completely overlooked our forward positions and the approaches to them for about a thousand yards back. The 125th Brigade took over all the front line on the Divisional Sector, the 126th and 127th Brigades resting in reserve and preparing for the coming attack. On the day of the relief the 427 Company moved into huts in a wood near the village of Prayelle, and took over all work in the forward sector. At this time there were three iron and one raft footbridges across the river.

Our first orders on taking over the sector were to help the 125th Brigade in any bridging work they might require to maintain forward communications, but principally to concentrate on collecting material from any source in the neighbourhood, and preparing to erect on some coming night a tank bridge over the Selle river where the main Briastre road crossed it—the old masonry bridge at this point had been completely wrecked by the Germans. Sufficient material was collected and being prepared on the 13th and 14th insts., when the work was handed over to a New Zealand field company.

Late on the evening of the 15th the company was asked by the 125th Brigade to erect a bridge that night in the northern portion of their sector. No previous reconnaissance had been made for a suitable site or for material near by. The night was very cloudy and dark. Throughout the night, and especially in the early hours of the morning, the enemy shelled the village of Briastre, where all the preparation work had to be done, heavily with both gas and H.E. shells. The bridge, however, was successfully erected and only one casualty in both sections used for the work was sustained—Lance-Corporal Henderson, an N.C.O. who had served with the company continuously since 1914, was killed.

On the 16th definite orders were received from C.R.E. as to the bridging requirements for the coming attack. The 427 Company was to concentrate on bridging work alone. The bridging scheme was to erect four more footbridges on the nights of the 17th and 18th and to prepare to erect four more on the 19th, the night previous to the attack, making thirteen bridges in all on the divisional frontage of 1500 yards. Also on this last night two pontoon bridges to take all wheeled transport and field-guns were to be thrown across as near as possible to a main road. As four of the five existing footbridges were on the southern side of the divisional sector most of the new bridges were to be erected on the northern portion, where at water level the river was a little over 20 feet in width at the narrower parts. For this reason the quickest and most convenient footbridge was obtained by using German telegraph poles, which were over 30 feet in length and averaged about 9 inches to 1 foot in diameter. Two poles placed about 3 feet apart formed the road-bearers, and the pathway was obtained by nailing 1-inch boards across the poles. On the southern sector, where the river was wider, the bridges were formed of about two to three trestles with duck-boards for the roadway. Both types were fitted with handrails.

On the night of the 16th the line of the Selle river on the divisional front was reconnoitred and the sites for all new bridges were selected; on the next two nights four more bridges were erected according to plan and four others prepared and placed ready for erection near their sites. Besides these sufficient material was collected and prepared to make two or three more bridges in case they were required.

On the night of the 19th, the night previous to the attack, the remaining four bridges were erected and the route to each bridge from the nearest point on the road running in a northerly direction through Briastre near to and parallel to the river was taped out. Notice boards showing the number of the bridge with lanterns in front of them were placed at the head of every bridge. These precautions were taken to ensure the safe guidance of the infantry across the river to their assembly positions. Owing to a rapid rise—about 4 feet—of the river that evening the bridges north of the weir about the middle of our frontage on the river had to be extended and raised; the extra material that had been collected previously enabled this to be done without much difficulty.

The loaded pontoon wagons were brought down soon after dusk —their wheels had been padded with straw held in canvas in order to deaden the noise caused by their approach over the pavé roads in Briastre to the sites of the bridges. The gaps spanned by the two pontoon bridges were 53 feet and 42 feet. After completing the bridges they were screened from ground observation as far as possible by means of canvas placed on both sides of them. Their approaches over the meadow from the main road near the river were made hard with rubble from the destroyed houses near by.

The completion of all the bridges on the night of the 19th and their successful maintenance throughout the morning of the attack was carried out at a cost of six casualties—wounded only—in spite of considerable enemy machine-gun and shell fire, and of a gas concentration which compelled the wearing of box respirators for several hours during the night and early morning.

On the morning of the 20th the infantry crossed the bridges on their way to the assembly positions at 0200 hours, and attacked shortly after, making considerable progress. At 0630 the advance of the infantry enabled the artillery to cross the Selle by the pontoon bridges and take up more favourable positions on the east side of the river. At midnight, 20th–21st, we handed over the care of these bridges to the Divisional Pioneer Battalion.

On the 23rd the company moved to Solesmes. From the 24th October to the 4th November they remained at Solesmes resting, and organized recreational training formed a big part of the training programme. On the 4th November the company moved to Beaudignies, near Le Quesnoy, where it was billeted for the night. The following morning the march was continued to Herbignies, a village on the west side of the Forêt de Mormal; during the day, however, orders were received changing the destination to Le Carnoy, some distance further on. For the next two days the company worked on improving communications in the Forêt de Mormal. Big craters had been blown at the main cross roads in the wood, and the company worked on two of these; in one case the gap was bridged over, a Weldon trestle being used, and in the other a deviation road was made round the crater. On the 7th two bridges were built over a stream in the Forêt de Mormal, and that day the company moved forward to Le-Petit-Bayay on the east side of the forest. Early next day a light pontoon bridge was thrown across the River Sambre, and on the 9th morning the company moved into the village of Hautmont, and the erection of two bridges over the River Sambre was commenced, one a heavy bridge to take all traffic and the other an improvized trestle bridge. This latter was completed on the 11th, but the heavy bridge with the whole company engaged on it occupied four further days in erecting. It was built on an old weir or coffer dam which was constructed of $2\frac{1}{2}$-inch walings supported by $9'' \times 9''$ piles and filled in with clay. The top of the dam was about 6 inches above water level, and this was probably the normal maximum height of the river, as heavy rain had been falling for some days previously. There were several piles in the waterway and round about the dam, which had to be cleared away. In order to make the foundation as solid as possible the top boards of the dam were taken up and the space below was filled with rubble, the boards being then replaced. To afford support to the sides and ends of the dam, large stones and cement and plaster in bags were deposited in the water all round the dam up to the surface. To distribute the load over the dam piers were made over each pair of piles, thus making short bays at each end. The centre bay was 30 feet in length, sixteen rolled steel joists being used in this bay as road bearers.

About forty civilians were employed on the job, which took five days altogether. After the armistice had come into force on the 11th of November, bridging work was continued; on the 12th the erection of a bridge to take motor traffic over the Sambre River at Sous-les-Bois was commenced. The original intention was that the bridge should be built on the site of the demolished one, but the site was not suitable, and despite the additional roadwork entailed the most suitable site selected was 100 yards farther up-stream than the position of the original bridge. The total span was 82 feet, and was bridged in three bays, the centre and longest of which was 32 feet in length. The piers at the points of support consisted of box trestles made of $12'' \times 12''$ timber. Four 16×16 R.S. joists were used for road-bearers. The average working party on this bridge was 85 R.E., including some from an Army Troops Company and a Tunnelling Company, and 80 Infantry or Pioneers. This bridge was completed about the 1st of December.

On the 3rd December a pontoon bridge, which had taken all the traffic while the heavy bridge was in course of erection, was dismantled.

During the following week, the time spent on works was as far as possible limited to mornings only. The afternoon was devoted to organized recreational training and lectures on educational subjects and demobilization. On the 13th two sections were moved to Marpent to reconstruct a medium pontoon bridge, which was completed on the following day. On the 14th December the company commenced the march to the Charleroi area, the area allotted to the Division for the remainder of the period it was on the Continent. On the first night of the march the company stopped at Faubourg-de-Mont and the following day marched to Estinne-au-Mont. On the 16th the company moved to Anderlines, where it remained on the 17th, and on the 18th marched into Charleroi, occupying,

427TH FIELD COY. R.E.

with the other two field companies of the Division, the Jesuit College billets.

The company was in Charleroi from December 18 until April 3, 1919. There was much work to be done in the matter of improvements to billets for all units of the Division, and in addition the 4th Corps found plenty of work for the sappers in the concentration centres for demobilization, canteens for troops passing through Charleroi, etc. Pivotal men soon commenced to leave for demobilization, and amongst the early departures were C.S.M. W. Waterworth, D.C.M., and C.Q.M.S. H. Gilt, M.S.M. The sergeant-major left England in 1914 with the company, and though he saw most of the fighting, he never left the company. He was promoted 2nd-Corporal for his gallantry in the severe fighting in the Vineyard on Gallipoli, and his D.C.M. was equally well earned during the fighting in 1918.

C.Q.M.S. Gilt had an equally unbroken period of service to his credit, and what he did not know of "Q" work in a field company was not worth knowing. Few field companies can have been better looked after in the matter of rations, clothing and equipment.

The cadre of the 427 Company left Charleroi, on the 3rd April, for England, via Antwerp. It arrived in Antwerp on the morning of the 4th and left the same day, sailing for Tilbury, where the cadre disembarked early on the morning of the 6th, entrained for Oswestry that afternoon and arrived there on the morning of the 7th.

On the 8th and 9th all stores and equipment were handed over to the Demobilization Ordnance Officer at Oswestry Camp, and on the 10th the cadre entrained for Manchester, where it was met on its arrival by Col. Crook and other officers, and by friends and relatives.

PART IV
THE 428TH FIELD COMPANY, ROYAL ENGINEERS
1914–1919

CHAPTER I

EGYPT AND GALLIPOLI

AT the time when mobilization was ordered in August 1914, the 2nd East Lancs. Field Co., R.E., had already left for Carnarvon for the annual camp; they were immediately recalled, however, and reached Old Trafford less than twenty-four hours after their departure.

The following fortnight was a somewhat breathless period which it is not intended to describe in detail. Kit and equipment had to be checked and completed where necessary, horses had to be obtained, also some civilian wagons to complete the establishment of vehicles; a hundred and one details had to be attended to. Meanwhile we all tried to get used to the idea that we were in the army and might perhaps find ourselves fighting before long. Many had private matters to attend to also; arrangements to be made for a possible long absence from civilian affairs. Added to this was the general anxiety felt all over the country in all walks of life as to the progress and probable duration of the war.

Ultimately we went into camp near Bolton, and then came the question of volunteering for service abroad. As a natural consequence of this there had to be a certain amount of reorganization owing to the gaps caused by those who were unable to volunteer.

In a surprisingly short time, however, solutions were found to the various problems and difficulties, and after a most uncomfortable fortnight in this dreary and excessively damp camp near Bolton, orders were at last received to entrain. By eight o'clock that evening the company was duly aboard the train. We were not at all sure of our destination: daylight saw us gliding into Southampton Docks. There we found that the naval authorities had everything in readiness for our immediate embarkation. The officers and men, less a few drivers, were quickly settled down on R.M.S.P. *Aragon*, together with the vehicles; the animals, plus an extremely small number of drivers, on the s.s. *Messaba*, with Lieutenant Mackenzie in charge of both companies' animals and harness.

At dusk the liners slipped quietly down Southampton Water, and by dawn next day we were in the neighbourhood of the Eddystone. Here we stopped all day waiting for a collier and an escort.

About tea-time we set off—about a dozen ships in all—at the unholy speed of nine knots. The succeeding days were an agony to most, and hard work for those unaffected by the Bay. By the time we reached " Gib." all was well again, and the sunshine and the novelty of everything made everybody very happy.

After nearly three weeks at sea we anchored one morning off the timber wharves at Alexandria—this was where the fun really started. The temperature was 98° F., and we had no drill clothing or helmets until we landed; hence the two days we spent anchored in a dirty harbour were very trying. The second afternoon saw us alongside and unloading—a gang of " Gyppies " loaded our vehicles on to the train—amidst much noise and in the dark. We had a tiring but very interesting journey to Cairo, and pulled in to Kasr-el-Nil sidings late the next afternoon.

Here all was strange and new; barracks built by Napoleon and furnished later by the A.O.D. and also largely by nature—vast quantities of soap and paraffin were necessary to combat nature's additions to the beds. The fight was continuous throughout our stay, but as in other matters later experience taught us new methods, which gradually led to more success. As we were new to soldiering, and especially to life in the East, we spent fourteen days confined to barracks until we were smart enough to let the native see us. This was one incentive, but the *voice* of Major Wells was much stronger, and was even known later in the campaign to cause strong men to faint.

The wonders of Cairo are not to be described here, but it can be easily imagined how we enjoyed those evenings and even (let it be whispered) those nights out—the Pyramids in full moonlight—the wonders of Sakkara—the bazaars. In the meantime our days were spent in a hard routine of drill and infantry training.

About the 23rd October rumours came of Indian troops on the Canal, and on the 25th October two sections went to Kantara, and Company H.Q. and two sections to Kubri, near Suez. Captain Riddick, with the two companies' animals and bridging vehicles, etc., remained in Cairo.

The Kubri party arrived at Suez in the early morning by rail, and after breakfasting there marched northwards to their destination. Here the garrison was a company of the Highland Light Infantry, a regular battalion recently arrived from India. They gave us every help in erecting tents, and many a useful tip about campaigning in Eastern climes.

Work was begun at once on a floating bridge capable of carrying artillery across the Suez Canal, and subsequently detachments went to El Shatt, Shallufa and elsewhere to construct defences for small posts. The Sweet Water Canal, running parallel to the Suez Canal, was bridged by us at Kubri and Shallufa. The hours of work were long but pleasant, bathing in the Suez Canal was a constant delight, and there was much chaff and " back-chat " with passing ships. The Wessex Division passed us, eastward bound, and the *Sydney* (R.A.N.), which sank the enemy ship *Emden*, passed through the Canal on her way westwards. The H.L.I. departed for France in October, and the troops in the Suez zone were largely increased.

An Indian Brigade Headquarters was established at Suez, with largely increased garrisons at El Shatt, Kubri, Shallufa and intermediate posts. A company of Madras Sappers and Miners also arrived.

In these days we took the war very seriously, encouraged by endless rumours of Beduin forces lurking in the Sinai desert and ready to pounce on us. Only thus can we explain the night when the sentry challenged a suspicious object, received no answer and fired. Out tumbled the guard, more shots were fired, and Corporal Wielding proceeded to stalk the foe, only to find he was a stray camel ! Others shared our scares, and the infantry allotted us both alarm posts to occupy and patrols to perform. Lance-Corporal Redfern made our first capture, but as he proved to be the contractor for supplies to the local Egyptian coastguard detachment, we had to release him.

The coastguards received one day a large quantity of explosive, for no apparent reason. The Greek ferrymaster and our Syrian interpreter became palsied with fear as soon as they heard the news, so one night, whilst the dusky sentry slumbered on a heap of camel-forage, Major Wells and Captain Walker of the H.L.I., who happened to be passing his post, delved in the sand and took the explosive away to the infantry camp. Next morning the Greek and the Syrian arrived, white-faced and trembling, to report that the enemy had raided the dump in the night and stolen the gelignite, etc. They advised us to be ready for a horrible death at any moment, and for some time we enjoyed their terror. When the truth was told their relief was equally comic, for they tried to kiss the Major.

From time to time Australian and New Zealand troops passed through the Canal, en route to Alexandria and Cairo, and at least once when a Sunday church parade had just concluded greetings were hurled at us literally in the form of all the ship's store of hymn-books.

A trip to Suez was our only possible relaxation. One of the sappers who had a good voice used to get a pass occasionally to Suez to sing a solo in the R.C. church there. Carried away completely by the music (or something stronger) he was one day brought back under escort, with many unkind things said against him by the police !

Brother Charley of that town was a great friend, and secured us the loan of a piano for sing-songs. He also raffled the piano, but we had no luck.

The company received much kindness from Dr. and Mrs. Creswell of Suez. The Doctor arrived in camp early our first morning at El Kubri with much quinine, everybody being dosed. Private Ryan, R.A.M.C., was given a supply, and as long as it lasted every officer, N.C.O., and man had to take his ration whether he liked it, wanted it, or not. At one time a bundle of socks and shirts was sent weekly to Mrs. Creswell, who, with the help of other ladies in Suez, darned and mended them for the men of the company.

Duty also took us occasionally to Suez, and Sapper Twemlow, one of the handiest and most experienced men in the unit, did useful work on the structure of a floating searchlight operated by the Royal Navy.

At Kantara the two sections found a large native village with two or three decent houses, a camel stable and some native camel coastguard hutments, a telephone line across the desert, a battalion of 1/4th Ghurka Rifles and a detachment of the Coastguard Camel Corps.

We pitched our camp after tremendous efforts across the soft sand with a G.S. wagon, and then started to consider how we were going to tackle the making of a swing floating bridge across the Canal. We managed to secure for the purpose some large coal lighters, enemy property, commandeered accordingly, and towed to us from Port Said by an enemy tug with a prize crew aboard from H.M.S. *Swiftsure*, the guard-ship there.

After a lot of hard work and a great deal of assistance from the ever helpful Canal Company the bridge was completed.

Meanwhile Lieutenant Mackenzie of the 1st Field Company had organized the supply by tank-boats of filtered water to all posts near us. About this time we managed to secure a German tug. Lance-Corporal Wolstenholme was made skipper and Sappers Lloyd and Kelsall were the crew. As long as we kept to our own piece of the Canal nothing went wrong, and we had a glorious time. Unluckily we sent the tug to Port Said, and knowing nothing of harbours it went ashore. A picquet boat from the *Swiftsure* towed her off. Our crew had a fine time on the ship for a couple of days, and then came back to camp a trifle crestfallen with a nice but slightly sarcastic chit, from the commander of the *Swiftsure*, about the proper spheres of naval and military activity.

In the meantime our Indian garrison grew, and the Ghurkas went away to France; 27th Punjaubis, 14th Sikhs, 93rd Burmas, Bikhanir Camel Corps and the Coastguards remained all under General Cox, plus one Mountain Battery, R.A.

This meant large defence works and the great joy of demolishing the village, etc. The mud-hut village was very quickly removed by the Indians, with little or no help. Camel Corps married quarters gave us a wonderful fire one night, but some real good stone camel stables did prove a snag. Gelignite was the only explosive we could get, and we could not tell anybody, but actually we had never seen any gelignite before. In this dilemma we laid small charges and gave large warnings not to approach, with the result of practically no damage done; next time we put quite decent charges and still no serious damage. Then the Indians laughed, and we put half a case in each charge, and having forced them to a reasonable distance let go; the Indians did not stop running for quite a long way, and when they did come back there was no camel stable.

At this time Turkey inconsiderately declared war; this had the effect of doubling our work by daylight and keeping us all out in the

428TH FIELD COY. R.E.

trenches by night. This went on for about a month; in the end some Imperial Service Indian Cavalry arrived and relieved us of our night duties, largely, perhaps, in return for our kindness in sharpening a jewelled scimitar of the Rajah, who was in command.

Christmas was now drawing close, and fortunately the British officers of the 14th Sikhs came to our rescue and gave us cold roast turkeys and sausages (for all ranks), whilst we found the necessary beer and cigarettes.

Christmas Day really started with Christmas Eve, when we provided a Carol Party, which whilst entertaining was entertained too well.

Christmas Day provided a wonderful series of native sports, including polo, on S. and T. mules, with a football. This was, probably, the best day the men had at Kantara—a full and satisfying real English Christmas dinner, the Indian sports, the Canal, and the ships with their searchlights passing up and down after dark.

We had by this time a Sweet Water Canal water supply working with a pulsometer on the west bank supplying troughs, etc., on the east bank; we also started up, and later worked, a ship's searchlight set requisitioned from Port Said.

One feature of this period was the passage home, up the Canal, of captured German ships with prize crews—these always drew a cheer—and also the P. & O. and Orient, who threw us dozens of tins of cigarettes.

It was about Christmas time, or possibly later, that a Sikh doing his ablutions very luckily barked his toe on a chain found to be fastened to a mine which was got clear just in nice time in front of the approaching P. & O. mail.

As evidence of the quality of the work we put in, it is to be noted that the bridges at Kubri and Kantara, although built in a great hurry for a short period of use only, were both still in service when we came back in January 1916.

Early in December, much to the sorrow of all, a very sad accident occurred to a water-boat, the boiler of which exploded on the return journey to Kubri from Suez, and killed Lieutenant Woods, Sergeant Mellor, Corporal McLeavy, Lance-Corporal Butterworth, and Sappers Greenhalgh, Moscrop and Nugent, who were travelling back to their camp. They were buried in Suez Civil Cemetery, and later, in 1916, headstones were erected by the company and a brass plate placed in the English church at Suez.

On January 5 we were withdrawn to Cairo—the 1st Field Company joining the train at Ismailia, thence travelling together to Kasr-el-Nil and barracks again.

January was a month of Divisional Training, *i. e.* field-days on the Suez road east of Abbassia; this involved the R.E. in a march to Abbassia one day, a bivouac on an icy cold desert, a long and trying field-day, a very long march back, and a cold late supper.

Lieutenants Allard and Angus of the Egyptian Government service joined us in Cairo, and, having been fitted out locally, revealed the

H

scanty resources of the Cairo shops. Lieutenant Allard's R.E. brass buttons bore Queen Victoria's monogram instead of King George's, whilst, in lieu of the sealed pattern sword, he trundled about a huge Egyptian Army cavalry sabre.

Towards the end of January we trekked to Heliopolis and went into camp on the Race-course alongside the R.A., and on February 2 entrained for the Canal again under the eagle eye of Lieut.-Colonel Tufnell, G.S.O. 1, of the Division; this officer endeavoured to cut down our baggage and stores, but failed owing to the conversational powers of the senior officers, who led him firmly but quietly away. The doctor's orderly distinguished himself on this occasion by driving the doctor's large and cumbersome kit to the main station at Cairo instead of to Pont de Koubbeh station, our entraining point.

Arriving at Ismailia, we went into camp by the bathing-machines, and a very jolly place it was.

The majority of our work was now at Bench Mark, the deepest cutting on the length of the Suez Canal. The infantry here at first were the 5th Ghurkas and later the 51st Sikhs; the work was cut-and-cover tunnels through the crest of the hill, the normal defences, and flares. Every morning early—very early—we sailed out across Timsah in a tug, had lunch out there at midday, and towards the evening sailed back.

Early in March two sections were sent to Ferdan, where the defences were very much as we had left them, when last we had them as part of the Kantara sector; the 33rd Punjaubis soon arrived, and an elaborate programme was detailed.

The R.E. estimate of time, materials and labour, rather daunted them at first, but nevertheless we rapidly set to work and settled down to a daily programme.

The conditions of life at Ismailia deserve a reference. The barracks in Cairo were bug-infested, and the Terrier had come to regard discomfort caused by insects as a necessary part of soldiering, so that when he slept on the sandy soil at Ismailia and was again badgered, this time—as he thought—by sand-fleas, he did not worry. Nevertheless, a long day's work and a sleepless night soon proved together a heavy trial for any man, but matters were only brought to a head by an outbreak of spasmodic fever which laid one after another low, and brought them into the hands of Captain Webster, R.A.M.C. (known unofficially to most of the R.E. as "Nobby," and ever afterwards a trusty friend), who had a hospital in Ismailia in a former inn or auberge, which latter title gave it its name. Eventually we learnt that the illness was Relapsing Fever, and the sand-fleas, so-called, were lice. Thus did we contract a friendship (?), never properly shaken off until we were demobilized. Thresh disinfectors were called in and clothes and equipment were well baked, but little good seemed to result. Flies, lice, mosquitoes and fleas, with an occasional scorpion, and once a cloud of locusts, kept us all mindful of the Pharaonic plagues, and encouraged the saying that Egypt was indeed a land of sun, sand, sin and sorrow. Some of the com-

428TH FIELD COY. R.E.

pany's horses were sent from Cairo, and a groom was one day seen at Bench Mark trying to water his horses from the Suez salt-water Canal. As he explained, they drank all right from the Sweet Water Canal in Ismailia, and what was the difference? Some, on the other hand, were heard to compare the town and Lake Timsah to Blackpool-by-the-Sea.

Church parades were for some time held in the open air at Ismailia. The lack of instrumental accompaniment and the faint-heartedness of the choristers caused a senior officer to describe the service as " a lot of bally bees buzzing."

Work was much hampered by lack of material. Cement-sacks served as sandbags (and when filled with sand took some moving), whilst Egypt and the Sudan sent all spare corrugated iron, which wasn't much anyhow, and had apparently been in use since Pharaoh & Co. built the Pyramids.

Engineer rates were adjusted as each sapper's skill became better known, and many an argument of the industrial world was debated in the desert. The climax was reached when a sapper, who was a non-unionist, gave his frank opinion, in very emphatic language, of an N.C.O. who *did* belong to a union. Military discipline had then perforce to be asserted, but Sapper Eachus, D.C.M., showed later in Gallipoli that his courage was even more fiery than his words.

The Lancashire men soon learnt to chat in half a dozen different lingoes, Arabic with the boot-blacks, French with the Canal Company's employees, Hindustani with the Indian troops, and so on, whilst, in dealings with the Anzacs, " bonzer " and " cobber " were not unknown terms. Sappers with working parties of Indians would christen the men Wall-eye, Sambo, Ginger or Grogblossom, for example, and the Indians might then be heard quoting these same names in all seriousness.

One of these pleasant nights at Ferdan after the 33rd Punjaubis had put away their gramophone, which had been playing on the Canal bank to the R.E., and the detachment had all got well to sleep, they were awakened by machine-gun bullets going through the tops of the tents. They turned out and lined the defences " according to plan "; it was merely a raid, but there was quite a bit of rifle fire, and the Turks had a camel gun. The raiders stumbled in the dark on a small post of Indians, the entrenchments for whom had been prepared by us twelve hours previously for the 2nd Rajputs, who then held Bench Mark. Hundreds of rounds were fired by either side, but dawn revealed no corpses.

On Sundays our men used to go into Port Said for the day, and generally had a pretty good time with the bluejackets there. Towards the middle of April they brought back news of the R.N.D.— then in harbour at Port Said. We were naturally full of rumours, and rather interested in the peculiar features of the R.N.D., who, whilst being very much volunteer soldiers, were trying to look like sailors, and neither the bluejackets nor our own men would in consequence speak to them. These rumours culminated at the end of

April in definite orders for the company to concentrate at Ismailia. So the two sections at Ferdan were packed on to barges, good-bye said to the Indians, handing over reports made, and they sailed for Ismailia.

Captain Carver had gone to Cairo to look after the movement of the transport, and Major Wells was temporarily indisposed and in bed, so that the sudden move was an exciting operation. However, we entrained in good order at Moascar, near Ismailia, on the evening of May 4, and after a night-journey reached the Alexandria timber-wharves once again at about 8 a.m. There Captain Carver and Lieutenant Bull met us with the horses and vehicles, having travelled with H.Q. R.E. from Cairo.

A Gyppy party was supposed to do the loading, but did not arrive owing to a frequency of Saints' days—and being some other sort of feast day made the British seamen strike. The latter's troubles were quickly settled, and by mid-afternoon we had loaded ourselves, H.Q. R.E. and a Field Ambulance on board, and were free to listen to some wounded Australians (the first returns) from Gallipoli ask us, "Are you downhearted?" "No!" we roared back. "Then you jolly soon will be," came the answer as the ship with the wounded passed us.

Evening saw us away, and also saw arguments as to sleeping quarters. It was a good trip, although one R.A.M.C. private fell down a hold, having toppled over backwards trying to spring to "attention" when the Major gave the word on the C.O.s morning inspection. We also had a very successful concert, largely due to Lieutenant Fairhurst and "Bendigo of Nottingham" from Pickston. The real amusement occurred over hair-cutting; the edict went forth to remove *all* men's hair; some did and some didn't, so Lieutenants Allard and Gracey thought an example would do good, and shaved off their own. Their entry together into the saloon at dinner time nearly caused a riot, and although the sacrifice proved sound, both afterwards and as an example, they got told off by their seniors and were the ship's joke for the remainder of the voyage.

After rather a pretty day dodging through the rough islands of the Greek Archipelago we sailed one morning up past Imbros to Anzac—we were quite close enough to see the Australians ashore along the top of the cliffs. After an hour at Anzac we were ordered back to Helles and cast anchor there behind the line of battleships some time in the afternoon. It was a marvellous sight—the deep blue sea with sandy beaches and cliffs, the greenish uplands, and behind the Straits the snow-capped mountains of Asia Minor. The sea itself was literally covered with liners, and between the liners and the peninsula a row of battleships merrily fired away at Achi Baba. The liners were discharging their cargo of men, animals and wagons as quickly as possible into lighters, rafts, ships' boats, trawlers, Thames pleasure steamers—any old thing that would float. On the second afternoon a lighter came alongside, and Major Wells, Lieutenant Gracey and C.S.M. Thomas, with the company's horses and practically

428TH FIELD COY. R.E.

nothing else except about twenty drivers, were taken away by a trawler to " V " Beach and landed after dark—over the remains of several lighters, planks, odds and ends tied on to the River Clyde—on to the beach, whence the only landing officer there implored them to move on and get out of the way; they could go anywhere but not stop there. So after C.S.M. Thomas had rescued all the animals but one that was trying to make Constantinople through the Straits, they moved off up the beach and lay down for the night between some ration boxes and Indian mule-carts.

At dawn the Major sent Lieutenant Gracey on a reconnaissance to find out what was to be done next. So he went to Lancashire Landing and found the Major-General trying to shave in the A.A. & Q.M.G.'s water without his noticing, and was duly told to go to ——, but not ask them any questions as they did not know the answers.

Thus to Major Lawford, whose Signal Company was so wedged in between a 60-pounder battery that it was almost dangerous to move in his camp. By this time it was about 8.0 a.m., and on the way back to " V " beach a camp site was pegged out and a couple of men left to sit on it; luckily the Major had started, and they just cleared " V " beach before the morning hate. The animals were now put on a line, some grub for animals and men got, and then Lieutenant Allard rolled up. This decided the Major, who now proceeded to go aboard and get the remainder off. It was late afternoon when the Major left the party; at dusk they had the doubtful joy of seeing the ship steam rapidly away. Such behaviour by vessels was by no means unusual at the time, for as there were practically no hospital ships, transports had often to turn back with wounded.

The two officers were a little bit frightened at the prospect of starting a campaign with seventy-six animals, little or no harness or rations, one C.S.M., twenty-five men and themselves. However, they settled down to get some sleep, and were awakened in the middle of the night by the arrival of the Major with the remainder of the company, less Sergeant Walker, who had taken a wrong turn, and did not arrive till dawn.

It was now raining and the company had to settle down to sleep in the open under ground-sheets. A certain liveliness was caused, due to the fact that the Major took off his boots and covered them up with a neighbouring waterproof sheet, which happened to belong to Lieutenant Allard. The latter, who at the time was up and about, returned later and pulled the waterproof sheet over himself. Consequently the light of day revealed the Major's waterproof boots full of water and not leaking any! Then for the first time did Lieutenant Allard really learn the terrors of war.

Captain Carver and Lieutenant Gracey had an exciting day persuading various R.N. people to rescue lighters containing our stores, etc., and the starving guards on them.

The 1st Field Company landed on this day, and we handed over some of our horses to them, theirs being sent back to Alexandria. The next day we moved up to Pink Farm and dug ourselves nice

little graves to sleep in. These were very necessary to avoid the
"overs" at night, when we slept by night, and the shrapnel by
day, when we slept by day. Next day No. 4 Section moved to
Geoghegan's Bluff and had their first exciting times with the 7th
Manchesters; the remainder stopped at Pink Farm and worked on
the central road.

Shortly after that the Division took over the centre, on either
side of Krithia Nullah; we had the left side, and the 1st Field Company the right side. The forward sections lived in what was called
afterwards the Redoubt Line, and was then about 300 yards from
the front line.

The first night there it rained and rained and rained. The trenches
became liquid mud; they passed it down with shovels till it reached
the nullah bed. The 10th Manchesters in the same trench sent a
nice little chit along to our end of the trench, when the rain stopped,
asking for advice as to what to do about it—answer sent: "Get out
of it, if you can." Hence standing joke against the sappers. The
same rain-storm flooded out the dug-outs at Pink Farm, and proved
a striking lesson to all as to the intense and local nature of tropical
storms, for soon after the rain had ceased a man working at Divisional
H.Q., about a mile away, returned to camp and announced that
they had no rain there at all. The lesson then learnt was applied
to the design of many works the following autumn. The infantry
greeted us when we joined them in the line as the lads who had
come to dig the trenches for them. Until our numbers were reduced
considerably and sufficed for supervision and little more, we certainly shifted much earth daily, and, thanks to practice, were twice
as useful at sapping proper as any one else. Gradually, however,
the infantry learnt that they had to do things for themselves—with
a shovel as much as with a rifle and bayonet.

Water conservancy and sanitation were matters which had to
be learnt from the very beginning by troops who always before had
relied upon the water company and municipal engineers for such
things.

Headquarters at Pink Farm was by no means lazy. C.S.M.
Davies "ran" a grenade factory, whilst the joiners prepared barbed-
wire "knife rests," a good example being thus set, in the field, to
the Ministry of Munitions then being created at home. One lightning
strike occurred amongst the munitioneers, but it was not of the
usual type, being caused by some one hitting a detonator with a
hammer.

Manchester men are fond of music, and many an evening was
beguiled by glee parties of No. 1 Section, including "Stiffy" Smith,
as a rule, singing "Casey Jones," or, when feeling really cheerful,
"The Ghost of the Old Violin."

Fear of cholera and typhoid led to disinfection of all the water
we drank, although for some time the taste of chemicals was attributed
to the dead mule buried near the Pink Farm well.

The few drivers and horses we had with us were kept busy for

428TH FIELD COY. R.E.

some time, trying to find a quiet spot. Most of the cosy nooks had a battery near them, and drew fire accordingly.

These days in late May were busy, and far busier were the nights. On several nights our line was advanced, the same system always being used. The party went forward the required distance and dug themselves in, mostly in disconnected holes, which were joined up the following night; the party remaining out in their holes during the intervening day. On the second night of each advance, as well as connecting up the holes to make a continuous trench, communication trenches were made. Having once got a reasonably deep trench, it could be improved during the succeeding days.

Lieutenant Angus had an exciting night with No. 1 Section about this time, fitting up barbed wire above the waterfall in the nullah; otherwise it was very hard work on a very hard ration and a very hard bed when you got any sleep.

Still, we then, and afterwards till August, believed we were winning, and any little hardships were hardly noticed. Casualties, however, were by no means few.

At first, before we did the advancing by going out and digging in, we tried sapping forward, but it was dreadfully slow, and the accurate sniping of the Turks made work at the sap-head dangerous. It was therefore abandoned, but later we used this method for completing some communication trenches on the right of the nullah.

After several night advances the line was brought to within about one hundred and fifty yards of the Turkish defence system, and then dawned the 4th of June, on which day a big attack was carried out.

About half a dozen sappers were detailed to go with the first assaulting troops, with gun-cotton torpedoes, to break the Turkish wire, which consisted of two belts of knife rests. They were not, however, of much use.

The actual attacking troops were in two waves, and were followed by working parties in two more waves. Two sections of the 2nd Field Company—one on each side of the nullah—went with the third wave, or first working party; and the other two sections—again one on each side of the nullah—with the fourth wave, or second working party. The infantry part of these working parties was supplied by the 6th Lancashire Fusiliers.

An Advanced Company H.Q., consisting mainly of a dump of stores for wiring, etc., was established in the nullah close to the Redoubt Line, and about two hundred yards behind the line from which the advance started. To this place messages for Major Wells were to be sent, and here also Captain Carver and C.S.M. Davies were to remain. Major Wells himself went forward on the left of the nullah early in the attack, about the time when the third wave were advancing, to investigate the situation in regard to the amount of consolidation required. No. 3 Section, forming part of the fourth wave on the left, were astonished, while waiting to go forward, to see the Major arriving from the forward direction! He assured them that things were progressing well, and that No. 4 Section with the third wave had reached the first Turkish line without much difficulty, and were about to start work. There was a pretty heavy shrapnel fire at this time, though it would hardly compare with a heavy "barrage" as practised later in France. It was rather surprising that we had so few casualties from shrapnel in crossing the old "No Man's Land," most of them occurring later, and being the work of snipers.

Captain Carver meanwhile left the stores dump in the nullah to go forward on the right in the same manner as the Major had done on the left, with a view to obtaining information as to the situation, and possibly helping in the consolidation of the captured position. Before long he was wounded badly whilst in our most advanced line, from which he was extricated after hours of waiting, only to die in a Casualty Clearing Station. The company in him lost a most gallant officer and one who endeared himself to all ranks.

By the time the attack had got through the first two Turkish lines, the sappers were with the infantry first line, and soon found themselves clean and clear through the whole Turkish system; from both sides of the nullah one could see into Krithia without any serious opposition. The right, however, had to fall back to the third line of the Turkish system so as to conform to the line on the right of the divisional front. On the left of the nullah the advanced troops began to dig in slightly further forward. This left a gap unmanned; moreover, the numbers had by this time been very much reduced and the strength on the left did not amount to much more than a hundred and fifty, on a rough count. The C.R.E. and Major Wells came forward up the nullah in the evening, and after consultation with them the line on the left was withdrawn to the third Turkish line to correspond with that on the right. At the same time, in view of the very depleted strength, the R.E. sections were ordered to remain with the infantry in the front line during the night. One had the rather uncomfortable knowledge that there were few, if any, men behind, and one hoped that the Turks would not counter-attack. At dawn, however, they did and were repulsed; and for an hour or so we had some nice target practice on individual Turks trying to get back to Krithia.

Meanwhile the gap between the left and right of the nullah had not been properly filled, and the enemy penetrated and began to fire at us from behind. This was stopped by building barricades—a job which lasted practically all the next day (5th June)—thus forming a defensive flank to join up the two sides of the nullah.

We were all tired out, the casualties during the two days had been heavy, and life had been rather more exciting than most of us liked. However, a night at Pink Farm was sufficient to set us up again, and on the 6th June three sections went forward—No. 1 to the old "forward billet" near the Redoubt Line, Nos. 2 and 3 further forward to live in a trench called Stretford Road, which had been the British front line just before the attack.

428TH FIELD COY. R.E.

On the night of June 6–7 occurred the affair of the " old Turkish Redoubt." This small isolated post was within our line, and after consolidation had begun was reoccupied by Turks getting into it from the nullah. The 8th Lancashire Fusiliers cleared them out, and themselves experienced heavy counter-attack. When night came they appealed to Lieutenant Angus, in our neighbouring front line (which he had just come to strengthen with a working party), to give engineer assistance. The circumstances decided him to call for volunteers, and there are in our history few more splendid incidents than this one. All the volunteers were lads of about twenty-one or less, but across the open to the Redoubt they went, worked all night, and before dawn came handled their rifles vigorously against enemy attacks. The rising sun found hardly one, R.E. or L.F., who was not either wounded or dead.

Sapping was begun from our front line to the Redoubt, so that the wounded might be got away and supplies and S.A.A. be brought up. It was in this work that Sapper Eachus exposed himself so daringly to fire and eventually was wounded. His handling of an infantry working party on June 4, when he displayed both energy and courage, had already brought him into notice.

Sappers Hinsley, Barlow and Knott died gloriously. Sapper Harold Smith was wounded, and both he and the other survivor, Sapper Pollitt, received the Distinguished Conduct Medal and promotion. After two years of repeated applications the D.C.M. was awarded to Sapper Eachus also, whilst Sapper Paterson, who was conspicuous in helping him, received the thanks of the Divisional Commander.

New communication trenches were dug, H.Q. for battalions made, and there was a good deal of nasty work with wire and loopholing and strengthening barricades. A little later we had an exciting night, when one of our barricades was overwhelmed by the enemy, and every one except the Turk ran out of ammunition half-way through the night. On another night some work had to be carried out in conjunction with a battalion of the R.N.D., and their colonel caused some astonishment by approaching in the dark and calling out to an attendant satellite : " Is that you, Taylor? Have you got the Headquarters? Then put it there," indicating a slight hollow in the ground, into which the obedient Taylor sank with the Headquarters (an ordinary field service correspondence book).

The newly arrived 52nd Division took over the line for a few days, relieving our infantry. The sappers, however, remained, largely because they knew the front so well that their presence was invaluable to any new troops, and the 52nd Division R.E. had not landed.

On the return of our own infantry mining detachments were formed by the R.E. from the miners available in the battalions, and later Lieutenant Boyes, of the 4th East Lancs., was put in charge, working under Major Lawes of the R.N.D. These detachments did very useful work, and rapidly put in a sound defensive scheme.

A good deal of sapping was now done, several new lengths of communication trenches being dug in this way. The enemy snipers were very keen on the sap-heads, and great care was necessary when at work there. Early in July Lieutenant Bull was visiting a sap one morning, and stopped a moment too long at a dangerous corner to tell an infantryman at the sap-head to keep his head down. He had scarcely uttered the words when he was himself shot through the head and killed, adding one more to the gradually lengthening roll of good men lost—good men whom we could ill afford to lose.

Later in the month the infantry were again relieved for a short period, this time by the 13th Division, and once again the R.E. were left to act as guides, philosophers and friends to battalions who were new to the game. They were a fine lot, and later distinguished themselves at Suvla Bay. Whilst we were with them, however, a jumpy man amongst their sentries one night mistook Lieutenant Jones for a Turk and fired, wounding him badly.

Thus we come to the latter end of July. The 13th Division left for Suvla, although we did not know whither they had gone. Indeed, we knew nothing; but once again, in spite of the flies, the heat, the frogs and the moonlight, the rumours of impending Turkish attacks, we were quite certain that something big was imminent and that we were about to win.

During all the time spent since landing, and indeed right up to the evacuation of the Peninsula, the few drivers and horses we had were fully occupied, the water-cart having to be replenished frequently, stores fetched from the beaches, and rations, tools, etc., carried forward to the trench system. The mounted men suffered casualties, like the rest of the unit, and it was no mean loss when C.S.M. Thomas, Farrier-Sergeant Robinson and Sergeant Graham in turn went off to hospital.

The 2nd Field Company draught horses were second to none on the Peninsula, and great credit was due to these N.C.O.s and the drivers. They were detached well in rear for a long time, and used to be sent up in rotation to be inspected at Pink Farm. When any horse looked at all "tucked up" the farrier-sergeant used to go to the Mobile Vet. Sec. and demand linseed. This would be refused, whereafter he would go daily to the vet., Captain Stokes, saying, "The Major says he must have linseed," and sticking to it till he got it. Captain Stokes did not forget this, and afterwards at Suez the company built him, to his great joy, a specially good stable for his sick lines.

The landing at Suvla Bay now took place, and to assist our troops there a series of operations were carried out by some of those at Cape Helles, including the East Lancs. Division. An enemy attack, we subsequently learnt, had been timed for the same date and on the same portion of the trench system, and our own costly attack achieved little.

428TH FIELD COY. R.E.

On August 6 we attacked on both sides of the nullah and fought it out all day. Our opponents were some of the finest Turks of the Adrianople garrison. The sappers were detailed to proceed in small parties with the attacking infantry, but, owing to the fact that the Turks gave little, if any, ground, the sappers simply got mixed up and fought with the infantry. Casualties were very heavy. The attacks and counter-attacks, fire of the guns, machine-guns and flying pigs were continuous all day until dark. We had a lively night, putting in again a number of land mines removed for the attack and patching up the battered defences.

The fiercest fighting occurred in or round an old vineyard, and the struggle for its ownership continued long after the general battle had ceased.

The ground was by now baked hard by the fierce sunshine, and broke the hearts of any who had to dig in it. One night as we were trying to consolidate our gains in the vineyard an R.E. party went out wiring. A few yards away a grenade duel was in progress, and as the trenches twisted greatly in that neighbourhood shots seemed to be fired in all directions possible. Before a couple of minutes had elapsed one of the party (Sapper Robinson, G.) was dead and another wounded. The latter made for cover, and in bringing back the dead man one of the remaining couple (Lance-Corporal Swift) was killed, whilst the fourth of the party got a bullet through his breast pocket, shirt and coat-sleeve, harmlessly, however. All this happened in a very few minutes. As cover was regained stretcher-bearers were passing, and gave the news of some 1st Field Company men a little further up the trench who had also just been killed. An infantryman of the East Lancs. Regiment was heard to comment thereupon to his chum : " Dost know what R.E. stands for ? Tha' doesn't ? Why, Royal 'Ellguts, lad." Praise from the infantry is in any case sweet, and was probably merited at that moment, when one seemed genuinely to stand in the guts of Hell, amidst the blaze of explosives, the din of battle and the anguish of the stricken.

Swift and Robinson were buried in our little cemetery at Pink Farm, but many another had to be interred where he fell, or only too often lay in the open amidst the scrub and heather, unseen by or inaccessible to his comrades.

A few days later the Division, this time including the R.E., were withdrawn to the Pink Farm neighbourhood for a rest. We had some glorious bathing in Morto Bay, and generally a very good time for a couple of days.

Inoculation against cholera was introduced about this time, but, being optional, some objected to it. These were therefore segregated and obliged to fend for themselves, being regarded as a danger to others. Although Sapper Owen, H., an excellent cook, was amongst them, the joys of camping out soon palled, and the party quickly returned to the fold with all its home comforts.

Then came the orders to take over from the 29th Division.

EAST LANCS. R.E. HISTORY

The two field company commanders with attendants hurried up to take over, but found the London and West Riding R.E. Companies already departing. Of the third, a Lowland Field Company, only one subaltern remained, and he was busy closing the Orderly Room, so regretted he could not escort them round the works. The handing-over was effected in a few minutes, and with the aid of a sketch on the back of an envelope. Thereupon all the effectives of the company, less H.Q., which remained at Pink Farm, moved up to a hollow near Geoghegan's Bluff in Gully Ravine (otherwise called Saghir Dere).

Since July the sappers had ceased to be organized in four sections, as our total working strength only equalled a single complete section. To keep things going constantly we worked in three eight-hour shifts daily.

The trenches at this side of the Peninsula were much the same as the ones we had left—the defence against mining was, however, useless, as we soon found out to our cost. The 2nd Field Company sector extended from the R.N.D. left through Border Barricade across the Gully to a point in Inniskilling Inch, where the 1st Field Company carried the line to the cliff at Fusilier Bluff. The work was additional wiring, which was badly needed everywhere, trench repairs also badly needed now the weather was beginning to break, opening up of communication trenches, which were in a very bad way, the narrowing of all fire trenches, water supply, and other jobs.

We had a particularly rough time in a sap running out of Border Barricade.

One little laugh we all enjoyed. We had been wiring on our right front and had asked the R.N.D. to be careful and not shoot us (as they tried to sometimes), since their flank sentries could see a part of our front as well as their own. We finished, came in and told the R.N.D. officers (who did not trouble to see that their sentries understood); a little later Johnny Turk came out, and under the noses of the R.N.D. sentries removed the R.N.D. wire from its posts.

Between the former British front line and the existing one lay a maze of battered Turkish trenches through which, thanks to the cover afforded by the ravine, there was no need to pass in going backward and forward. The only ones to explore them were the R.E., whose officers might often be seen conducting select parties round the most gruesome sights they could find in the Boomerang and other trenches, whilst Corporal Kinley and others drove a brisk trade in curios and mementos with a certain Field Ambulance.

Reinforcements of officers and men were now arriving, unfortunately not as many as we should have liked. They succumbed more easily, too, to the different ailments by this time well-established in the expeditionary force than did those who had become accustomed and inured to them.

With eggs from Bulgaria and a ration of flour many a tasty dish was cooked, whilst from time to time even tinned fruit was obtain-

428TH FIELD COY. R.E.

able, given away at a nominal price by philanthropists disguised as Greek traders.

Then the first mine went up at Border Barricade. A long period of suspense and sudden bursts of effort had to be made to block the gaps each time and seize the lips of the craters. This carried us to the middle of October. The Major went away with jaundice the day the first mine went up, Lieutenant Angus was killed helping the consolidation of the second, Corporal Wielding, our jester always, was also killed, and many another good fellow. We were absolutely helpless, although the miners did their best, and could only listen and wait and then rush in and secure the best position we could and consolidate.

We had very little material and very few sandbags; a good many of these were the efforts of good ladies and were about the size of a vanity bag; sometimes, alas, open at both ends !

The Turks added another joy to the day and night by making a reply to our flying pigs; this consisted of a heavy artillery brass cartridge case mounted on a stick and fired from a length of gas-pipe (from Gallipoli Town). It was filled with any old iron as slugs and a percussion nose-cap fitted to fire a bursting charge.

During October, Major Wells being still away in hospital, Major Montefiore took over command of the company for fourteen days. He landed, thoughtfully bringing with him chickens, rolls and bottled Bass for lunch, in case the officers' mess had not been warned of his advent ! Evening found him revelling in bully-beef and tea like the rest of the company, a wiser and a sadder man as regarded the mess catering. The 1/2nd West Lancs. Field Company had arrived meanwhile, to become the third field company of the Division. After acclimatizing themselves, they took over both companies' front sectors, as they could very easily do, at the end of October. We retired to Gully Beach, improved our quarters and continued to work each night on the reserve line at the Zigzag.

This last phase of life on Cape Helles was the most pleasant; the entrance of Bulgaria became rather noticeable from the increased gun-fire, but thanks to everybody's exertions we had better quarters than we had ever had before. We still had work every night, wiring, digging, etc., but pretty comfortable days.

Towards the end of October the South-Eastern Mounted Brigade joined the Division. Sturdy troops, and drawn from farming and hunting districts, in the pink of condition, they presented a great contrast to our war-worn men, sick from every ailment imaginable.

On November 15 with very little notice the first rain came. Border Barricade, made of sandbags, in the bed of the Ravine, was washed away, and through this gap in our front line were washed dead bodies, much débris, and a young donkey. For a short while the stream ran, feet deep, down what was our main road to the firing-line, and then subsided.

Some Indian Army tonga cart drivers with their transport were attached to us at this time, and Major Wells was very active in getting them an issue of winter clothing. To show their gratitude they brought him, next time they slaughtered a sheep, a plateful of smoking entrails and prayed that the light of the countenance of the Protector of the Poor and Giver of Justice might ever shine. The brothers Echlin made a voluble counter-attack in Hindustani, and all parties emerged from the episode with credit.

In November and December, apart from the making and maintenance of defences, the work of the company was chiefly the construction of winter quarters, with the aid of inadequate materials and weary working parties, and the maintenance of road communications within the Ravine.

Sapper W. Murray was detailed to build winter quarters for Major-General W. Douglas, the Divisional Commander, who visited him frequently to observe progress. When Murray, who hailed from Auchtermuchty or thereabouts, discovered that the General was one of the Douglases of Killiecrankie or something of the same sort, a volley of " Hoots-toots, mon ! " " Och aye," and so on, rent the air, and every day thereafter Murray gave the Divisional Commander a thirty minutes' lecture, at the point of the trowel, on the use of manure in mud mortar, and kindred topics.

One night Lieutenant Barrington and No. 3 Section were out in the open working on trenches near Frith Walk (also called from its nature Filth Walk). Suddenly a star-light rose in the air and remained there for a while, illuminating everything, whilst Briton and Turk exchanged rifle-shots. " Drop down, men," cried the officer, and himself flopped to earth. As he did so he felt a sharp stab in the leg, so told Sergeant Johnson, who was near him, that he had been hit. The wound was not excessively painful, and he was congratulating himself on having received it so calmly, whilst they lifted him into the trench, got ready the iodine and field dressing and tenderly bared the rent flesh. Alas, well-embedded in our young hero's hide was nothing more than a stout thorn from a bush !

December passed away fairly smoothly, except for the classic sea wall built by Lieut.-Colonel Cox of the Ambulance, condemned by the Major and strafed by the Colonel because the stone came from the official (but useless) pier, and scorned by the Chief Engineer of the Corps because it had not been improvised from, say, bhusa missa (chaff) and incinerated bully-beef tins.

No history of Gallipoli is complete without some reference to the blizzard, which descended on us when all seemed so fair, and made life an agony for the enfeebled sun-soaked troops. The company, however, thanks to its settled quarters and organization, suffered less than most, much being owed also to the gifts of warm woollen clothing, mufflers and mittens, which arrived at this time from well-wishers in England, whereas the army supplies arrived a few days too late. Welcome cases of tinned fruit and milk, chocolate, cigarettes, soups, etc., came also from friends in Egypt, London and Lancashire, cheered us greatly, and made our Christmas fare

428TH FIELD COY. R.E. 111

something like the real thing. Snow on Achi Baba and the freezing of all the pumps completed the picture.

The road in the Ravine bed became worse and worse, but with insufficient labour little could be done to remedy matters. Eventually the 29th Division, from Suvla, took charge of it for a few days and employed large parties on it with some (temporary) success.

The weather gradually grew stormier, and from time to time half rations only were issued. Meanwhile came the news of the evacuation of Anzac and Suvla—first a rumour, then something more definite, and the glare of the huge bonfires. Then we were to be relieved by the 13th Division, but still no news of evacuation, which seemed incredible. Then definite orders to go and days of packing our equipment in cases, etc. Then actual evacuation, destroying our own and other people's wagons, etc., and last, but not least, being guides, at " V " Beach, to the 13th Division because the East Lancs. R.E. had been so long on the Peninsula, though there were few enough left.

Meanwhile the King's Christmas message had been read to us, reminding us that the year had ended as it began, in toil, bloodshed and suffering. How far, if we had only known it, were we still from our goal!

Our night to go away came suddenly enough; one party had a fearful job getting our stores into lighters at " V " Beach, and then joined the Major with the remainder of the company on the road to Lancashire Landing, and sat in a ditch round a tent there for hours listening to the arrival of Asiatic Annie's children on the beach below us. Our turn came at last, and we moved down on to the beach along a frail wooden jetty on to a " beetle," as the self-propelled R.N. barges were called.

When the lighter was fully loaded there were still two large sacks to be brought aboard, one of potatoes, the other of hymn-books, both the property of a Manchester brigade padre. He could only take one, he was told; which would he have? "Good gracious!" he replied, "I couldn't leave the potatoes at any price. Shove them aboard!"

There crowded together like flies we clung, whilst the engine throbbed and the naval man said he had no orders to move. A shell from Asia came so close at last that some fell overboard and all were splashed with spray. This settled the matter, and we gradually drew out and sailed away to the *Redbreast*, lying about a mile away. Out there the sea was roughish, and round and round we circled trying to embark on the dark side of the ship. The naval man and the *Redbreast* interchanged such a beautiful flow of language during this that we quite enjoyed it, but were nevertheless pleased when we did get aboard, and after some delay sailed away. We were glad to get away, but very sorry to go.

Morning saw us still steaming away, and shortly before midday we anchored in Mudros harbour, after passing an ominous crowd of hospital ships. The main body went ashore at once, one officer and a few men being left to have lunch and unload the stores under the direction of Major Connery, the veteran Q.M. of the 1/9th Manchester Regiment. Major Connery was an Irishman, he had been a soldier and a quartermaster all his life, so it can be imagined we had a pleasant but a busy time unloading into the " beetle."

Captain Webster of the R.A.M.C. was there, and wished to put all the Ambulance stores on top and the R.E. and infantry in the almost inaccessible inside of the " beetle " : a word from the R.E. (whose stores were at the bottom of the *Redbreast*) to their old ally Connery settled that, and it is said that " Nobby " Webster was so wild that he threw his own automatic pistol into Mudros harbour, thinking it belonged to the R.E.

Then we had lunch, the men feeding luxuriously on the rations of the 5th East Lancs. (which battalion had no unloading party), and the officers drinking medical comfort stout (" Nobby " was too wild to notice). At last we were complete, and were towed to the pier at Sarpi just as it was getting dark. Here a thoughtful Staff had provided six G.S. wagons in place of thirty, to carry the brigade's stores and baggage. The A.S.C. officer in charge asked for the Brigade Transport Officer; Connery promptly answered " Here " and took the six wagons, giving the R.E. one, the 10th two, and keeping three for himself. " Nobby " then said what he really thought to Connery, the A.S.C. officer and the rest of us, but all to no good purpose.

We had quite a decent camp at Sarpi, between the Australians and the 52nd Division. The C.R.E. ordained an early morning before-breakfast parade the next day for all except Field Officers, and we all grumbled. The day after that, at the same ungodly hour as our parade, a pipe band of the 52nd Division did a half-hour stunt performance on a patch of ground adjoining Colonel Tennant's tent; the connection seemed obvious, anyhow our parade continued and so did " the music." The next thing was a divisional football tournament, and the R.E. did very well.

Meantime detachments of the 42nd Divisional R.E. had been taking part in the final phase at Cape Helles. An officer of the 2nd Field Company describes it as follows—

Early on Saturday, January 8, orders were received that the final evacuation of Cape Helles would be carried out that night.

The R.E. forward preparations had been practically completed for some days, and the work on the left sector had included the construction of controls at points which the various infantry parties would pass on their way to the respective beaches.

Barbed wire obstacles and gates to fill the gaps in the wire at the controls were in readiness, and small parties of sappers were detailed to place " gooseberries " and other wire obstacles at selected points in the main communication trenches after the passage of the infantry.

Gully Ravine had been almost impassable owing to heavy rains,

428TH FIELD COY. R.E.

and a series of small bridges to take infantry in single file had been constructed, and the road demarcated by sandbags throughout its length.

The day was spent in the destruction of surplus vehicles and stores and the burying of ammunition, etc., and in the course of the afternoon the West Lancs. Field Company moved away from the bivouacs near Geoghegan's Bluff towards the embarkation beaches.

Two R.E. officers and about twelve sappers were left behind to carry out final duties, and these parties reported at dusk to the Officers-in-Charge Controls.

These control posts were situated at several points in the main communication trenches leading from the firing-line, and they were connected by telephone with Headquarters at Gully Beach and " W " Beach, so that those responsible for the evacuation might know when the last parties passed through the controls. Only then was permission given to the sapper parties to close the communication trenches with the barbed wire obstacles.

Shortly after midnight the last parties of infantry passed through the controls, and the gaps in the wire entanglements were then closed.

Candles were lit in the centres of the piles of stores at the Brigade Headquarters at " Y " Ravine and the Zigzag, and dumps in Gully Ravine at the Eski Lines, after which messages were sent to Headquarters as to the completion of the work, and orders to leave the control stations awaited.

On receipt of these orders the parties at the controls moved to Gully Beach, where the infantry were found lined up in three queues waiting the arrival of the boats.

The bulk of the men were embarked on the first boat, but the second went aground owing to the rough water, and as it was impossible to refloat her she was abandoned, and instructions eventually came through from Headquarters at Lancashire Landing for the remainder (about 160 all ranks) to proceed to Lancashire Landing, where another boat was in readiness.

The tramp to Lancashire Landing along the beach took some considerable time, and it was 4 a.m. when the party finally clambered into the waiting boat, which proceeded to Imbros, arriving at 8.30 a.m.

Later in the day the various parties re-embarked for Mudros, where they rejoined their units.

After something like a fortnight, chiefly spent in sleep and trips about the rather barren and dirty island, we at last embarked on the s.s. *Egra* for Egypt once more.

CHAPTER II

EGYPT AND SINAI

AFTER a voyage of three days we reached Alexandria and entrained for Cairo. Detraining at the sewage pumping station sidings, after tea and buns, kindly provided by some Cairo ladies, we proceeded by tram to Mena Camp, near the Pyramids. All our tools, stores and baggage came along behind on innumerable little donkey carts.

Up to then we had regarded ourselves as a bit shabby perhaps in our clothes, but nothing serious; but now really we discovered why they had sent us to Mena—so we set about getting decent clothes from Cairo for officers and men.

At Mena Lieutenant Walker rejoined us with the animals of the 1st Field Company and of the West Lancs. Field Company. We had some pleasant days at Mena, spent in getting clean again and then in visiting our old friends in Cairo.

It was very pleasant, but did not last long; a few days saw us packed up again and arriving at Tel-el-Kebir, a great tent and hut camp with a street of weird and wonderful shops made of old packing-cases, etc.; it looked just like a newly sprung-up town in Western Canada. Two or three days here spent in wandering about the old battlefield—the Egyptian trenches can still be seen—and we were on our way by train again to Shallufa on the Suez Canal. Into camp once more on the east bank ("in Asia" as the Canal Company say), and animals on the west bank, a swing floating bridge to operate.

We relieved, at Shallufa, the 46th Divisional R.E. who with the rest of that Division returned to France after a stay in Egypt of three weeks only! The air was dark with their curses as they wended their way back to the snow and slush of the Somme, which they thought previously they had quitted for good. Just as things were beginning to look a bit too much like peace No. 4 Section was sent to Geneffe to make defences. Subsequently Headquarters and the remaining three sections moved to Geneffe, following the Brigade H.Q., and No. 4 Section moved with the 1/10th Manchester Regt. to Ashton Post, nine to ten miles east of the Canal on a desolate deserted sand ridge.

Then came the great pipe "stunt"; miles of pipe had to be laid in a great hurry, and in a remarkably short time this was done; only a part of the company was engaged on this, the remainder doing a good deal of work on the defences at Ashton Post and Geneffe.

In February the company marched to Suez and went into camp

428TH FIELD COY. R.E.

with the other companies, and a draft from Southport arrived shortly afterwards.

The camp at Suez was made up of bell and E.P. tents, and was, although dusty, sufficiently near Suez to be quite pleasant after so many months' isolation. The company was employed in the erection of double matting roofed huts for the East Lancs. Brigade. Work commenced very early owing to the increasing heat; the infantry supplied what skilled assistance they could. The doctor inoculated all for cholera. The West Lancs. Field Company departed. The heat became daily more unbearable.

At last, in June, when the huts were practically finished, the Division moved and with it the field company by rail to Ferdan, and thence by march route to Abu Uruk, the camp in the hills at the rail, road, and pipe head, east of Ferdan.

In crossing the pontoon bridge over the Canal, six mules were drowned.

At Abu Uruk we relieved a company of the 11th Divisional R.E., then moving to France.

The remainder of June and most of July passed away pleasantly enough here in a tent camp. There was a great deal of both maintenance and new work to be done on the railhead defences, which consisted of a series of outlying posts linked together by their "fields of fire." The previous arrangements with regard to water supply, and especially water storage, at these posts, were altered and considerably enlarged.

Towards the middle of July the C.R.E. considered that the field companies should be given some opportunity to train in bridge work, and accordingly No. 1 Section was sent to the Canal bank to live with the newly arrived 3rd Field Company stationed there, and practice pontooning. To the disappointment of the remaining sections, before No. 1 had completed its schooling, the company was moved to Kantara, marching via Ferdan. It stayed one night there and marched the following morning to Hill 60, a few miles east of Kantara.

Here we had an inkling of what the next few months were to bring. Soon after our arrival all the company vehicles, most of the animals, and the greater portion of our equipment were sent back, under the charge of Captain Courtis, to the base at Kantara. The new establishment was to fit the company for mobile work on the desert. Fifty-five camels were supplied, sufficient for all the transport work of the company. Only certain tools, of which a very complete list had been prepared, which were considered necessary for future work, were to be carried. Besides these, we were to carry, as part of our permanent equipment, well-lining material and canvas troughs and a Norton-tube pump.

The new equipment was not long in arriving. The camels were taken over a day or two after we arrived at Hill 60. The next few days found us training hard at well-sinking and also trying various ways of loading the camels in order to arrive at the most suitable distribution of loads and most speedy method of loading.

By this time it was known that the Turks had advanced to the vicinity of Katia, and that an attack on our railhead defences at Romani was imminent. The 126th Infantry Brigade Group, with which we were brigaded, formed the Divisional Reserve and moved forward to Pelusium the day after the battle of Romani. After this decisive victory the Anzac Mounted Division pushed the enemy back to Mazar, and the 52nd Division formed the protective troops at railhead, as the railway and pipe lines progressed, with the result that 42nd Divisional H.Q. returned to Pelusium about August 15. The 42nd and 52nd Divisions now took it in turns to form the supporting division to the cavalry and rail construction work, and the sappers were fully employed on water reconnaissance, being spread out on a broad front and well ahead. The Norton tubes enabled tests to be made very rapidly, and the medical officer, specially attached to these reconnaissance parties, made his analysis of the water on the spot, so that tests for salinity and probable yield were marked on site and the results sent on to the C.R.E. During this trek across Sinai, the company lived in bivouacs made of laths with each man's second blanket stretched across, against heat by day and cold by night. One or two mounted N.C.O.s remained with Company Headquarters to look after the Egyptian camel drivers, and to take charge of and guide the small ration and water convoys which had to be sent from Company Headquarters, or railhead, to the outlying sections. Other work that fell to our lot was the erection of 2300-gallon canvas tanks at each successive railhead, to hold the drinking water that was sent up in tanks on the railway, laying of wire netting "roads," erection of canvas troughing at the wells, whatever their saltness, for the use of horses and camels. In addition, sapper supervision was provided on the considerable defence works carried out by the Egyptian Labour Corps at each station as the line progressed, with a view to the minimum number of troops being required on the lines of communication.

At the end of August, Lieutenant J. P. Echlin, with No. 3 Section, was engaged in the neighbourhood of Oghratina sinking Norton-tube wells in search of the best sites for wells; after some days of this work the sinking of the full-size wells (usually $4' \times 4' \times 16'/20'$ deep) was commenced. A few days later Divisional H.Q. and the 126th and 127th Brigades moved forward into the new area, and the company put down a large number of wells in the Oghratina Hod and between Negiliat and Kilo 60 on the new railway.

About a month later the main body of the Division retired to Romani and Mahamdia, but two sections of the 2nd Field Company, with a portion of the 126th Brigade, moved forward to Bir-el-Abd, where much time was put in on the defence works. The remainder of the company moved at the same time to Kilo 60 with Headquarters and remainder of 126th Brigade. It was from this point that further water reconnaissance parties went out to Mageibra and Bayud, and made exhaustive surveys of the neighbouring "hods."

"Hod" was the local Arabic term for a water-bearing depres-

428TH FIELD COY. R.E.

sion in the sand, usually identified by date-palms growing there. In recognition of the company's efforts certain irreverent Staff Officers christened the Major "Hod Pasha," and so nearly deprived him of his rightful title, "Bombardier."

From Kilo 60 the company moved forward by stages to Salmana and Abu Tilul, very often by rail, as the Major had a way of obtaining trucks for bulky R.E. stores, in charge of which there was usually a large R.E. party! At the latter place, in November, the company with both pain and pleasure learnt of the promotion and appointment of Major Wells to Lieut.-Colonel as C.R.E. of the 52nd Division.

At this time few, if any, Territorial R.E. officers had been appointed C.R.E. of Division, and the selection of Colonel Wells was a high compliment both to Colonel Wells and the company. Captain Riddick of the 1st E. Lancs. Field Company took over the command.

The early days of December saw the company at Maadan or Kilo 128, preparing wells in the plain which led up to the El Arish defences. A great deal of work was done, and the supply, naturally very slight, greatly developed by the evening of the 20th December, which found the whole Desert Column of two Infantry Divisions and a Cavalry Division wedged tightly into a long valley near by. The night brought disappointing orders : no advance was necessary, the enemy had fled. So we lit fires of scrub to warm the cold night, and rapidly the valley lit up and disclosed the great mass of troops.

Daylight came, and with it even more disappointing orders to march back to Mazar. This we did, and took over the maintenance of the many wells and construction of blockhouses and defence works.

Christmas came, and with it a sandstorm, but it was nevertheless celebrated as well as we could.

After Christmas the Division advanced again, and the 2nd Field Company went for a few days with the East Lancs. Brigade to Kilo 139 or El Bittia, and thence marched into El Arish. There we occupied a camp on the western side of the town; it was the site of camps from time immemorial, and so was very dirty.

The 52nd Divisional R.E. and the 1st and 3rd Field Companies had already done the majority of the work required, and so it remained for us to be bombed from the air and rest as much as possible.

Some days so passed, and then glorious news—the Division was to go to France.

Hasty days of packing up, and then a long and sandy journey on the railway to the horse-lines camp at Kantara; many tales to tell the drivers; much excitement for all. Then we moved by rail to a camp near the timber sheds at Alexandria, and after some days of refitting, packing the wagons and so forth, and enjoying the novelties of a town again, we embarked to sail for Marseilles.

Last, but not least, our official name had been changed before leaving from 1/2nd East Lancs. Field Co., R.E. to 428 (East Lancs.) Field Co., R.E.

CHAPTER III

FRANCE

(*March* 1917—*March* 1918)

THE company reached France in two portions in the first week of March 1917, a few riding horses, the company vehicles, and one dismounted section with the drivers arriving first, followed within two days by the O.C. with the remainder of the company.

At Marseilles, billeting parties at once entrained for the north, and a first acquaintance was made with the luxurious travelling arrangements provided for troops on French railways. The inner meaning of the words *Halte Repas* had not been realized by us whilst in the East, but those unlovely halts at early dawn or in the middle of the night will never be forgotten. At Marseilles we also made acquaintance with the French scale of rations, amongst which were Pork and Beans. This should have been called Beans and perhaps Pork ! There was nothing excessive about the speed of the journey, as we took five days to cover the distance from Marseilles to Pont Remy, near Abbeville. Nearing Paris we ran into a snowstorm, and as few of the carriages had windows intact, it seemed a cold procedure compared with our last rail journey in Egypt.

Within a week we were billeted at Limeux, near Abbeville, with the 427 Field Company in the same village. Officers and men struggled hard with the language, and with that peculiar form of it as used by the ancient *Garde Champêtre*, who seemed unable to understand the efforts of the best of us.

A busy time then ensued; Captain Courtis made frequent visits to Abbeville, and in his inimitable way got the right side of remounts, and drew wonderful pontoon teams; he also selected several active chargers, one of whom he christened " Boxer " on account of his way with his fore feet. Bicycles and ordnance stores generally were collected together to complete the unit equipment to establishment on the French scale.

Meantime an officer and several N.C.O.s who had been attached to the 1st Division in the line near Dompierre returned to the company on the 17th of March, and the O.C. went up the line on the following day for an attachment which lasted three or four days.

The German retirement of March 1917 had now begun, and the C.R.E. ordered training in bridging to be practised—he himself gave lectures to officers and N.C.O.s at his headquarters at Hocquin-

428TH FIELD COY. R.E.

court, and the company during the day was trained in rapid use of the service trestle and pontoon equipment.

The weather was very unfavourable for troops coming from the East. It rained and snowed alternately for several weeks, and it was poor consolation to be told that the winter was a record one for rain. But in spite of all this, there was very little sickness.

Leave commenced at this time, and Corporal Whitehead left first for his ten days. Many of the men had left home in 1914 as mere boys, and on their return to the company stated that their relations at home had almost failed to recognize them. In many cases this must have been perfectly true, for boys of nineteen had become men of twenty-two with nearly three years' war experience to their credit.

It was at Limeux that a French interpreter was attached to the company for duty. He lived with us for nearly three months, and occasionally rode a horse which he could not readily control. He was seen one evening galloping madly along the pavé road between Limeux and Hocquincourt, as if the whole German army were behind him, and begging, nay beseeching, the animal to stay his pace. The company subsequently attempted to teach the interpreter to march.

Before leaving Limeux claims by the civilians poured in. No. 4 Section was accused of ruining untold quantities of grain by sleeping on it, and a certain officer who would keep his horse in a separate stable was presented with a stiff account for damage to the plaster wall. Two or three sappers with a trowel and some mud soon put things right, and the experience gained was well worth the money eventually paid. The company has been "canny" ever since where claims have been concerned.

Towards the end of March the company went to Erondelle, a village on the Somme, for bridging, where parties of the two other field companies also assembled. Captain Courtis was appointed Commandant of the School, and some useful bridging practice was carried out.

The excellent billet at the Mairie (where Nos. 3 and 4 Sections lived) made us loth to leave, but orders for a move soon came.

The company water-cart almost failed to accompany us, as it was at Abbeville in process of being altered to carry petrol tins, an innovation to ensure a more rapid distribution of water. Corporal Pickston and Sapper Henshaw, however, completed the job in time, and the latter was then unfortunately left behind suffering from synovitis of the knee, and was never able to rejoin. His mighty efforts at Suez in the company football matches when playing full back will be remembered by all who watched his bulky form moving across the ground to counter the efforts of a precocious 427 or 429 forward.

On the 4th of April the company entrained at Pont Remy for an unknown destination; the staunch efforts of Nos. 2 and 4 Sections in putting the pontoon wagons on the flats were most praiseworthy; whilst Sergeant Cottrell and his men pushed and shoved, the voice of Sergeant Boughey could always be heard, shouting, "Prepare to heave—HEAVE!" Probably Sergeant Boughey was in specially fine voice, as instead of going "up the line" he was bound for home on leave.

We detrained at Chaulnes on 4th April, and marched to Dompierre through thick snow, slush and mud, occupying deep dug-outs and Nissen huts, which a few days before had been a part of the front system, but which, owing to the German retirement, had now become a back area. The following day the march was resumed via Péronne and Doingt to Le Catelet, where the company was destined to remain for some weeks under the orders of the C.E. 3rd Corps, while the remainder of the Division was employed behind on roads.

Our work consisted of building a new Corps Headquarters in the orchards and grounds immediately surrounding what had once been a very fine château. The latter had been blown sky-high by the Boche prior to his departure, and there was only a farm or bailiff's house left standing. This was subsequently re-roofed and made available for "A" Mess. About forty-five Nissen huts, two hospital Nissen huts and two Adrian huts were ultimately erected, and the company earned a reputation with the C.E. for good and rapid work. Memoranda with reference to huts poured into the company office at this time, including innumerable drawings of Nissen huts, signed by a certain 2nd Corporal Newcomb of the E.-in-C.'s staff. This N.C.O. had apparently set himself the task of sketching Nissen huts from every conceivable angle, and the results were circulated to all concerned in their erection. The company lived in the remains of some old buildings near the château and then in tents, until they were ordered to move a short distance to Bias Wood. Whilst in tents some members of the company made praiseworthy efforts to keep warm by installing stoves, which, however, were not allowed to remain owing to the danger of fire. It certainly seemed no sort of weather for life under canvas, as we still had to put up with snow and frost.

Whilst in Bias Wood the 126th Infantry Brigade sent to us for attachment twenty-five men and one officer per battalion, and this system was continued with the exception of short intervals when in rest until the arrival of the Divisional Pioneer Battalion in February 1918.

Some members of the company learned something of craterfilling hereabouts, whilst others learned the true and inner meaning of the word "potter" as defined by Brig.-General Schreiber, the C.E. 3rd Corps.

The company also learned how "scrounging" of material should be done by "Storm Troops." Two battalions of Scots and Grenadier Guards moved into the area on the night of the 13th of April, and immediately set to work to dismantle many of the Nissen huts then in course of erection. Early on the 14th the air became electric, but the O.C. had a friendly chat with Viscount Gort, commanding

428TH FIELD COY. R.E. 121

the Grenadiers, as to the correct procedure, and the pilfered material was quickly restored.

Hatred of the Boche was more deeply impressed on our minds by the awful devastation of the country, by the open and desecrated graves of Cartigny Cemetery, and by the wanton destruction of trees and orchards, which were hideous and hateful to look upon.

As work on the Corps camp slackened off towards completion, new work on roads was expected, but the Division was by this time due for its initial experience in the line, and this came about early in May. The 3rd Corps moved into their new quarters before we left, and we saw the panelled and painted huts actually used.

On the last day of April 1917 the company marched from Bias Wood through Buire, Tincourt and Marquaix to Villers Faucon, where we lived in open bivouacs in the fields for some time, marching up nightly for work on wiring in front of Ronssoy. The infantry still considered it to be purely an R.E. matter to do all the wiring for them, and at this time every available sapper was turned out, whilst huge infantry carrying parties brought up the material from the rear. Tombois and Guillemont Farms will be remembered in connection with this sector.

Villers Faucon was found to be too far away from the line, and quarters were found for the company in cellars, stables, etc., at Ronssoy. A heated argument between Captain Courtis and the subalterns as to whether the water-cart should be allowed in Ronssoy is worthy of record, the point of view of the gallant captain being that it were better for the company to be short of water than that the water-cart (of which the captain was inordinately proud) should be allowed to run the risk of being damaged. For a short time during our stay in Ronssoy village an 18-pounder battery lived just below us on the forward slope. After considerable activity on its part the Boche became irritated, and put down such a successful shoot with 5·9's that our gunners decided to move to the reverse slope behind the village. The Boche fire was extremely accurate, and though billeted so close to the battery we suffered no casualties as a result of the duel. Afterwards by forbidding all transport in the village during daylight and controlling all movement, the billets became quite a health resort. All trees had been cut down, but the gardens were very interesting to those who had not seen an English spring since 1914, and the nightingales sang as one came in during the early hours after a night's wiring or digging. About the 17th May the Division was relieved by the 2nd Cavalry Division, and moving north, went into the line in the Trescault (Havrincourt) sector. The company moved to Metz-en-Couture, passing one night *en route* at Fins, where Corporal Hunt, hungering for dinner after unaccustomed marching, poured petroleum on the fire to hasten culinary operations, with disastrous results to Sapper Bray's eyebrows and chest.

After working from Metz for several days the company moved into Havrincourt Wood, comfortable wooden shacks being erected.

Here the company suffered its first casualties in France. On June 4 Lieutenant Saint and Sapper Hampson were both killed, and Corporal Cliffe (afterwards awarded the D.C.M.) was wounded whilst gallantly attempting rescue work. Lieutenant J. P. Echlin also behaved with great gallantry and coolness on this occasion. C.S.M. Davies and Sergeant Cottrell (the latter had " run " No. 4 Section, including its officer, for nearly three years) left the company to everybody's regret to take up R.E. commissions, and Sergeant Boughey was transferred from No. 2 to No. 4 Section.

On June 11 the front-line work in front of Havrincourt was handed over to the 429 Field Company, and the company moved back into reserve at Ruyaulcourt. Lieutenant Echlin and No. 3 Section explored wells and renovated billets at Bertincourt. Some good work was done here in clearing wells, especially at the Brewery, where, after a lot of hard work, Sapper G. F. Yates cleared the old pump barrels from the bottom of the well shaft, 60 to 70 feet deep, thereby allowing us to run one of the chain Hélice pumps driven by a petrol engine. It was sometimes difficult to explain to Colonel Slaughter, the A.A. and Q.M.G. of the Division, technical reasons for delay and why such jobs could not be done more quickly, but before the Division left the area there were model baths completed at Ytres, Bertincourt and Ruyaulcourt; in fact, the company became so expert in this work that the Divisional Concert Party had a try at showing up the weak points in our standard design. Nos. 1 and 4, besides building baths at Ytres and Ruyaulcourt, made considerable preparations for a large hutting scheme to house at least another division in the three villages of Ytres, Bertincourt and Ruyaulcourt. These ultimately proved to be some of the initial preparations for the Cambrai offensive of November, 1917.

Captain Courtis and the transport lines were housed at Ytres during this period, and Lieutenant Welch arrived to do duty with the company in place of Lieutenant Saint.

At the end of the first week in July, the Division came out of the line to go into rest for divisional training in G.H.Q. Reserve, and the company moved via Ytres to Bihucourt, removing again in three days thence to Courcelles-le-Comte, of which place all who were then with the unit have pleasant memories. The company was under canvas in an orchard; good football grounds were available, and many fine games were played. It was here that a very famous game of football took place between Officers and N.C.O.s versus other ranks, and Corporal Pickston wrote a most humorous account, chiefly at the expense of the officers and C.Q.M.S. Young. It was here, also, that Corporal Pickston used to address gatherings in the orchard on summer evenings on " Life in Canada " or " Life in New Zealand," narrating his narrow escapes from " bits of pink chiffon " and the like.

At Courcelles we also obtained " by purchase " a gramophone, which for a time, at any rate, nobody was allowed to touch except Lieutenant Kennard; this restriction was removed later, and the 'phone could be heard any night up to midnight and sometimes after at the N.C.O.s mess.

The company now came to know very well such places as Logeast Wood and Ablainzevelle, which became still more familiar in March and April 1918 under very different circumstances. It was rather a remarkable coincidence that some trenches which were roughly dug for demonstration purposes at this time for the 126th Infantry Brigade, were on March 26, 1918, actually held by the field company when escorting the divisional artillery.

The company put in some very useful training during this period. Lieutenant Welch and No. 4 Section constructed a very fine cut-and-cover dug-out in the ruins of the Beet Factory, and we learnt what a lengthy proceeding such work was, and how insecure when completed compared to concrete protection or tunnelled dug-outs. All sections had practice in demolitions, the effect of bangalore torpedoes on barbed wire defences, also in loading pack animals, and a vast amount of work was put into the improvization of pack saddlery for the 126th Brigade. The C.R.E. inspected the transport, and warned the drivers that there were stirring times ahead.

On August 21 the company marched to Mailly-Maillet, via Ablainzevelle, Bucquoy, Puisieux, Serre and Mailly-Maillet Sucrerie, all places which we were to know in 1918 under very different conditions, and thence the next day to Beaucourt-sur-Ancre, where it entrained and arrived at Proven about midnight. Here Sapper Atkins fell off the railway platform and injured his back, and went to hospital. But he declined to go to England, and rejoined the company at Béthune in January 1918.

Early the next day the march was continued to Watou, and billets were occupied in the vicinity. Passes into Watou were granted freely; too freely, indeed, for two well-known characters from No. 4 Section were on one occasion unable to find their way back to camp, which resulted in their being very prominent for several evenings under the care of the orderly sergeant.

From Watou advance parties consisting of the O.C. and a number of officers and men, went to Ypres by lorry to learn the geography of the sector which was to be taken over from the 15th Division.

On September 1 the company marched to Poperinghe; thence, H.Q. and three sections proceeded by rail to Ypres, the remaining section and the transport lines being billeted alongside Divisional H.Q. at Brandhoek.

The old dug-outs in the ramparts at Ypres, in which the three sections were now quartered, were immediately on the right of the Menin Gate. It might be called a sultry spot, and for discomfort the quarters took a lot of beating. Everything was as it had been for the last two years; there was no ventilation in many of the dug-outs; they were damp, and had only five feet of headroom, and were collapsing in places and infested with rats. They had the redeeming feature of being safe, for though direct hits from some of the hostile heavy artillery shook things up, the old earthen ramparts with their brick facings withstood the worst the Boche could do; and though the gas-proofing in those days consisted of a blanket hung in very haphazard fashion in front of the dug-out entrance, the chances of being gassed during the constant and heavy gas-shell bombardments were very slight.

Field company work was done either during the night or from daylight at 5.0 a.m. to 11.0 a.m., and it consisted chiefly in laying duckboard tracks to points as near the front line as possible, and maintaining those already laid. There were no trenches. Some work was also done in strengthening Battalion Headquarters at Wilde Wood. This and similar work consisted of a steel rail shield over what had now become the front of an old enemy concrete pill-box. This was the only type of cover available, for with the exception of the two tunnelled dug-outs for Brigade Headquarters, at Mill Cot and James Farm, there were no habitable tunnelled dug-outs in the sector. The ground was so waterlogged that power-driven pumps had to be kept going in these day and night.

Preparations were now made for the attack which the 125th Infantry Brigade was to make on the three pill-boxes opposite our front, viz.: Iberian Farm, Borry Farm and Beck House. Large carrying parties were required each night to get wiring materials from the Frezenberg Ridge to Square Farm or Low Farm, and it was an unpleasant business going through the heavy barrage which the enemy put down at frequent intervals during the night on the duckboard tracks. There was no opportunity of going by another route, as the ground on the Frezenberg Ridge itself was so churned up by heavy shells that it was hardly traversable even by day except by the tracks. Sapper H. Jackson was killed while on this work, and he showed by his gallantry that, while far from strong physically, he was brave and cheerful up to the last. The drivers will always remember the Potijze Road to the point just beyond Bavaria House, where transport nightly dumped the loads of wiring materials, duckboards, etc. The company was fortunate in suffering no casualties during the operations connected with the attack, but Corporal Fox and Lance-Corporal Bardsley were wounded one night at the Menin Gate, when starting off for work. Sapper Atkinson, store-keeper of No. 8 Section, was unfortunately killed by a fragment of an aeroplane bomb in Ypres, and Driver Yates was seriously wounded in like manner when going through Vlamertinghe on a motor lorry. Captain Courtis also received a wound in the arm which took him to England, and he was never able to rejoin the unit.

Those who were with the company at this time will not readily forget the Belle Vue or Crystal Palace effects from 8.0 p.m. onwards, when our own and the enemy artillery really became active. Above the constant flashes from the fire of our own 18-pounders could be seen the beautiful signal rockets used by the enemy to report O.K. or the reverse. These varied from coloured stars to golden rain. At daylight all this activity ceased, and it was possible to sit down beside the Zonnebeke Road behind the Frezenberg Ridge, and wait

428TH FIELD COY. R.E.

for daylight and the strafe to cease. Half an hour after daylight, one could walk down to Square Farm or Low Farm or our front-line posts without hearing a shot fired except from some early morning sniper. And in one's walk back to the ramparts, there was usually a good covey of partridges to be put up between Cambridge Road and the Menin Road along " J " Track. The swans in the moat round the eastern ramparts of Ypres might be seen quietly swimming, though our own 60-pounders were within ten yards of the water's edge.

Lieutenant Oxley came to the company at this time, and joined the three other officers in their tiny dug-out 12′ × 9′ × 5′ in which the rats ran nightly over one's bed. His name will always be connected with a famous spot called Sans Souci, though at this stage it is feared the operations there belied the name.

On the night of September 5, the Menin Gate was dosed with gas shell to the tune of some thousands, and though no ill-effects resulted at the time, most of the men who worked about camp had to be evacuated two or three days later as a result of going about their employment in the still poisoned atmosphere.

The company was relieved by a field company of the 9th Division on September 16, and proceeded to Brandhoek; on arrival there, it was found necessary to order two sections up once more to re-erect the screening on the Menin Road. The party left Brandhoek about 3.0 a.m. and worked on the road until midday. Things were becoming more active on both sides as a result of the coming offensive on our part. Our 60-pounders and 6-inch and 8-inch howitzers were blazing away. There were several warm rejoinders from the enemy and a number of casualties on the road, but fortunately Sapper Lynn was our only casualty, and though seriously wounded he made a good recovery. It was typical of the C.R.E. (Colonel MacInnes) that he accompanied the O.C. Company on this little expedition, and spent his time walking up and down the Menin Road encouraging all ranks to push on with the work.

On September 20 the company moved with its brigade group to the coast sector, billeting at Wormhoudt, Teteghem, and La Panne on the way. After a night at La Panne, the company moved to Oost Dunkerque Bains, where it was quartered in shelters of various sorts amongst the sand dunes. Here we took over from the field companies of the 66th Division, who were about to go into the Ypres Sector, and to do such excellent work on the Passchendaele Ridge. The coast sector was a very pleasant change after Ypres. Hostile artillery, especially long range, was pretty active, but it was a fine bracing climate, and up till July 1917 had been a very quiet sector in the hands of the French. As soon as the B.E.F. took over, things began to liven up. After the enemy attack in July, there were no bridges to maintain over the River Yser, so sapper work consisted chiefly of maintenance and repair of roads and tramways, and the "boyaux" or covered trenches, which the French had built.

Some old veterans, such as Sappers Twemlow, Murray and McGill, were dispatched to the base as unfit about this time.

On October 6 the company was relieved by a field company of the 41st Division, and the 42nd Division took over from the 32nd Division in the right flanking sector, which included the town of Nieuport, and its maze of waterways and bridges. All three field companies were now on forward work, the 428 Field Company being responsible for the right brigade sector with some thirty-eight bridges over the various canals. For this work, and the improvement of front-line trenches (all breastworks), three sections of the company, under Lieutenant J. P. Echlin, lived at Tricar Dump, on the site of which a neat cottage now stands, near White House on the Bruges Road. The shelters here were of the flimsiest description, and considering the enemy shell-fire activity and his low-flying planes at this time, it is wonderful that there were actually very few casualties in the advanced billets. Corporal Goldstraw was, however, wounded, and all in the company were grieved to hear later that he had died of his wounds.

Company H.Q. and the remaining section lived further back at a large farm near Wulpen.

Lieutenant Turner Jones had come to the company for one of his periodical visits at this time, and had been at the transport lines, which were near Coxyde and situated in a sea of mud which threatened to engulf them. It was a wretched billet which quite prevented the fostering of the spirit of pride in the animals and vehicles generally displayed by the mounted ranks of the company, and which so quickly reasserted itself under the improved conditions after the move south. Lieutenant Jones was recalled to the 429 Field Company as second in command on the 18th of November.

From the transport lines to the advanced billets was a journey of about eleven miles each way, and the transport of rations night after night was a considerable strain; the ration wagon took anything from ten to fourteen hours to complete its task. The C.Q.M.S. had an amusing experience on one of these trips. Taking the rations one night to some men of a Tramway Company who were attached, he was met in the lane by one of them who had been sent to guide them clear of a large shell hole. When near the shell hole the guide started walking backwards and giving instructions to the driver as to the course he had to keep. All of a sudden the guide disappeared, but there was a yell and then a voice floated over the scene shouting, " Stop, stop, for God's sake stop, I am down the —— hole myself."

Apart from bridge maintenance, the construction was commenced of some concrete pill-boxes for machine-gun crews, and those in charge of the large carrying parties found that the job of piloting 100 men for two trips to Nun or Nice Walk (a matter of one and a half miles), each man carrying a 60-pound bag of sand, cement, or gravel, was no enviable one. To negotiate a narrow, slippery, and heaving cork-raft bridge with this load on a pitch black night was a difficult matter for any man, and, of course, the enemy had the tracks and bridge crossings taped to a nicety, and

428TH FIELD COY. R.E.

frequently put the latter out of action. To provide for this, and to ensure prompt repairs, three sapper patrols were put on to inspect all bridges for repair work thrice daily.

Other concrete work was done on the Veterinaire O.P., on Regimental Aid Posts, and on some elephant shelters. An advanced Brigade H.Q. was commenced at the Brickworks, midway between Wulpen and Nieuport. This work was only started seven days prior to the relief by the French Division, and the 126th Brigade Headquarters Staff did not for one moment expect that these shelters could be made habitable in time; however, Sergeant Kinley, Corporal Boyes, Lance-Corporal Lamb and their party decided otherwise, the unexpected happened, and Division ordered Brigade Headquarters to move in for the two final days of our stay in the sector.

The hand-over to the French Field Company was rather a lengthy business, but on November 18 the 428 Field Company concentrated at Wulpen Farm, and at 5 a.m. next morning we were marching through Oost Dunkerque, reaching Adinkerke at 10 a.m. where we embarked, proceeding by canal through Dunkerque to Bergues. A march of fifteen miles brought us to Wormhoudt. The arrival of the transport after their thirty-mile march the same evening will not readily be forgotten by a good number of the company, for, thanks to a pitch black night, sodden ground, narrow lanes with deep ditches, and an outlandish farm as the company billet, by 10 p.m. all bridging vehicles and the G.S. wagon were badly ditched.

On the 20th the march was resumed to Zermezeele, on the 21st to Staple near Ebblinghem, and on the 22nd to Glomenghem, west of Aire, where a few pleasant days were spent and where every one and the vehicles got a wash, and most of the company enjoyed roaming about the old town of Aire.

A peculiar skin disease was noticed here on one of the animals, and this was no doubt the beginning of the serious outbreak of mange which affected almost the whole of the company horses in February 1918.

The inhabitants of Glomenghem were very friendly, as they had recently had Portuguese troops billeted on them, and it was understood they were very pleased with the change. There were " sing-songs " in the small château, and on the 25th a short service taken by the O.C.

On the 27th the march was resumed to Robecq. On the 28th Essars was reached, one and a half miles east of Béthune, and after a few days there the company moved into the best billets it ever had in France at Le Quesnoy.

Though only three and a quarter miles from the line the billets for men and horses were excellent, and hardly ever shelled. Béthune, only two miles away, was a pleasant old town with everything almost normal, as it was at this time very seldom shelled. At Le Quesnoy there joined the company a new officer who had previously served in the ranks, and who knew many of the sappers. One evening this officer was detailed to pay the company, and took the opportunity to greet some of his old comrades. It would be interesting to know which one received an extra thirty francs that night for shaking hands with that newly-arrived officer. It appears that the business of shaking hands became so engrossing that the officer somehow mislaid that amount.

The company, after a short period of " Q " work whilst in reserve, took over work in the right brigade sector, of which the La Bassée–Béthune canal formed about the centre. The trenches, though in good order, were not provided with any defence works capable of withstanding an offensive, and the Division set itself to remedy this state of affairs. Tunnelled dug-outs north of the canal in 428 Sector were impossible owing to water level being so near the surface, so vast quantities of sand, gravel and cement came into the R.E. dump at Gorre by barge and were taken forward nightly to Harley Street. From this point they were distributed to Oxford Terrace and Marylebone Road for construction of pill-boxes for machine-guns or Company H.Q., and to the Village Line, and to Kingsclere Battalion H.Q. for making shell-proof elephant shelters for garrisons of the various localities. The following table gives some idea of the quantity of concreting materials required.

CONCRETE WORK IN RIGHT SECTOR OF LA BASSÉE FRONT, SHOWING MAN LOADS FOR EACH JOB IN HAND.

Average weight of Sandbags, 60 lbs.
Thickness of concrete on top or enemy side, 5 feet.

Job No.	Name of Shelter.	Internal Dimensions of Dug-out.			Material (Sandbags Full).			
		Lgth.	Wth.	Max Hght.	Shingle.	Sand.	Cement.	Total.
1.	Spoil Bank Keep	8' 9"	× 4' 9"	× 5' 3"	2645	1323	712	4680
2.	Oxford Terrace No. 1 Coy. H.Q.	8' 9"	× 4' 9"	× 5' 3"	2784	1392	744	4920
3.	Oxford Terrace No. 2 Co. H.Q.	8' 9"	× 4' 9"	× 5' 3"	2784	1392	744	4920
4.	Orchard Keep Co. H.Q.	16' 0"	× 7' 0"	× 5' 3"	3925	1963	1048	6936
5.	Kingsclere Bt. H.Q. Buzzer Stn.	7' 9"	× 4' 9"	× 5' 3"	1525	763	360	2648
6.	Pill Box II. Tower Res. Trench	10' 4"	× 4' 9"	× 5' 3"	1907	953	476	3336
7.	Pill Box III. Nr. La Bassée Road	10' 4"	× 4' 9"	× 5' 3"	1907	953	476	3336
8.	Pill Box IV. Marylebone Road	10' 4"	× 4' 9"	× 5' 3"	1907	953	476	3336

GIVING A TOTAL IN MAN LOADS OF 34,112.

428TH FIELD COY. R.E.

Whilst at Le Quesnoy, advantage was taken of an Army Order allowing N.C.O.s of long service overseas to be exchanged with suitable N.C.O.s then at home, and accordingly Sergeant Graham left for the U.K.

His replacement duly reported for duty and astonished everybody by stating in broad Scotch that he knew nothing of horses, and was not likely to be of much use on the Transport Lines. Corporal Howard at once took over the duties of Transport Sergeant, whilst " Jock " Wilson understudied Sergeant Johnson in No. 3 Section.

The 427 and 429 Field Companies were at this period infected with a dread disease known as " Lost-store-itis," and the O.C. spent several hectic hours questioning the nimble Captain Allard of 427 Field Company as to the disappearance of company bicycles outside shops in Béthune. We had reason to be glad that the defaulting units were let off lightly, as the disease recurred at a much later date amongst ourselves.

C.Q.M.S. Young proceeded to the U.K. for a month's well-earned leave, and whilst he was away Corporal Moores and Sergeant Howard filled their oil store, with good results to the company harness.

The Divisional Concert Party's theatre was close to the company billet: for the " Xmas season " they put on a very good pantomime. The Divisional Canteen also was in the village: it was a novelty to find such things accessible to troops working in the line.

On the 20th of December a blow was received on hearing that the C.R.E., Lieut.-Colonel D. S. MacInnes, was leaving the Division —he was loved by all for his fearlessness and for his tremendous energy, which carried him from his office to the front line at all hours of the day or night. Colonel MacInnes was never so happy as when on his rounds of inspection, and he was as considerate as he was keen.

Lieut.-Colonel R. E. B. Pratt, D.S.O. (the new C.R.E.), arrived on the afternoon of the 20th of December, and a few of the company officers went to the H.Q. of the 429 Field Company to renew acquaintance with him—most of the officers and many of the men had met him on the Suez Canal at Ferdan in June 1916, when in command of the 86th Field Company, R.E.

Work in the front system was proceeding at a ding-dong pace, and the dismounted men proceeded to work daily along the La Bassée Canal Bank to Pont Fixe and Harley St. Dumps. C.S.M. Garnett evolved a scheme for the constant use of the company cycles, and at this time a cycle for two men would have been none too many.

Small parties of men lived at the two forward dumps, and were perfectly happy until Sapper Hargreaves joined them. Sapper Hargreaves always drew fire, and this was no exception, as one day he complained of headache and was then to be seen with a bandaged head where he had been hit by a shell splinter.

Corporal Lomax headed a keen and determined band of gas-proofing enthusiasts, and under his guidance most valuable work

K

was carried out on all tunnelled dug-out entrances throughout the forward system.

Preparations for Christmas proceeded apace, and when it arrived a thoroughly enjoyable day resulted. No. 3 Section succeeded in beating No. 2 in the final of a sectional tug-of-war. Lieutenant Oxley was snowballed in the midst of carrying out his daily duties. The enemy was not forgotten, and the gunners and gas experts gave him a playful reminder on the night of the 24th. A few officers who thought they could sing, accompanied by Corporals Moores and Kirkpatrick and Sapper Sharples, serenaded the N.C.O.s Mess and the 429 and 428 officers' messes.

Lieutenant Oxley was no mean musician, and he also developed quite a faculty for verse-making. We quote below his parodied verses of the well-known part song, "We left the Baby on the Shore," which was rendered by a party at the concert on January 25, given by the three field companies at the Gorre Brewery, where the 429 Field Company was billeted.

"Just over in yon trench old Fritz is sitting,
    Fritz is sitting,
Feeling sorry that he ever named 'the Day,'
He still has got to learn his lesson,
    learn his lesson.
That tearing scraps of paper doesn't pay.
That the rights of little countries be respected,
And that Kultur and that sort of thing must cease,
And only when he's learned that lesson,
Will we ever think of making Peace.

"The water in the trench is slowly rising,
    slowly rising,
Yes. Rising as it never rose before,
    rose before,
We were feeling weary, very weary,
As we humped our loads and then went back for more.
The Sergeant quietly is sleeping,
Sleeping where he never slept before,
    slept before.
So when we get around the corner,
We'll dump out half the shingle on the floor,
Yes, we'll dump the shingle on the floor,
A thing which we've never done before,
But we got a lecture from the Major,
So we'll never try that game on any more.

"Across the sea there is an Island,
    is an Island,
Where the folk have got a bad attack of blues,
    got the blues,
'Cos they think that there's a scarcity of rations,
    short of rations,
And the shoppers have to stand all day in queues.
So soon they'll realize that there's a war on,
A thing that they've never done before,
    done before.

428TH FIELD COY. R.E.

And as we out here have got to stick it,
We don't want to hear them whining any more.
Yes, we all of us have got to stick it,
Stick it as we never did before,
So let those at home just stop their grousing
And buck up and finish off the war.

"The long awaited time is coming,
           time is coming,
When the Forty-Second's going out to Rest,
           out to Rest,
And then we'll polish up our buttons,
           clean our buttons,
Brush our tunics, clean our belts and look our best.
There'll be lots of Musketry and Bayonet Fighting,
Gas Drill, Sloping Arms, and Forming Fours,
           Forming Fours,
And then to prevent us getting rusty,
We shall clean the Tools and sharpen up the Saws.
Yes, that's what they call Divisional resting,
We have often heard that fairy tale before,
And when the General inspects us,
He'll mistake us for a ' Pukka ' R.E. Corps."

On the 4th of January news came to hand of the first British decoration awarded to an officer of the company, and all ranks were gratified to hear of Lieutenant J. P. Echlin's Military Cross as being a thoroughly well-earned reward. This officer left the company on January 24 to become second in command of the 427 Field Company. He took with him the affection and esteem of all his comrades.

Lieutenant Lord joined the company shortly afterwards as the reinforcement.

Other awards at this time, all splendidly earned, were the M.S.M. to C.Q.M.S. A. J. Young, and the Belgian Croix-de-Guerre to Corporal Boyes, B., Lance-Corporal Hardman, W. H., and Sapper Cottriall, J.

About the middle of January, after a spell of very hard frost, a rapid thaw with heavy rain set in, and at once most of the trenches became impassable. All work on the "localities" and on concreting ceased, and every available man of the 127th Brigade was put on to clearing trenches. In addition the C.R.E. arranged for nearly 200 men of the 1/5th S. Lancs. (Pioneers) and three sections of the 422 Field Company, R.E. (all from 55th West Lancs. Division) to assist. By the month end we were able to recommence concreting, and the South Lancs. Pioneers tackled Willow Drain, which was supposed to drain the front-line trenches into the La Bassée Canal.

On February 13 the 423 Field Company of the 55th Division took over all work, and we came under the C.E. 1st Corps for work on tunnelled dug-outs at Noyelles, Sailly, and Cambrin, strengthening of cellars at Noyelles and the provision of new artillery observation posts in the Fosses at Noeux-les-Mines.

No. 3 Section, under Lieutenant Lord, went off on detachment to Sailly Labourse and stayed there until the work to the south was completed, including a large amount of wiring round Noeux locality. The work on tunnelled dug-outs was novel to the company, and great interest was taken in it, and we had the able assistance of " B " Company of the 1/7th Northumberland Fusiliers, the Pioneer Battalion now attached to the 42nd Division.

No. 2 Section was out for records at Cambrin, and two splendid dug-outs resulted in a very short time, but owing to striking water at Sailly, Lieutenant Welch was obliged to concrete his elephant shelters and the two shafts.

During March further progress was made with these tunnelled dug-outs and O.P.s of various kinds, and a large tunnelled dug-out was made for a Divisional H.Q. just north of the Béthune–Beuvry Road. All this time the enemy artillery was increasing in volume daily, and back areas such as Le Préol and Beuvry were bombarded constantly with heavy howitzers. It was pathetic to see the French villagers (nearly all women and children) who had lived securely though so near the firing line, since 1914, now packing what household goods they could on handcarts or even perambulators, leaving their homes and most of their belongings to certain destruction.

Amidst all these alarms the company, after a violent attack of mange amongst the horses which lasted for over a month and which carried off over 80 per cent. of the animals, prepared horses and vehicles for the Divisional Transport competition.

The mange was very serious, as it entirely crippled the company in case of a move being ordered hurriedly, and it was a very fortunate thing that all the animals had been replaced prior to the 22nd of March.

The mange had its humorous side—the C.R.E.'s orders were most stringent and included the despatching of a special message to him nightly to certify that certain orders had been read out to all mounted ranks. The drivers were detailed in two detachments, the first to groom and look after the infected horses, the second to look after those so far without symptoms of the disease. All clothing was stoved and the drivers for at least one day were obliged to ape the Scotsman and to keep themselves as warm as they could in their shirts.

But in spite of all these disadvantages Lieutenant Oxley, Sergeant Howard, the drivers and company wheelers had the satisfaction of seeing their hard work recognized, when the C.R.E. selected the G.S. limber to represent the R.E. at the Show. However, the enemy decided otherwise, and Lieutenant Oxley and his prize turn-out were recalled from D.H.Q.

CHAPTER IV

FRANCE

(*March* 1918—*April* 1919)

THE Division had been at eight hours' notice to move for over a week, and at 7 p.m. on March 22 orders came for the expected move. Night-shift parties were recalled, and between 7 p.m. on the 22nd of March and 6.30 a.m. on 23rd, all stores and vehicles were packed. At the latter hour the company, less transport, marched to Busnes, where it embussed, proceeding with 127th Infantry Brigade via St. Pol, Frévent, Doullens, along the Arras road to Adinfer Wood, where we left the busses at 1 a.m. on the 24th and bivouaced on the road-side. The transport arrived about 11 p.m. on the evening of the 24th. The company now, unknown to itself, formed a large part of the divisional reserve, and at 1.30 a.m. on the 25th of March instructions were received by the O.C. to turn out every available man immediately (including all but ten drivers) to act as infantry escort to the divisional artillery. With a limber for picks and shovels and the company's pack animals with Lewis-guns and spare S.A.A., etc., we proceeded ahead of the artillery through Douchy and Ayette to the depression just west of Courcelles, where the gunners unlimbered. The roads were blocked with transport of all kinds, such things as 6-inch guns or 12-inch howitzers all moving west and making it difficult to get forward.

The company moved about with the divisional artillery to positions south of Logeast Wood, again to Courcelles, and finally to low ground south of Ablainzevelle, where two sections rested, whilst the other two lay out all night in front of the guns. On the 26th early two sections relieved the other two, and at once a general retirement began, in which the company took part. Fresh positions were taken up by the artillery on the eastern edge of Essarts village near the crucifix, and the line finally stabilized just east of Bucquoy in the afternoon of the 26th. Later in the evening the company was ordered to move into Essarts, where the R.E. and Pioneer Battalion formed the Divisional Reserve, being concentrated there during some very heavy fighting.

Essarts was heavily shelled, and Lance-Corporal McQuinn and Sapper Stevenson were killed by enemy shell fire on the 28th. The company transport had moved to Pommier late on the 25th, and had joined the 126th Brigade Transport on the 26th at St. Amand.

On the 27th the company marched up to Bucquoy after dark, and wired in front of the 127th Brigade. On the evening of the 28th the company moved up through Bucquoy to support trenches west of Ablainzevelle.

At 10.30 p.m. on the 29th of March, the Division was relieved by the 41st Division, and the company proceeded *via* its rear headquarters at Essarts to a map reference just west of Gommecourt, which turned out to be the old German front line of 1916 with very fine deep tunnelled dug-outs.

Sergeant Johnson proved himself once again to be a strong man—on this occasion he carried a keg of rum from the line to Essarts, and during the hour's halt at this place the company would have drunk his health had they known whom they had to thank.

Orders about this time were frequently countermanded, and not much useful work was done in consequence.

The transport during this time was at Couin, but moved to Souastre on the 2nd of April. Two days' work were now put in by the company on the " purple " or reserve line system, east of Gommecourt, and this consisted of organizing carrying parties for wiring materials, and also the wiring of the purple line localities. At 5 p.m. on the 1st of April the company again went into the support trenches west of Ablainzevelle, being attached to the 1/5th East Lancashire Regiment. An important section of front-line trench was dug on the succeeding nights with infantry and pioneer assistance.

On the 8th of April the 457 Field Company of the 62nd Division relieved the company, which marched *via* Monchy-au-Bois and Bienvillers to Souastre, where lorries met and conveyed the company to Pas.

Pas was like Heaven after the rough experiences of the preceding sixteen days, and a general cleaning up was entered upon, though we still had the burden on our shoulders of being under one hour's notice to move, day or night.

Shortages of kit were investigated, and that wonderful word " Adinfer " has saved many a sapper's account from being debited with losses.

The G.O.C. 42nd Division inspected the company on the 11th of April, and on the 12th the dismounted portion of the company moved to a bivouac east of Coigneux, and known as J. 16. a. The other two companies were also there, and the work was the digging and wiring of strong points in the neighbourhood of the Château de la Haie. A 7·5-inch naval gun mounted on a broad-gauge railway truck came to the point where the company was bivouacked, and gave a display of quick-firing every evening, and at daylight, its objective being probably Bapaume; it was a mighty objectionable neighbour, and we were not sorry when it donned its cap for the night and cleared off.

On April 15 the company relieved the 154 Field Company of the 37th Division in Gommecourt Wood, and occupied the same quarters as between 30th of March and April 1. For three weeks

428TH FIELD COY. R.E.

the company struggled hard to improve the defences and communications in this sector, and three main strong points were dug and wired—they were Salmon Point, Julius Point and Gommecourt Locality.

Corporal Brocklesby and a party did a lot of hard work on the repair and maintenance of the tramways, by means of which rations and R.E. materials were trolleyed to the line nightly.

The company was housed below ground, in a large continuous series of tunnelled dug-outs, and rations were normally received at the "back door" of the series, which considerably reduced the risk to the company transport.

Rum Trench, Biez Switch, High Street, and all other well-known haunts of the company were rapidly improved, and made passable, though the weather for the greater part of this period was all against rapid and efficient work.

On the 28th of April, the O.C., Major Riddick, handed over the command of the company to Captain Entwistle. Before leaving he expressed to a few of the N.C.O.s in the dug-out his great regret at leaving such well-tried comrades, and his appreciation of the splendid support they and the whole company had given him during his period of command. Captain A. N. Walker rejoined as second in command on vacating his position as Adjutant R.E. at D.H.Q.

Several casualties were suffered, amongst them Corporal Whitehead (wounded), who was later awarded the M.S.M. for the excellent work he had done whilst with the unit. On May 5th Sappers Greenwood and McLeod were killed while proceeding to their work, and their loss was greatly felt by all in the company. Greenwood was an original member of the company and a splendid tradesman, and he was much respected by all his fellows in No. 2 Section. The two bodies were taken to Couin and buried there.

On May 6 the company was relieved by the 421 Field Company R.E. of the 57th Division and again marched to Pas, where we bivouacked in tents in a beautiful wood just above the village. Training was commenced, and a little work relieved the monotony of it. Baths were put up at Hénu and Pas, and a rifle range was completed at Mondicourt.

News came to hand that Sergeant Kinley had been awarded the M.M., and the officers thoughtfully stayed indoors when at a late hour the gallant sergeant and his intimates returned to their leafy bower—it was a source of general pleasure to learn of Sergeant Kinley's honour.

The Army of the U.S.A. began to show itself whilst we were in Pas. They were a fine lot of men, though there were reputed to be ten or a dozen different languages spoken in the ranks. They were keen to learn their job in the shortest possible time, and their presence whilst training alongside gave us a greatly increased confidence in the ultimate end of the war.

The whole company went through a course of musketry at Pas, the results being quite satisfactory, and most of the afternoons were given up to games and running—Corporal Boyes showed his latent powers by running with the best of them and always made a point of finishing the course—this despite his fifty odd years. Towards the 20th of May training gave place to work on tunnelled dug-outs at Couin and Château de la Haie, and on hutting at Halloy. On the 30th Lieutenant Oxley left the company to take up an appointment as Adjutant to C.R.E. Fifth Army Troops; the transport of the company owed a lot to his painstaking work, and he left us all sorrowing when he went.

Lieutenant Hall also left through sickness, and was never fit to rejoin. The Divisional Commander presented medal ribbons on the 26th of May, and amongst the company recipients on this day were Sergeant Kinley, Corporal Boyes, Corporal Hardman, and Sappers Cottriall and Jackson, R. C.

Rumours of a further spell in the line came to nothing, though Lieutenant Taylor and a party proceeded to the 502 Field Company to see the work in hand; but on June 3 an advance party went to the H.Q. of the 2nd N.Z.E. at Bus-les-Artois, and the company moved to the woods east of Bus village on June 7, taking over the camp of the 154 Field Company R.E., who had previously left for the south.

Lieutenant K. H. Read joined the unit at Pas, and his lectures on camouflage became a by-word and were, indeed, very illuminating. The company transport at this time occupied an excellent field off the Bus–Louvencourt road.

The company, being in reserve for the first part of this period, explored the catacombs under Bus Château, which was used as Divisional Headquarters. No. 2 Section were set to work on mined dug-outs at Fort Bertha, a mined dug-out with a pop-up at a point near Colincamps, etc., whilst No. 4 Section, under Lieutenant Marr, were attached to the R.A. for dug-out work.

An intensely interesting time ensued, which will have pleasant memories for all, as the camp was a tented one at the edge of a wood, with a good playing-field hard by—cricket and football were indulged in every night, and the shift work on dug-outs, etc., was so arranged as to give all men their turn.

Corporal Pickston distinguished himself by engaging an enemy plane with a Lewis gun, and his report speaks for itself.

To O.C., 428 FIELD COMPANY, R.E.

Report of Lewis Gun in Action.

During the exciting episode last evening our Lewis gun was in action all the time the " Bosh " plane was in range.

From the moment he left the shelter of the cloud on his mad dive for our balloon he was raked from stem to stern by our machine-gun on the broadside.

After changing magazines, during which all records were

broken, Sergeant Howard had a duffy as he left us, peppering his behind and making feathers fly.

We hit him for sure, and I'll bet my next leave that the plane and its occupants are as full of Tracer armour-piercing bullets as a Porcupine is of quills.

There were *no* stoppages.

We were out during his visit with nothing on save the little short shirts one gets from the baths, as we had turned in rather early; but it was a touch and a go to our not trundling that Bosh plane into salvage this morning.

We have no glasses down here, which is a great disadvantage.

If he was brought down (as *we* did it) we would like to put in a claim for the £20 and the month's leave. Corporal Brooke, R.A.M.C., despite the Geneva convention, brought up ammunition.

(*Signed*) H. V. PICKSTON, Lce.-Corp. and L.G.

Pickston, however, was far from well, and he was soon afterwards evacuated to the base, whence he was transferred to England, where he died in hospital. Corporal Pickston was part and parcel of the company for almost four years, and his loss was keenly felt by all. Besides being a highly skilled tradesman and an indefatigable worker—he was never content unless he had one of the bridging vehicles under extensive repair—he was a source of encouragement and help to officers and men—on account of his ready wit, his smile, and his never-failing good-humour; his recitals of the " Boxing Parson of Nottingham " and his stump speeches, which hit officers and men alike, never failed to cause enthusiastic applause from his hearers.

Further interesting work was now taken in hand, including corduroy and macadam roads near the new D.H.Q. alongside the Bois de Warnimont, constructed in case of a further big enemy offensive. The R.A.M.C. came in for a good deal of attention in this sector, and the work done consisted of evacuation and rest huts at Louvencourt Station, two large gas-proof shelters at the dressing station at Bus to be used in case of enemy gas bombardment, and also a large elaborate clearing station on the left of the Bus–Bayencourt road—this was a heavy job, necessitating the use of a large quantity of rails to form a false roof, the whole being built up on a heavy sleeper framework—deep revetted approach and exit trenches communicated with the road. The famous Euston Dump, near the Sucrerie on the Mailly-Maillet–Colincamps crossroads, provided most of the material required for the work.

Towards the end of June work was gradually extended more and more into the forward area, the improvement of Beer and Canterbury trenches was undertaken, and a further tunnelled dug-out for the machine-gunners was commenced.

The tunnelling companies undertook the bulk of the dug-outs which were constructed in this sector to an extent never before thought of, and the company took them over to complete such items as bunking and stairways, etc. The Divisional Commander's intention was to have at least one tunnelled dug-out in each of the defensible localities, commencing with those on the reserve or support lines of defence in the divisional area, and gradually carrying the work to those localities close up to the forward system. Between Cork Trench and Bertrancourt village in the right brigade sector alone there were thirty-four dug-outs completed, under construction, or planned.

On the 1st of July shift work was commenced on a concrete M.G. pill-box in a farm building near Colincamps in J. 80. b, to which materials and water were carried every night by motor lorry. Corporal Boyes and his men showed great keenness, and surprised the many Staff Officers, who came to inspect operations very regularly, at the rapid rate of progress. About ten tons of material per day were put into this job, and it took about eighteen days to complete, with the addition of an Artillery Observation Post superimposed upon it. As this farm building remained untouched by enemy shell fire, one cannot help wondering what the farmer decided to do on his return to his farm with a monolithic structure concealed in his barn with five-foot walls on top and sides, and whose foundations went three feet below ground level.

About this time Sergeant Kinley returned from the Army Musketry School with a special mention on the results of his work.

Large infantry parties were employed daily on the various strong points under construction by the company, of which the chief were Fort Bertha, Orchard, Cutting, and Mustard Points, Crimea Locality, and Shrine West and East. Several of these localities were arranged in depth to a flank facing south, and it caused humorous comment when the neighbouring right division was found to be adapting our localities to fire north; however, it was all to the good, as showing that each division was ready for eventualities to a flank.

The Division was still expectant of an attack in strength by the enemy, and the Alarm Post for the Divisional R.E. in case of alarm was made known to all, but the successes of the French Army in the south gradually relieved the tension, and really caused one to believe that our extraordinarily strong system of defences would never be required. This decided change of opinion came about towards the middle of July.

The Moir Pill-Box erected in Coigneux Valley near Courcelles-au-Bois is worthy of mention, as it afforded a lot of pleasure and scope to our camouflage officer, who spent much time in trying to convince the C.R.E. of the merits of his methods, whilst the O.C. endeavoured to be impartial.

The Reserve Brigade now received attention in the matter of quarters, and numerous " C " type elephant shelters were put up for their accommodation.

428TH FIELD COY. R.E.

Rumours of relief by the 57th Division were persistent, but came to nothing.

Lieutenant Baldwin now joined the company, and Corporal Fox and several other old friends left owing to sickness, chiefly from influenza.

August found the company fully recovered from the influenza epidemic and in very good form, and busy with the erection of baths at Bertrancourt and Courcelles, valuable experience of petrol engines and chain Hélice pumps being gained at the latter place.

Whilst talking of baths and delousing chambers we must not omit to record the story of Colonel Slaughter and the shirts.

In the opinion of " A " and " Q " at D.H.Q. clean shirts were above suspicion, and the expression of any doubt on this point was not " playing the game." But the sappers in 428 Field Company were quite rightly very particular, and declined to exchange their shirts at the Divisional Baths if they were not sure of getting as good a shirt as the one handed in. On this occasion some " clean " shirts were brought to the O.C. and were safely delivered by him to Colonel Slaughter. The result in " Q " office was a general stampede for the door, with shouts of " Take them away ! "

During these summer evenings Sapper Humphries still bowled over after over at night, and officers practised fancy strokes against imaginary cricket balls. Teams from the 57th Divisional R.E. and the 25th Divisional Artillery came and fell to our prowess, and Corporal Fry and his wasp-like gang of drivers often came to try their luck at football.

Our drivers always had a big idea of themselves as regards football, and there was often a considerable amount of blood-letting when they tackled a team from their more lowly brethren the sappers. On these occasions Driver Peak would arm himself with as much food as he could carry, including a tin of " Ideal " milk, to which he would firmly attach his lips, only letting go to utter an ear-splitting yell as " Stenn " or " Erb " collided with an adversary and brought him to grass.

We do not like to record it, but we believe that C.S.M. Waterworth and his gang of 427 stalwarts beat us at cricket, using our tackle with which to inflict the defeat. Those 427 fellows thought no small beer of themselves, but we contend that Captain Echlin did his best for his old unit by neglecting to score.

Towards the end of the second week in August the enemy began to make slight withdrawals on our immediate front, and on the 21st he was definitely pushed out of his position by our infantry. Our work now was to mark and patrol forward tracks, and to excavate a trench from Maillet Sucrerie for a four-inch water main going east over the ridge towards Serre, the work being necessarily done by night. On the 23rd the dismounted portion of the company moved forward to Courcelles for two nights, and on the 25th to Puisieux, the enemy being now definitely on the move eastwards. A water-point of considerable importance was made at Mailly Maillet

Sucrerie on the 23rd and 24th, and the repairs to the pump and engine there were a cause of considerable anxiety to all concerned. For some time great efforts had been made by the Divisional R.E. to get the old oil engine and deep well pump at the Sucrerie to work once more, and it should have been in use on the 22nd. But spare parts had to come from an Electrical and Mechanical Company, R.E., who lived twenty-five miles behind the line, and when one of the studs of the main gland broke, it took thirty-six hours to get a new one. Consequently the first supply of water for this important water-point had to come up in big tanks on the broad-gauge railway track. In all this work the company had the invaluable assistance of Captain Codling and his sappers of the 142 Army Troops Company, R.E.

On the 25th all work in the Colincamps area was left far behind, and the company was engaged (after its march) on the repair of the wooden plank road between Puisieux and Miraumont and a water-point at the latter place. The transport joined the company on the 26th, and from this date onwards was never far away from Company H.Q. The tents which had been in use during the whole summer were transported at each successive move, and saved much time and labour in the preparation of new quarters. A large enemy dump was taken over at Miraumont, and pumps were dismantled at Courcelles and other places in the back area and brought forward. On the 29th a section was attached to the 125th Brigade for work on a defence line at Loupart Wood, but the enemy still retired, so nothing was actually done. The following day the whole company moved forward, the Transport under Lieutenant Baldwin to Miraumont, and the Company H.Q. to a point between Irles and Warlencourt-Eaucourt, whilst No. 3 Section rejoined the company from Loupart Wood. A new watering-point was at once commenced at Warlencourt, which later was developed into an excellent installation, consisting of baths for officers and men, horse troughs and water-cart fillers, the whole being supplied by a chain Hélice power-driven pump at a well which the enemy had unsuccessfully attempted to destroy. The plant was capable of delivering 500 gallons per hour. The work at this stage was to complete watering-points indicated and located by the two forward field companies, and to put down the necessary pumps, tanks and troughs to meet the demands of the Division.

The orderly room staff displayed their efficiency as sappers in these stirring times, and never failed to fix up a complete office within a short time of arrival. The animals were put to great strain, but they had had liberal additions to their forage during the summer in the shape of green clover, thanks to the energies of Lieutenant Taylor, Sergeant Howard, Corporal Moores, and others, so they were in good form for their work. It is wonderful how a Field Company moves—an hour or two before the column pulls out it seems impossible to stow everything away, and it needs a keen eye to circumvent the tendency in some quarters to collect surplus kit.

428TH FIELD COY. R.E.

We once had a sapper in Egypt who for months carried about a pair of roller skates in this way, and another who carried a so-called bullet-proof waistcoat.

Drivers were the worst offenders, and it was a smart dodge when the C.Q.M.S. fitted them all out with sandbags to enforce a reduction and a standardization of kit.

Further wells were now put down in the Pys Valley, and wells in back areas were dismantled and stores taken forward—the whole system now being worked on the leap-frog system, under which the C.R.E. decided when wells were no longer required by keeping a patrol to report on the numbers of animals watered daily. This system worked extremely well, and a great saving in the use of stores was the result—such things as petrol engines, belt and chain pumps, pumps L. and F., tanks, troughs, etc., being far too valuable to be left behind a day longer than was necessary.

On September 3 the transport moved up to Pys from Miraumont, and on the following day proceeded to Thilloy, whilst Company H.Q. went forward to a wood at Villers-au-Flos.

Immediately after the 126th Infantry Brigade took Riencourt a power-driven belt pump was put down there, and later a similar plant at Barastre, Sergeants Kinley and Boughey with their men doing excellent work at the former place, and carrying on through the night to complete the new engine with storage tanks and troughs. Canvas belting was used for the first time at this place to bring the water to the surface, but it was found to be unsuited to deep wells, as the great weight of water tore away the fabric of the material and caused not infrequent stoppages.

Small parties were sent almost daily to render assistance to the Divisional Headquarters, and Corporal Pollitt should know something about these matters if we have another war.

Odd men had been left behind in charge of various wells and stores *en route*, but they rejoined as soon as possible on finding the rations not to their taste in what had now become the back areas.

On the 6th of September the company marched back to Pys, handing over work to the 1st Company N.Z.E., the New Zealand Division having taken over the line from that day. We were inspected by the G.O.C. 42nd Division on the march, and experienced a long slow tramp at the rear of the Divisional Infantry.

A period of rest and training followed, and Lieutenant J. Taylor joined from the base. Musketry and Lewis-gun instruction were given, and the afternoons were given up to games and recreational training.

Most of us visited the divisional open-air theatre, which was designed by Lieutenant Read and erected by No. 1 Section, it having 6 trusses with a span of 35 feet without pillars, and being built solely of 1-inch boarding with wire tension members.

The advance was proceeding meanwhile, and on the 18th September a party proceeded to Havrincourt Wood to inspect work in hand by the 153 Field Company of the 37th Division. The following day the company moved up to Lebucquière, where an unpleasant night was spent in an old hutted camp near a cross-roads which the enemy subjected to fire throughout the night. As a result one of the riding animals injured itself and had to be shot.

On the 21st the company moved up to Havrincourt Wood, taking over from 153 Field Company, R.E., and at once set to work on a well at Trescault, working day and night shifts. This area was the identical one which the company knew so well in June 1917, but a year of war and more especially the Cambrai fighting had altered for the worse all the villages and Havrincourt Wood, and the enemy in his retreat had blown in most tunnelled dug-outs. The company's quarters on the western edge of the wood and a mile west of Hubert's Cross were not too healthy, as the enemy was searching for ambushed Tanks. Corporal Patrick on one occasion tempted the company out of its holes by appearing with his travelling canteen, but upon a mule being hit he had to beat a hasty retreat. Several of the cooks were slightly wounded, including Sapper Radbourne more severely, but we were glad to hear of his speedy recoverery.

We were now the forward company, the 429 Field Company having gone into reserve, and work on water provision proceeded apace. All dug-outs were reconnoitred, map referenced, and gas proofed, and some were repaired, whilst full details were sent in to C.R.E. so that all possible shelters for the attacking troops might be used in the approaching attempt upon the Hindenburg Line. The well at Trescault was by this time seventy-five feet deep with four feet of water, and a chamber was now put in to receive a turbine pump as soon as this could be obtained from 4th Corps. When this pumping set eventually arrived at the Trescault well it was greeted with a lengthy and heavy shelling, and the feelings of those in charge can be imagined as they saw the Trescault Water Supply forming Aunt Sally for the enemy. But no damage was done, and immediately things quietened down, the pump was lowered the seventy odd feet, and shortly afterwards put to work.

At 5.20 a.m. on the 27th the infantry stormed the Hindenburg Line.

Parties of sappers reported at left and right Brigade Headquarters to mark out tracks, and further small parties were attached to the infantry for dug-out reconnaissance and dealing with booby traps. The N.Z. Division took over on the 28th of September, after the 42nd Division had captured Welsh Ridge, and five road mines were removed in Trescault village on the same day.

Dug-out reconnaissance and gas proofing formed our main source of activity for the next few days, but on the 29th well reconnaissances were undertaken in the villages of Beaucamp and Ribécourt, and water was exploited at the latter place on the following day, whilst a divisional twelve-spray bathhouse was commenced at Trescault. There were difficulties in getting the power-driven pump to work satisfactorily at the latter place, and until further deepening was carried out, we had to use some of the small wells in Ribécourt,

428TH FIELD COY. R.E. 143

which, although in 6th Corps area, were really the only possible water supply for the Divisional Artillery east of Trescault.

On the 1st of October an officer and several N.C.O.s proceeded to Masnières and Crèvecoeur on reconnaisance of the River Escaut or Scheldt. This party extracted forty charges from a couple of road bridges on the canal and reconnoitred the new country. The company meantime completed the baths at Trescault and assisted the 142 Army Troops Company, R.E., in the repair of the water main from Metz-en-Couture to Trescault.

On October 4th the company moved up to Trescault, carrying on work on water supply there and at Ribécourt, and endeavouring with the assistance of a company of the 1/7th Northumberland Fusiliers (the Divisional Pioneer Battalion) to make the Trescault–Ribécourt road passable.

During the next few days things slackened off somewhat, and a standard trestle for heavy bridging was prepared for practice purposes, as we were now leaving the dry, chalky country of Picardy and approaching a country of rivers, and there appeared to be the probability of considerable bridging work having to be carried out. Meantime the engine house at the Ribécourt water-point was completed.

On the 8th October preparations were made for a further advance, and No. 4 Section under Lieutenant Marr was attached to the 126th Infantry Brigade for forward work as the advance progressed. On the 9th the company marched to a point near Lesdain, via Villers Pluich and La Vacquerie, where it bivouacked, collecting surplus water supply stores from Ribécourt. The next few days were spent in collecting the N.Z.E. bridging equipment from the Escaut River and taking it forward to Jeune Bois on the Caudry–Cambrai Road, in locating booby traps in Esnes and in sign-boarding water-points, whilst on the 12th the whole company marched to Jeune Bois via Beauvois, and at noon commenced work on a new water-point at the Brasserie.

This water supply became very useful, as the old German baths were quickly put in order and a large storage tank erected, which supplied water-cart fillers and troughs in the street.

Further water-points were installed at Jeune Bois and Aulicourt Farm (commonly known as Oilcloth Farm). The boiler and steam plant at the Beauvois Brasserie now replaced the Petter engine, and on the 15th of October a fourth water-point was installed at Herpigny Farm. The whole of the company's work at this juncture was water supply and its maintenance, the 427 and 429 Field Companies respectively making themselves responsible for bridges and roads generally. The enemy had retreated to the Selle River and had left huge craters at all important cross-roads, which meant large infantry working parties, and much horse transport had to be found to ensure rapid repair of the roads.

Preparations for the battle of the Selle River were now put in hand, and all preliminary work completed, with a view to proposed new water-points at Viesly and Briastre. The company, being now definitely on water work exclusively, had the services of an expert water tester lent by the Field Ambulances, who did most useful work; he was better known to the Division as a trick dancer and sleight-of-hand merchant, and was often to be seen at the Divisional Concert Party.

No. 4 Section during this time had developed the baths at Aulicourt Farm for the 126th Brigade, and had also put down a waterpoint at Prayelle.

On the 20th of October the battle of the Selle took place, and as soon as possible an officer and a section proceeded east of the river on water reconnaissance. The points at Viesly and Briastre were quickly put in working order according to plan, and Lieutenant Lord and No. 3 Section put down an extraordinary combination at Viesly, using a portable steam engine which was found and turned on to the service of working a vertical pump. As the N.Z. Division had once again leapfrogged the 42nd, the time between the 22nd and the end of October was spent quietly at Jeune Bois clearing up, resting and patrolling water installations still in use in the area, whilst many sappers were still detached running power pumps and baths; this constant detachment of odd men caused Sergeant Hunt and Sapper Foster a lot of work in the B213 return, and they saw to it that the O.C. did not overlook his men.

The 428 Field Company and the 1/2nd Field Ambulance shared the commodious quarters at Jeune Bois, and one ought to mention that old friend and medical adviser to the company, Captain "Nobby" Webster.

Captain Webster knew the 2nd Field Company in those early days on the transport *Aragon* in 1914, and again on the Gallipoli peninsula, when he held in check the plagues of dysentery, jaundice, and septic sores which had brought the company to about a quarter of its establishment. Doctor "Corpl. Brooke" was an able second in all this work.

On the 31st of October preparations were made for a R.E. Horse and Transport Show, whilst parties were engaged in the erection of a Boxing Ring at Divisional Headquarters. The drivers did not love Transport Shows, and the sappers had to afford a little assistance in getting things ready—it reminded one of a children's party and the boy who only washed his neck when he was going out—but 428 did not intend to be beaten by the 427 Field Company, though the latter *did* carry their grooming tackle on the horses' necks; our transport officer thought it risky, and had long ago had little bags made to hold such easily mislaid articles.

Lieutenant Petry now joined the company and took charge of No. 1 Section. Sergeant Edge and his crew had long since despaired of retaining an officer more than a few weeks at a time, as they repeatedly sent him sick or found him another job. However, Lieutenant Petry commanded No. 1 Section from this date until the end of our journey.

The Sports and Transport Show of the 1st of November were a

428TH FIELD COY. R.E.

great success. We won many items, but the 427 Field Company, under the guidance of its horsy leader, attracted the eyes of the judges more often than ourselves—but it was a fine day and thoroughly enjoyable. The mounted N.C.O.s did themselves great credit, and we ran the 427 Field Company to a close finish.

On November 4 the company moved by march route to Solesmes, which was full of troops, principally from the 6th Corps on our left, and on the next day the march was continued in wretched weather to Le Quesnoy, recently captured by the N.Z. Division ahead.

From November 4 to 6, therefore, no work was done by the company, which was employed solely in marching from Jeune Bois to Le Carnoy, except to make forward reconnaissances of water supply and roads, work which, thanks to the rapidity of the advance, was of no value.

On November 6 it became imperative to get traffic through the Forêt de Mormal, so the company was ordered to make a crossing over a blown culvert at N. 29 a 8.4. Sections were detailed to work in six-hour shifts, commencing at 16.00. A pontoon wagon and a ten-horse team were turned out and sent to Maison Rouge to collect one Weldon Trestle with two bays of superstructure, which were then taken up to the job, one horse being wounded *en route*. The first relief erected the trestle and superstructure, the second relief made the bridge foundations and shore transoms safe by means of crib piers, and commenced to improve the awkward approaches. The third relief completed the approaches, but owing to the constant stream of traffic commencing soon after dawn this relief had to remain and maintain the bridge, which was several times broken. Owing to the company being again ordered to move, this party under Sergeant Edge could not be relieved, and worked for twenty-four hours without a break.

On November 7 there was little or no work, but the company moved to the region of Petit Bayay, and on the 8th two sections were ordered out to Hautmont to examine roads, railways, locks, and buildings for mines and booby traps, but no actual work was done until the next day. On the 9th November the whole company concentrated at Hautmont, and at 10.00 commenced to erect pontoon bridges of a temporary nature over the River Sambre. It was decided to bridge the lock with a girder bridge 18′ 6″ span slightly on the skew, and to cross the river or spillway proper with a pontoon bridge. To obtain a deviation road on the S.E. bank a large coal dump had to be moved, and for this the C.R.E. obtained a crowd of willing civilians, who worked almost continuously until the job was through. A company of 1/7th Northumberland Fusiliers (Pioneers) was employed on the road approaches to the bridge, and the Frenchmen also assisted in collecting stores.

Girders were plentiful, but it was difficult to obtain any quantity of timber. By 20.00 both bridges were completed except for screening and the handrails on the pontoon bridge.

The river was in partial flood, so the ramps on to the pontoon bridge were easy.

L

146 EAST LANCS. R.E. HISTORY

The following day (November 10) it was decided to improve the footbridge over the debris of the demolished masonry bridges for the use of civilian foot passengers, who naturally wished to cross the river, which divided the town about equally into halves. This work was commenced and finished off with handrails and steps on the following day. The 427 Field Company was also ordered to build a tank bridge alongside the existing pontoon bridge erected by us, in which work one of our sections rendered assistance, and was given the job of erecting the tank bridge over the lock. This was completed by the evening of the 13th of November, but in the meantime the great day had arrived, and a telegram was received at 8.30 a.m on the 11th from Headquarters R.E. which announced the Armistice as follows—

G 113   11

Hostilities will cease at 11 o'clock today AAA Troops will stand fast on the line they occupy which will be reported by 125 Infantry Brigade to D.H.Q. AAA 125 Infantry Brigade will maintain existing defensive precautions AAA No intercourse of any kind will be allowed with the enemy until further orders AAA Addressed to all concerned.

(Signed) E. C. B. KIRSOPP, Captain,
for Lieut-Colonel, G.S., 42nd Division.

Some old German baths were discovered, but with no water supply immediately available. This was obtained, however, by using a well in the adjacent brewery, pumping by L. and F. pumps into existing tanks and heating the water by means of the brewery boiler. The baths were in running order by the evening of the 11th November.

Although the Armistice was not entirely unexpected, it came nevertheless as a great shock, and was one of those events in our lives which is only realized and fully grasped after a lapse of time. There was no excessive hilarity but rather a deep sense of relief, and one scarcely knew what to do or say.

Work, of which there was plenty for R.E. and Pioneers, proceeded as usual, and one felt that it would have been a splendid finish to the great advance had our forces been allowed to clear the enemy right back into his own territory.

Later in the day of the 11th November the following Special Order of the Day by Major-General A. Solly-Flood, C.M.G., D.S.O., was sent to all units—

" The Armistice proclaimed to-day has brought the operations in which the Division was engaged to a premature conclusion.

" Generally speaking, the recent fighting was not of the violent nature in which you have previously taken part and so greatly excelled. At the commencement of the operations, however, it was sufficiently severe, and the conditions imposed

428TH FIELD COY. R.E.

by the Forest of Mormal and the bridgeless River Sambre were such as to call for the highest soldierly qualities.

"After long marches at night in bad weather over boggy forest tracks, although cold and wet, hungry and tired, you attacked and defeated the enemy with your customary indomitableness.

"When the history of the war is written your efforts, commencing in the Forest, then forcing the passage of the bridgeless River Sambre in the face of severe enemy fire, and culminating in the capture of the town of Hautmont, will rank very high among the exploits of soldiers during this great war.

"I consider that the Divisional Motto has once again, probably for the last time, been entirely upheld.

"Officers, N.C.O.s and men of all arms and services in the Division, I am proud to be your Commander, and to be able once more to thank you, in the name of our King and Country, for your gallant deeds and your steadfast loyalty.

"A. SOLLY-FLOOD,
"Major-General,
"Commanding 42nd Division."

11*th November*, 1918.

From the 12th of November work proceeded daily, on the maintenance of the Sambre bridges, on running of baths, and on the salving of bridging material. The transport moved into a large empty factory near the river, and all efforts were directed towards making all ranks comfortable.

A Divisional Laundry was put into running order by the adaptation of a portable engine, and work was carried out on a Boxing Ring, on the Divisional Theatre, and on the general cleaning and painting of the transport vehicles.

A number of men went sick at this time, amongst them Lance-Corporal Brocklesby, who was thought to be just suffering from feverishness and the general influenza. Later on, however, news came to hand of the corporal's death. His loss was deplored by the whole company, for Corporal Brocklesby was one of the most popular junior N.C.O.s in the unit.

The rest of the month was passed in recreation of one kind and another, with a little work on destruction of enemy explosives, etc., but Hautmont was not an attractive town, and the weather was damp and cold, so that most of us would have been glad if the Division had been ordered to march into Germany. However, this was not to be our fortune, though at one time there were strong rumours of such a move.

Lectures on "Demobilization" were given by officers specially sent from 3rd Army for the purpose, and this subject naturally formed a great part of the conversation of all of us.

On December 1, His Majesty the King passed near Hautmont on

his visit to his Armies, and a detachment of officers and men proceeded to the Maubeuge–Avesnes road to see him pass.

We were now awaiting definite instructions to proceed to Charleroi, and on the 6th No. 2 Section proceeded there via Binche and Fontaine L'Evêque, coming under the orders of Major Hanmer, of the 429 Field Company.

No. 1 Section on the same day proceeded to Vieux Reng to bridge craters there and at Elesmes. On the 10th No. 3 Section reported to Major Hanmer at Charleroi, proceeding by motor lorry, and afterwards went forward to Fleurus, whilst two days later No. 1 Section also reported at Charleroi—the three sections now there doing advance work on hutting and improvement of billets, etc., preparatory to the arrival of the Division.

Company Headquarters moved on the 14th under the orders of the 126th Brigade, and arrived at Charleroi on the 18th, having spent one night each at Lameries and Binche, and two at Fontaine L'Evêque. Company Headquarters and dismounted ranks were at once settled in the Jesuit College, and the transport took up its quarters in a factory at Damprémy.

The company now came under the orders of its own commander, and work proceeded apace for the 127th Infantry Brigade, the R.A. and Divisional Headquarters, and consisted simply of camp and billet improvements.

Lieutenant Whitehead joined the company from England, and at once made himself acquainted with the multitudinous army forms in connection with demobilization. This officer also carried out a heating scheme at the town swimming baths—normally only used in summer — and general improvements at one of the town's theatres, which was taken over by the Division in preparation for the pantomime.

We had two days' holiday at Christmas, with an unusually fine round of festivities—the College Hall was gaily decorated and used for a dance on Christmas Eve, whilst excellent fare was enjoyed by all on the following day. Our Divisional Commander and Colonel Riddick set a hot pace for dancing, both of them kindly looking in upon us during the evening and also making an inspection of the decorations in the morning.

January saw us with a huge orderly room staff battling bravely with demobilization matters, and endeavouring to settle as equitably as possible the order of priority for going home.

We had no sports ground, and indeed had little time for games, being still kept busy with hutting and odd jobs up and down the countryside.

C.S.M. Garnett was one of the first to be sent for under special instructions from home—as a pivotal man—and he left to our great regret. This warrant officer was later awarded the M.S.M., and it is a thousand pities we had not the news of this well-earned honour before he left us. C.S.M. Garnett was a man of rare capabilities, a quick thinker, and a keen organizer.

428TH FIELD COY. R.E. 149

Space will not allow us to mention each man by name as he left the unit, but we gradually despatched personnel to the Concentration Camp, and soon became much depleted in numbers. Sergeant Johnson assumed the duties of C.S.M., but left us in a short time, to be in turn replaced by C.Q.M.S. A. J. Young, who fulfilled his dual role in his own convincing style. The disposal of the animals had not commenced at this time, so it was impossible to free any drivers, but the veterinary authorities classified the horses and mules into groups, and we had to be content to await events.

In February the reduction of personnel proceeded very quickly, and a fair proportion of mounted men went away as a result of the reduction in the number of animals, which had by this time started. The employment of some German prisoners of war at the transport lines permitted a further reduction of our own mounted ranks.

Periodical dances were held in the College Hall, and some diversion was created on the 19th February by a fire at Divisional Headquarters hard by. The R.E. took part in the quelling of this outbreak, and the damage was not extensive.

Early in March all stores were carefully checked and stored in the infantry barracks, and great credit was due to C.Q.M.S. Young, Sergeant Edge, and the men who worked under them for the careful and methodical way in which this work was carried out.

On 22nd March Sergeant Edge (who had volunteered for service in the Army of Occupation) with thirteen other ranks proceeded to join the 1st Divisional R.E. in Germany, and we were all glad to hear that Sergeant Edge was quickly promoted to the rank of Q.M.S.

The departure of this party reduced us to " Cadre B," which was the strength at which we were to return to England. On April 2 we left Charleroi by train at 7 p.m. for Antwerp; there was a busy day prior to entrainment in moving wagons and stores to the station and loading them on to the train. Remaining in the hutted embarkation camp until April 5, we embarked on that day, and landed at Tilbury Docks on Sunday morning, April 6. Thence we went by train to Oswestry, where all stores were handed in. Those whose homes were not in the Manchester district were despatched to their destinations, and the remainder entrained for Manchester, where they were met at Exchange Station by Colonel Crook, Lieut.-Colonel Riddick and a host of relations and friends. Certain boxes of orderly room papers and records were sent off to Seymour Grove, Old Trafford, and we then dispersed to our homes, the 428 Field Company, R.E., having now ceased to exist.

There remains little to record, and so, before the chapter is closed, we may well reflect awhile. We had been a band of men brought together by the common cause of national defence, and we were similar to hundreds of other units scattered to the four corners of the earth. Nevertheless as a unit we possessed an individuality of our own, for whose origin we must search the earlier pages of our history. It is difficult to imagine a finer body of men of all ranks than the original company which left England in September, 1914. Following faithfully the leadership of Major Wells, and inspired by a lofty sense of duty, they set up a standard of determination and unselfish endeavour which served as a guide to successive reinforcements throughout the war. The result was that the entire company always pulled together, tackling any and every task which faced them with the single aim of doing the job and doing it well. All honour, then, to those pioneers who blazed the trail we trod.

PART V
THE 429TH FIELD COMPANY, ROYAL ENGINEERS 1915–1919

CHAPTER I

EGYPT AND SINAI

THE 429 Field Company, R.E., was first formed at Southport on December 2, 1915, being then known as the 1/3rd East Lancs. Field Company, R.E. It was formed from the Third Line Depot, East Lancs. R.E., which had been at Southport since the end of August 1915.

At first purely a draft-finding depot consisting of three field companies at three-quarters war establishment, in December the Third Line Depot supplied this complete field company at full strength.

The ultimate object of the 1/3rd Field Company was to be the 3rd Field Company of the 42nd (East Lancs.) Division, the original East Lancs. Territorial Division, which had hitherto had only two East Lancs. Field Companies. After formation it remained at Southport training with the Third Line Depot until the departure of the latter to Carnarvon; the 1/3rd Field Company then moved on the 28th of January, 1916, to Crowborough, Sussex. Captain F. E. Button was at this time in command of the unit. At Crowborough this company joined the three field companies and signal company of the Second Line East Lancs. T.F. Division—the 66th Division—and training was continued under their C.R.E., Lieut.-Colonel H. A. Fielding.

At Southport we had lived in billets, but at Crowborough we were put into huts, this being for many their first experience of real army accommodation. In spite of cold weather we had quite a good time at Crowborough, and March found us still there, working on field works; the trenches were so perfect in design and regular in construction that it seemed the only thing necessary to complete the job would have been to wallpaper them. The weather continued very wintry, and for the most part there was snow on the ground.

On the 20th March the whole of the 66th Division, and the 1/3rd Field Company with it, moved to Colchester, where the R.E. were quartered in the Cavalry Barracks, which, though old, were quite convenient and comfortable. The barracks boasted a fine square, on which were held many " posh " parades. Here the divisional R.E. band functioned on Sundays, so well that many local friends of the fair sex attended regularly.

On one occasion when the 2/8th Manchesters were formed up on their parade ground ready to proceed on a brigade march, one of the pack horses belonging to this company—a huge animal—broke away from a small driver, charged the troops on the square, and scattered the infantry in all directions, strewing picks and shovels in its wake, and finally came to a standstill with its head in the sergeants' wet canteen. Talking of the latter, though not included in the list of daily orderly duties, it was apparently always necessary for the regimental orderly officer, the R.S.M., and the orderly sergeant, to approve of the beer that was sold there.

During the greater part of our stay at Colchester we were confined to barracks under Period of Vigilance restrictions, owing to the naval landing scare, and "Prepare to move" and "Stand to" orders were frequent. Consequently the promenade upon the open space called Abbey Fields and adjoining the barracks, became the only form of outside recreation during these periods, and the company realized for the first time how comfortable G.S. wagons and lorries were to sit in. Zeppelins were seen over the town on two or three occasions.

Early in April a great reconnaissance of a portion of the coast was made by two officers and several N.C.O.s, with a view to constructing extensive defence works, but to our great disappointment this came to nothing.

The cavalry riding school and the open-air jumps—*i. e.* "the lane" —were a source of great enjoyment to all mounted people except a very few. Any grey dawn Captain Button might have been seen stealing into the school for a little quiet tuition on "Dobbin" by Corporal Hamilton. The latter did everything, except sticking up bills, to advertise his cavalry experience in the 6th Dragoon Guards.

The senior N.C.O.s of the company also attended a select class under Corporal Hamilton as riding-master, and this provided much amusement. Sergeant Gray picked out a nice quiet-looking little horse and set out in quite the approved style round the school. On the command "Halt," Sergeant Gray said "Halt" very persuasively to his horse, but without avail. He repeated this polite request in a louder tone, but unfortunately a motor bicycle just outside the riding school started back-firing. The horse immediately commenced to "trot out," and then broke into a canter, and Gray took up a more forward position—in fact he hung round the horse's neck, calling out: "Stop it! Stop it! one of you, stop the thing! Get hold of it! Can't one of you do something?" The audience was convulsed. All good things come to an end, however, and before long Gray was deposited on his back and the animal secured.

Training in all branches of R.E. work went on steadily, and No. 1 and 2 Sections erected a long trestle bridge on dry land. There was considerable rivalry between the 1/3rd Field Company (commonly known as the "One and three-pennies") and the companies of the 66th Division, and there was a certain amount of quiet satisfaction when it was noticed that a section of the 2/2nd Field Company took a whole day to assemble a service trestle.

Stores and horses now began to arrive. Quite a number of the

429TH FIELD COY. R.E.

latter came from the North Devon Yeomanry, who were being dismounted, and these were so good as to cause the other companies to cast envious eyes on them. In fact the C.R.E. and the adjutant both selected chargers from our remounts.

Every one heard with great regret on the 24th April that C.Q.M.S. Newton had died in hospital from diphtheria, and the following morning all the senior N.C.O.s were sent to an isolation camp; 2nd Corporal Linney and Lance-Corporal Ferguson together functioned as C.Q.M.S. for a time. Both did so well that they surprised themselves and the company.

About this time the company was inspected by Brigadier-General A. W. Roper, Inspector General of R.E., with a view to ascertaining if it was ready for service overseas. It must be admitted that we were only just beginning to learn the contents of a tool-cart.

On May 9 the 66th Division and the 1/3rd East Lancs. Field Company, R.E., were inspected by Lord French. We had been marched out along a little country lane, where we awaited for six hours in the pouring rain the arrival of the great Field Marshal. C.S.M. Evans provided a little diversion while waiting by trying a ride on a horse, which put him over its head on to the further side of a small brook. Quite suddenly the Field Marshal drove past in a closed car. The whole column was ordered to turn about and return to barracks, and then the fun began. It was pointed out to the Brigade-Major that it was impossible to turn a pontoon wagon with a six-horse team in a twelve-foot country lane, but without avail. All the horses went mad, and after strenuous efforts and charging up banks and into meadows we arrived back at Colchester about 10.0 p.m.

Another inspection of the Division and the 1/3rd Field Company by members of the Russian Duma took place two days later. A very " posh " march-past with full transport followed the review. It was observed that just before the inspection one or two officers found difficulty in keeping their horses still, and hurried exchanges were made with N.C.O.s in the rear. Many facetious remarks were exchanged while we were standing easy prior to the inspection, notably when one driver in answer to a query as to how we should recognize our illustrious allies, replied that they would probably have snow on their beards; there were also many allusions to the rapidity of movement down Colchester way of the " Russian steamroller."

The R.E. sports on the 17th May were a great success. Though Sergeant Gray had laboured hard to train sprinters and runners from the 1/3rd, they let him down, and though of course we all said that the one and three-pennies had won the barrel-piering competition on points, the award was in favour of the 2/1st Field Company.

On the 18th May there was yet another inspection—by General Robertson this time. He found us very busy at pontooning and bridging (on dry land), and there was much uneasiness among the officers and senior N.C.O.s in case the general might ask a leading question, but he passed without comment.

It now became known that we were soon to leave for Egypt, and from this time onwards all available officers, N.C.O.s and men were hurried off on final leave. Owing to short notice this leave was lamentably short, and in some cases only allowed a few hours at home. An advance party, consisting of Lieut. Bateman, with Corporal Marsden (the only available man in barracks at the time) as his batman, left for Southampton on the 29th May. Incidentally it may be mentioned that this gigantic advance party rolled up at Alexandria about ten days after the rest of the company, having been taken to Salonica by mistake.

On the 18th May Major Lawford came from the 3rd Line Depot at Carnarvon to take command of the company. We left on the night of 31st May, after having a full-dress parade, and inspection by the G.O.C., 66th Division. On this parade were included sun helmets (some with and some without puggaree), vehicles and all horses. That is to say, all horses went on to the parade ground, but some insisted on leaving it before the appointed hour for dismissal, in spite of their riders' efforts. It was, nevertheless, a brave show, though many pith helmets almost fell off on the command "Sla-o-o-IPE!" given in Major Lawford's best style.

One or two refractory mules were lost on the way to the station, and scouts were out looking for them. One man, who shall be nameless, accidentally found one of them, and gave it a good thwack with a stick as a reminder that we did not want it with us: he then returned without it. Our worthy transport officer picked up sufficient decent horses on the quay-side at Southampton to make up deficiencies.

We embarked on the s.s. *Georgian*, and sailed at 8.0 p.m. on June 1. Major Lawford was O.C. troops on board, and organized innumerable boat-drills. These and the daily bath were the chief diversions during the voyage. There was an impression that the daily bath under the ship's hose was organized for the amusement of the officers, as they all watched the spectacle, while a subaltern checked off the names on a nominal roll.

Censorship of letters started at this time, and many men took the opportunity to let the officers know what they thought of them; home truths were the order of the day. One unfortunate driver mentioned in a letter that whenever a horse died the meat ration increased, which he thought suggestive. This shocking insinuation was ruthlessly tracked to its originator by an energetic censor, and punishment was meted out. Such are the drawbacks to a sense of humour! Later, when every one had become accustomed to the censorship, lively incidents like this did not occur. It would appear, nevertheless, that at least one officer continued for some time to read letters with the utmost care, for many months afterwards he remarked to a sapper: "You know, most of the letters are piffle, but I really enjoy reading yours."

Another feature of the voyage was, as might be expected, a certain amount of *mal-de-mer* of unpleasant memory. This was especially

429TH FIELD COY. R.E. 157

pronounced in the case of one sergeant, who had leave ashore at Malta, but had to be dumped in the customs house for three or four hours, while his two friends were searching in the streets that go uphill and then down, for the wherewithal to slake their thirst. However, nothing could be found, so honours were more or less even. We remained at Malta from 9.0 a.m. on June 9th till 1.30 p.m. on the 10th.

Right pleased we were to reach Alexandria on the 13th June. We disembarked the same day and spent the night in the dirty old Camp " A," Gabbari, among the ants. This Camp " A " is not a place one would choose as a health resort, and the great heat and general conditions upset a number of us. Lieutenant Kendall caught measles, of all things. It was said that this was due to wearing shorts, and certainly Lieutenant Kendall's shorts were not ordinary shorts, but he never wore them again.

Alexandria, of course, proved to be full of interest, and the long tram-ride down Sister Street was an education in itself.

When the company got its marching orders on June 27, every one was delighted to leave Camp " A," but this joy was short-lived when we found how hot it was at El Ferdan, where we joined the 42nd Division. This was our first glimpse of the Canal and the desert. We liked the former because it provided us with cool baths—in spite of the jelly fish—and with a topic of conversation for hours when a ship passed through, but we had no use for the latter until we had cultivated a taste for its charms. At El Ferdan Sergeant Cowsill commenced to try his hand as Company Sergeant-Major, and Corporal Fitchford was made sergeant of No. 3 Section.

Things looked much rosier on July 3 when the company crossed over to the east bank and took over a delightful camp from the 86th Field Company, commanded by Captain R. E. B. Pratt, whom we were afterwards to meet in another capacity. Though unaccustomed to the great heat, the company laboured manfully on hutting : one would have thought that we built enough huts for a million men. Corporal Craig distinguished himself on this work by his skilful handling of " Gyppies " with a stout piece of $4'' \times 2''$ timber, as we had a number of them working for us. We paraded at 4.0 a.m. daily, and spent the middle of the day resting and sleeping when the flies didn't make it impossible. Our spare time was taken up with watching camels at work and play, and G.S. wagons complete with teams frolic off the bridges into the Canal.

Later in July the " Hush-hush " stunt was started. This was a preliminary canter for the Desert Column, and there was much talk of camel racks and practice in loading camels with water, stores, etc.

These schemes took definite shape when the company had camels complete with wallahs dished out to them at Hill 40, whither we had moved via Kantara on the 24th July. At Hill 40 we joined the 127th Infantry Brigade for the first time. On the 26th July we moved on to Gilban, via Hill 70. It is said that, while Major Lawford was standing without a collar or tunic and minus rank badges, inspecting our first well-sinking job at Gilban, an unwitting infantryman came up and addressed him as " Corporal," much to every one's amusement.

No. 4 Section were always rather exclusive, and whether it was due to their section officer or to Sergeant Gray is not certain, but they always did things which no one else did. About this time they ran rather a good line in note-books. They had innumerable note-books. Each sapper had at least one. Sergeant Gray had probably about a dozen, and one would not care to say how many Lieutenant Kendall had. The uses of these note-books were many and various, and there is reason to believe that some of them were used for purposes which would have surprised the Army Printing and Stationery Department had they come to their knowledge.

The company moved to Pelusium on August 3, and here we first heard the noise of battle in the form of the sound of distant guns at Romani. During the night large batches of Turkish prisoners began to arrive, escorted by the somewhat wild-looking Australian Light Horse and New Zealand Mounted Rifles.

On the 5th August half the company moved to Katia, the other half moving up a day or two later, and for perhaps the first time in our lives we experienced what thirst and sunstroke were, and how trying it was to march on soft sand. Our Brigade, the 127th, was just in time to extend on the ridge, and fire a few shots; then, worn out with the march, the Brigade sank down to rest for the night beside dead Turks and camels, whilst the R.E. dug wells furiously. Unfortunately C.S.M. Cowsill went down with dysentery at this time.

Our chief work here was well-digging, mainly for camel-watering, for most of the horses and their drivers had been left behind at Kantara. Here, too, we first made the acquaintance of Fritz, the Taube, who visited us regularly every morning at breakfast, for the specific purpose, so Sergeant Gray said, of bombing the wells which No. 4 Section was making.

The Division, which by this time had foregathered, moved back to Romani on the 14th, and we hailed a mail, including parcels of food, with great delight. The 3rd Field Company had an opportunity of extending its acquaintance with the other two field companies, and many old friends were discovered. Work on the Romani defences and a certain amount of training chiefly occupied our time, and here we first had the assistance of the Egyptian Labour Corps. Lieutenant Farrell went to the base from Romani.

At the end of the month the first real water reconnaissance took place from Oghratina. The party consisted of a section from each field company, each having a medical officer attached. One of the latter, Lieutenant Vandandayne, became Jester-in-Ordinary to the detachment, and the easy way in which he borrowed horses and camels, and scattered them over the desert, and his subsequent ingenious excuses, were nearly sufficient to upset Colonel Mozley's gravity, when he was questioning Lieutenant Vandandayne about the loss.

One day the party encamped at a spot where they expected to remain for a few days, and it was decided to use one of the long lengths of " fileries " (4" × 4" timber) which had been so troublesome to the camels, as a guide-post, and to erect it on a high level close to the camp on the following morning, so that parties returning from work could easily find the camp. The post was duly erected, but unfortunately it happened to be the same day that Lieutenant Kendall, pursuing his policy of educating his section above all others, decided to make a surveyor of Lance-Corporal Craig. As a matter of fact, the Scotsman is rather heavy and getting on in years, and was not at all grateful for the interest taken in him, the result being a whole day spent in climbing hills. Anyway, Lieutenant Kendall found that there was another hill in the neighbourhood—about two kilos away—which was higher than the one on which the guide-post was erected. So he had the post moved to the higher level. The result of this was heard about 10.0 p.m. the same night, when some " misguided " persons found the camp after making a minute search for it around the guide-post. By the way, can't soldiers swear?

The site of the wells under construction being some distance from the camp, every sapper's great ambition was to ride a camel—either solo, or with one or two more sappers—to work.

Wild dogs came into the camp at night, and were so cheeky that one or two moonlight hunts with fixed bayonets, clubs, etc., were organized. No mighty hunter was discovered among the detachment, consequently there was no dog to augment the bully beef and Machonochie.

There was something very marvellous about the way the railway crept up to Oghratina (Kilo 60) from El Rabah (Kilo 51). It wound its way over the desert like a huge rattlesnake, heralding its approach with the collective chattering of hundreds of " Gyppies," and its speed was really remarkable.

On the 12th September the Division, which had meanwhile continued to rest and train at Romani, moved up to Oghratina, and took up the line which the R.E. reconnaissance party had marked out with many signboards and plans. Work on wells and water supply generally continued, this company working mostly in " No. 3 Valley." Experiments were made to see what percentage of salt camels would jib at in their water, and it was found that some of these extraordinary creatures would drink water containing 1300 parts per 100,000.

Major Lawford went to take over the duties of C.R.E. consequent on Colonel Mozley's departure on leave on the 26th September, and Captain Button assumed command of the company.

Some very beautiful dawns and sunsets were observed, Lieutenant Kendall being particularly affected by their remarkable colouring. The evenings were further made pleasant by a quartette in the 2nd Field Ambulance. Every night this little party rendered some choice selections, which sounded so good that every one stopped to listen. The R.E. choir also functioned on those nights in which beer was sold, but it was very nice to listen to, whatever the motive power. The company moved back with the Division on the 11th October to Romani, and the 52nd Division went forward.

On the 17th October a party went to the rest camp at Sidi Bishr for a week. Lieutenant Kendall and No. 4 Section detachment were at this time out on a water reconnaissance in the Katia district. One of the "stunts" of this party was to make tea, coffee, etc., with each sample of water, and report on its palatability.

Another water reconnaissance detachment, consisting of Lieutenant Bateman, a medical officer, and No. 2 Section, an infantry party and some E.L.C., left for Bayud and Mageibra on the 30th October. This detachment found very good friends in the Yeomanry (Gloucesters, Warwicks and Worcesters), especially when on two successive days the ration convoy from Company Headquarters failed to turn up at the "half-way point," Corporal Hamilton having lost his way.

Corporal Hamilton's system of finding his way to the detachment to take rations to them, was to mark the route with pegs and posts the first time he went, when of course he had a guide. For all subsequent journeys he relied on these marks. Unfortunately one day a sandstorm obliterated all his marks, and the result was that he completely lost himself. A message was received by " visual " through signals in the evening to say that the detachment had not received their rations. The C.R.E. was informed by wire that the ration convoy had lost itself, and all patrols were told to look out for it. Eventually it rolled up at Company Headquarters—not having found the detachment, and not having delivered the rations—about 8.0 a.m. the next morning. Corporal Hamilton was warned as he came into camp that Captain Button was waiting for him, and was in a smouldering condition. Corporal Hamilton had picked up on the desert an old Turkish musket, so he decided to use this as a peace offering. Approaching Captain Button as though nothing had happened, he showed him this musket and opened the conversation by saying: " What do you think of this, sir ? I've just picked it up." The remainder of the conversation is not our affair.

Returning to the subject of the detachment, however, they found during their trek a new Hod, or water-bearing depression, which they promptly named and notice-boarded "Hod el Southport." The whole trek was made by compass, working to a somewhat obsolete 1/100,000 scale map.

On the 30th and 31st October, the main body of the company moved back to Negiliat via El Rabah.

Later the Division moved up to Khirba, and Nos. 1 and 2 Sections went on detachment to Bir el Abd, and found the bulk of the 52nd Division there. On the 22nd November the whole Division marched to Salmana. No wire roads had been laid up to this time, and the marching was found a little strenuous. A brew of tea on the march proved a great stimulant, and tea came to be regarded more as a food than a beverage. The 52nd Division was for the time being left behind, and the 42nd Division moved on to Abu Tilul on the 23rd, and to Mazar on the 24th November. These moves were very well

429TH FIELD COY. R.E.

executed with advance, flank and rear guards, and a cavalry screen, bivouacking at night.

Arriving at Mazar, the 127th Brigade, to which the 1/3rd Field Company was affiliated, took up advanced positions, and it was rumoured that there might be some Turks in the Magara Hills on the right. The Brigade was told to expect an aerial bombardment, and every one feverishly dug-in his bivvy. It was now getting cold at night, and bivvies took on a more protective form, *i. e.* groundsheet or canvas in place of matting, palm leaves, etc.

Colonel Mozley returned from leave, and on the 25th November Major Lawford came back to the company. The E.F. Canteen moved up about this time.

Water supply was now assuming larger proportions, and wells were dug in batteries. The company had the southern group in hand, and also had the job of putting in working order some deep-well pumps left behind in a damaged condition by the Turks. A big survey of the eastern portion of Mazar was also undertaken. At Mazar we met the 1/1st Field Company at football, and of course beat them.

During well-sinking operations here, Sergeant Gray had the misfortune to lose a " spearpoint " of a Norton tube well, and when the company moved he had to stay behind to recover it, being supplied with a daily working party to dig it out. About two years later, while on leave in Manchester, he was walking along Market Street, and one of the infantrymen who had worked on this digging job—also on leave—saw him, and to the astonishment of the citizens, and the discomfiture of Sergeant Gray, he shouted across the street to ask whether he had found his bit of pipe yet.

The company was ordered to move on 2nd December to railhead, some six or eight kilos out (Kilo 125), which was being guarded by the 1/5th East Lancs., to prepare water supply and mark out positions for the move forward of the Division. On the march on this occasion the company was organized with advance, flank and rear guards, etc. So highly organized, in fact, that the various guards used up nearly the whole company, and the main body consisted of about sixty camels with native drivers. Smoking was forbidden (the march started in the evening), and there was to be no talking above a whisper. Lieutenant Kendall, who was with the main body, found one " Gippy " driver smoking a cigarette, and spent about five minutes telling him all about himself and his ancestors—in English. Finally, he seized the cigarette, and flung it on the ground. The driver, quite unmoved by this flow of oratory, of which he understood not one word, picked up the cigarette, and went on smoking. Lieutenant Kendall, with his mental equilibrium completely upset by this lack of appreciation of his fine phraseology, demanded angrily whether the man couldn't understand plain English !!

On arrival at railhead, it was found that the cavalry and camel corps screen was quite close, and there was a certain amount of mild excitement in the situation, as the Turk was thought to be not far away. Consequently, every one was ordered to keep his rifle or revolver constantly handy. We worked here in conjunction with the Australian Field Squadron, and on the 7th December moved over to the Australian Light Horse Brigade Camp at Gererat. Two companies of the Scottish Rifles (52nd Division) were attached to the company as pioneers, and did good work.

The drinking-water supply was very scarce, and men had to go out for a whole day with only half a bottle full of water, which had to allow for making tea. One party of No. 4 Section, however, under Corporal Brightmore, stated that this was quite all right, as they daily met a water reconnaissance party of Turks, who were so shocked by this state of affairs in the British Army that they insisted on supplying a dixie-full of water every day. Of course, it would be Corporal Brightmore's party, and it would be No. 4 Section.

The camp at Gererat is worthy of note, being, from its natural position in the folds of the sand dunes, at the same time picturesque and good from a defensive point of view. Here the Taubes again got busy, and strict orders as to lights were enforced. The company, consequently, had one or two sing-songs in the dark—weird but enjoyable—and it should be noted that the rum ration was particularly good at this time.

On 18th December we moved to Kilo 129½. Here the divisional R.E. carried out probably their biggest water undertaking, two infantry and two cavalry divisions and Camel Corps all using the many troughs which had been hastily constructed to receive water from the tank train.

On 20th December we rejoined the Division, which had now moved up to Maadan, and assembled that evening and slept in the open ready for the advance on El Arish; and everything pointed to an engagement. On this night we had the first issue of candles there had been for a long time, and the sight of innumerable candles and fires dotted about all over the desert was really wonderful. Whilst lying out on the ground many troops and camel convoys passed and repassed over the bivouac sites, and certain men in the company are said to bear the print of camels' hoofs on their faces to this day. This, however, is a scurrilous libel on some perfectly harmless faces.

Early in the morning of the 21st it was announced that " Johnny " had evacuated El Arish, and the Division moved back to Mazar; this move gave us our first experience of marching on a wire road, and we found it very helpful. At Mazar we managed to have an enjoyable Christmas dinner on such fare as could be procured from parcels, and from the E.F. Canteen. The orderly room staff and friends regaled themselves on tinned fruits, milk, biscuits, cake, cocoa and coffee, and were ever afterwards known as the Pineapple Chunk Brigade. The statement that they drank both cocoa and coffee is entirely their own, and it is not known whether they drank the two mixed, or which one they drank first, and what was the result. The senior N.C.O.s repaired to the bivvy of the C.Q.M.S., fortified themselves with beer, and, it is rumoured, with a more

429TH FIELD COY. R.E. 163

than ordinary ration of rum, and subsequently serenaded the officers with Christmas Carols, or such as they were in a fit state to remember. The first line of each carol came out bravely enough, but there seemed to be a wild diversity of opinion as to the second line, and the carol was given up in favour of another one. However, such as they were, they served their purpose; and a high authority, who ought to know, states that Sapper Broadbent slept out that night, owing to the presence of a very senior N.C.O. in his bed.

The month closed with rain, thunder and lightning, and for a time it was very cold. Early in January 1917 the company preceded the Division up to El Arish to take over from the 52nd Division. Lieutenant Kendall was nearly drowned at El Bittia (Kilo 139) on the way up through the collapse of a very scientific bivvy which he had constructed.

On the 8th January Lieut.-Colonel Mozley went sick, and Major Lawford again took over the duties of C.R.E., Captain Button taking command of the company. "Fritz" once more started to worry us with his Taube machines. We put down at El Arish an elaborate system of wells near the camp, and they were generally looked upon as the best thing of the kind that we had done. Though only a couple of hundred yards from the sea, the water contained only a small percentage of salt (40 per 10,000). Another big survey of the whole area was undertaken.

Rations, forage, R.E. stores, etc., now began to arrive by sea, being landed in lighters from the cargo boats. The railway station grew to gigantic proportions.

Though El Arish is but a poor little village, our first sight of it gleaming white through the green foliage of tamarisk, olive and other trees, with its flat-roofed houses, and its one or two minarets, reminded us of the pictures we had seen of Biblical villages. Down the Wady El Arish ran a small stream which nourished quite a fair plantation of fruit trees, the wady mouth being very picturesque with palm trees growing within a few yards of the sea. All these were pleasant sights to eyes that had grown somewhat tired of the unending desert, only relieved by hods and occasional patches of scrub.

One night at El Arish, Sapper Johnson, formerly the third-line bandmaster, who had lately joined the company, was on guard, and had occasion to ask his way to the C.S.M.'s bivvy. In some manner he was directed to the officers' quarters, and entering Major Lawford's bivvy, he demanded in a loud voice to know where the C.S.M. was to be found. A voice came from underneath the blankets: "Who are you?" Reply: "Oh, I'm Johnson." Again the voice asked: "And who's Johnson?" Reply: "WHAT! Don't you know JOHNSON? Who are YOU? Just a minute while I strike a light." He struck one, and quickly blew it out. Then—he went out.

The company, less No. 2 Section, moved back on 13th January to Kilo 142 to dig more wells, and the C.R.E. moved up with Divisional Headquarters to El Arish on the 17th. The next day the vicinity of the camp was badly "strafed" by 'planes, and it is said that some E.L.C. rushed into the sea to avoid the bombs, and were drowned. They certainly used to flock down to the sea-shore at dusk every day and dig themselves in.

On the 20th January it was recorded that at the wells made by the company at El Arish, the following were watered : 1530 camels at 10 gallons each, and 350 horses at 9 gallons each (three times during the day—average 3 gallons a time). Total for the day—18,000 odd gallons.

On the 22nd January we returned to El Arish with the 127th Brigade, and received orders to move out to El Burj to prepare wells for a further advance of infantry. On the way out General Sir Philip Chetwode, the Desert Column Commander, and all his staff, overtook us, and Captain Button had to accompany the general. Greatly to his discomfort he was given a fiery Australian horse to ride for the occasion, and arrived in camp later in a very exhausted condition in consequence.

In front of the camp, which was sited in a picturesque tamarisk grove, were a squadron of Light Horse and some Camelry, who were very amused by our restrictions on lights at night, whereas they had big fires burning all night. So, by way of a little leg-pulling, they warned us that Turkish patrols were in the neighbourhood, and that there were also a number of cut-throat natives about. Consequently, we increased the night guard on the camp to enormous proportions.

The wells were sited near the shore, and a road about a mile long had to be constructed from the caravan route to them. This was made of wire netting interlaced with tamarisk, so as to form a sort of carpet. Not, however, as some suggested, to avoid hurting the poor camels' tender feet.

A bombshell fell in the camp on the 28th January in the shape of the arrival of some 52nd Divisional R.E. officers, who stated that they had come to arrange about taking over. They brought a rumour to the effect that the 42nd Division was to leave Egypt, and naturally there was considerable speculation as to its destination; but it was generally thought that it would be Salonica or France.

The company returned to El Arish on the 29th, on the night of which a "khamseen" occurred, and on the 31st, an advance party, consisting of Lieutenant Sinclair, Sergeants Linney and Fitchford and some others, of whose names there appears to be no record, departed, and we were pretty certain that it was for France. The move to Kantara was made a day or two later by rail in instalments. This was usually a tedious journey, as derailments were frequent; in this case, however, we did not have any trouble of this kind, and the trip was accomplished in eleven and a half hours.

By the 3rd February the companies had all foregathered at Kantara. The title of the company was now changed from the 1/3rd East Lancs. Field Company to the 429 Field Company;

the 1/1st and 1/2nd Field Companies at the same time taking the numbers 427 and 428 respectively.

On the 5th February we marched to El Ferdan, and the following day we went on to Moascar Camp. Here the divisional R.E. remained with the Division for five days, making tented camps and receiving lectures on "How things are done in France," and generally polishing up. The popularity of the ancient game of "House" was revived. Leave was granted to Ismailia. Flashes, or distinguishing patches, were first issued during our stay here, and were worn on the sleeves.

The R.E. left the infantry at Moascar on the 12th February, and went off by train to Alexandria, a much more interesting place; the only drawback was that we were installed at Gabbari Camp "A," of unpleasant memory. Colonel Mozley returned to the Division, and on the 13th Major Lawford therefore resumed command of the company. The chief occupation at Gabbari consisted in getting passes to the town, but occasionally we checked stores during the day, and we also learned a new and wonderful drill for unlimbering and limbering-up tool-carts; the preparation of this drill caused the C.R.E. and the R.S.M. several sleepless nights. It should be added that here the three companies paraded together for the first time.

CHAPTER II

FRANCE

(*March* 1917—*March* 1918)

EARLY in March the companies embarked in instalments for France, the main body of the 429 Field Company sailing on the 4th on board the s.s. *Menominee*. The crossing was a somewhat adventurous one, owing to submarines and bad weather, and no one was sorry to land at Marseilles on the 12th March. There were occasional submarine alarms during the voyage, and at one of these times, Lieutenant Kendall, expecting to have to spend a few days in an open boat, rushed into the officers' mess, and ordered Lance-Corporal Pettener to have some sandwiches made for him at once. It is not known whether he made any arrangements for a supply of liquid refreshments also.

After a train journey lasting forty-nine hours, we arrived at Pont Remy, and marched to Hocquincourt, near Abbeville, where we had our first experience of billets and of France. The long railway journey from Marseilles, although cold and none too comfortable, was in a way quite interesting. It was good to be in a Christian country once more, and it was very interesting for those who could do so, to try the effect of "school-boy" French on the civilians. Sometimes it worked, and sometimes it didn't. The train stopped on the bridge at Dijon for an hour or more, and the civilians, including many young ladies, seemed to want to cultivate our acquaintance. The number of souvenir buttons and cap badges (generally from some one else's cap) thrown down to them was enormous, and no doubt the C.Q.M.S. had a lot to say about it afterwards, when new ones were demanded to replace them. At Hocquincourt there was still snow on the ground, and the roads were inches deep in mud, and we began to think that the clean sand was not so bad after all; every one felt the cold very keenly.

We were kept very busy at Hocquincourt training, and being instructed in rapid wiring, and other matters concerning trench warfare. The new divisional sign had to be painted on all the vehicles; the company equipment had to be made up to the new mobilization store table; bicycles, tin hats, and respirators were drawn, and altogether C.Q.M.S. Walker had one of his busiest times. Major Lawford put up his extra pip here, and became Lieut.-Colonel Lawford. Lieutenant Sinclair and party returned on the 17th March from the 1st Division to whom they had been attached, and Colonel

429TH FIELD COY. R.E.

Lawford took a small party " up to the war " for five days to have a look at it.

No. 4 Section under Lieutenant Kendall left at this time to work at the Fourth Army School at Flexicourt. They rejoined the company later at Chuignolles. During their move, two of their tool-cart horses sat down in the middle of the road, and refused to move. While they were stuck there with a despairing driver wondering what to do next, and several sappers feeding them on biscuits, an A.S.C. officer appeared on a horse, and asked what the trouble was. On being told, he inquired to what unit they belonged. " R.E." he was told. " Ha-ha-ha ! The brains of the British Army," he said, and rode off laughing. Nice people, the A.S.C. ! !

A bridging school under Captain Courtis of the 428 Field Company, assembled at Erondelle on 26th March, and Nos. 1 and 2 Sections of the 429 Field Company were included. It broke up on the 28th, however, as we had to move forward. The two sections rejoined the company at Merelessart, and the following day we marched to Pont Remy and entrained for Chuignes, which was just behind the line recently evacuated by the Boche in his retreat. Detraining, we marched to Chuignolles. The transport moved up the whole way by road, under Captain Button. During this march Sapper Cook, the saddler, and some others found a house one night, which they thought would suit them well as a billet. It was dark at the time, and when they had settled down inside they found it draughty. Cook was always very particular about his bivvy or billet, no matter where it was, and he spent a long time making the door draught-proof. Having done this to his satisfaction, he settled down for the night; on waking in the morning, he found the real cause of the draught. The house had only three walls.

At Chuignolles, we had a French hutted camp in the R.E. Park, but on 31st March, Nos. 1 and 2 Sections moved up to Herbecourt, and lived in some old French dug-outs. One dug-out was occupied by Sergeants Evans and Linney and Sapper Thompson, and their reports on the behaviour of the rats were received with the usual pinch of salt by the rest of the company. They declared on one occasion that one had been seen to come in, put on its spectacles, look round, blow out the candle, and make off with it; while another one stole a greatcoat. The odd thing about this was not so much the tale itself, as the fact that there had been no possible means of obtaining an overdose of liquid refreshment.

While in these dug-outs also, Sergeants Evans and Linney made themselves responsible for calling at 3.30 a.m. a party going to Maricourt (Divisional Headquarters). During their rounds of the dug-outs, with which they were not too familiar, they knocked loudly at one door, and were astonished to receive, instead of the usual military reply, an invitation to " Come in." Investigating this extraordinary phenomenon, they discovered the C.R.E. sitting up in bed with a night-cap on (this is their tale) inquiring in his own inimitable way to what he was indebted for the honour of this early morning visit. At 3.30 a.m. that sort of thing is a little trying to all concerned, so they withdrew hurriedly.

The roads were in a deplorable state, and with a brigade or so of infantry as working party, the half company was fully occupied in trying to improve their condition. The weather was fearful, and snow, hail, and sleet swept continuously over the bleak and barren country.

On Easter Sunday, 8th April, the company moved up to Péronne, about three weeks after the evacuation by the enemy. Here we worked on roads, repaired buildings, made our first acquaintance with craters, and searched for booby traps and mines. We also met the 48th Divisional R.E., who said that we looked as brown as niggers. One hundred infantry with four officers were attached to us at this time as pioneers. This became later a sort of permanent working party, and except for short intervals while we were out of the line, we had a party of this size attached to us until early in 1918, when the Division had a pioneer battalion allotted to it. At Péronne, also, we had a roads officer named Johnson, who was promptly nicknamed " Massa " by the C.R.E.

The first leave allotment was received with great joy, and Captain Button left for England on the 14th April. The weather began to improve wonderfully, and when the Division went forward to take over the line from the 48th Division on 1st May, spring had come to stay. The 429 Field Company went to live in cellars in the village of Epéhy which, like all the others in the neighbourhood, was a heap of ruins. We soon found that Epéhy was a very unhealthy place, and as a first experience of front-line work on this front, it was a most unpleasant one. We had our first casualties while at Epéhy, and those who were there will probably never forget the day when so many good fellows were killed through a shell landing in a cellar where No. 3 Section lived. Fifteen were killed or died of wounds as a result. This was on 13th May, and with the exception of those who died in hosiptal, they were buried the following day in the cemetery behind the village.

Lieutenant Nicolson joined us at Epéhy, and had an unfortunate experience with a carrying party one night. They set out forty strong to carry wire and pickets up forward to a wiring job, Lieutenant Nicolson leading. Having some difficulty in finding the site of the work, he decided to have the material dumped until he found the exact place. Word was therefore passed back that all the wire and pickets were to be brought along to where Lieutenant Nicolson was standing, and were to be dumped there. All that arrived was two coils of barbed wire, the party having got tired of carrying the remainder and dropped it en route.

On the 15th May, Captain Allard came to us as second in command, as Captain Button went to hospital and later to the R.E. Base Depot, Rouen, as O. i/c Workshops. A few days later, we left Epéhy, and moved further north, the Division taking over the line in the Havrincourt Wood sector from the 20th Division. The 429

429TH FIELD COY. R.E.

Field Company went into Dessart Wood, near Fins, with two sections living forward in Gouzeaucourt Wood. This part of the front was quieter than Epéhy, and our camps in the woods were never shelled. The great objection was the distance we had to walk to our work up forward. We had a certain amount of wiring to do, and this was practically the last place where we took any considerable part in front-line wiring. On one night, the entire company and its one hundred attached infantry were employed on one wiring job. On this particular night, a newly-joined officer caused a certain amount of amusement. Having been told to be sure that he had the work properly organized, and being uncertain how much the company knew about this form of wiring, he went through a very long process of trying to detail every man to his exact job before starting out, explaining at some length what every one had to do. This naturally gave rise to some almost audible smiles. Corporal Craig finally put a stop to this performance by explaining that he had done this sort of job many a time before, and that the men knew all about it. After all these precautions, things did not work out as well as they might have done, as the party carrying up the wire was not large enough, with the result that there was not sufficient wire on the job to keep all the company employed, and a great number of them were never got to work at all. This has ever since been treated by some people as a vast joke, but most of the men concerned saw nothing funny in it at all, as they had a long walk up forward in the dark, and a long walk back, all for nothing. Fortunately, the infantry, who had asked for this job to be done by the R.E., were fairly satisfied with the amount of work that was done.

On another night, Captain Allard and a small party were interrupted in their work by a patrol of the enemy while they were setting out a line for wiring, and Sapper Foxcroft was wounded by the officer of the patrol. We did not get him back until the summer of 1918.

Colonel Lawford went on leave as soon as we arrived at Dessart Wood, and Captain Allard was therefore in charge of the company during this period. This company had had no previous experience of Captain Allard, and one or two people who had formed the habit of going through life rather drowsily, found themselves suddenly jerked into wakefulness and activity. Several N.C.O.s and men still experience a little shudder when they hear his name mentioned, and begin to wonder what they have done wrong lately. There is no doubt that the company was all the better as a result of making his acquaintance.

When Colonel Lawford returned from leave, we were in Havrincourt Wood; in the meantime, having stayed about a week at Dessart and Gouzeaucourt Woods, we had been back to Bus for a few days and had then gone up into Havrincourt Wood to work on a tramway. When the move from Bus up to Havrincourt Wood took place, the horse-lines went to Ytres, No. 4 Section going with them to make a camp for the drivers. Timber from ruined houses in the village was used to make huts, one of which later blew down in a gale in the middle of the night. Why No. 4 Section permitted themselves to build huts which could be blown over, is a mystery; probably it was the lack of the guiding hand of Lieutenant Kendall; it should have been mentioned, by the way, that he had left us at Epéhy.

The tramway in Havrincourt Wood, on which we went to work, kept the greater part of Sections 1, 2, and 3 and their attached infantry busy every night for about a week. At the end of that time, we handed it over to the 427 Field Company, and we then took over all the forward work of the 428 Field Company, No. 4 Section at the same time coming up from the horse-lines. While at work on the tramway, Sergeant Higgins had an encounter with an elusive Boche, or supposed Boche. Leaving the working party at work, he and Lieutenant Jones walked forward along the proposed route of the tramway through some long grass, to look at the ground, and see the work that had to be done, but they made the mistake of going more or less unarmed; the only weapons between them being one stout walking stick, and one bayonet. Approaching the support line trench, Lieutenant Jones, who was walking in front, was startled to hear Sergeant Higgins call out : "Hullo ! Hullo ! !" Turning round, he saw Sergeant Higgins dancing round a bush, and making frenzied thrusts into it with his bayonet, calling out the whole time "Hullo ! Hullo !" On inquiry, Sergeant Higgins explained that there was a man there. As there was no man visible, and no traces of any path through the grass by which he might have come or gone, the officer ventured to doubt this assertion. "I beg your pardon, sir, there is," was the indignant retort. "I saw him : he was looking out from this bush as you passed, and when I called out he turned and disappeared in the grass." On the strength of this, they visited a company commander in the support line, and suggested that he might like to have a search made. Although doubting the possibility of any one having got through the lines, he agreed that it was worth looking. So an N.C.O. and six men duly turned out to search, and began to prod inoffensive bushes with bayonets. The only result, however, was that Lieutenant Jones and an infantryman approached one bush simultaneously from opposite sides; the former prodded it with his walking stick, and the latter, seeing the resulting movement of the branches, prodded from the other side with a bayonet. Neither having seen the other, there was very nearly a nasty mess.

We remained about six weeks in Havrincourt Wood, and managed to make ourselves reasonably comfortable. Captain Allard produced a design for a standard hut to hold eight men. These huts were made of brushwood, of which there was plenty about; some of us, however, lived in tents. Work as usual was plentiful, and those who had to deal with the front-line trenches, found them muddy and unpleasant. On the 13th June, Sapper Flynn was unfortunately killed by a shell while at work in the front line, and Sapper Holt was wounded at the same time.

429TH FIELD COY. R.E.

Those of us whose work did not lie in the front line, had a better time, and struck some quite interesting jobs. No. 2 Section, for instance, had some work connected with water supply, and both No. 2 and No. 4 had some " Japanese Baths " to erect. This was an open-air bathing place on a kind of sausage machine principle. You put in a dirty man at one end, and he comes out clean at the other. Unfortunately, unless there was some one there to direct them which way to go, they always went the wrong way round, and upset the scheme.

The furnishing of a tunnelled Advanced Dressing Station by Lance-Corporal Pickles was another important item. Few people know all the details of the conferences that took place between Pickles and the medical people on the subject of how they should have their Advanced Dressing Station furnished. It is understood, however, that they all lived in terror of him, and that only very senior officers ventured to express any opinions on the subject. They were usually sat on, and the job was finished in the Pickles style throughout.

Another job that came our way was the digging of a lot of cable trenches, and at one time we had large parties of Guards working for us. Sergeant Gray was the man of the moment on these jobs, and he and the guardsmen used to measure the depth of trenches by their own height. As there is a good deal of difference between Sergeant Gray's five feet two inches and the six foot and over of the guardsmen, this produced at times some rather amusing " back-chat " on the subject of height.

One day Captain Allard, feeling that things needed stirring up a bit, sent for the orderly corporal, who happened to be 2nd Corporal Ogden. " What are your duties as orderly corporal? " asked the captain. After a few moments' thought, Ogden gave a resumé of what he did during the day, commencing at reveille, and finishing at " lights out," including parading orderlies, collecting the sick, etc., to all of which Captain Allard listened most patiently, as was his wont. In fact, it was this habit of patient listening which usually caused a man to get mixed, as he could count on every little bit of the conversation being stored up and probably repeated to him with more or less suitable comments. On this occasion, however, Ogden manfully waded through his day's work, and made it appear quite a lot. In fact, he persuaded himself that he was doing excellently, and that the job of orderly corporal was most important for the running of the company. Captain Allard, on completion of this recital, simply said : " All wrong, all wrong ! The orderly corporal's duties are to see that orders are obeyed."

Early in July, Captain Allard left us, and went as Brigade Major to the 176th Infantry Brigade, in the 59th Division. A few days later, we handed over to the 58th Division, and moved back to Achiet-le-Petit; there Lieutenant Bogle of the 427 Field Company came to us as captain. We had not been long at Achiet when Lieutenant Sinclair went sick, and left us, to every one's regret. Later, in 1918, we were sorry to hear that he had been killed while with the 66th Division. Lieutenant Hughes, arriving from home, replaced him.

At Achiet, the great idea in life was training and sports, and on the whole we had a very good time. We distinguished ourselves by winning a very fine cup presented by the C.R.E. to the winning company in competitions in Musketry, Rapid Wiring, and Football. In wiring particularly, Corporal Ogden's squad was far ahead of those of the other two companies. In football, though we beat the 428, we lost to the 427 Field Company. Unfortunately, the C.R.E.'s cup arrived two days before we moved from Achiet, and it had to be packed up again hurriedly, and sent home. Colonel Lawford made arrangements for its care until such time as we could all get together again at home. It has since been brought to the East Lancs. R.E. Headquarters at Old Trafford, Manchester.

We also had inter-section sports, comprising a large number of events, and extending over quite a long period. No. 4 Section finally won, though No. 3 Section ran them very close, thanks to Lieutenant Morrey's sprinting. The last event was a mounted tug-of-war, and No. 4 Section's drivers, headed by Lance-Corporal J. Robinson, came to the rescue, and won this event for them, thus just getting ahead of No. 3.

As to training, we did quite a lot of R.E. work, including some bridging, for which we went to Beaucourt-sur-Ancre for a few days; also on two occasions we were included in brigade attack schemes with the 127th Brigade. During one of these, No. 4 Section had a small forward dump of wire, etc., very far forward—in fact, too far forward—and there congregated vast carrying parties, and two pack horses. The 1/8th Manchesters had their Battalion Headquarters at the same place, and as it was only just behind the line from which the attack was to start, and on a comparatively high piece of ground, it was of course rather ridiculous to suppose that things could have been carried out that way in an actual attack. The Divisional Commander, riding round, saw the absurdity of the situation, and wanted to know the why and the wherefore. He opened his attack on the R.E. party, and had quite a lot to say about it. Talking to the section officer, he concluded his remarks as follows : " My dear boy, don't you realize that you and your men would be pushing the daisies up by this time. You would be absolutely useless. As for those pack-horses, send them home; they'd have been dead long since." Then he passed on to the 8th Manchesters to tell them all about their misdeeds. The pack-horses were accordingly despatched to the place where Colonel Lawford had established his Company Headquarters, with a note to explain their untimely demise. They remained with Colonel Lawford for the rest of the day, and enabled him to get his own back. For, during the afternoon, the Divisional Commander saw them, and wanted to have them used for some purpose in connection with the scheme. Not recognizing them as those he had seen before, he asked for them. Colonel Lawford thought it would be very inconvenient to send them on this particular job, so he refused on the grounds that they were dead. As they were obviously very much alive, the general wanted an explanation; but, on being told that he himself had ordered them out of action, he retired in good order and left them.

It was at Achiet that the ceremony of "orderly room" was relieved of some of its solemnity by a certain driver who was charged with breaking branches off a cherry tree, contrary to standing orders. A witness gave evidence that he had seen the branches broken by the accused. The following then took place—

O.C. (to witness): "You say you saw the accused break some branches?"

Witness: "Yes, sir."

O.C. (to accused): "What have you to say?"

Accused: "I didn't break any branches, sir; I might have snapped off a few twigs by accident."

O.C.: "What do you mean by twigs? How do you draw the line between them? When do you say a twig becomes a branch?"

Accused: "I suppose in years to come, sir."

This startling answer took the O.C. so completely by surprise that all he could do on the spur of the moment was to remand the case until the next day.

We left Achiet on the 21st August, and went to Ypres, travelling most of the distance by train. We moved first to a hutted camp just outside the village of Bouzincourt, which is near Albert, and entrained two days later at Aveluy. While at Bouzincourt, some people managed to get into Albert, and Colonel Lawford had some tin whistles bought there; the idea being that each section should have a sort of tin-whistle band, trained by Sapper Carter of No. 3 Section. This did not materialize, as Sapper Carter was wounded soon after our arrival at Ypres.

Our experience of Ypres was limited to three weeks, but it was sufficient to learn what a particularly objectionable spot it was. No very noteworthy incidents occurred during our stay there, but the motor cycle issued to us—as was usual for field companies in that sector—provided Colonel Lawford with a constant source of amusement. He was generally to be found with a valve in one hand and a spanner in the other, while his conversation was of carburettors rather than of camouflage; of oil pumps rather than of trench pumps.

The greater part of our work here consisted of clearing out old Boche dug-outs, which were in a fearful state; very obnoxious work. The horse-lines, at Brandhoek, had a bomb unpleasantly near them one day, and a pontoon was damaged. Up forward, gas was the chief trouble, and Sappers Harvey and Whealing went to hospital gassed, while Sapper Carter was wounded by a shell splinter.

The next sector we went to after Ypres was on the coast, Company Headquarters being in Nieuport Bains. Here we took over from the 66th Division, and met several old friends amongst them. The billets were quite good—in cellars of hotels, etc., all connected up by tunnelled passages, and having entrances from a covered trench leading up from the Laiterie Royale about a mile back, where there was an R.E. dump.

There was talk of a " push " in the near future, and with a view to taking part in the crossing of the Yser, a party under Lieutenant Hughes went to Furnes to practice pontoon rowing drill in gas masks in the canal there. Nothing came of this, however, and early in October we moved into Nieuport itself, taking over from the 32nd Division, while the 41st took over the coastal sector. While on the coast, one was reminded a little of Egypt, as there was quite a broad belt of sand dunes running about half a mile inland from the sea.

In the Nieuport sector, we remained six weeks. The company billets were in some huts built into a railway embankment by the French. Fortunately they were strongly built, and had quite a lot of overhead cover, for we had to put up with a good deal of shelling from time to time. The arrival of rations in the evening was a time often chosen by the Boche for a little display of hate, and it was a trying time for drivers. The road all the way up from Coxyde, where the horse-lines were situated, was liable to be shelled, but no great disaster ever occurred so far as we were concerned. In this we were very fortunate, as night after night we had strings of G.S. wagons bringing up stores for us, as well as our ration wagon. There were of course some close shaves, and on one night in particular the ration wagon had a very hot time while it was being unloaded at Company Headquarters. Lance-Corporal J. Robinson, who was in charge of it, was afterwards awarded the Belgian Croix de Guerre for his conduct on this occasion.

Corporal Hamilton, when he came up with the ration wagon, always managed to strike a bad night, and a shell splinter grazed the side of his head one night while he was waiting at Company Headquarters. Colonel Lawford and the C.S.M. were standing near by, and running up to them he said, " What shall I do ? What shall I do ? What would you do ? " " Wash it off," said the C.S.M., laughing. " It's all —— fine for you two —— standing there laughing at me," said Corporal Hamilton, " but I've been hit in the clock."

We had only been at Nieuport a day when we lost Corporal S. C. Mort and Lance-Corporal Wright, a loss which we could ill afford. Corporal Mort was an extremely capable N.C.O., and had been transferred a short time previously from No. 4 to No. 1 Section, to act as section sergeant. Wright, though he had not long been a lance-corporal, was one of the most promising junior N.C.O.'s. They were with Lieutenant Hughes visiting a patrol whose duty was to keep an eye on some bridges which were subject to shell fire, report damage, effect small repairs, etc. Walking along a trench, the whole party were practically blown out of it by a shell falling just behind them. Lieutenant Hughes got off with wounds, and was not long off duty, but the other two were killed outright. They were buried at Coxyde the following day.

429TH FIELD COY. R.E.

The attached infantry did not live with the company here, but lived in the town itself, in a building which had some strong cellars. Fortunately there were a number of such buildings, but it was at the best an unpleasant town to live in.

On the whole, the work at Nieuport was probably the most trying the company ever had. It involved the maintenance of a number of bridges, of which the most objectionable were three horrible little floating foot-bridges made of cork floats and duckboards. Being vital to the holding of the front line, they naturally came in for a good deal of shelling, and as they were about 320 feet long, they were not difficult to damage. Hardly a day passed without one or other being broken, and even when this did not happen there was constant work required to maintain them in passable condition. Bad breaks often necessitated parties being turned out in the middle of the night, and no one could be sure when he went to bed that he was going to get a decent night's sleep. These three bridges were known as Putney, Crowder and Vauxhall bridges, but as well as these there were a large number of others to be maintained. The others, however, were not shelled quite so much as these three.

For repair work under shell fire one particularly bad day, when all three bridges were broken, Lieutenant Nicolson was awarded the M.C. and Corporal Brightmore, Sappers Rylance and Bennett the M.M. On the 8th November we had the misfortune to lose Sapper Galpine, who was killed on bridge work.

At one time when Vauxhall bridge was out of action, it was necessary to get a cable across the river in order to get on with the repairs. There were four wire cables for each of these bridges, the floats being attached to them, but on this occasion all the cables were broken. Sapper T. Wright volunteered to swim across with a rope; not at all an inviting job in that cold weather, but he managed it successfully, and so enabled the repairs to be completed very much quicker than would have been the case otherwise.

A bridge casualty diary was kept, and the following extract from it (from 19th October to 8th November) shows how frequently these three bridges, Putney, Crowder and Vauxhall, were damaged. It also contains references to other bridges.

Bridge.	Damage.	Time.	Date.	Repaired.	Time.	Date.
PUTNEY	Floats, duckboards,	1.0 p.m.	18.10.17	Repaired & opened	12.20 p.m.	19.10.17
	Handrails	5.20 p.m.	18.10.17			
VAUXHALL	Floats, duckboards, & handrails	2.45 p.m.	18.10.17	Repaired & opened	4.0 a.m.	19.10.17
,,	1 float waterlogged	3.30 p.m.	19.10.17			
	Float & duckboard	9.10 p.m.	19.10.17			

Bridge.	Damage.	Time.	Date.	Repaired.	Time.	Date.
VAUXHALL	Waterlogged & hit by shell-fire all day		20.10.17			
,,				Repair work carried on intermittently between shell fire		21.10.17
Bridge Dump	Shelled. Gunnels damaged		21.10.17			
VAUXHALL	Still impassable		22.10.17	Repairs continued		22.10.17
CROWDER	Float & duckboard	4.20 p.m.	22.10.17	Repaired	1.5 a.m.	23.10.17
PUTNEY	1 float	4.20 p.m.	22.10.17	Repaired & opened	5.55 pm.	22.10.17
,,	Float & duckboard	10.0 p.m.	22.10.17	Repaired & opened	1.0 a.m.	23.10.17
VAUXHALL				Passable. Repairs not complete	8.45 a.m.	23.10.17
,,				Repairs completed	2.25 p.m.	23.10.17
CROWDER	1 float	2.25 p.m.	23.10.17			
,,	2 floats. Direct hits	4.15 p.m.	23.10.17	Repaired & opened	4.55 p.m.	23.10.17
PUTNEY	½ float hit	4.15 p.m.	23.10.17	Repaired	8.30 p.m.	23.10.17
DAM 66	Damaged. Passable		23.10.17	No repairs		
CROWDER	Slight damage by tide		24.10.17	Repaired	10.30 a.m.	24.10.17
,,	Float & gunnel	2.15 p.m.	24.10.17	Repaired	7.30 p.m.	24.10.17
23	Trestle & two duckboards	2.15 p.m.	24.10.17	Repaired	5.30 p.m.	27.10.17
VAUXHALL	Floats, gunnels & duckboard	3.0 p.m.	24.10.17	Repaired & opened	7.0 p.m.	25.10.17
46	Roadway damaged	2.45 a.m.	25.10.17	Repaired & opened	9.50 a.m.	25.10.17
56	Slight	2.45 a.m.	25.10.17	Repaired & opened	9.50 a.m.	25.10.17
25	Duckboards	9.0 a.m.	25.10.17	Temporary	7.0 a.m.	26.10.17
				Repairs complete	2.45 p.m.	26.10.17

429TH FIELD COY. R.E.

Bridge.	Damage.	Time.	Date.	Repaired.	Time.	Date.
ROWDER	Float, cable, gunnel & duckboards	3.20 p.m.	26.10.17	Repaired	10.53 p.m.	26.10.17
22	Roadway	2.15 p.m.	27.10.17	Repaired	4.0 p.m.	27.10.17
UTNEY	2 floats, gunnels, & duckboard	2.15 p.m.	28.10.17	Repaired	8.30 p.m.	28.10.17
AUXHALL	2 floats, gunnels, & duckboard	3.0 p.m.	28.10.17	Repaired	9.30 p.m.	28.10.17
,,	Float, duckboard, gunnels & handrails	5.15 p.m.	29.10.17	Repaired	9.45 p.m.	29.10.17
46	Duckboard broken	5.30 p.m.	29.10.17	Repaired		30.10.17
UTNEY	4 floats, gunnels, duckboards; cable broken	3.0 p.m.	30.10.17	Repaired	4.0 a.m.	31.10.17
22	Roadway	3.15 p.m.	31.10.17	Repaired	9.45 a m.	1.11.17
Bridges	all correct		2.11.17			
24	Approach & handrail		3.11.17	Repaired	8.15 a.m.	3.11.17
AUXHALL	2 floats, gunnels, duckboards	10.30 a.m.	3.11.17	Repaired	5.30 p.m.	3.11.17
ROWDER	Float, gunnel, & duckboard	7.20 p.m.	3.11.17	Repaired	9.30 p.m.	3.11.17
28	Roadway. Slight		4.11.17	Repaired		4.11.17
29				New handrail		4.11.17
AUXHALL	Float, gunnel & duckboard	4.20 p.m.	4.11.17	Repaired	7.0 a.m.	5.11.17
ROWDER	Float, gunnel, & duckboard	4.20 p.m.	4.11.17	Repaired	11.15 a.m.	5.11.17
All bridges passable			6.11.17			
All bridges passable			7.11.17			
BRIDGE OF SIGHS	2 shell holes in roadway. Structure of bridge intact	10.15 a.m.	8.11.17	Repaired	4.20 p.m.	8.11.17
UTNEY	Duckboard. Slight	5.0 p.m.	8.11.17	Repaired	5.30 p.m.	8.11.17

Another job which was perhaps more unpleasant than these bridges was " Dam 66," but this was not long in our hands. It involved concreting, generally under shell fire. The 427 Field

Company, who took it over from us, had several casualties on it.

Amongst other things, we put up an aerial ropeway across the Yser, and there was one occasion when Lance-Corporal Edsforth was left suspended in mid-air within about a foot of the water, because the party hauling him across found the shelling too hot and had to stop hauling. His opinions on the subject were interesting, but quite unprintable.

A concrete O.P. which we constructed in a ruined house close beside the company billets had an element of uncertainty about it, though there were never any accidents there.

We had several men wounded at Nieuport, but fortunately most cases were slight. For the work done while we were there, Colonel Lawford was awarded the Belgian Croix de Guerre, and so also were C.S.M. Cowsill and Sapper Spaven, in addition to the other decorations already mentioned.

We left Nieuport on 19th November, handing over to the French. Captain Bogle went to hospital sick the day before we left, and subsequently went to England, and we never got him back. Colonel Lawford, two days before we left, went to act as C.R.E., as Colonel MacInnes was going on leave.

We next went to Gorre, in the La Bassée sector, and here we had what was perhaps the best billet for a company working in the line that one could find in France; that is, Gorre Brewery. It was not only that it was a brewery actually in operation, though one might expect that to be some attraction, but it was a really good billet, and was handed over by the 130 Field Company of the 25th Division in excellent condition. Even the horse lines, for once, were good.

The march down there from Nieuport took altogether nine days: the first day by lorry from Coxyde—though we had to march to Coxyde from Nieuport—the next four days marching. This brought us to La Roupie, just outside Aire. We spent two days there, and then finished off with another two days' marching. A rather formidable march, but it passed off quite well, in spite of some rain on the second and third days. The stopping places were: first night, near Teteghem; second night, Wylder, in the Wormhoudt area; third night, Zermezeele; fourth night, La Nieppe; fifth, sixth and seventh nights, La Roupie; eighth night, Mont Bernenchon. We moved for the first five days with the 125th Infantry Brigade, and after that came under the orders of the 127th Infantry Brigade.

At Teteghem we had a little difficulty with our billet, as we were allotted a farm, and an infantry company were allotted the same farm. After a certain amount of argument, we both managed to fit in. The transport had difficulties on the first, second and fifth days, and did not get in until late. The chief source of trouble was pontoon wagons getting ditched on narrow roads, though on the first day this was not the cause of the delay; on this day it was a case of missing a guide and losing the way.

At Mont Bernenchon there was some trouble with an old lady at one of the billets. One of the section cooks, being short of firewood, inquired where he was to find some; being told to try and find some for himself about the village, he went and found a gate. It made excellent firewood, no doubt, and the section got their evening meal, but unfortunately the place where the gate was taken from was close beside the owner's house. The owner rose up in her wrath and demanded payment. It was decided to make a new gate for her, and on arrival at Gorre, Lance-Corporal Broadbent and his workshop men got busy and made her a very fine one, much better than the original. Broadbent himself went back with it to fix it for her, and he and the lady were, of course, friends for life. It is understood that the quality of her beer (or was it wine?) was distinctly above the average.

Speaking of cooks, what extraordinary people they are on a move! We march all day, and at the end we get into a more or less uncomfortable billet, praise Heaven for small mercies, and prepare to settle down for the night, the only disturbing thought being how many —— miles we have to go the next day. But the cooks all this time are cooking our dinner. They are probably short of firewood, and have no proper cookhouse, but in an astonishingly short time they produce a meal. Nobody knows how they do it. After that they think about some water for breakfast in the morning. Some time in the evening they get to bed. Breakfast is sure to be ordered by some heartless individual at the head of affairs for some unearthly hour in the morning, and in the cold grey dawn the cooks are up, lighting fires (still with no firewood, and probably no matches) and getting the breakfast ready. Then they spend a feverish time packing up their gear and getting it loaded on the transport; and finally, when the company parades to march off, an irate C.S.M. wants to know why they are not ready at the proper time. And so the day's march starts again.

La Bassée was an interesting, and on the whole a quiet, sector— a great change after Nieuport, and almost as good as a rest. We did a great deal of concrete work, more than we did in any other sector; and some very strong shelters built by Messrs. Paul, Gray & Co. in the front line in Givenchy village were quite out of the ordinary. The work of the company in general was very varied, but individual men worked for long periods on the same jobs, and did not see much variation in it. Drainage was quite a problem in itself, and there was a vast system of drains and ditches, the main one being known as the Suez Canal. This drained out both ways from the centre of our sector, running to the right into the La Bassée Canal, and to the left into the Portuguese sector, and finally into the River Lawe.

There was also a fair amount of screening along roads to be looked after, and for a time we did some work on gun-pits. Dotted about all over the sector were various keeps and redoubts, which were arranged to hold out in the event of a hostile attack. Each one had water storage arrangements, and this came under our supervision. For supplying water to the neighbourhood of the front line there were three pipe lines. These occasionally gave trouble, either as a result of shelling or through frost.

We were in this sector two and a half months, and during part of the time there was a severe frost; the subsequent thaw brought considerable trouble. Trenches caved in and became impassable, roads got into a shocking state; and, as has just been mentioned, there were difficulties with the water supply.

The three outstanding incidents of this period were: first, the unfortunate day when the horse lines were shelled, and Drivers Jones and Walker were killed, and Muldoon, Snelson and France were wounded; secondly, Christmas, which was celebrated by an unusually large feed and a concert; thirdly, the raid at Givenchy by the 1/9th Battalion, Manchester Regt., in which Lieutenant Chapman, Lance-Corporal Collins, and six sappers of the 429 Field Company took part.

This raid was a great success, and Collins and Tudor were awarded the Military Medal for their share in it; at a later date, T. H. Johnson was also awarded the Military Medal for the same thing.

Although there was plenty of front-line work here, the only casualties we had in this sector were the drivers already referred to, and Sappers Cook and Burslem. The former of these was wounded by a shell while working at some new trench mortar emplacements, and we were sorry to hear later that he had died in hospital. Burslem was slightly wounded at the advanced R.E. Dump at "Windy Corner," where he lived and had charge of the dump.

On February 13, 1918, we came out of the line, and moved to Les Harisoirs, behind Béthune. This was a very muddy place, and after a week another move took place into Hinges, where Divisional Headquarters was situated at that time. On the 14th March we again moved—to Oblinghem—as Hinges was then required as a Corps Headquarters by 11th Corps, who were just returning from Italy.

At this time mange was prevalent among the horses of the Division, and we did not escape it. The drivers' nightly catechism was a great feature of the measures taken to stamp it out. At 6.0 p.m. each evening the drivers had to be paraded at the orderly room, to have certain facts about mange read over to them by the O.C. After the reading of the "lesson," something like this used to take place—

O.C.: "Now, who's responsible if mange breaks out—you or the veterinary officer?"

Chorus: "We are, sir."

O.C.: "And if you think a horse has mange, what do you do?"

Chorus: "Isolate it, sir."

O.C.: "And what next?"

429TH FIELD COY. R.E.

Chorus : " Report it, sir."
O.C. : " And how do you know when a horse has mange ? "

But here the chorus was not very uniform. They all wanted to express themselves differently, and it usually ended in one or two of them struggling through a long answer which ended by saying that the horse would "respond" by twitching its mouth as if it were pleased when scratched.

There were days at Hinges when one Kanolty used to retire to a distant field with a trumpet and a packet of cigarettes, and at intervals between cigarettes, discordant noises would float down the wind. It was perhaps a pity that after all this practice he did not sound stable calls every day. Perhaps, on the other hand, it was just as well.

At Hinges, also, the batmen distinguished themselves by discovering a sort of salvage dump in the top floor of their billet. The lady of the house had apparently collected enormous quantities of army clothing and stores. The result of this was a raid on the premises carried out by the military police and the gendarmerie, assisted by the local Maire, in which they unearthed about a G.S. wagon-load of socks, cardigans, shirts, and other clothing and stores—including even some bottles of pickles !

Another incident was the affair of the matches. Late one night a wire was received ordering all matches to be isolated immediately. Colonel Lawford thereupon ordered all matches to be collected at once. This was about 10.30 p.m., and sleeping sappers found themselves rudely awakened and being asked to hand over matches forthwith. Sort of " Stand and deliver " business. It turned out afterwards that something had gone wrong with a consignment of matches of one particular brand, and they were considered to be unsafe, so this order had been sent out pending further investigations.

During all this time there was a great deal of work going on in preparation for the expected enemy offensive. Round the villages of Lestrem, Locon, Zelobes, etc., miles of wire were put up; while at Vieille Chapelle on the River Lawe, and between Gorre and Béthune on the La Bassée Canal, pontoon bridges were prepared for hasty erection.

CHAPTER III

FRANCE

(*March* 1918—*April* 1919)

WHEN the offensive opened further south on 21st March we were still at Oblinghem, and the first we heard of it was on the evening of the 22nd. About 9.30 p.m. orders came for a move the following morning, and as Sections 2 and 3 had just been sent to Noeux-les-Mines to work under the C.E., 1st Corps, and part of No. 4 Section was away at Burbure erecting a Y.M.C.A. hut, these detachments had to be hurriedly recalled. It had been previously arranged that in the event of such an emergency a motor lorry would report at the church to move our surplus stores to a central dump at Gonnehem. Within a very short time of the receipt of the order, the lorry duly turned up, and all stores which could not be carried on our own transport were sent off by this means to Gonnehem, two sappers going with them to look after them. All night long the preparations for the move went on. Sections 2 and 3 and part of No. 4 did not reach Company Headquarters until the early hours of the morning of the 23rd, but shortly before 9.0 a.m. everything was ready and we left.

The transport went off separately under Lieutenant Hughes, and the rest of us marched to Labuissière, where we embussed with the 125th Infantry Brigade. After travelling all day in lorries we finally reached Adinfer, and marched from there to Ayette, where we settled down between 10.0 and 11.0 p.m. under hedges for the night.

The next fortnight was a time of continual anxiety, frequent movement, and little sleep. Reviewing it after the passing of months, one is struck by the fact that we did singularly little useful work. We spent most of the 24th at Ayette, and a site was selected for the horse lines at Douchy-lez-Ayette, the transport being expected in the evening. In the late afternoon we moved up to take over the line from the 40th Division. The position of the line was uncertain and was constantly changing, and owing to a miscarriage of orders we did not meet the guides of the field company which we were supposed to relieve.

These guides should have been met in Logeast Wood at a place called Forest Lodge, but as they did not turn up it was decided to go on to Gomiecourt, where at least one of our own infantry brigades was known to be situated. On arriving at the railway bridge north of Achiet-le-Grand station, however, reports were received to the effect that the line was moving back and was now quite close, and there appeared to be some doubt as to whether it would be possible to reach Gomiecourt.

The 429 Field Company, with the 427, which was also moving in the same direction, were therefore disposed along the railway embankment, while the two O.C.'s went forward to Gomiecourt. Reaching the Château without difficulty, they found the headquarters of two brigades, and it turned out that the line was not so close as had been supposed. From Brigade Headquarters instructions were received to move the two field companies further north, and dig in along the railway cutting immediately west of Gomiecourt.

Touch was also established with the 40th Divisional R.E., and the matter of the carrying out of the relief was settled. We remained in the railway cutting for the remainder of the night, and until late in the afternoon of the 25th, the line, so far as we could judge, being more or less stationary. It was, as a matter of fact, during this time that the infantry of the Division were making a name for themselves, and possibly history for future generations, by holding on and making counter-attacks against great odds. We saw nothing of this, however, and could only judge how things were going by the amount of shelling that went on. At first there was no shelling near us; then we noticed that Gomiecourt was being shelled slightly; then this increased to very heavy shelling, and various people who passed us going to and from the village appeared to find great difficulty in getting in and out of it. Later still we had some shelling near us in the railway cutting, and several batteries of our own field guns took up positions in a field behind us, and started to fire rapidly. Shelling of Courcelles-le-Comte then started and gradually increased in volume.

The railway metals were, of course, still bright, and signals in working order, and it was curious to think that so short a time before there had been leave trains running along this identical line, while here were we dug into the bank of the cutting and trying to look fierce, waiting for the enemy, and Courcelles, to our left and slightly behind us, was being shelled to bits.

During the afternoon Colonel Lawford and Major Mousley both received orders to report at 127th Brigade Headquarters, and it was then found that the Brigade had moved out of Gomiecourt, and had established their headquarters at a place more in the open and less liable to heavy shelling. It turned out that a retirement was to take place, and in the late afternoon we moved back into Logeast Wood and spent the night in a camp of Nissen huts. The situation round Achiet-le-Grand was at this time rather obscure, and some people said that it was in the hands of the enemy. Apparently this was not the case, however, and it does not appear to have been occupied by them till early the following morning. During the day of the 25th, while waiting in the railway cutting, some people had been into Achiet and had found the E.F. Canteen evacuated, but still full of stores, and they brought back with them some cigarettes and other useful things—such as a tin or two of Café au Lait; while during the night Colonel Lawford and Lieutenant Nicolson went forward from Logeast Wood to 127th Brigade Headquarters, and had to pass quite close to Achiet in doing so, and it was apparently not in enemy hands then.

Early the following morning (26th) we received orders to withdraw to Essarts-lez-Bucquoy, as the whole line was being withdrawn to Bucquoy.

The transport, meanwhile, had missed Douchy on the night of the 24th, and in the early hours of the morning on the 25th had arrived at Ablainzeville; later the same day they moved back through Ayette to their appointed site at Douchy. From here they were able to get some rations and deliver them to the company during the early hours of the morning of the 26th, just before the move back from Logeast Wood to Essarts.

When this withdrawal to Essarts took place the transport lines had to go there also, and orders were therefore sent to Lieutenant Hughes to get away to Essarts as quickly as he could. They packed up and got on the move in record time, and leaving Sapper Roebuck in charge of a small dump of stores which they could not carry, they passed through Ayette to Bucquoy, and so back to Essarts, from where they were sent still further back to Bienvillers-au-Bois. It was fortunate that they were so quick getting on the move, as this road which they used was the only one which was known to be in passable condition, and necessitated moving forward to Bucquoy, and then turning back to Essarts. Had they been half an hour later, it is doubtful whether they would have got through Bucquoy. As it was, the only trouble they had was a bomb which fell unpleasantly near them as they were passing along the road between Ayette and Bucquoy. Roebuck and his stores were got back by another route later.

The retreat on this part of the front was now over, for the line at Bucquoy resisted all further attacks, thanks to the infantry of the 42nd Division; up to this time we had done nothing that could be called useful work. Our activities may be shortly summarized as follows : we had dug some recessed bits of trench in the side of a railway cutting; we had had three casualties; and we had captured three prisoners. The casualties were Sapper J. T. Evans, J. Holdsworth and Pioneer A. Smith. Sapper Evans was thought to have been only slightly wounded by shell fire while crossing the open from Gomiecourt railway cutting back to Logeast Wood on the afternoon of the 25th. He walked to the dressing station, and we were astonished as well as grieved to hear later that he had died in hospital in England. Sapper Holdsworth was only slightly wounded, and Pioneer Smith went off with shell-shock. The capture of the three prisoners was due to Sapper Fielding and another sapper, who were cycling through Logeast Wood towards

429TH FIELD COY. R.E. 185

Achiet-le-Grand on the morning of the 26th, looking for the headquarters of the 427 Field Company to deliver a message. They met these three Boche walking along in the opposite direction. It was not clear how or why they came to be there, but they were duly bagged and handed over to those interested in the species.

There followed a most uncomfortable time, and it was found necessary to alter our rôle several times. First, we were to get defences constructed; then we were to go into the line with the infantry; then that was altered and we were told to rest and be prepared for any old thing; then we were to do some wiring. We did actually spend two days in the line, as will be explained presently.

From the 26th to the 29th March was spent in this uncertain manner, sometimes doing some work in the front line, improving trenches, sometimes working for the support battalion of the 127th Brigade, making them some weatherproof shelters, etc., and on the night of the 29th March we left Essarts at 11.0 p.m. and moved into Gommecourt Wood, where we went into some old German dug-outs. During the 30th and 31st March and the 1st April the line was held by the 41st Division. This did not mean a rest for the 42nd, however, as we had to work on defences in the neighbourhood of Essarts. It was just about this time that Essarts began to get really unpleasant, and from now onwards it was subject to very heavy shelling. It was fortunate for us that we moved out of the village when we did.

When the 42nd Division went back into the line on the night of 1st/2nd April, the 429 Field Company went into the line with the 1/10th Manchesters, and remained there with them for two days. After that it was found possible to employ us definitely on defensive works, and accordingly we left the 1/10th Manchesters, and went back again into old dug-outs. These were not the ones we had occupied for the previous three days, but were quite near them, and were in a wood called Pigeon Wood, which joined on to Gommecourt Wood. Here we remained until the 42nd Division finally left the line on the 8th April, on which date we handed over to a field company of the 62nd Division, and moved back to Hénu.

During the period 26th March to 8th April we had done a fair amount of useful work in various ways, mostly on a defensive line called the " Purple " line between Essarts and Gommecourt, but it was disjointed work, and somewhat scattered.

Our transport had not had such a bad time as that of some other units, but it was by no means an enviable job taking rations up to the company when they were anywhere near Essarts. The main road up from Bienvillers through Hannescamps and Essarts to Bucquoy was heavily shelled, more especially between Hannescamps and Essarts, where there were a large number of batteries of field guns close beside the road, and any transport which had to pass along that part of the road had a very bad time. Our own horse lines moved on the 2nd April from Bienvillers to Souastre, and remained there until the whole company went to Hénu, when, of course, the horse lines came too.

On the whole we seem to have come very well out of a very trying time; our greatest troubles were lack of sleep, and during the latter part of the time bad weather and inky black nights.

We were not long at Henu. We had time to have baths, and to be inspected by the Divisional Commander at Pas, and then we had to go and work on a defensive line known as the "Château de la Haie Switch." For this purpose we lived in bivouacs on the side of a hill west of Sailly-au-Bois. The drawback to this place was a railway gun, which used to come up almost daily to fire from a railway just behind us, making a frightful noise. This gun went by the name of "Copper-knob." Later, several other railway guns appeared in this locality.

On the 16th April we moved from these bivvies into Sailly itself, where we lived in cellars, with Company Headquarters in the Mairie, and simultaneously the Division went back into the line in the Hébuterne–Gommecourt sector, taking over from the 37th Division; we therefore found ourselves working round Hébuterne.

Sailly at this time was reasonably quiet. About once in four days the Boche used to let it have about ten minutes of small shells, generally in the evening, and during one of these bursts a shell landed in a house of which the cellar was occupied by some of No. 1 Section, and wounded three of them—Lance-Corporal Penney and Sappers Waller and Malone. Penney went to hospital the next day and did not return to us, as he went to a cadet school when he got home. Malone was rather badly hit, but Waller was soon all right again. Later, after we had left it, Sailly got rather badly knocked about. This was not surprising, for during April the number of guns in the neighbourhood increased to enormous proportions, some of them being almost in the village itself.

Hébuterne was no sort of place to stand about in, although it was nothing like as bad as Essarts had been. The only man who was ever known to enjoy it was Sergeant Gray, but that was because it had an old mill in it, with a certain amount of machinery. However, it was later, in June, that he really came to find this out.

On May 1st Lieut.-Colonel Lawford left us and went to the 15th Corps as C.R.E. Corps Troops. He had been in command during the whole period of the company's active service, and after this long association one felt lost without his familiar figure, and it took some time to get used to the sensation of having a new O.C. Major Riddick was appointed to succeed him in the command, but did not actually join us until 31st May, as he was attached temporarily to the 126th Infantry Brigade. During the early part of the month we moved back into Couin Woods, and the Division came out of the line for a month. During this month at Couin there was a good deal of work done on defences round the Château de la Haie, Sailly, Bayencourt, etc. Among other items we had some tunnelled dug-outs to make; this was the first time we had had much of this work.

429TH FIELD COY. R.E. 187

On going back into the line on the 7th June we took over from the New Zealand Engineers a camp west of Sailly, which was practically on the same spot as where we had bivouacked for a few days in April; the place from which " Copper-knob " used to fire. This had been made into a really comfortable camp by the New Zealand people, and " Copper-knob " had ceased to fire from this position, so it was quite a pleasant place in which to live. The camp consisted of a large number of small huts built into the side of a bank. Some of them had rather appropriate names, and others were soon christened.

" Teetotal Tavern," for instance, was occupied by Sergeant Evans and Corporal Brightmore. Corporal Marsden, of course, went into " Umlanga's Retreat," and among No. 1 Section's huts one was soon called " Waugh-Lorne Cottage." No. 4 Section went one better and produced " Gas-proof Chambers " with a list of tenants on the door. These were—

Ground Floor :	Prof. H. R. Norman	The unlimited supply company.
1st Floor :	Inspector Hitchin	The human sleuthhound.
2nd Floor :	Geoff. Tudor	The professional shadow.
3rd Floor :	T. Wright	Sick Reporter to Heapy's Weekly.
4th Floor :	A. Cooper, A.M.I.C.E., A.M.I.M.E., A.M.I.E.E., A.S.S.	Advice given free.

This particular hut also claimed at one time to be the " Royal Hotel "—Proprietor : Jeff. Tudor, licensed to sell Wiggie's tea, pies and army duff.

Speaking of Wiggie's pies, by the way, reminds us that while we were in this camp, an influenza epidemic started, and a fair number went to hospital, Wigglesworth among them.

The horse lines were behind Bus-les-Artois, and Divisional Headquarters in Bus village. The horse lines blossomed out with white posts and ropes all over the place, and looked like a sort of exhibition garden city. The horse lines of the other two field companies were adjoining our own.

Our drivers at various times have had mascots of one sort or another, generally dogs; but at this time they had a sapper as a mascot. He was generally known among the drivers as " His Nibs," and lived at the horse lines, where it was thought he could make himself more useful than he could with the company, as he was more or less medically unfit to do a lot of marching to and from work.

The horse lines were to be seen at their best, however, on days when the O.C. visited them. The Q.M. stores in particular sprang into great activity. As the O.C. usually went for the main purpose of seeing the horses, he did not generally go round the rest of the camp until he had been round the lines. His arrival in the camp, therefore, was the signal for Sapper Lowden to get busy in the stores; and while the O.C. was looking at the animals, Lowden dashed round the stores and straightened things out, hiding anything that was better not seen, and sprinkling chloride of lime lavishly on the floor. This was completed just in time for the entry of the O.C. into the stores. As he entered Lowden would be standing in a corner leaning against a table, ostentatiously doing nothing, just sufficiently " at ease " to enable him to come smartly to " attention."

They would then exchange remarks on the flies and fly-papers, the quality of the bacon, and the quantity of the vegetable ration. Every one present was perfectly aware that every one else knew that the whole business had been carefully " staged " for the occasion, and every one winked at some one else behind other people's backs. The party would then pass on to the cook-house, where Drivers Brown and Gill had been arranging things in a similar manner. There, Brown would be discovered stirring something in a dixie, and Gill would be putting some wood on the fire. Everything would be exactly as it should be, and as in the stores there would be some very freshly-sprinkled chloride of lime on the floor.

When Colonel Pratt left the Division on 21st June Major Mousley was at first appointed acting C.R.E., but as he went sick, Major Riddick had to go from the company to act as C.R.E. After a few days he was definitely appointed C.R.E. and made Lieut.-Colonel, so we were left without an O.C. until Major Hanmer came to us from the 5th Division on the 17th July.

The most unfortunate thing that occurred to us while in this sector was a shell in the camp on the morning of 2nd July. There was some light shelling going on in the neighbourhood, and about 8.0 a.m. a shell landed in our camp on top of a hut occupied by four of No. 1 Section, and they were all four killed outright. They were Holland, Kershaw, Royles and Tomlinson. They were buried at Bertrancourt the following day. There were also two others wounded by the same shell—Burslem and Stevens-King. The latter was sleeping in the drawing office next to the orderly room, and the orderly room itself was badly knocked about, papers being torn up in an extraordinary manner, and a cash box with a lot of notes in it being destroyed; the N.C.O.s mess was completely wrecked.

At the time of our taking over this sector it was still thought possible that the enemy might attempt another big attack, and there was therefore a great deal of work to be done on defences, consisting largely of wire, new earthworks, and a number of tunnelled dug-outs. The place was also remarkable for the large concentration of guns of all calibres, but during the summer their number was gradually reduced as the probability of a big hostile attack decreased.

For a time we had dealings with Hébuterne again, but about the end of June this was handed over to the New Zealand Division, who went back into the line on our left. The front of the 42nd Division was then slightly contracted so as to leave Hébuterne out. While dealing with Hébuterne the Gray wire-reeler was produced. The cause of this was that we received nearly all barbed wire on very big coils, which were difficult to handle. So we wanted an apparatus to reel it off on to smaller reels. Sergeant Gray got busy with his derelict mill, and produced a remarkable thing which looked like a cross between a lathe and a sewing machine. This had numerous accessories : spindles of several sizes, bolts, nuts, wheels, handles, etc.

By selecting the correct spindles in combination with the right wheels, bolts, nuts and handles, it was possible to wind any kind of wire from any size of reel on to any other size of reel. Unfortunately, there was only one man who knew which was the correct spindle for any particular reel, and that man was Sergeant Gray. So that, when he left it, it is unlikely that it was used much. Sapper Hitchin had a good deal to do with its construction, but he was never seen to manipulate it afterwards.

One of the great sights of Hébuterne was Lieutenant Paul and Sergeant Gray parading the streets. Other and lesser mortals generally walked in trenches, as there was no knowing when the Boche would start shelling. At times, however, one would hear footsteps and conversation coming down the street, interrupted occasionally by a bursting shell. One heard this sort of thing—

" Exactly ; that's the thing to do, Sergeant Gray."

" Mumble, mumble, mumble."

" You go over straightway and have a look at that other well, and I'll meet you at the crater."

" Mumble, mumble, mumble."

Then round the corner they would come, the long and the short of it. Heads would look out of dug-outs, to be hurriedly withdrawn as a shell whistled over. But they had seen, and the word would go round that all was well. No. 4 Section was functioning, and every one was reassured. Battalion commanders sat down to lunch with an easy mind. Gas-guards went to sleep again.

In July Corporal Craig distinguished himself by inventing a new wiring drill for erecting high, wide, wire entanglements, which the 4th Corps Commander wished to have used. We were told to instruct the infantry in the matter, and as we didn't know anything about it, we had to invent something ourselves. Corporal Craig ran a little school of infantry N.C.O.s, and when one day the 1/10th Manchesters had a competition between their companies in wiring, he helped to judge.

August found us still working on defences, but when the enemy retired a little, early in the month, and evacuated Serre, some tracks had to be made across country over shell-holes to allow transport to get forward. On the 21st the great advance began.

For the first two or three days of the advance we worked on tracks, with the exception of one N.C.O. and two sappers attached to each of the attacking companies of the 125th Brigade. Unfortunately, we lost some of these men during these operations : Lance-

Corporal Machin being killed, and Sappers R. Bailey and Carnell being wounded.

On the 24th August, the company began to move forward, and our work was then mainly road and water reconnaissance. On the 29th, Lance-Corporal J. Mort was wounded, and on the 30th Corporal Farquhar, both of them while out on reconnaissance work. On the night of 30th/31st August, the company billets at La Barque were shelled, and we had further losses, Sappers Carter and Deedman being killed, and Crossman and Burden wounded. Lance-Corporal Jenkinson was afterwards awarded the M.M. for his conduct on this night.

On the 31st, there was still further trouble, for the horse lines, then near Pys, were shelled, and an infantry officer who was attached to us for work on wells—2nd Lieut. Tankard, of the 1/5th Lancs. Fusiliers, was killed. On the whole, this advance was somewhat costly to the company; Epéhy was the only other place where we had so many casualties in so short a time.

During the early days of September, similar work continued; the company moved up to Barastre, and sections worked as far forward as Ytres. Lieutenant Eastwood, returning to Company Headquarters after a day's work forward, was one of the greatest spectacles of the twentieth century. He generally appeared with his tin hat tilted over his eyes, a pipe in his mouth, foul tobacco in the pipe, pushing himself along with an enormous stick. On being asked by the O.C. what sort of a time he had had up forward, he invariably answered : " Hell, sir ! "

On the night of the 5th/6th September, the Division came out of the line, and the 429 Field Company moved back to Pys. After an unbroken spell of thirteen weeks' front-line work, a rest was a welcome change, even though it involved a great deal of training—usually a dull business. It was, however, much less dull than might have been expected, and as we made a short rifle-range close beside the camp, there were plenty of shooting competitions. There was also a certain amount of football, although the ground all round was badly shell-holed, and it was impossible to get a really level ground anywhere. Every one trained. Even the cooks, batmen, and orderly room staff appeared occasionally on parade, and felt very lost in that unwonted situation.

On the 22nd September we went forward to Lebucquière, the Division taking over the line at Trescault from the 37th Division, and preparing for the next push, which came on the 27th September. At Lebucquière we lived in a camp of Nissen huts which had been built during the previous winter and had been knocked about a good deal during the March retreat and the subsequent advance. However, we made ourselves reasonably comfortable, and were not seriously bothered by shelling, although there were occasional high-velocity shells not far away.

We were the rear of the three field companies, and did not see much of the push of the 27th September, either in preparation or

429TH FIELD COY. R.E.

in execution. It was on this day that the Hindenburg Line was captured in front of Trescault. We sent two sappers to live with each battalion of the 125th Brigade, and two to Brigade Headquarters, to give any assistance they could in case of dug-outs having to be made gas-proof or similar small jobs requiring to be done. A letter was received afterwards from at least one battalion to thank us for their able assistance. Apart from these few sappers, our work both before and after the push was mainly on water points and baths.

After the 27th, the Division was relieved by the New Zealand Division, and remained roughly speaking where it was, while the New Zealand Division went on pushing up to the Escaut Canal.

The 429 Field Company went to Bertincourt, and then on to some old dug-outs in front of Trescault near the Hindenburg Line. The horse lines went to a site just outside Havrincourt Wood. No. 3 Section then went back to build a Divisional Reception Camp between Bertincourt and Ruyaulcourt. They took with them their tool-cart, of course, and caused some amusement by un-limbering it and making properly dressed wagon lines by arranging the two halves side by side propped up on posts.

We were not long near Trescault, as the New Zealand Division pushed on across the Escaut Canal. Late at night on the 8th October we received orders to move at 7.0 a.m. the following morning. Our first orders were to go to Bois Lateau, a little short of the Escaut Canal, but by the time we arrived there (about 11.30 a.m.), word had come through that the line was far ahead, and we went on to Lesdain, south of Cambrai, where we found rather uncomfortable quarters in a valley just outside the village. No. 3 Section rejoined the company late at night. The roads at this time were bad, although the weather was inclined to improve. On this particular day, it was quite fine, and it was interesting to see the observation balloons travelling forward.

We spent three days at Lesdain, Divisional Headquarters being at the next village further forward—Esnes. The New Zealand Division were meanwhile continuing the advance, and pontoons were urgently required, so we had to remain at Lesdain a day longer than we should otherwise have done, to dismantle pontoon bridges from the Escaut Canal, pack them up, and take them forward to a place near Beauvois.

Moving up on the 12th October, the 429 Field Company went to live at a place called Jeune Bois, on the main Cambrai–Le Cateau road; the 42nd Division at the same time took over the line on the River Selle from the New Zealanders.

Jeune Bois was a large farm with several other houses adjoining, and was about an equal distance from Beauvois and Caudry. Caudry was somewhat of a novelty to those who had occasion to go there, as it had civilians living in it—the first civilians we had seen since the advance started in August. There were also some at the villages nearer the line: Briastre, Viesly, and Quiévy, but most of them evacuated these villages and went to live in Caudry. Our work while at

Jeune Bois was mainly filling in road craters, of which there were some particularly big specimens in the neighbourhood.

It was by this time fairly obvious to most people that " pushes " were going to succeed one another fairly quickly, and on the 20th October the 42nd Division again advanced, carrying the line well across the River Selle. Although the 429 Field Company were not taking any very great part in this advance (the 427 were the forward company), we had the misfortune to lose Lieutenant Chapman, and also had 2nd Corporal Collins and Sapper Lamb wounded. These and another sapper—Newsom—had gone through Briastre at about 6.30 a.m. on the 20th, four and a half hours after zero, their job being: first, to get some notice boards erected at bridges over the Selle; and secondly, to go forward and reconnoitre the main road into Solesmes, as it was believed that a railway bridge had been blown up at the point where the railway crossed the road, and the road was thought to be blocked. As the party went through Briastre, heavy shelling started about the centre of the village, and they had almost got clear at the south-east corner of the village when shells started to fall near them; and one, landing in the road beside them, killed Lieutenant Chapman, and wounded 2nd Corporal Collins, and Sapper Lamb. Newsom was badly shaken but untouched. Lieutenant Chapman was buried the following day at Beauvois, in the civilian cemetery. This was the only occasion on which the 429 Field Company had an officer killed, and his loss was felt keenly by all ranks, more especially by his own section—No. 3.

Another party, taking on the road reconnaissance job, found two bridges blown across the road at the entrance to Solesmes. Our next job was, therefore, to move them. This company tackled one, and one of the tunnelling companies took on the other. As it was a matter of considerable urgency to get the road clear for the advance to continue, this had to be done by using explosives, splitting up the girders into small pieces.

The road was finally cleared in time to allow traffic to pass on the morning of the 23rd October, when the Division did another attack, and then immediately handed over again to the New Zealand Division, who carried on the pursuit almost to Le Quesnoy.

On the 24th October we moved up into Solesmes. Solesmes was the first place since March in which we had been billeted with civilians. At this time it was occasionally shelled by a H.V. gun, but this never did us any harm. We did a little training here, and on the 1st November, the Divisional R.E. had some sports and transport competitions at Prayelle, near Viesly. As the 427 and 429 Field Companies were both living at the time in Solesmes, and the 428 were back at Jeune Bois, it was not easy to find a suitable ground, but Prayelle was chosen as being about midway between them.

The last advance started on the 4th November. This was set in motion by the New Zealand Division, and the 42nd followed up and took over from them on the night of the 5th/6th. The function

429TH FIELD COY. R.E.

of this company was to be prepared to take on any job of any magnitude which the leading company (427) might be unable to tackle, as it was imperative that the 427 Field Company should keep well up forward, and should not be delayed long in their advance. To get into touch with any such job with as little delay as possible, we had an officer attached to the 427 Field Company. This was 2nd Lieut. Stevenson, who had only lately joined us.

We moved forward to Le Quesnoy on the 5th November, and when our advance party arrived there that morning, they found a band belonging to the New Zealand Division in the main square playing the Marseillaise and other airs, while the inhabitants of the town stood or danced round, many of them weeping with joy at their deliverance.

Beyond Le Quesnoy, we had to pass through Mormal Forest, which we found to be a most unpleasant place, the roads through it being abominable. A number of road craters had been blown, and these necessitated bridges or road diversions. It was nevertheless easy to see that in time of peace it had been a very beautiful forest.

This last week of active operations was a very trying time for every one, owing to the bad weather, continual marching, and the great amount of work which had to be carried on at the same time. The drivers had, perhaps, a harder time than most of us, for they had to turn out at all hours of the day or night, after long marches, and go back miles through Mormal Forest to bring forward more pontoons. It was anticipated that pontoons would be required to bridge the River Sambre, and those of the New Zealand Engineers were kept as far forward as possible, in case our own should prove insufficient. As far as the 429 Field Company were concerned, we did have to put a pontoon bridge across the Sambre at Boussières; also a service trestle bridge was required across one of the craters in Mormal Forest, and another across a small stream called the Ruisseau de la Fontaine, about a mile short of Boussières. In connection with the bridge at Boussières, a road diversion had to be made, and for this work we borrowed a large number of wheelbarrows from the inhabitants. The Maire was asked if he could find about ten; but he must have sent forth an order calling for every wheelbarrow in the place; they came rolling up in shoals. Indeed, the inhabitants, though spending most of their time eagerly discussing the situation, and speculating as to the end of the war, were only too delighted to be able to help us in any way. Probably, the mere suggestion of wheelbarrows being required was sufficient to send them all scuttling home to fetch any crazy, ramshackle apparatus on one wheel, or even half a wheel.

While it lasted, this seemed to be a good push to be out of, but when it finished, and we realized that we had been taking part in the last push of the war, we could not fail to be glad that we had been in it. The armistice on the 11th November found us living near Maubeuge. Sections 3 and 4 were forward at Ferrière-la-Grande, working on bridges across the River Solre, and living in front of the outpost line of the Division, with only the cavalry in front. The remainder of the company were on the outskirts of Louvroil, on the Maubeuge–Avesnes Road.

People sometimes ask what we did when we heard of the armistice. Well, we did nothing out of the ordinary; we just carried on with the work in hand. On the morning of the 11th, we at first heard only a rumour. It did not sound very impossible, as it was obvious that a climax of some sort was approaching; nevertheless, one did not lightly accept rumours of this sort, and the various parties went out to work wondering what was really going to happen. The official message announcing the armistice came during the morning when nearly every one was out working; and the first real confirmation of the rumour that most of us got was when Major Entwistle of the 428 Field Company came up from the C.R.E.'s Headquarters in Hautmont to see how bridging was progressing at Ferrière, and brought the definite news with him. This was at about 10.15 a.m., three-quarters of an hour before the armistice actually came into force.

Most people did not realize at once that this was really to be the end of the war; for all we knew, the war might start again later. It was only after we had thought about it a little, and had heard all the details of the armistice terms, that we saw that a resumption of hostilities would be almost impossible. In any case, we had urgent work to get on with, so had not much time for jubilation, even had we felt so inclined.

A few days after the armistice, we moved back into Hautmont, and remained there with the rest of the Division until early in December. Bridge repair work at various places continued, and about the end of the first week in December, we became considerably split up. No. 1 Section, with a section from each of the other field companies, went to Charleroi to prepare accommodation for the move thither of the whole Division; and the other three sections went to a village called Vieux Reng to do some more bridging; the transport lines remained at Hautmont.

By the 18th December, however, we were all together in Charleroi, where the field companies lived in a Jesuit College called the Collège du Sacré Cœur. The next question was: how to arrange a suitable Xmas dinner. The divisional canteen managed to supply a limited number of turkeys; and thanks to the strenuous efforts of Sergeant Ellis, who spent a busy week searching the district for foodstuffs and for plates and similar utensils, we managed to have quite a good spread. This was followed by a dance and whist-drive, in both of which the other two field companies also joined.

The only thing that mattered now was: how to get demobilized as quickly as possible. There was still plenty of work to be done, mostly in connection with the accommodation of the infantry, so time did not hang so heavily on our hands as it might have done otherwise. Nevertheless, most people had only one thought, and that was Home.

429TH FIELD COY. R.E.

During January 1919, demobilization got into full swing, and by the end of February we were almost down to cadre strength, *i. e.* the nucleus whose job was to bring home the stores and vehicles. It would take too much space to record the departures of individual officers and men; suffice it to say that the cadre finally left at the end of March, in charge of Lieutenant Paul, who was made an acting Captain on his appointment to the command, proceeding via Antwerp and Tilbury to Oswestry, where the stores were handed in and checked. The last remnants of the unit then dispersed : all those for Manchester travelled together with the Manchester men of the other field companies ; and at the railway station in Manchester, with the last farewells of comrades, and the greetings of friends who had come to meet us, our war service ended.

PART VI

SHORT HISTORY

OF THE

42ND (EAST LANCS.) DIVISIONAL SIGNAL COMPANY, R.E. ON ACTIVE SERVICE. 1914–1919.

MOBILIZATION, EGYPT, GALLIPOLI
(1914-1915)

THE East Lancashire Divisional Signal Company was mobilized on the 5th August, 1914, under the command of Captain A. N. Lawford, R.E. (T.). Headquarters and No. 1 Section assembled at the R.E. Headquarters, Seymour Grove, Old Trafford, Manchester, and by 10 a.m. every N.C.O. and man had reported, with the exception of two or three who were travelling from distant towns.

The remaining portion of the company, Nos. 2, 3 and 4 (Infantry Brigade) Sections, joined their respective Brigade Headquarters, or assembled with the battalion from which most of their personnel were drawn.

On August 20 the Division moved under canvas, Company Headquarters, No. 1 Section and No. 3 Section at Bury, No. 2 Section at Turton, and No. 4 Section at Littleborough.

After three weeks under canvas, training and fitting out, orders were received for the Division to proceed to Egypt; the response to the appeal for volunteers for Imperial Service was excellent, and practically the whole company agreed to serve abroad wherever called upon to go; the standard of physical fitness was high, and few were rejected as medically unfit.

The whole company concentrated at Chesham Camp, Bury, on September 7, and three days later embarked at Southampton on the Donaldson liner s.s. *Saturnia*, together with the Lancashire Fusiliers Brigade Headquarters and the 6th and 7th Lancashire Fusiliers.

The horses, cable wagons and transport in charge of C.S.M. Campbell and a small detachment embarked on another vessel.

The officers of the Signal Company on leaving England were—

Captain A. N. Lawford, R.E. (T.), in command.
Lieutenant G. L. Broad, R.E. (T.), No. 1 Section.
2nd Lieutenant R. S. Newton (6th L.F.), No. 2 (Lan. Fus.) Section.
2nd Lieutenant G. N. Robinson (4th E. Lancs.), No. 3 (E. Lancs.) Section.
Lieutenant C. H. Williamson (7th Man.), No. 4 (Man.) Section.

It took fourteen large vessels to carry the Division overseas, with a battleship and cruiser as escort.

The voyage was an interesting and memorable one, and undertaken without mishap to any vessel.

Alexandria was reached on September 25, and the following evening the Signal Company detrained at Abbassia, Cairo, and took possession of the old Polygon Barracks lately occupied by the Camel Corps School.

The company quickly settled down to its new conditions and its hard period of training for the next seven months: riding and driving, foot drill, cable laying, visual signalling, musketry and technical lectures all had their part, and prepared for the combined Brigade and Divisional operations which took place later on the vast open desert, traversed by the Cairo–Suez road, on the edge of which Polygon Barracks stood.

Clear atmosphere and continuous sun brought heliograph work into common and daily use for very long distances, and such landmarks as Numbers 2 and 3 Towers on the Suez road, Flagstaff Hill, Virgin's Breast and Gebel Ahmar were seldom without their visual signal stations.

One of the first tasks allotted to the company was the organization of signal communications in the Defence of Cairo scheme, as a precaution against the breakdown of civil telegraphic communications in Cairo, and with the large Imperial wireless station at Abou Zabaal, fifteen miles distant. This was constantly practised, by heliograph and limelight, under the supervision of Major Lawford, now promoted.

Large classes of Infantry Signallers were held at Polygon, and trained by the Brigade Section Officers and N.C.O.s, and the standard of signalling throughout the Division greatly improved.

On October 31 two cable detachments with a complement of motor-cycle despatch riders were sent to Ismailia for work on the Suez Canal defences. The chief work was the laying of a cable line from Ismailia to Kantara, a distance of approximately twenty-five miles. This line was worked and maintained by company telegraphists and linemen, and proved of great importance and value in the defence of the Canal against the Turkish attack in the following February. The Divisional Signal Company motor-cyclist despatch riders were the first ever employed as such on active service in any operation beyond Europe.

Early in 1915 the War Office increased the establishment of the company from approximately 150 all ranks to 208, with a proportionate increase in horses, vehicles and equipment. The new establishment provided for an R.A. Headquarters detachment, an additional cable detachment, an increase in the number of motor cyclists, and a considerable strengthening of the Infantry Brigade Sections, which were issued with telephone equipment and pack mules.

With the exception of the officers, all the personnel of Nos. 2, 3 and 4 Sections were transferred to the Royal Engineers.

To bring the company up to its new strength a large draft of men arrived from England in March.

The Signal Company took part in the several divisional route marches through Cairo and its environs, including the memorable one on March 28 before General Sir Ian Hamilton, who was then preparing for the landing on Gallipoli.

After seven months strenuous training the company was in a high state of efficiency, when the call came for more serious work at the end of April.

With only twenty-four hours' notice No. 2 Section embarked with the Lancashire Fusiliers Brigade at Alexandria on May 1, and landed at Cape Helles, on the Gallipoli peninsula, on May 5, being sent straight to the firing-line in support of the 29th Division.

This section had forty-eight hours' continuous work, under severe fire and quite in the open, with only such equipment as could be carried off the transport by hand.

By May 9 the two other brigade sections had reached the peninsula, and the following day Headquarters and No. 1 Section disembarked and carried out the difficult task of landing horses, wagons and stores under constant shell fire without loss.

The first bivouac of Company Headquarters was on the edge of cliffs above Lancashire Landing, but a move inland was quickly made to the position selected for Divisional Headquarters, where a Signal Office was formed, in tents *d'abri*, in the early hours of May 11, and a D5 cable laid by barrow from the 8th Corps Headquarters, and worked by a vibrator.

A section of the front line was taken over by the Division from Australian troops on the evening of the 11th, the Lancashire Fusilier and Manchester Brigades being in the line and the East Lancashire Brigade in reserve.

Existing communications, such as they were, were taken over by the brigade sections and rapidly improved.

The cable detachments laid D5 cable lines to each of the Brigade Headquarters, all worked by vibrator with inter-communication by means of a commutator.

For several hours the instruments were working out in the open, but towards nightfall shallow trenches had been dug, and were covered in by means of tents *d'abri*. Heavy rain fell almost the whole night, causing conditions to become very unpleasant. The lines were rapidly duplicated, and a small local telephone exchange system rigged up. Lateral lines were laid to the 29th and the Royal Naval Divisions. French and artillery liaison lines were also provided, whilst the Corps later ran a single air line from "W" Beach in substitution of the original D5 line.

In addition the company had to provide a large party to reinforce the 29th Divisional Artillery Signals, who had suffered heavy casualties in the landing and the early days on the peninsula.

At this time the countryside was a mass of bloom, and the air fragrant with the homely smell of lavender, wild thyme and other wild flowers more or less familiar. The linemen often waded knee-deep in the luxurious vegetation, fields of poppies, yellow and scarlet marsh mallows, cornflowers, clover and young maize, whilst the tree crossings were held up by the walnut, fig, mulberry or olive tree.

Wild life was plentiful, chiefly represented by numerous small birds, hares, tortoises, partridges, snakes, lizards and so forth, not forgetting a multitude of frogs. On a few occasions eagles evidently from their eyries on distant Asiatic mountains flew majestically over the peninsula surveying the invading army with distant curiosity.

The Divisional Signal Office was moved to a fresh position on the 21st May, occupying some old trenches about 400 yards eastwards. The Signal Offices on the peninsula were seldom fixed in dug-outs in the manner later adopted in France, owing to lack of timber and other material, but the best possible use was made of deep trenches, with recesses for each operator, and as much head cover provided as the scanty materials available would allow.

D5 cable was invariably used, poled where most necessary across tracks, and through the area of reserve trenches and bivouacs which quickly spread out over the toe of the peninsula, but for the most part laid on the ground, and on the sides of the nullahs leading to the Infantry Brigade Headquarters. After the first few days it was realized that cable wagons were totally unsuited to the local conditions owing to the broken nature of the ground, and to the fact that they were a too-obvious mark for enemy artillery: the dominating height of Achi Baba giving the enemy perfect observation over the whole of our small area.

Consequently, "Barrows drum wheel universal" now became exceedingly valuable items of equipment; at times it was found possible to use a steady horse for haulage, but as this led to many barrows being smashed when crossing obstacles the linemen generally had to man-handle them.

In the forward trenches lines were laid by hand, men carrying coils of about 200 yards of cable each, but in some of the wider trenches, such as the Eski and Redoubt lines, the barrow could be taken fairly easily.

A very heavy rainstorm on the evening of May 25 played havoc with the communications of the brigades in the line; the Krithia Nullah was turned from a gently flowing stream into a raging torrent in a couple of hours, the Lancashire Fusiliers Brigade Headquarters were under four feet of water for several hours, and the Signal Office and most of its equipment completely washed away; to make matters worse two of its operators were badly wounded whilst endeavouring to construct a new office. The relief of the East Lancashire Brigade by the Manchester Brigade took place during the storm under very great difficulties.

Preliminary work in connection with the battle of June 4 was now in hand, and all lines were thoroughly overhauled and extensions made to the Brigades' Advanced Headquarters.

It was whilst engaged on this work on June 3 that Sergeant C. E. Williams won the first D.C.M. awarded to the company, whilst in charge of two strong parties laying cables forward along the Krithia Nullah. All day long the enemy had shelled this main communication route, which was congested with all kinds of traffic.

42ND DIVL. SIGNAL COY. R.E.

One of the working-parties was caught by two salvoes which killed two men, wounded another, and smashed up the cable barrows and killed a horse. Sergeant Williams with splendid courage and determination reorganized his men, and by force of personal example carried on and finished the job.

During the severe fighting commencing on June 4 the whole of the Signal Company had four or five days' strenuous and unceasing work, both the brigades participating. The Manchester and Lancashire Fusilier Brigades had Advanced Headquarters in the support trenches, and these were connected up to the Division through their rear headquarters, and to their artillery groups. A central visual station was formed near the Manchester Brigade Headquarters at a point known as MV in the Redoubt Line for direct visual communication to Divisional Headquarters; this proved of great value owing to the constant damage to lines by shell fire.

The linemen, both brigade and divisional, had a particularly hard time of it, and there were many casualties.

The Division had now received a numerical title, and became the 42nd (E. Lancs.) Division, the old divisional signal call of GN (Geneasla) giving way to YDB : the three Infantry Brigades became the 125th (Lancs. Fusiliers), 126th (E. Lancs.) and 127th (Manchester), with the signal calls of ZLE, ZLF and ZLG respectively, all other units received recognized signal calls also.

On the morning of the 16th the enemy guns were especially active, and five of the headquarter horses were killed in a few minutes, but by the ready assistance of officers and men the remainder were got away from their position in the open, and " dug in " without further casualty.

" Asiatic Annie " and other guns across the Straits now became very troublesome, and caused many alterations in the siting of " dug-outs," but the company had no casualties from this cause, though there were many narrow escapes.

One enemy gun firing from Asia provided an interesting example of the time of flight of a shell, as it was not long before it was discovered that about twenty-eight seconds elapsed between the sound of the gun being heard and the arrival of the projectile : this gave ample time for the wary to get under cover.

During the battle of July 12 and 13, when the 52nd and Royal Naval Divisions, together with the French, made an attack on the Turkish trenches, the cable lines of the attacking division were all broken, but those of the 42nd Division were successfully maintained intact and proved of great assistance.

The battle was mainly observed from the 42nd Divisional O.P., and the General Staff expressed their high appreciation of the working of the line and communications.

Early in August the Division, after only a few days out of the line, took over the northern sector of the Allied line from the 29th Division, from the coast at Fusilier Bluff on the left and across the great Gully Ravine. Divisional Headquarters were at the mouth of the ravine on the edge of Gully Beach; the Signal Office here was in a sand-bagged shed, roofed, and under the protection of a steep bank.

Lines to brigades were still worked by vibrator, and to the Corps by sounder; in addition there was a small telephone system consisting of a twelve-line exchange, with lines to the Corps, brigades and principal Staff Officers.

By the end of the month the whole company was very low in strength owing to the large amount of sickness, the chief causes being dysentery, jaundice and septic sores. Lieutenant G. L. Broad was admitted to hospital, also C.S.M. Nuttall, and shortly afterwards the O.C. company, Major A. N. Lawford, fell a victim to sickness, and left 2nd Lieutenant A. Roberts, the senior officer at Company Headquarters, in temporary command.

It was about this period that the office telegraphists had a very hard time. Owing to pressure of work and shortage of staff each operator had to perform alternate eight-hour reliefs, meal reliefs and many odd fatigues in addition; many were sick with diarrhœa and septic sores, but none complained, their one object was to see that all the messages were transmitted quickly and correctly. Office telegraphists and drivers are not often in the limelight of publicity, and unfortunately their devotion to duty is too often overlooked.

The work of the motor-cyclist despatch riders was at all times heavy, but particularly so in this sector, where they did excellent service. The night journeys up the Gully, often flooded and deep in mud, were indeed arduous, and machines suffered severely, but thanks to a good artificer they were kept in condition; after a time, some relief to the motor cyclists was given by the brigades in the line each providing two mounted men for the night duty.

The command of the company was assumed by Captain R. W. Dammers, Sherwood Foresters, on October 10.

A poled route was erected up the Gully, consisting of eight lines of D5 cable used as loops. This route, owing to its course on the rough, steep sides of the ravine, was very difficult to erect, and great credit was due to Sergeant Willcock and his party of linemen for the efficient manner in which the work was completed. This line suffered severely from shell fire, but worked well through some violent storms, in spite of the heavy cable and weak poles supplied.

The brigade sections erected D5 cable throughout their areas, on short cross-arm poles in the Gully, and stapled to the sides of communication and fire trenches, all lines being duplicated and in some cases triplicated.

At one period the Corps ordered all trench lines to be run in grooves cut in the side of the trenches and supported by wire staples, but this method was quite unsatisfactory with the lower insulated cables on account of earthing due to the dampness of the soil.

Visual signalling on the peninsula had only a very limited scope owing to the uneven nature of the ground, and the almost entire lack of cover from enemy observation; on the coastal sub-sector, however, considerable use of visual was made by the brigade sections in maintaining contact with the Navy for the direction and control of gun fire.

The snow blizzards and hard frosts in November and December caused heavy casualties amongst all ranks suffering from a decreasing vitality and lack of any but the scantiest shelter. Such luxuries as Rest Camps, well-stocked canteens, and Y.M.C.A.s did not exist on the Gallipoli peninsula. The brigade sections suffered probably the most, and except for the splendid aid of attached infantry signallers, many of whom afterwards transferred to the Signal Service, would not have been able to carry on; certainly a small draft of men from England assisted to fill some vacancies, but the majority had had little training and were not fit to stand the rigours of the campaign.

A recreation those at Divisional Headquarters or in reserve could enjoy was the magnificent sea bathing, but even here many were killed whilst enjoying a swim.

Announcement was made early in December of the award of the Military Cross to Lieutenant G. L. Broad, and of the D.C.M. to Sergeant C. E. Williams of No. 1 Section.

The end of the Gallipoli campaign came suddenly; the evacuation of Anzac and Suvla in December only strengthened the belief that we should " hang on " to Cape Helles, so that orders for the Division to embark for Mudros before the end of the year were assumed to mean simply a few weeks' well-earned rest; No. 2 Section of the company was the first to leave on December 28, embarking with the whole of the 125th Brigade on one small steamer, followed by the other brigade sections as the infantry were relieved; Company Headquarters and No. 1 Section reached Mudros on January 3, 1916, leaving only a small detachment to work the communications up to the end.

All the vehicles and heavy stores were burned, and many horses destroyed to prevent them falling into enemy hands.

The company went under canvas at Mudros, the brigade sections remaining attached to their brigades.

By this time it was common knowledge that the evacuation was complete, and that our work on the Gallipoli peninsula was at an end.

THE RETURN TO EGYPT AND ADVANCE TO EL ARISH

1916–1917

THE 42nd Division spent about a fortnight under canvas on the island of Lemnos, and the Signal Company, with all other units, enjoyed the change after eight months on the peninsula, the freedom from constant gun and rifle fire, and the opportunity to take exercise without restriction.

The next move was back to Egypt; Company Headquarters and No. 1 Section embarked on January 16 after a tremendous rainstorm, and the remaining sections accompanied their brigades. Landing at Alexandria, the Division entrained for Cairo, and encamped at Mena, under the shadow of the world-famous Pyramids, the whole of the Signal Company having arrived by the 22nd inst.

After a brief and welcome rest at Mena Camp, Cairo, the company proceeded to Shallufa on the Suez Canal on the 2nd February, 1916, and immediately commenced work in connection with the Canal Defence scheme. An armoured cable across the Canal connected to permanent lines on the west side provided the necessary channels to Corps H.Q. at Port Tewfik. Strong points were constructed out in the desert, and these were joined to H.Q. by means of ground cable D5. Some of these lines were from twelve to fifteen miles in length. Similar lateral lines were also laid. Communication with the Indian Division on the right at El Kubri was effected by means of an air line.

There was much scope for visual signalling in this sector, and the brigade sections maintained constant visual communication between the desert posts and Headquarters, and our extreme left at Geneffe, by heliograph and lamp.

The burying of D5 cable in the sand, in the vicinity of camps and bivouacs, was tried, but owing to the dampness of the sand under the dry crust this was not successful.

Early in February a strong draft from England arrived, and the company was made up to strength in personnel; a number of remounts, vehicles and other equipment, to replace those left on the peninsula, were issued.

A good deal of training was carried out, and the men's health and strength improved rapidly; several khamseens, with an ever-increasing abundance of flies, tried the patience of all ranks at times.

On April 3 the company moved to Suez, where the whole Division went under canvas for training and re-equipping.

The headquarters of the company were close to the Freshwater Canal, about two miles from the town.

Here, communications were quite simple, as all units were in fixed positions, and except on manœuvres the work was only a matter of routine.

Some very useful training was carried out on the desert west of Suez, though the intense heat restricted the hours of training to early morning and evening.

Further reinforcements arrived, and the excellent Ordnance Depot at Suez fitted out all sections with first-class equipment, both technical and personal.

Captain Dammers being invalided home in May, the command of the company was taken over by Captain C. H. Williamson of No. 4 (Manchester Brigade) Section.

42nd DIVL. SIGNAL COY. R.E.

The restful period at Suez came to an end in June, when the Division again took over a section of the Canal defences further north, comprising the Canal Posts of El Ferdan and Ballah, with its headquarters at El Ferdan.

Communications were taken over from the 11th Division, and were on a most extensive scale, the two large desert posts at Ferdan Railhead and Ballybunion occupied by the 126th and 125th Brigades had very large systems of communications, and the Signal Sections responsible had as much as they could do to cope with the work entailed. One brigade section had 100 miles of cable to patrol and look after, with frequently over 300 telegrams per day through its office, and in addition was responsible for a very large D.R.L.S.

The concentration of the Turkish forces on the northern route across the desert caused the Division to be moved north to Kantara at the end of July, after handing over to the 54th Division.

In a few days the march eastwards commenced, all units being mobile with camel transport and a minimum of equipment; horse transport broke down entirely on account of the great heat, lack of water and difficult nature of the desert traversed.

August 4 saw advanced D.H.Q. at Pelusium, where the Division concentrated, but by this time the "Battle of Romani" was over, and the enemy in full retreat; the following day at dawn the whole force moved forward.

After a hard struggle a D5 cable line was taken to Royston Hill, where a Divisional Report Centre was established, but the achievement proved the death warrant of the ordinary cable wagon for use on the desert.

Later communications were established from Mount Meredith, and the next day an improvised camel transport for cable enabled direct touch to be obtained with the G.O.C. on the move.

After a most trying march in intense heat and over exceedingly rough ground the oasis of Katia was reached, the Signal Office was quickly established and the brigades linked up once more.

Many of the men arrived at Katia in a state of physical collapse, but the requisite reliefs for the office were found and all messages disposed of. The few telegraph operators available carried on magnificently, their dogged devotion to duty being worthy of the best traditions of the Royal Engineers.

The line to Advanced Corps Headquarters at Kantara now consisted of about fifteen miles of semi-permanent air line, and some fifteen miles of D5 ground cable worked by vibrator.

After a brief stay in the oasis of Katia, the Division went into rest, leaving Katia on the 14th August and proceeding by march route to Pelusium, which was reached early on the 15th August. A period of rest, varied by training, followed. Visual signalling now formed an important feature of all communications, and a great deal of attention was given to exercising the company in heliograph, flag and lamp work, and also in the employment of camel transport for desert operations generally.

September 9 again saw the Division moving east, proceeding by easy stages to Romani and El Rabah, arriving at Hod El Negiliat, where D.H.Q. was established on the morning of the 11th. Two of the brigades moved further east to Oghratina and beyond. Communications consisted of duplicated ground lines to each brigade, and a line to Corps followed the permanent route along the railway, which was now pushing eastward very quickly. The weather conditions were almost ideal. Operations against the enemy were confined to occasional affairs of outposts and patrols, in which the cavalry and camel corps only were concerned. A few bombing raids by the enemy occasioned a little local excitement at odd times.

One Brigade, the 125th, was at this period on the Canal holding the Kantara Section Defences, where its Signal Section was fully employed in maintaining a very large area of communications reaching from Port Said to Ballah and Ballybunion.

In October the Division concentrated at Mahamdiya, a very pleasant spot on the edge of the Mediterranean, north of Romani, where the company had a very easy time and thoroughly enjoyed the excellent sea bathing, whilst many of the men had a week's holiday at the rest camp established at Sidi Bishr, Alexandria.

Another change of command took place at the beginning of November, when Captain Williamson, who had recently been awarded the Military Cross, transferred to the R.F.C. and was succeeded by Captain S. Gordon Johnson, M.C., of the South Staffordshire Regiment.

Preparations were now in hand for the formation of the mobile force known as the Desert Column, of which the 42nd Division formed a part, and before the end of the month the Division was in bivouac at Mazar, holding defensive outposts protecting the advancing railway.

The Brigade Signal Offices were all fairly close to D.H.Q. and internal communications were easily maintained, but the distance from the Canal was now great, and semi-permanent lines became a regular feature.

A class of visual signallers was formed at Headquarters, which at a later date became the Signal School for the Division.

The projected attack on El Arish on December 19 proving abortive owing to the sudden evacuation by the Turks, the company spent Christmas at Mazar, and moved forward with the Division to El Arish in January 1917.

After a week or two in bivouac at El Arish the Division was ordered to return to the Canal for preparation to proceed to France. A large camp was taken over at Moascar, by Ismailia, where the Signal Company had to equip itself for its campaign on the Western front.

THE COMPANY IN FRANCE
(1917–1918)

TOWARDS the end of February 1917, the Division completed nearly two and a half years in the Near East and voyaged by units and brigades from Alexandria to Marseilles. Before leaving Moascar a farewell march past took place at Ismailia before the Commander-in-Chief, General Sir Archibald Murray, in which the Signal Company took its place at the head of the column.

The Signal Company did not concentrate for this voyage, but left Nos. 2, 3 and 4 Sections to travel with their respective Brigade Headquarters.

Company Headquarters landed at Marseilles on March 3, and at once proceeded north, with the Division, to prepare for its final phase on the Western front.

The change of temperature from the heat of the Egyptian deserts to the severe frost and snow of March 1917 in France was keenly felt by men and animals, but the remarkable stamina and sound physical condition of all ranks of the company prevented much sickness.

The first experience in the front line, after a period in reserve in the devastated Péronne area, was gained in April at Roisel and Epéhy.

There was not that elaborate system of communications here that was called for in subsequent operations. Two lines to each brigade were hurriedly laid, and a small local Exchange Telephone System was organized for D.H.Q. proper.

The first decoration, a Meritorious Service Medal, awarded to the Division in France was gained by Corporal S. Eccles, a motor-cyclist despatch rider, who rode fifteen miles in order to deliver a despatch although suffering from a fractured ankle sustained *en route* as a result of an accident. Corporal Eccles was the first D.R. of the company to be decorated.

Leaving Epéhy the Division moved northwards and took over the Havrincourt Wood Sector, with D.H.Q. at Ytres. The enemy were now well established in the famous Hindenburg Line, and there seemed every prospect of a lengthy stay in this position.

Immediate steps were taken to perfect the divisional communications, and a semi-permanent route was built from Ytres forward to the south-west corner of Havrincourt Wood, where a shell-proof test point was constructed. From here ground lines were laid in duplicate along the edge of the Wood to each brigade. In addition a buried cable, six to seven feet deep, was laid through the wood to the proximity of the brigades. This was the first deep buried cable put down by the company, and singularly enough afterwards proved to be the last buried cable used by the Division, being invaluable in the tremendous battles leading to the breaking of the

P

Hindenburg Line in September 1918. Permanent lines ran from D.H.Q. to Corps.

The brigade sections greatly improved their forward communications, and though risk of breakdown of lines to battalions was brought to a minimum by duplicate and alternative routes, an elaborate system of visual from front to rear by means of daylight signalling lamp and shutter was organized and maintained.

Frequent practice of lamp signalling from the front trenches to observation balloons in the rear was carried out. In this sector also the first practical use was made of Earth Induction Sets and Trench Wireless by the brigade sections of the company.

By this time, the formation of two signal sub-sections for carrying out the communications of the Field Artillery Brigades of the Division had been effected, the whole of the divisional artillery communications being under the charge of Captain G. N. Robinson, with an officer commanding each sub-section.

Captain A. Roberts was now second in command of the Signal Company.

Early in July 1917, the Division was withdrawn from the line for rest and training, and marched to the Achiet-le-Petit area, at which place D.H.Q. was fixed, the three brigades being located at Gomiecourt, Courcelles and Achiet-le-Grand.

Full advantage was taken by the Signal Company of this opportunity, under ideal conditions, to instruct all ranks in the latest signal methods, it being fully realized that, efficient as the company had been in Gallipoli and Egypt, it had not had the advantage of the best and latest equipment as supplied to the Signal Service in France, nor the opportunity of attending the excellent Signal Schools in vogue there.

All ranks realized this and worked hard to make themselves thoroughly efficient. "Communications in the Attack" were practised by the brigade sections with their battalion signallers almost daily, until it was done "according to the book" even to the last pigeon.

The Divisional Signal School for training and refreshing infantry signallers, which had gradually taken shape after the arrival in France, was in full swing under the command of 2nd Lieutenant A. J. Ellis, and did a large amount of most necessary work.

In addition to systematic courses of drill, discipline and riding, the company found relaxation in sport, and under the direction of Major Johnson organized and carried out a full day's "sports," which included driving, riding and jumping events, motor-cycle races, and best "turn-outs" in men and horses.

Another innovation was the formation of the Signal Company's Concert Party under the title of "The Blue Birds," who secured an immediate and lasting popularity.

This pleasant period came to an end late in August, when the Division moved north into Belgium and took part in the Passchendaele operations in front of Ypres. Divisional Headquarters were at

42ND DIVL. SIGNAL COY. R.E.

Brandhoek with an Advanced Signal Office and Report Centre in the ramparts at Ypres.

The communications taken over were in a very bad state owing to the terrible condition of the ground and the enormous amount of shell fire on this front.

Strenuous efforts were made to improve the existing buried cable system from Brandhoek to advanced D.H.Q. and thence forward to Cambridge Road.

To supplement the buried cables an overland armoured cable was laid forward from the ramparts to brigades, but the constant shell fire soon rendered it useless and beyond repair. At Ypres all communications were patchy and extremely difficult to maintain, and the linemen had a particularly hot time, and several decorations were awarded.

A lamp signalling station was established at the ramparts, working through to all brigades with fair success. The wireless efforts were of small value, but the carrier pigeon service proved eminently successful and surprisingly quick and reliable.

In the attack made by the 125th Brigade on three almost impregnable "pill-boxes," the only communication No. 2 Section were able to maintain from the front line for over twenty-four hours was by pigeon, all other means proving absolutely useless.

A great many casualties were sustained whilst in this sector, gas poisoning cases being very numerous. The casualties due to gas in the personnel manning the Advanced D.H.Q. station in the ramparts was 90 per cent.

In September the Division moved from Ypres to the coast, and took over the extreme left sector of the Allied line, where communications were comprehensive, and included a great mileage of wire and cable consisting of semi-permanent overhead routes, ground and buried cables, wireless, pigeons, dogs and the usual despatch-rider letter service.

For the left section of the Corps front, D.H.Q. was at St. Idesbalde, but on moving to the right section, which included the town of Nieuport, D.H.Q. was moved on October 7 to Coxyde Bains, with an Advanced Divisional Signal Office at Pelican Bridge.

After a time, however, owing to the persistency of enemy shell fire, it was found necessary to move the Advanced Signal Office to trench dug-outs adjacent to the lines occupied by the Belgians on our right.

The Signal Office at Coxyde Bains was a substantial well-built affair of timber and iron, with sand-bag walls well sited and protected by sandhills. Traffic in the office, although lighter than at Ypres, was still fairly heavy—upwards of 400 messages a day—in many cases very long ones passing through.

Although there were no large operations undertaken by the Division in this sector, it was by no means a quiet one either in the forward line or the back areas, and the company suffered several casualties.

Corporal Hart, who on several previous occasions had shown entire disregard of danger, again did a gallant deed by carrying Pioneer Hardaker, who was badly wounded whilst working with Hart on line repairs at night, a distance of over a mile in a shelled area to safety and for medical attention.

The forward communications of the brigades were very difficult to maintain in this area, the town of Nieuport, through which ran many brigade lines, was shelled continually, but the greatest difficulty was the maintenance of lines across the Yser canal, which called for all the ingenuity, resource and patience which the brigade sections possessed.

Carefully screened daylight lamps proved of great assistance to telegraph communications to and from battalions.

With the long dark nights and riding without headlights, the despatch riders had a very trying time, particularly in the areas about Pelican Bridge and the artillery groups—Sykes' for one—on the left, which were well forward and under direct observation. Several cycles were smashed up by shell fire, and Corporal Rawlin became a casualty for the third time.

Following the example of well-established precedent, as soon as communications became established and the troops well sheltered, the Division again trekked, being relieved by the French about the 19th November. Moving by easy stages, the Division arrived on the Béthune–La Bassée front and established D.H.Q. at Locon, relieving the 25th Division on November 27.

The front seemed particularly tranquil after Ypres and Nieuport, and it was curious to see guns in action in and about farms and houses still occupied by the civilian population, who often carried on with agricultural work within easy range of the enemy's field-guns.

In this section communications which were taken over had apparently undergone little change during the preceding two years, and consisted of an open trestle pole route to the brigades and, in some instances, to Battalion Headquarters, together with armoured cables laid in and along the La Bassée Canal and the ditches and dykes draining the surrounding country. Buried cable, open field cable of every known type, wireless and visual provided for every contingency except that of prolonged battle.

The existing buried cables were very often only about a foot deep, and were occasionally placed in iron pipes. The ditches were freely used and served as a kind of open trench and helped to protect the cables from shell fire.

Deep buried cables were put down at important points, all open routes were greatly strengthened, numerous derelict routes were tested out and made good and used for alternative means of communication. The Signal Office was moved from the railway station to the cellar of the château opposite, and arrangements were made for reserve communications in the event of a retreat being necessary.

No difficulty was experienced in maintaining communications, as there was very little enemy activity, and the only casualties were those sustained by No. 2 Section when the 125th Brigade H.Q. at Loisne was hit by several 5·9-inch shells. On this occasion the Signal Office staff was wiped out, Corporal R. Cox being amongst the killed. Here again Sergeant Watters distinguished himself, most gallantly dashing into the Signal Office and carrying out the wounded under heavy shell fire.

Generally speaking, the La Bassée front was the quietest held by the Division in France, though the night bombing in Béthune and its outskirts was severe, and very trying to those in billets or in reserve.

The Signal School which had been carried on in Coxyde Bains was continued in a large building on the edge of Béthune under the command of Captain R. S. Newton, M.C., assisted by a very able staff of N.C.O. instructors from the company and the infantry battalions. Large numbers of officers and men were trained as signallers and many sent on to Corps and Army Signal Schools to qualify for instructors' certificates.

"The Blue Birds," under the able direction of Corporal Flaws, continued to produce excellent entertainments, and increased their popularity.

The 55th (West Lancashire) Division took over our line on the 15th February, 1918, and the Division went into reserve in the area about Chocques, the Signal Company, after a short period at Hinges, making its headquarters at Lenglet. The Divisional Signal Office was established at Labeuvrière, where practically the whole of the office staff, for several weeks, was provided by infantry signallers who were under training at the Signal School. This unique experiment worked fairly satisfactorily, and had the advantage of not only greatly increasing the efficiency of a number of battalion signallers, but relieving the divisional operators for drill and physical training, which stood them in good stead in the strenuous days to come later.

During the company's stay at Lenglet, special training was carried out in all branches of signal work. Cable laying, air line, jointing, permanent line work, drill, physical exercises, theory and practice of telegraphy, telephony, wireless and visual all having due attention.

The company was inspected by the Divisional Commander, Major-General Solly-Flood, C.M.G., D.S.O., who warmly complimented the Commanding Officer on the men's fine appearance and general turnout.

FRANCE

(1918)

THE pleasant days at Lenglet were abruptly terminated on March 23, when the Division moved south by motor transport, to help in staying the enemy offensive then fully launched. The

Signal Office was opened at Basseux on the 23rd until 3 p.m., and then moved forward to near Adinfer Wood, being established again by 6 p.m., when the infantry of the Division began to arrive and proceeded a few miles forward.

On the 24th a move was made to Monchy-au-Bois, when the company transport and mounted men arrived by march route.

On this day the Division took over part of the line in front of Gomiecourt, and the following day D.H.Q. moved forward to Bucquoy. A Divisional Report Centre was established at Gomiecourt, and communications were obtained by two ground cables, one running on each side of Logeast Wood, by visual, and wireless.

The enemy attacks developed about 9 a.m. on the 25th. The W.T. Station at Gomiecourt was soon put out of action by a series of direct hits, and later on the cable lines were destroyed by shell fire, and all attempts to restore them failed with heavy casualties. The visual transmitting station was destroyed by a direct hit, thus gravely interrupting visual communication, and after 1.30 p.m. the only means of communication left was by motor-cyclist despatch rider.

At 2 o'clock cable detachments moved forward, leaving fresh lines which were never utilized, as the brigade had moved to a fresh position. Captain Harmer was severely wounded near Gomiecourt, and was only saved from capture by the devotion of Corporals Folwell and Duffy and Sapper Beresford, who carried him into safety.

Communications were now in a terribly confused and incomplete state owing to the frequent moves of all units, and the constant change of Divisional and Corps areas.

The despatch riders again proved absolutely indispensable, and provided practically the only reliable means of communication for three days. Where all distinguished themselves, it is difficult to specify individuals, but Motor-Cyclist Corporals Roscoe, Baldwin, Gregson and Flaws, who were all awarded the Military Medal, most readily occur to memory. The youngest despatch rider, Pioneer Richardson, was killed at Gomiecourt, together with several of the 125th Brigade Wireless Telegraph detachment.

As will be naturally realized, the brigade sections of the company, both infantry and artillery, came in for the brunt of this severe fighting, suffering very heavy losses, and becoming completely exhausted by the time they were withdrawn from the line early in April.

Of the many decorations awarded to the brigade sections for bravery and exceptional work under fire, perhaps the most noteworthy was the D.C.M. earned by Second Corporal W. Williams of No. 4 (127th Brigade) Section.

At 6 p.m. on the 25th D.H.Q. moved to Fonquevillers, where a buried cable route was picked up and communication re-established with Corps, one pair of twisted cable being laid from Bucquoy to Fonquevillers via Essarts, Bucquoy being used as an Advance Report

42ND DIVL. SIGNAL COY. R.E.

Centre. The Advanced Divisional Signal Office moved in from Bucquoy the following day after being in "No Man's Land" for about twelve hours. Before leaving the Signal Office at Bucquoy all possible shelters were burned and all stores safely got away. The motor transport proved invaluable during these operations, and enabled the company to move with its headquarter signal equipment almost intact.

The lines laid from Bucquoy on the previous day were cut at Essarts, and an Advanced Divisional Report Centre was established there by Lieutenant A. J. Ellis, later awarded the M.C., who had been left in charge at Bucquoy. Unfortunately this position was within the enemy barrage, and as a result the cable lines were constantly cut.

On the 26th D.H.Q. again moved further back and was established at St. Amand by 6 p.m. the same evening, and remained there until April 2.

Duplicate lines were laid from Advanced D.H.Q. to Essarts, and from Essarts to the brigades in Gommecourt Wood, Corporal Hart's detachment being particularly prominent during this period of extreme activity.

Strenuous efforts were necessary to keep these lines (too often put down at the trot and along heavily shelled roads) intact. Test points in cellars or behind some stout wall were established at convenient intervals of about half a mile for a distance of two miles from Essarts. Two linemen were stationed at each point, and by dint of ceaseless activity and with splendid devotion to duty, the lines were kept fairly intact. As soon as possible direct lines were laid across the open country and away from roads and tracks, which proved a distinct improvement, making maintenance much easier.

The Division, now sadly depleted in strength and greatly exhausted, was withdrawn from the line on April 7 and placed in reserve for a brief rest and an opportunity to reorganize and re-equip. The Headquarters of the Division were established in the château at Hénu from the 2nd till the 7th April, and then at the neighbouring château at Pas-en-Artois.

This period of rest finished on April 16, when the Division took over part of the line immediately to the right or south of Bucquoy, with Headquarters at Couin, and an Advanced Divisional Signal Office at Fonquevillers.

Forward communications to Fonquevillers, and the brigades in the region of Sailly-au-Bois, were at first provided by ground cables, but early steps were taken to locate and bring into use the old buried cables laid down two years previously during the battles of the Somme. Corporal Folwells and Fox and Sapper Beach were very much to the fore on this job, their efforts proving most successful. Sufficient cables were made good to provide for a great improvement of all forward lines, and many routes were fully duplicated.

Visual and wireless were largely employed in this sector between the Division and Infantry and Artillery Brigades; these communications were under the charge of Lieutenant P. C. Fletcher, who was now in command of all the "alternative communications," which ranged from the latest wireless equipment to pigeons, dogs and rockets.

The despatch riders still played a very important part in the scheme of communication, and as the wires were often blocked with very long operation messages, the motor cyclists were frequently called upon to undertake extra runs, and never failed to deliver their despatches in the shortest possible time.

The N.C.O.s and men at Advanced D.H.Q. carried on a difficult task splendidly and responded to every call.

The linemen under Corporal Hart constructed a buried cable route from here to the brigades, by working only at night, and then only with rare luck as regards serious casualty.

The telegraph and telephone operators were sorely taxed by heavy traffic with exceptionally long and complicated messages which were handled with wonderful speed and accuracy. Several of the men refused to be relieved for a brief rest at Company Headquarters, being determined to stick to their job as long as the Division was in the line.

From the time of leaving Lenglet the transport of the company, both horsed and mechanical, had been severely taxed. With constant movements, numerous outlying detachments, and great consumption of technical stores on new works, the drivers had many long and arduous duties to perform. The men, however, were equal to any and every emergency, and backing up the efforts of an exceptionally well-organized quartermaster's department under C.Q.M.S. G. H. Millner, saw to it that every man was fully rationed no matter where he was stationed. Some of the drivers seemed to have an uncanny knack not only of finding their way across unknown and difficult country, but of "winning" all manner of useful stores *en route*.

Early in May the Division was relieved and went into reserve, D.H.Q. being again established at Pas. Whilst here a great deal of signal work was carried out in connection with possible defensive action, and battle positions for D.H.Q. and all brigades were selected and fully connected by duplicate air lines and cables. In addition comprehensive tactical exercises were carried out so as to familiarize all ranks with the anticipated requirements, and drastic steps were taken to ensure mobility.

The month spent at Pas was a very enjoyable one for all ranks, the weather conditions were ideal, and the practically unspoilt grounds of Pas Château and the surrounding country afforded a pleasant change from the ruins and desolation further forward. Numerous boxing contests took place, and "The Blue Birds" performed almost nightly.

The attachment of an American regiment to the Division for training purposes brought both operators and linemen into contact with our allies from U.S.A.

On June 6 the Division again moved into the line, relieving the

42ND DIVL. SIGNAL COY. R.E.

New Zealand Division in the sector Hebuterne–Sailly-au-Bois–Colincamps, with Headquarters at Bus-les-Artois.

The system of line communication on this front was mostly buried. This cable system, although two years under ground, was in excellent repair, except the joints, which demanded a lot of attention. It consisted of twenty-five pair lead-covered cables and in some cases D5 twisted. In the case of lead-covered cable, it was difficult to provide the means of repair, as that particular class of cable had become obsolete for buried work, being replaced by armoured cable. The insulation of the D5 cable had in many cases perished, and was therefore very earthy and difficult to work.

Owing to heavy shelling, the Brigade Headquarters were moved back to more secure positions, and at very short notice the company put down buried cable systems to the brigades on the right and left. Each buried system consisted of three seven-pair lead-covered and three seven-pair armoured cables.

The electrical communications were supplemented by wireless, pigeons, and dogs, together with a visual chain and the D.R.L.S. system; rockets were experimented with and used to a limited extent. These methods of alternative communication had by this time been brought to a high state of efficiency.

The Divisional Headquarters being moved back to Authie for tactical reasons, necessitated another buried system to a point about half way between Authie and Bus. From there a lead cable was suspended on existing air line poles back to Authie.

On the 15th of August D.H.Q. returned to the château at Bus-les-Artois, and immediate preparations were made for the offensive, which culminated three months later in the defeat of the enemy. The buried cable was still further exploited, and old test points in the front line were re-opened.

After the enemy's defeat and retirement on August 21 the buried cable routes were extended by means of ground lines laid out from hand barrows, and communication was quickly obtained as far forward as the Advanced Battalion Headquarters, and the Advanced Divisional Report Centre.

Wireless and visual stations were established at Serre.

D.H.Q. moved forward to Colincamps on the 24th, taking over dug-outs in the Chalkpit vacated by the right brigade.

The brigades and artillery groups were connected up by ground lines which ran forward by two routes, connected by two lateral lines in the vicinity of the Brigade Headquarters.

On the 23rd a line was laid from Serre to Miraumont Dovecotes, where an Advanced Divisional Report Centre was established. The cable detachment in charge of C.S.M. Willcock had a most difficult task, but completed the line before dark without mishap.

The lines from Miraumont were extended to near Bucquoy on the 27th, by Sergeant McCarthy, who had two cable carts and one or two linemen, the working parties being provided by attached wireless men. This job was a difficult one, across country pitted almost every yard with great shell holes, and covered with barbed wire and every obstruction imaginable.

Lines were now laid from Beauregard Dovecote through Miraumont and Irles to Loupart Wood, where the Advanced Divisional Report Centre was finally established at a point about half a mile west of the Wood.

The brigade sections and sub-sections, during this advance and continual fighting, did splendid work without exception, not only maintaining communication by some means or other between their headquarters and constantly moving units, but also giving great assistance to Company Headquarters in the difficult task of keeping in touch with the Division.

About a week later the Headquarters of the Division were moved to near Bucquoy, and then to Grevillers close to Bapaume, where the command of the company was assumed by Major P. A. Foy, M.C., in succession to Major S. Gordon Johnson, D.S.O., M.C., who had been appointed to the command of the Fifth Army Signal School. For nearly two years Major Johnson had commanded the company, and brought it to a high state of efficiency by his ability and personal influence; his thoughts were ever for the comfort and well-being of his men, and it was with universal regret that his departure was witnessed.

The advance still continued, the forward communication from the Advanced Divisional Headquarters now consisted of one line through Loupart Wood, across the Bapaume–Albert Road, through La Barque to a point beyond Buchanan's Cross; this line was used on the 29th inst. by two battalions in the line, the 126th Brigade Headquarters and two Artillery Brigades; Riencourt being taken by the Division on August 31.

The whole Division was withdrawn from the line on the 5th September, and went into rest for a few days, Headquarters being established in some old German ammunition dug-outs close to Riencourt (Bapaume).

The question of further supplies of cable was now becoming a serious problem, and day after day cable wagons were sent back over old battle areas for salvage purposes. The salved cable was carefully gone through, overhauled and jointed.

Whilst in rest at Riencourt considerable attention was paid by the new commanding officer to the discipline and smartness of the company at Headquarters, and drill and ceremonial parades took place daily, with the result that any sign of slackness consequent of the recent mobility and scattered detachments was quickly effaced.

Following our advancing infantry, the company moved to Velu Wood towards the middle of September, when the enemy was back at the old Hindenburg Line.

A previous division had laid the lines, in this area, on the French system of ground stakes, and although the system had some points in its favour, it proved a source of trouble when the tanks commenced to move forward.

42ND DIVL. SIGNAL COY. R.E.

The buried cable through Havrincourt Wood, which had been laid by this company in the previous year, was rapidly brought into use and proved invaluable in the successful assault against the Hindenburg Line.

The next move of Company Headquarters was to near Trescault on October 8, when, owing to the forward movement becoming so rapid, there was only a single line to each brigade. On the following day Headquarters were at Esnes, the New Zealand Division having gone forward, leaving the 42nd in reserve.

On the 12th October D.H.Q. marched to Beauvois-en-Cambresis, and again took over its part of the front line. Ground cables were laid forward to the brigades, and subsequently poled.

The Signal School which had latterly been carried on at Bus was now brought forward and established under great difficulties of food and fuel in a farm in this vicinity.

The Selle River positions were successfully attacked by the Division on the 20th, when all forward communications were by ground cable.

The cable wagon continued to play an important part in the communications of the Division, and it was found possible to lay cable from the wagons by the most inexperienced men, the more skilled personnel being employed in maintenance and placing lines in safe positions.

Many casualties were suffered at this time in the brigade sections, and the company lost many valuable N.C.O.s and men, and a most capable officer in Lieutenant H. T. P. Moore, M.C., who was killed whilst commanding an Artillery Brigade Sub-section.

On the 5th November Advanced D.H.Q. moved from Beauvois via Beaudignes to Potelle Château, near Le Quesnoy. Communications were not improved, the Division moving almost immediately to the south-western corner of the Forest of Mormal. Owing to an epidemic of influenza in the company, Corps Headquarters were asked for assistance, as over fifty per cent. of the company had become casualties, but none arrived.

After stiff fighting in the Forest, the Division moved forward rapidly, the 126th Brigade entering Hautmont on the 8th, and D.H.Q. was established at Haute Rue (at the north-eastern corner of the Forest) on the same day, communications being maintained by ground cable to the brigades and artillery. Despatch riders, wireless, pigeons, and dogs continued to be used as alternative means of communication.

During the advance through the great Forest of Mormal the 126th Infantry Brigade suffered heavy casualties, and for a short period its Signal Section, No. 3 Section of the Company, commanded by Lieutenant H. G. Brown, M.C., abandoned communications and assisted to man the front line.

Divisional Headquarters moved forward to Hautmont on November 9, and two days later hostilities ceased.

An advance of over one hundred miles had been made, following a retreating enemy fighting bitterly all the time, and communications between all the various headquarters and their units had been maintained, almost without fail, by the Signal Company. To have done so under the best conditions would have been no mean effort, but to have achieved it under all the difficulties of battle, and over some of the worst possible country, was a feat to be proud of, and on arriving at Hautmont the company felt that it had done its best in this the last chapter of the Great War.

The Signal Company concentrated its personnel at Hautmont, and soon afterwards proceeded by march route into Belgium to Charleroi, where the 42nd Division was established as part of the army in support of the advanced troops on the Rhine.

The civilization of the town of Charleroi appealed to all ranks, after the experiences and discomforts of the past few years, the luxury of respectable billets, the attraction of shops, and the pleasures of cafés and cinemas all helped to make life in Charleroi quite pleasant for a time. Visits were paid by many of the company to the Field of Waterloo, to Brussels, and other places of interest, and Christmas 1918 was celebrated by the company according to the highest traditions of the British Army.

During its service abroad many honours and decorations were won by members of the company, but none were more richly deserved than the M.C. awarded in Egypt to Captain R. S. Newton, the M.C. and Bar awarded to Captain A. Roberts in France, or the awards announced at Charleroi of the D.C.M. to Company Sergt.-Major H. Willcock and the M.S.M. to Company Quartermaster Sergeant G. H. Millner.

Early in 1919 the process of demobilization commenced, and continued rapidly in the company, until only the cadre was left to return to England in March 1919, and so bring to an end the period of service in the Great War of the 42nd Divisional Signals.

PART VII

66TH DIVISIONAL ROYAL ENGINEERS

CALENDAR OF MOVEMENTS

Date.	H.Q. 66th Divisional Signal Co.	H.Q. 430 Field Co.	H.Q. 431 Field Co.	H.Q. 432 Field Co.
1917	Landed at Le Havre, 28/2/17	Landed at Le Havre, 28/2/17	Landed at Le Havre, 2/3/17	Landed at Le Havre, 2/3/17
March 5				Lambres
March 7		Le Hamel	Calonne	
March 8				Beuvry
March 10			Béthune	
March 16		Gorre		
March 17			Le Préol	
April 1	Béthune			
April 19	Locon			
June 22		Le Hamel		Marles-les-Mines
June 24	Chocques			
June 25		Dunkerque		
June 26	Coudekerque-Branche		Bray Dunes	Petite Synthe
June 27		Oost-Dunkerque Bains		Oost-Dunkerque
June 28			Oost-Dunkerque Bains	
June 29		Nieuport Bains		
July 10	Rosendael			
July 16		Coxyde		Oost-Dunkerque Bains
July 18	St. Idesbalde			
July 19			Nieuport Bains	
Aug. 5			Near Furnes	
Aug. 27		Nieuport Bains		
Aug. 28			Oost-Dunkerque Bains	
Sept. 3		Oost-Dunkerque Bains		
Sept. 4			Nieuport Bains	
Sept. 18				Nieuport Bains
Sept. 19			Oost-Dunkerque Bains	
Sept. 24		Bray Dunes		Ghyvelde
Sept. 25	La Panne		La Panne	
Sept. 27	Renescure	" Ridge " Wood Ypres	" Ridge " Wood Ypres	
Sept. 28				" Ridge " Wood Ypres
Sept. 29				
Oct. 3	Godewaerswelde			
Oct. 4	Winnezeele			

EAST LANCS. R.E. HISTORY

Date.	H.Q. 66th Divisional Signal Co.	H.Q. 430 Field Co.	H.Q. 431 Field Co.	H.Q. 432 Field Co.
Oct. 6	Brandhoek			
Oct. 7	Ypres			
Oct. 12	Winnezeele			
Oct. 20	Renescure			
Oct. 25		Poperinghe	Near Brandhoek	Brandhoek
Oct. 26		Racquinghem	Racquinghem	Racquinghem
Nov. 1		Hondeghem	Hondeghem	Hondeghem
Nov. 9		Kruistraat	Ypres	
Nov. 10	Ypres			Kruistraat
Nov. 22		Berthen		
Nov. 23	Reninghelst	Staple		
Nov. 24	Hazebrouck			
Nov. 26			Sylvestre-Cappel	Morbecque
Dec. 8				St. Marie Cappel
Dec. 14				Ypres
Dec. 15	Blendecques			
Dec. 16		Ypres	Ypres	
1918				
Jan. 11				Potijze
Jan. 13	Ypres			
Feb. 6		St.Jan-ter-Biezen		
Feb. 9			St.Jan-ter-Biezen	
Feb. 10			Watou	
Feb. 11	Couthove Château			St.Jan-ter-Biezen
Feb. 16		Proven	Proven	
Feb. 17		Guillaucourt	Le Quesnel	Proven
Feb. 18	Villers-Brettoneux			Vauvillers
Feb. 28				Montigny Farm
March 2	Nobescourt Farm	Roisel	Milieu Copse	

March 21 to 30—66th Division engaged in rearguard actions with left wing of Fifth Army—R.E. used as infantry.

March 30	Boves	Boves Wood	Boves Wood	Boves Wood
March 31	Pissy	Amiens	Amiens	Amiens
April 1		Saleul	Floxicourt	Floxicourt
April 2	Bellancourt	Ergnies	Ergnies	Ergnies
April 3	St. Ricquier			
April 5		Millancourt	Millancourt	Millancourt
April 11			St. Leger-les-Domarts	St. Leger-les-Domarts
April 12			Vaux-les-Amienois	Villers Bocage
April 13		Famechon		
April 21	Tilcques	Longpré		Vignaucourt
April 22		Cormette	Longpré	Longpré
April 23			Leuline	Audenthun
April 26	Nielles-les-Blequin	Coulomby	Morbecque	Staple
May 2		Arrest		
May 3		Bethencourt-sur-Mer		

66TH DIVL. R.E.

Date.	H.Q. 66th Divisional Signal Co.	H.Q. 430 Field Co.	H.Q. 431 Field Co.	H.Q. 432 Field Co.
May 4	Friville-Escarbotin			
May 11			St. Marie Cappel	
May 12		Nibas		
May 20			Cohem	Cohem
May 21			Helfaut	
May 22			Bilques	St. Quentin
May 25		Courcelles		
June 9		Machiel Area (Bois de Crécy)		
June 20		Pierregot		
June 21		Mollieus-au-Bois		
June 22	Bernaville			
June 23			Les Ciseaux	
July 9				Mazinghem
July 16		Berteaucourt		
July 17		Pont Remy		
July 22		Loziéres		
July 23	Gaillefontaine			
Aug. 14				Molinghem
Aug. 16		St. Maurice		
Aug. 28			Steenbecque	
Sept. 9				Gonnehem
Sept. 20	Le Cauroy	Sars-les-Bois	Marles-les-Mines	Boyaval
Sept. 21			Berlencourt	Denier
Sept. 28	Fouilloy	Vaire-sous-Corbie	Vaire-sous-Corbie	Vaire-sous-Corbie
Sept. 29		Eclusier	Eclusier	Eclusier
Oct. 2	Montauban	Combles	Combles	Combles
Oct. 3		Epéhy	Epéhy	Epéhy
Oct. 4	Combles			
Oct. 5		Villers Faucon	VillersFaucon	Villers Faucon
Oct. 6	Ronssoy	Bony	Bony	
Oct. 7				Bony
Oct. 8	Bony		Beaurevoir	Bellevue Farm
Oct. 9	Beaurevoir	Serain	Avelu	Avelu
Oct. 10	Maretz	Maurois	Maurois	Reumont
Oct. 20	Serain			
Oct. 21		Le Cateau		
Oct. 23			Le Cateau	Le Cateau
Nov. 2	Le Cateau			
Nov. 5	Landrécies	Landrécies	Landrécies	Landrécies
Nov. 6	Maroilles	Basse Noyelles	Maroilles	Maroilles
Nov. 7	Taisnières	Dompierre	Taisnières	Marbaix
Nov. 8	Dompierre			Le Petit Fuchay
Nov. 9		Solre-le-Château		St. Hilaire
Nov. 10	Solre-le-Château		Solre-le-Château	Solre-le-Château
Nov. 11		Beaurieux		Sivry
Nov. 14		Solre-le-Château		Solre-le-Château
Nov. 16				Montbliart
Nov. 18	Froidechapelle	Montbliart		Cerfontaine
Nov. 19	Philippeville	Villers-deux-Eglises	Philippeville	
Nov. 23		Philippeville		

Date.	H.Q. 66th Divisional Signal Co.	H.Q. 430 Field Co.	H.Q. 431 Field Co.	H.Q. 432 Field Co.
Nov. 24	Waulsort	Aguimont	Waulsort	Miavoye
Dec. 15				Huy
Dec. 16	Ciney	Marche	Ciney	
1919				
Feb. 11		Achêne		Taviet
March 3		Ciney		Ciney
May 21	Cadres left for U.K.			
June 13			Cadres disbanded at Ciney and personnel sent to Marchienne-au-Pont-Charleroi for demobilization	

PART VIII
66TH (EAST LANCS.) DIVISIONAL ROYAL ENGINEERS
1914–1919

WHEN the "First Line," or original East Lancashire Division, left Bolton and Bury for Egypt in September 1914, there remained at Bolton a small number both of officers and other ranks, who for various reasons were unable to accompany the Division abroad: some were medically unfit for active service overseas, and others unable for business and other reasons to volunteer immediately for foreign service. These detachments, which were left by all units of the Division, remained at Bolton till October, training as best they could with the little equipment the Division had not taken with them. The training that could be carried out was very limited in extent, and this, together with their sudden separation from their comrades, made the life of all ranks somewhat cheerless for a time. In October, however, a move was made to Winstanley Park, Wigan, and soon after this, recruits for all units began to arrive. About this time the C.R.E., Lieut.-Colonel C. E. Newton, was transferred to the T.F. Reserve, having reached the age limit for the active list, and Major H. A. Fielding took over command, being promoted Lieut.-Colonel.

Meanwhile, recruiting had been proceeding vigorously at the R.E. Headquarters at Seymour Grove, Old Trafford, and a large body of men had been got together there, including several N.C.O.s who had formerly been in the East Lancs. R.E. and had rejoined.

Early in November the units from Wigan moved into billets in Southport, and on the 14th of that month all recruits still at Seymour Grove went to Southport to join them. The companies could now be properly organized once more, and became part of the "Second Line" East Lancs. Division. The field companies became respectively the 2/1st and 2/2nd East Lancs. Field Company. The strength was about 75 per cent. of the full establishment in personnel, and various drafts of recruits from Old Trafford during the next few weeks brought this up to approximately full strength, though horses, vehicles, stores, and rifles were still lacking. For some time the R.E. units had only sixteen horses and two G.S. wagons between them, while there were barely enough rifles to arm the guard at the R.E. Headquarters in Duke Street. During this time, when the guard was mounted, they had to take over from the old guard not only the latter's duties, but their rifles also, the number of rifles being insufficient to arm two guards simultaneously. This was the subject of a certain amount of facetious comment by other units. As a matter of fact, the other units were not very much better off, for they had been going through exactly the same process of formation as the R.E., but when any rifles became available for issue, the infantry units naturally had the preference.

After a short time some Japanese rifles were issued for drill purposes, and a considerable number of picks and shovels were acquired; also, large quantities of bridging stores were obtained from the old headquarters at Old Trafford. This enabled training in infantry drill, musketry, bridging, and trench construction to be carried out. Of the regular Sergeant Instructors of the permanent staff who had been with the East Lancs. R.E. at the outbreak of the war, four had gone abroad with the First Line, and only Sergeant Spanner remained. When the Second Line became a complete division, he acted as the R.E. Regimental Sergeant-Major, and was of very great assistance in training all ranks, more especially in bridging. Of the officers and N.C.O.s of the original division, only a few had remained behind, and the new ones had to learn the work themselves, and endeavour to teach it to recruits at the same time; a regular warrant officer was therefore invaluable.

Bridging was done mostly in the Marine Lake, earthworks at first on the Birkdale Sandhills, and later at Shirdley Hill, where the use of a field was acquired. It was difficult in the flat surrounding country to find a field sufficiently high above sea-level to permit of earthworks being dug without reaching water. This training was varied by occasional route marches, but was still hampered by the lack of wagons and horses and proper field and signal company equipment. The majority had never seen a pontoon or a tool-cart, and had only a hazy idea as to the tools and stores carried by a field company or a signal company in the field. The lack of horses made it impossible to give proper instruction to the mounted ranks, who spent most of their time in training with the sappers. The signal company had to content themselves mainly with " flag-wagging," as they had no other equipment.

Thanks mainly to the efforts of Major Carlyle, a band of fair size was formed, and performed very creditably with Corporal Smedley as bandmaster. Owing to the shortage of khaki cloth at this stage, the dress of the units was a curious mixture. Some men did have khaki; others were issued with the old scarlet uniforms from Seymour Grove, but these were used chiefly for Church Parades and similar ceremonial occasions, the working dress of the majority being civilian clothes, or a mixture of that and some form of uniform—blue trousers and a civilian coat and cap being quite commonly seen.

Since the whole Second Line East Lancs. Division was at Southport, several inspections of it by outside inspecting generals were necessary, both as a part of the training of the Division, and also for the purpose of ascertaining progress. The turn-out of the R.E. on these occasions was always smart, and compared very favourably with that of other units. A few drafts of reinforcements were sent overseas to join the First Line in Egypt, one exceptionally large one going to the Signal Company in March 1915.

At the end of May 1915 the whole Second Line Division was moved to a hutted camp at Crowborough, Sussex. At this time the companies were in possession of a more reasonable number of horses, and shortly after arrival at Crowborough they received practically all their wagons and equipment, so that they could now train on more satisfactory lines. Later in the year it was decided that the Second Line should be kept intact as a complete division, with a view, so it was understood, to proceeding abroad as such at some future date. In order that the training and organization of the units should not be interfered with, it was necessary to discontinue sending drafts of reinforcements abroad to the First Line (which was now called the 42nd Division), and consequently a Third Line was formed as a training depot, and Major Carlyle left the Second Line to take command of this. In October 1915 the R.E. organization of a division was altered from two to three field companies, and the third field company for the Second Line (the 2/3rd East Lancs. Field Company) was provided by sending a large draft from the Third Line Depot to Crowborough. In November all divisions in Great Britain were numbered, and the Second Line became the 66th Division.

On March 20, 1916, the whole of the 66th Division was moved from Crowborough to Colchester, where the R.E. units were accommodated in the Cavalry Barracks, which had just been vacated by the 20th Hussars. Until July 1916 there had been no adjutant in the 66th Divisional R.E., but about that time Captain Morgan was appointed to that post. About the same time, too, Lieut.-Colonel Fielding, after a prolonged illness, was transferred to the T.F. Reserve, and Lieut.-Colonel Guggisberg was appointed C.R.E., 66th Division. Training continued without very many noteworthy incidents. There was naturally a great deal of speculation as to when the 66th Division would go abroad, but it was not until 1917 that this came about, the long-desired orders to move to France being received during the last days of February.

The field companies moved separately to Southampton, and thence crossed to Le Havre, where one night was spent in the rest camps. From Le Havre the companies travelled by train to villages between Aire and Béthune, and got their first chance to practise the long, detailed but well-thought-out maxims of the C.R.E., Lieut.-Colonel F. G. Guggisberg. During the next few days the remainder of the Division arrived, and the whole being concentrated the field companies moved forward and took up billets in Gorre, Le Préol, and Beuvry respectively. The sector taken over by the 66th Division was one which had not materially altered for a long time, and with its long and complicated trench system and " boyaux "—all in seemingly hopeless disrepair—was almost ideal to complete the training which the companies had been taught in England. With the greatest energy and goodwill all ranks set to work to clear and revet the decaying " boyaux " and trenches—but here we soon met our enemy the " Minnie," a feature of this sector, and as we soon found, the cause in large part of the difference between these trenches and our model ones at Colchester. Still, "Minnie" or no "Minnie," the field companies struggled with the problem, and progress was soon made. The trenches, "the boyaux," the tram-lines, etc., all began to improve, and the companies very soon settled down. About the 20th of March the 66th Division side-stepped and took over the Hohenzollern Redoubt sector. It was at this time that the command of the 480 Field Company was taken over by Major W. Garforth, R.E. The hard work and normal routine were broken also by two raids which the R.E. accompanied much to their joy with mobile charges, and in which they did much damage to the Boche dug-outs, etc. Major R. H. Joseph, in command of the 432 Field Company, was very unfortunately wounded, and the command was given to Major E. C. Graves, and Major P. H. Sharpe, R.E., arrived to command the 431 Field Company, R.E. This interesting period came to an end in June, and at the end of that month the 66th Division was withdrawn, and having entrained in the Chocques area was taken north to the area around Dunkirk. Here the 66th Division remained, but as usual the sappers did not stay with them, and a few days later were on their way to the line, which had been but recently taken over from the French and extended from the coast near Lombartzyde to the south side of Nieuport, where the Belgians took it over. The next halt was in the neighbourhood of Oost-Dunkerque, a pleasant little village, not then damaged very much. The halt was short, the 480 Field Company being sent up immediately to Nieuport Bains to join the 1st Division R.E., and work in the reserve area, while the 431 and 432 Field Companies at the same time were attached to the 32nd Division holding the line east of Nieuport itself. The sappers now had a taste of what had the reputation of being a "bad sector." Preparations for a British offensive on a large scale were in progress, and repairs to dams and bridges, together with the construction of gun positions, observation posts, dumps, shelters and light railways, followed one another in endless succession. In spite of many difficulties, and harassed daily by incessant enemy shelling, the men stuck to it well and got through any amount of work, remaining cheerful at all times, however depressing the conditions. After about a month of this exhausting work under bad conditions the climax came on the 10th of July, when the enemy delivered a very heavy and sudden attack on the 1st Division and drove them back to the west bank of the Yser. This attack was accompanied by a very heavy bombardment which extended as far back as and behind Oost-Dunkerque. All units in the area suffered casualties, but the situation was rapidly restored with unfortunately the loss of our positions on the coast east of the Yser. Very shortly after this the 66th Division was brought up from Dunkerque and the field companies rejoined their own Division, and with it took over the new coast sector at Nieuport Bains. As may be imagined, the defences in this sector, but recently occupied

LA BASSÉE SECTOR. THE BRICK STACKS.

NIEUPORT, SHOWING REMAINS OF PUTNEY AND CROWDER BRIDGES AND RUBBER HOUSE IN THE DISTANCE.

NIEUPORT BAINS AND RIVER YSER.
(From an Aeroplane Photograph.)

66TH DIVL. R.E. 233

as a front line, were far from adequate, being merely the remains of the old French reserve lines, etc. Nieuport Bains is built on the sand dunes lining the sea with low-lying marshy fields behind; these two factors had seriously damaged even those defences that did exist, and added much to the difficulties now to be overcome by the 66th Division field companies, who were assisted by an Australian Tunnelling Company, attached for making deep dug-outs (as deep as possible in the sand dunes). Thus there followed a very interesting and hard-working time whilst new defences rapidly took shape, and the old cut-and-cover "boyaux" were repaired and maintained. Also and no less important, the 10th D.C.L.I., who had joined us as Pioneer Battalion, kept open the pavé road from Oost-Dunkerque Bains to the Laiterie. The billets were good—rear billets in or near Oost-Dunkerque Bains for all three companies and forward billets in the electrically lit cellars of Nieuport Bains; these last, being near the work and with grand piano complete, were especially popular. The 432 Field Company also had two sections in old French dug-outs near the Laiterie which they shared with a field battery which nearly always broke their short hours of slumber. Shortly after this preparations began again for a grand attack on Ostend to follow the hoped-for success at Ypres, and for this the R.E. were to play an important part in crossing the Yser. The scheme provided for pontoon bridges to be erected by the 430 and 431 Field Companies, who were also to provide parties to accompany the attack and for a number of Berthon boat ferry rafts (made on a plan designed by Lieutenant Beaumont) to ferry across two brigades of infantry to commence the attack. This entailed endless collection of stores, detailing of plans, reconnaissance, and training by sections in a camp near Furnes. This was a delightful rest, and both the sappers and pioneers attached for the purpose became rapidly proficient in the handling of Berthon boats and pontoons. Two special rehearsals were carried out at Nieuport, and proved exceedingly realistic (Berthon boats only). All this preparation was under the eye of Lieut.-Colonel E. N. Mozley, D.S.O., R.E., who was assisting the C.R.E., Lieut.-Colonel G. C. Williams (who had succeeded Lieut.-Colonel F. G. Guggisberg, appointed to command a brigade of infantry in June). Colonel Mozley's eye was piercing, but his questions were even more so, as the 42nd Division R.E. could testify. The ordinary work was continued all through, and only portions of each company were trained in turn at Furnes. The attack at Ypres did not, however, prove at once successful, and so the operation was temporarily postponed. Major E. C. Graves received an appointment with a field survey unit and Major R. L. Gracey came from the 42nd Division to command the 432 Field Company. But although postponed the original and rather hurried plans were not complete, and so were gradually extended and improved, and much reconnaissance of the Yser, etc., was carried out. The weather improved and was perfectly glorious in August and September, and those who could manage it had some very pleasant excursions into La Panne and also occasional baths. This period was really a very happy one—plenty of hard work but good billets; the only real drawbacks were the occasional heavy shelling, the high velocity shells, and bombs which wrought havoc in back areas at night especially. Thus time passed on towards the third week in September. Plans for relief were now got out and much joy was experienced when it was learnt that we were to be relieved by our First Line Division, the 42nd, who very shortly arrived from a three-week spell in Ypres and took over from us. Each field company then marched out with its affiliated brigade group via Coxyde Bains and La Panne to Ghyvelde or Bray Dunes, and after two or three days spent largely on gas drill and games the companies were embarked on bus convoys, which after some minor mistakes delivered them into the very thickly populated area of Ridge Wood—Vierstraat, where they were rejoined after even more minor escapades by their rations and mounted sections, which had preceded them by road. A day spent at Ridge Wood, and the companies marched towards Ypres. The 430 and 431 Field Companies marched with the Pioneer Battalion and the C.R.E. to a damp and rather unhealthy camp at Goldfish Château on the main road from Vlamertinghe to Ypres, and the 432 Field Company into dug-outs, etc., in an old soap works opposite the Cathedral in Ypres itself. The mounted sections were billeted in that much-bombed hamlet, Vlamertinghe, where they subsequently spent many harassed nights.

 The work on which all three field companies and the Pioneer Battalion were to be employed was a " slab " road from Wieltje to Spree Farm and on again via Kansas Cross to Gravenstafel. This was commenced right away the next morning. Each day lorries carried the parties from Goldfish Château up to a point just past St. Jean, starting just about dawn or before and working till about 2 p.m.; 432 Field Company being nearer had to employ their own pontoon vehicles if they wished to avoid walking, which they soon did after several marches on the pavé up through St. Jean.

 The work was done in full daylight once the dawn had completely broken, and at first the weather was very good; this was all right in one way, but in others it increased the accuracy of the enemy gunners, whose attention in the salient was quite sufficient even in bad weather. Nevertheless the road progressed very rapidly indeed, the greatest hindrance being the continuous stream of men, animals, rations, and water-carts across the men at work and the constant repairs to work already done. Still at last the third Battle of Ypres seemed to be moving on again, and although the work was hard, the shelling heavy, the billets poor and bombed and shelled at that, the slow but sure stream of prisoners and the rush on the bigger days made every one full of hope and anxious to push the road on. Tempers were not even lost when on arrival at dawn one day it was found that an 8-inch howitzer had in its

YPRES.
(From an Aeroplane Photograph.)

ZONNEBEKE CHURCH.
(From an Aeroplane Photograph.)

anxiety to get ahead walked off the end of the road into the mud. In order to avoid delay a temporary road had to be built round it, and it was only after many unsuccessful attempts to remove it that the combined efforts of gunners and sappers finally triumphed. The drivers had nearly as exciting a time as the sappers—they helped on the road in the afternoon and carted hundreds and hundreds of slabs up to and around the very lively neighbourhood of Spree Farm. Gradually as October advanced the weather grew worse, and as progress was made with the road, the daily tramp to and from work became longer. To shorten the latter the Goldfish Château Camp was moved up to Salvation Corner—a more convenient spot but no improvement as regards home comforts. Soon after the move the 430 Field Company were unfortunate in losing their O.C., Major Garforth, as the result of a bomb-wound in the arm received whilst entering his dug-out. The " Corps " now demanded that the rate of progress of the road should be increased, and the 49th Divisional R.E. and a company of New Zealand engineers were sent up to help. The heavy strain on all ranks was beginning to show, and orders for the relief of the 66th Divisional R.E., who had been at work on the same job for more than a month, were welcomed.

The move took place in two stages, first by march route to an area around Brandhoek and thence by bus convoy to Racquinghem. Here the billets were very good indeed and the people very nice and kind. The field companies were just about to settle down to enjoy themselves when news arrived that Sir D. Haig would inspect the whole Division, including the R.E., in two days' time. The infantry had been out and cleaned up for at least a fortnight. The R.E. had been in longer and had only just got out—no one had much in the way of cleaning materials, and nobody's kit was by any means as good as it had been before going into Ypres. Still the men set to, and with their usual cheerfulness managed to get quite fit and decent in time.

The inspection duly took place on the St. Omer–Aire high road, and the companies marched past the C.-in-C. quite well just outside Racquinghem to stirring music provided by the band of the 10th D.C.L.I. Shortly after this the 10th D.C.L.I. were taken away from the Division, much to our sorrow and theirs, and as soon as this move had been ordered the R.E. were moved also to the neighbourhood of Hondeghem—quite decent billets, but scattered and not so pleasant as Racquinghem. Here the C.R.E. distinguished himself by laying the trail of a paper chase. He laid five false trails—the men tried only two and then tried a near-by estaminet, whilst the C.R.E., Adjutant, and R.S.M. waited patiently at the other end to award prizes to the winners.

Major Garforth not being able to return to the Division, Major S. H. Morgan was appointed to command the 430 Field Company, and Captain C. A. West, M.C., R.E., joined a little later as Adjutant.

Whilst at Hondeghem a great fight was made against an epidemic of skin disease amongst the animals, which had broken out as a result of Ypres mud and the lack of clippers. The drivers of the 432 Field Company had a particularly hard time, which, however, was turned to very useful account by teaching them what to look out for and how to avoid it on future occasions.

May we in passing ask how it was that horse-clipping machines were never included in mobilization store tables for a field company?

A short week here, however, and the Division was off again for Ypres—this time via an abominable rest camp at Westoutre and thence on a wet and particularly gloomy evening to Kruistraat, and camps which consisted of bits of bent and torn corrugated iron balanced over shell holes—430 Field Company were happy, however, as they managed to get into Ypres Post Office, a really good billet, whilst the other companies soon improved theirs, but that first night was a bad one. The new work was for the Division which was again in the line, and besides work in Ypres, of which all companies had a little, the 430 and 431 Field Companies worked on duckwalks, etc., leading up from Railway Wood to Kit and Kat and beyond into Zonnebeke. These were daily blown to pieces by the Boche and daily repaired by the sappers. The 432 similarly worked at Kit and Kat making timber platforms and placing 6-inch howitzers on them which were otherwise unable to fire owing to the mud; these were daily shelled off their platforms, and it was seldom that more than one howitzer in four was able to fire. Some shelters were also erected. The last and fiercest struggles of the third Battle of Ypres were now taking place, and as the month drew on and the weather grew worse, the shell fire increased to its greatest intensity since the battle commenced. Nevertheless the work was done, however many times destroyed, and cheerfully done at that, but there were few who did not heave a sigh of relief when the Division was once again taken out for a rest on the 22nd of November. The 430 Field Company and 431 Field Company went to their brigade group areas at Staple and Sylvestre-Cappel respectively, the 432 Field Company to Morbecque to complete the 66th Divisional Reinforcement Camp and the XXIInd Corps Schools. The companies worked on horse standings and additions to billets, and whilst they did so endeavoured to get the infantry to help themselves, as the sappers were sure not to remain out of the line long. This advice was taken to heart by some, but in many cases fell upon deaf ears, who were surprised to hear that a move back to the line was again impending on December 13th. Once again back into Ypres, but this time to quite good billets—the 430 Field Company at the Post Office again, the 431 Field Company in a camp just east of the Sally Port, the 432 Field Company in Baby Elephants near the Lille Gate. The work, too, was to prove equally attractive, and consisted in a new corps defence scheme which was required at once, as even then it was recognized that early the next year the Germans would be in a very strong position and all ground that had been gained in 1917 needed, therefore, good defences to enable us to keep the advantages gained, and if not, at least to keep untouched our original lines. The sector allotted to the 66th Divisional R.E. was from the Menin Road, through Anzac and Potsdam, to the Zonnebeke Road : the defence being one of posts of increasing size arranged in depth with a continuous line behind the belt of posts—the whole being wired in with double apron fences. The Maori Pioneer Battalion of the N.Z. Division undertook the wiring, the 66th Division Field Companies each took one-third of the front, and set to work on the posts; each post was to be provided with "pill-box" accommodation, in most cases by the conversion of German pill-boxes, but in some cases by new ones. Labour was provided by our own infantry. The posts and the wire very rapidly grew up, but the concrete work did not go quickly, largely because the weather very rapidly grew extremely cold and kept hard and frosty for a long period. The Boche pill-boxes were, however, dealt with to a certain extent, and the new system was quite well advanced when it was handed over to the 49th Divisional R.E. early in January, on the 66th Division taking over the front line on either side of the Broodseinde cross-roads. Christmas Day was bright and cold ; Ypres was covered with snow and looked almost pretty. The billets, thanks to the ruined state of Ypres, were cosy and warm with their ever-burning stoves, and the Christmas dinner was so abundant that one section at least decided to make two days of it. As regards work Christmas Day was only a half-holiday—but half or whole, every one enjoyed it very much. The Division having taken over the line again the companies' work was arranged so that the 430 and 431 Field Companies alternated between back area work around Ypres and frontline work on the left half sector north of the Broodseinde cross-roads. The 432 Field Company took over the right half sector of the front line and moved to a very nice Nissen Hut camp near Potijze; the other companies remained in the same billets. The weather kept very cold, but plentiful firewood, good huts, and plenty of work kept all ranks happy. The hours were the usual Ypres hours, *i. e.* before dawn to 1 or 2 o'clock and then the afternoon off to sleep or play. The front-line work was largely on new posts on the Broodseinde Ridge—new wire on the forward slope which, in spite of much sniping with field-guns, was done by day. This was easier and safer than doing it at night, when the enemy machine-guns would and did make any movement on the forward slope a dangerous matter; the field-guns of the Boche were nothing like as accurate as their machine-guns. Other work continued—with a tram-line—miles and miles of duck-walk, new and old—slab roads, and the hundred-and-one other things a field company has to do in such a place, the principal being drainage when the thaw came. The streams which formed the natural drains had long ago disappeared in the bombardment, and the land, except the sandy top of the ridge, was a mass of water-logged shell-holes. Some more concrete work was also done, and the services in Ypres included a very fine officers' club, several much-needed baths, and two new camps east of the Menin Gate. The shelling had also died down, and Ypres was rapidly becoming a nice, if dreary and dirty, sector; but as billets were good and work plentiful the companies were almost getting really to like Ypres, when in February the orders came to move back again. On the 6th the move started by brigade groups to an area of cold and desolate rest camps just west of Poperinghe. By the 10th the whole Division was clear of Ypres, and on the 16th and 17th the field companies were glad to entrain at Proven. The next day saw the companies detraining at Guillaucourt near Villers-Brettonneux, where, glorious to relate, it was warm and bright and the grass, unlike the salient, was green. There was no mud. The 430 Field Company settled down in Guillaucourt itself, the 431 Field Company settled much more luxuriously in the château of Le Quesnel, famous as Von Klück's most westerly headquarters, and the 432 Field Company found decent billets at Vauvillers. These villages were very comfortable, but slightly damaged by the 1916 Somme battle, the land but little cultivated and the inhabitants few; in fact, it was the last fringe of houses outside the desolation of the Somme.

It was ideal for troops at rest, however, and a week of fine weather quickly passed in games, paper-chases and smoking concerts (including quite a famous one at Vauvillers). A new battalion—1/5th Border Regiment—arrived to do duty as a Pioneer Battalion, and several officers, N.C.O.s and men of the field companies were sent to help and instruct them. As the month drew on the Division received its orders, and each company marched away eastward along the great St. Quentin Road with its affiliated Brigade of Infantry. A night was passed in a tent camp near Villers Carbonnel, and another night in hut camps near Vraignes. Thence the companies took over from their opposite numbers of the 24th Divisional R.E. about the 1st March: the 430 Field Company at Roisel, with a forward section near Templeux; 431 Field Company at Milieu Copse, with a forward section near Hargicourt; 432 Field Company at Montigny Farm, with two forward sections. The new sector was a large one, with all three infantry brigades in the line, and with little or no artillery. The R.E. work handed over included a golf course, an officers' club with garden, a very fine battalion officers' mess and a theatre, but the defences which every one wanted to see were difficult to find. The latter included an old and decayed outpost line—the same as was first taken up the year before—a poorly sited and made main line of resistance; a reserve or corps line with a good belt of wire, but the trenches 1 foot 6 inches deep; no deep dug-outs or other decent shelter, except at Templeux Quarries; no buried cables; no tramways, and roads in a very bad state of repair. Companies had two days before the C.R.E. and Divisional Staff arrived, and then after two more days spent in reconnaissance a new and necessary system of defence in depth was rapidly planned and started. Deep dug-outs were commenced for all the really necessary points, long lines of cable trench were begun, and the R.E.

and infantry were soon humming like bees at work. Thus began the fateful month of March. It was common knowledge that a big show was coming, but no one knew where; many thought in Champagne against the French, others that our line between St. Quentin and Arras would receive the blow. Anyhow companies knew they had only weeks or even days to do work which really would take months to do thoroughly. As the days passed the theatre of the coming attack became more obvious, and about fourteen days before it came it was fairly certain that the 66th Divisional sector would be in it. The speed of work was increased, the hours of the sappers and the infantry were lengthened, and surprisingly quickly a new and good main line of resistance was built up. It was never hoped to finish it, but a good attempt was made, and when the time came the new system proved the mainstay of the line. The last week of work in this sector was carried out under increased difficulties. Anxious to leave no stone unturned to defeat the enemy, should his attack fall on their part of the line, the Staff practised the Division nearly every night in manning its battle positions. Thus in addition to an increased amount of work by day, the sappers, like every one else, spent a large part of the night lying out at their alarm stations. Fortunately the weather remained marvellously good, and all ranks remained equally cheerful, certain of the result if they should really be attacked. Forty-eight hours before the actual attack a Boche N.C.O. deserted into the 66th Division area with this time definite news. Still the enemy remained so quiet and showed no signs of what he was doing that most did not believe it until about 4.0 a.m. on the 21st March the bombardment came down. Never even at Ypres had we heard the equal of this—never, not even when the Hindenburg Line was taken later in the year, was the sound so great or so overwhelming. Being now quite practised in alarm and battle positions the sappers turned out, only to find a mist so thick that they could not see a yard, and that the mist had a large percentage of gas in it, and nearer the front line an increasing quantity of high explosive.

The country in this sector is similar to that around Epéhy and Ronssoy, and is only just south of the sector occupied by the 42nd Division in May 1917—it is a land of high rolling chalk downs with long, narrow valleys, running east and west from ridges: such a ridge formed the main line of resistance. There are few streams, and the only military obstacles between the Hindenburg Line and the Somme are a number of sunken roads; imagine this open, almost treeless (except for a few copses) land all covered with a thick white mist, its valleys a mass of gas and mist, and the whole forward area heavily bombarded. The sappers in the forward billets and the company of the Pioneer Battalion there did extremely well during the day, but finally with the remains of the outpost line had to come back to the main line of resistance when the fog cleared about 1 p.m. The 430 and 431 Field Companies, less their forward sections, were used on the night of the 21st, and on the 22nd March to wire in the spitlocked Green Line from Bernes to Roisel; the 432 Field Company were used as infantry by Lieut.-Colonel G. C. Williams (the C.R.E. and appointed on the 19th to command temporarily the 199th Infantry Brigade); they were put in the line on the afternoon of the 21st, their forward sections remaining there.

Meantime the forward sections of all field companies had had some exciting experiences. The German barrage came down right along the line of the R.E. forward billets, which were about 1000 yards behind the front line. Gas was very thick, and respirators had to be worn from 4.30 till after 9 o'clock. All wires seemed to be cut at once, and no message was received at all at one forward post, which consisted of two sections of R.E. from the 431 and 432 Companies and a company of infantry. There was a large square space enclosed by high banks just by the billets, and this was defended until the middle of the day. The enemy got through on the left and used their machine-guns on the position from the rear, and our own shells were also dropping on the spot, but when the mist rose and the enemy could be seen driving in the line on the right flank, the infantry captain decided to defend a trench about 300 yards behind. Many men had been killed, but they must have done a lot of damage to the Boche. It was the first time that many of the sappers had really had a chance of getting their own back, and they were as happy as sandboys and full of fun, although at the time it didn't seem likely that they would ever get out of the place. The infantry captain, who was the last to leave the enclosure, was killed by a hand grenade, but the trench was held until the evening, when the sections again got in touch with the rest of the Division.

On the morning of the 22nd the mist was again repeated, and the bombardment was nearly as heavy. The enemy had penetrated a portion of the main line of resistance, but was nowhere through it, and throughout the day he was held on the Brown Line immediately behind the main line of resistance. During the late afternoon the 66th Division was ordered to withdraw through the 50th Division, which had come up to man the Green Line. This was done with several minor "scraps": the enemy advancing rapidly and in great numbers, quite like a football crowd on our heels. Each field company was now again concentrated, and after a hasty meal moved each with its brigade group into billets on the main road from Roisel to Péronne. But there was no rest here. The men were just lying down hoping for a peaceful night when orders were received for an immediate night march to the rear through Doingt and Péronne, thence out through the Faubourg de Paris and overland to Barleux. The main road here was one mass of lorries, guns, horses, and labour corps getting away; and now around the fires in amongst the ruins were ourselves trying to sleep in the cold and wet. A bit of breakfast at daybreak and a conference: result, sapper patrols on bicycles through Péronne to find out the situation, and sapper parties to all bridges to make certain that

66TH DIVL. R.E.

none were forgotten by the Corps troops detailed to destroy them. Each company found at least one uncared for, and when the patrols returned soon after with the news that the enemy was entering Péronne, these were blown, and just in time, at any rate in the case of the Biaches bridge. All the bridges the 66th Divisional R.E. blew were fully destroyed, but unluckily the Corps troops did not quite destroy the railway bridge into Péronne, and this added materially to the responsibilities of the defence, and gave one R.E. subaltern of the 66th Division an uncomfortable night with his men in a very gallant and partly successful attempt to fire and keep alight the bridge, whilst the enemy post at the other end did their best to stop them. The R.E. were now formed into part of a scratch battalion, and with the infantry lined the hastily organized defences from near Brie to Biaches along the west and south bank of the Somme. The enemy made several attempts to cross, and with field-guns, and especially with low-flying aeroplanes, made life exciting for everybody. Two days of successful defence found the men in very high spirits, but only to receive orders to go back again to the line Assevillers–Herbécourt, to conform to movements to the south and the very obvious enemy advance north of the Somme. This was quite a good line, but another break to the south moved us back again the next day through Becquincourt and Dompierre, and then past Foucaucourt to Proyart, to a line through Framerville and Vauvillers. A stand in each place, in which some of the R.E. assisted, was made, to cover the retirement and delay the enemy's advance. During this part of the retreat, parties of engineers were told off to set on fire the many huts, rest camps, hospitals, etc., that had been built along the main Amiens–St. Quentin road during the winter of 1917–18, and a heart-breaking task it was to see some of the better cared for Y.M.C.A. and Church Army huts that had served many a weary soldier as a haven of rest, thus sacrificed before the advancing enemy and sent up in flames. Vauvillers was lost next day, but a very gallant counter-attack was organized, and in spite of the enemy machine-guns was successful. Vauvillers was, however, exposed too greatly to the south, and the line had to be brought back to the railway east of Harbonnières. The counter-attack had, however, split up a big German concentration east of Vauvillers, and had thus amply repaid all. The Harbonnières line was good and held well, but although we did not know it the enemy had crossed the Somme behind us, and so before dawn next day we were hastily withdrawn and marched via Caix to Guillaucourt, and there lined the railway to the next village, facing this time north instead of east to meet the enemy on our flank. The enemy all too quickly occupied the high ground in our right rear, and, having machine-gunned us heavily, compelled the troops gradually to fall back again towards Amiens, and at nightfall a new line just east and to the south of Marcelcave was taken up. Here we spent a noisy night with plenty of 5·9's, and at dawn were attacked from the north; this attack we drove back quite

R

successfully, but an attack later in the day to the south of our line got through, and once again the line had to be swung back another mile or so. All the afternoon the enemy tried to get through us, but without avail, and as night drew on he ceased his attempts. Dawn again saw us at it, and to our horror our right flank again disappeared, causing another swing back. Thus the retreat went on, and by the afternoon of the 30th the line was in the outskirts of Hangard Wood, where at last we saw our friends the French on our right. At first we found it difficult to distinguish them from the enemy, but we quickly learnt the difference, and afterwards heard of their stands and difficulties to the south, in sympathy with which the last few days' retirement had taken place. This last afternoon it was decided to try and get back the enemy line about a mile to our east front, and the Division (which by now consisted of men and officers of nearly five or six divisions mixed) swung forward cheerfully to attack the enemy. We advanced a mile and got within a hundred yards of his guns and a great victory, only to be mauled by his light machine-guns on a slope from which to go back was the only course. As evening drew on a fresh brigade of Australians went through to try this counter-attack again, but like ourselves could not master that final hundred yards. This effort of men who had no rest from fighting for ten days—no wash and but little good food—will always stand out in the remembrance of all who were there and saw how the British soldier is really and truly never downhearted, and what is more, this attack stabilized the line and finally checked the enemy, who was unable to advance any farther. That night the Division was relieved, and the next day the men of the 66th Division were re-gathered into their units at Boves' Wood for the R.E. and Longeau for the infantry. At dusk the R.E. marched along the valley road, past endless lines of French lorries full of fresh troops, into desolate and almost abandoned Amiens, where billets were found in a Girls' High School, but recently a large hospital, and in consequence a very good billet indeed.

Although it was a retreat the R.E. and the whole Division may indeed be proud of what they had done—they had been ordered back before they came each time. The 432 Field Company had been infantry all the time, and had only detailed one or two small parties for R.E. work. Major Gracey, commanding it, was one of a very small number of officers of the Division who were in the fighting line from start to finish of the retreat. He more than earned the D.S.O. which he was subsequently awarded. The 430 and 431 Field Company sections in forward billets had done equally well on the first day, and like the other company, became infantry at Barleux. The Pioneer Battalion had proved once again its well-earned reputation as a first-class fighting battalion, and no one who was there will ever forget the bravery and leadership of its C.O., Lieut.-Colonel W. B. Little, D.S.O., M.C. Two nights in Amiens and once again the Division marched. The vehicles and mounted sections, it should be noted, had preceded the sappers throughout the retreat in a great convoy, and having been much bombed had safely arrived at Boves Wood. This time the 430 Field Company to bivouac at Saleul, and the other two field companies to poor and small billets at Floxicourt for one night, and then a train journey next day from Saleul to Longpré, followed by a long march to Ergnies, where all three companies found good billets in a nice clean little village very far from anywhere, but north of the Somme. Two days here and another move was made through St. Ricquier, the Divisional Headquarters, to Millancourt. Here the companies drew lots for billets, and the 432 Field Company drew the Château, whilst the other companies had to put up with farms. The weather remained good, and after much washing and cleaning, the companies were inspected by a new C.R.E.—Lieut.-Colonel G. J. P. Goodwin—who had just arrived to take the place of Lieut.-Colonel G. C. Williams, D.S.O., who had been promoted to command permanently the 199 Infantry Brigade.

Here at last we had leisure to count up our losses. Our best, both officers and men, had gone, amounting to about half of our original numbers. Many had been killed, others wounded; some of the latter were prisoners in enemy hands. But our leisure was not destined to last long. Speculation as to the future quickly became rife, and any hopes of a rest that may have existed were soon dispelled. Two companies were required at once for work under G.H.Q., and one only was to remain with the Division. The 430 Company was finally selected to remain, and the 431 and 432 Companies received orders to march the following morning. These last set out via St. Leger-les-Domarts and Vignaucourt, and after bivouacking for one night on the road reached Vaux-les-Amienois, and Villers Bocage respectively. The 481 Field Company billet was also the Advanced Headquarters of the Fourth Army, with whom Major Sharpe immediately got on very good terms in his own inimitable way. The 432 Field Company set up a nice little camp in two adjoining orchards, and were quite comfortable for a time. A few companies of Indians and Chinese labourers had preceded the 481 and 432 Companies by a few days, and were making efforts to dig a new line. It was the sappers' job to guide their efforts, site the new system as it grew, wire it, and see that the requirements of the M.G. Corps and gunners were properly worked in to the defence. The thing that mattered was time; hence every one was extremely busy, but the sappers had not so much to do until about the third day, when ample wiring materials were procured. Five or six days saw a big change; one line of trench was completed, another partially completed, and a large part of one belt of wire put up. A draft of officers and men arrived, and being added to the company's strength made every one feel very happy indeed, and a bit more like old times again. The only drawback to the camp at Villers Bocage was bombs. The enemy was not often over it, but one night he dropped a real big one in the middle of the camp. Luckily it was a delayed action fuze, and so, although it made a pretty big hole, did not damage any one. Just when the defences were beginning to take shape, and every one was getting into his stride with the actual work, the two companies once again had to move. Orders for the 432 Company came in at 2 p.m., and by 5 p.m. they were at Vignaucourt for the night. Next day they reached Longpré at 4 p.m., only to be told that they and the 431 Field Company, who had just come in after a nine hours' march, were just one day late, and that the rest of the Division had already gone north. After an uncomfortable and damp night in the goods shed at Longpré, the two companies were entrained before daylight the next day, and after a long but rapid journey, reached Wizernes near St. Omer that evening, and later on marched to Leuline and Audenthun, a few miles distant, where they were once more with their own Division, the C.R.E. and 430 Field Company being located at Cormette. Here the Division caught the prevailing "American Fever." Everybody dreamt of training Americans, though few took it seriously. For several days spare time was spent in reading awesome documents about their organization, and then, as before, orders came for 431 and 432 Field Companies to leave the Division. The 430 Field Company remained with the Division, and continued to do a great deal of good work in the way of camp services, etc., in various areas during May, June and July, when the 66th Division, which had been cut down to cadre establishment, was training an American Division, and later, in the same way, during the reconstruction of the 66th Division in the Gaillefontaine area in August and September. On April 26th, 431 and 432 Field Companies marched away from the Division. They were inspected by Lieut.-Colonel Goodwin, the new C.R.E., as they left, and this, though only the third time they had seen him, was destined to be the last, as when they finally rejoined the Division some five months later, he had left with a view to qualifying for the command of an infantry brigade. Their brief acquaintance with so capable a soldier was all too short.

The morning of April 27 saw these two companies encamped at Morbecque and Les Cinq Rues, near Staple respectively. In both cases the companies were under canvas, and the camps were "healthy" in all respects, though at Morbecque high-velocity enemy shells occasionally disturbed rest. Work was again upon new systems of defence which had been hastily laid out to meet the threatened attack on Hazebrouck, that important railway centre where the lines from Ypres, Armentières and Béthune all converge. British infantry in this case provided the necessary working parties, and the sappers were kept busy taping out trenches, wiring and revetting. As the system grew, the working area spread out to the north and south of Hazebrouck, and on the 11th of May the 431 Company moved to St. Marie-Cappel. It was at this time that the great fight for Kemmel was taking place, so the urgency, speed and energy required for the work can be gathered. Many French battalions passed by the camps, and very fine men they were—the pick, it was said, of the French army—men who had lately enjoyed a very well-earned rest since their defence of Verdun. As the situation to the

66TH DIVL. R.E.

east grew more settled, and the works grew more nearly complete, the centre of anxiety at headquarters moved a little further south, to the defence of the Lys Valley. And so both companies received orders to march, and met once more at Cohem—a delightful little village near Aire, where they spent one day together. The 431 Field Company then moved to Helfaut, and next day to Bilques; the 432 Field Company, after another day's wait at Cohem, moved to St. Quentin, a village on the outskirts of Aire. At St. Quentin the men were partially in billets and partially under canvas. The houses being all small, the billets were poor; but fine weather, closeness to Aire (which although badly damaged was not by any means abandoned), and a Corps swimming bath made up for this.

The 431 Field Company settled in a lovely wood and made a perfectly delightful camp. The work on this new line was similar in character to that on the line behind Hazebrouck, but included many more breastworks. The working parties were drawn from Chinese labour companies and a Portuguese brigade, which was a new and interesting experience for all ranks. The Chinese are excellent labourers, and there are few races who are their equals in this respect; they will do wonders if handled fairly and firmly, but they will do nothing at all if tasks are changed after work has begun; they have funny fancies; they want abundant water to wash in; they love hats and watches; they are kind and patient with birds which they always carry to their work, but they are barbarously cruel to other animals; they laugh and play like children, yet will refuse to work and go back to camp under an officer or N.C.O. as a protest against short rations. Their great amusement is gambling: it was no unusual thing for a man who had lost all his money to do two men's work the next day to make up his debts, whilst the creditor lay on the ground close by, smoking cigarettes and enjoying immensely his debtor's penance. The Portuguese are good workmen too. When once started upon a job they were "all out" to finish it in the shortest time possible. They always worked at lightning speed whenever "task work" was the order of the day. On one occasion it was reported "that cows during the night" had lifted the tape which had been put down by an R.E. officer the day before work was to start. The Portuguese soldier in his anxiety to be the first man to finish and get back to camp, could not wait for the R.E. officer to come and show him his task. Great was the surprise of that officer on finding an hour after work had begun, that a trench of marvellous trace had been completed to full section right across a wide field! The Portuguese like large shovels and to start work early. The sappers working with them had to be on the job at 5.0 a.m., but unlike the days spent at Ypres, by 9.30 or 10.0 a.m. the day's work was done, except for those detailed to trace out the work for the next day.

Thus with much hard work the summer passed pretty peacefully. 431 Field Company moved in June to Les Ciseaux, 432 Field Company in July to Mazinghem. Influenza laid nearly everybody low, but with luck and perseverance in nursing, very few left the units, and as July grew into August more drafts appeared, bringing the companies nearly up to strength again. Mazinghem and Les Ciseaux were both pretty little camps of tents and shelters; luckily situated away from larger camps, they escaped the bombs which were every night dropped in and around the area; the putting out of lights was a nuisance but necessary. The beginning of August saw the 432 Field Company moved into quite good billets in Molinghem, and later in the month the 431 Field Company to equally good billets at Steenbecque, where Captain Baines speedily built some very fine stables. At Molinghem the defences were part of the " Corps Lines," and were taken over from the 14th Division. Included in the work were some interesting schemes for the demolition, if need arose, of the steel works at Isbergues. Alarms and excursions did arise here, as the enemy was believed to be considering an attack; the two field companies became the nucleus of a defence force, and carried out some practices at manning trenches. Towards the end of the month the enemy, however, began to show signs of retiring, and so the 432 Field Company marched in heavy rain to some ruined houses between Hinges and Gonnehem. The work here was the defence by pill-boxes of the Hinges–Mt. Corbeau hill with the La Bassée Canal to the north of it. It was taken over from the 19th Division. It proved extremely interesting, and involved work on several monolithic and a number of block pill-boxes. By this time both companies were getting very tired of work on rear defences, especially as the enemy were known to be retreating and the British army advancing. The 66th Division had been almost forgotten, and so when orders were received on the 19th for a move south, the news was heartily welcomed and put fresh life into all ranks. The next day the two companies marched— 431 to Marles-les-Mines, and 432 to Boyaval : one a mining village and the other a quaint little country place. The next day, after a twenty-two mile march, they rejoined the now fully trained and ready 66th Division at Berlencourt and Denier, in the Le Cauroy area to the south-west of Arras. The 430 Field Company were at Sars-les-Bois, and many were the stories the companies had to tell each other after their four months apart. It should be mentioned here that the 66th Division had been out of the line continuously since April 2, and that during the summer two brigades had been entirely reorganized with troops from the near East. The South African Brigade had been incorporated to make up the full divisional establishment. The whole was under the command of a very distinguished and capable soldier, Major-General H. K. Bethell.

In the Le Cauroy area the field companies first became associated with the 9th Battalion Gloucester Regiment, which joined the Division as Pioneer Battalion under the command of Lieut.-Colonel E. P. Nares. The Gloucesters had had no previous experience of pioneer work, and so a party of one officer and four other ranks from each field company was sent to live with them for training. A similar number of infantry replaced the sappers in each field company.

66TH DIVL. R.E.

This arrangement lasted right throughout the final advance and last stages of fighting.

The field companies who had done little military training throughout the summer carried out here a series of route marches, and spent the time in polishing up and preparing for the line once more. But in spite of programmes of training and good resolutions, time was cut short, and a week saw them again on the move. The sappers this time went by train, and the mounted sections under Major Sharpe by road. The sappers detrained at Corbie in the dark, and marched in the night through the ruins of Corbie out into the valley of the Somme, where some little while after midnight the sappers found a short rest and a hot meal in the ruined farms of Vaire-sous-Corbie, which the mounted sections had reached the previous afternoon. An early breakfast after a short rest for the sappers, and the three companies marched again via Hamel and the road along the Somme through Cappy, which was remembered by the mounted sections, as it was here in March 1918 that the cellar of an estaminet was discovered, and at least one driver did the next stage in a pontoon and at a later date met his company commander. The companies were billeted next night in a German Divisional Headquarters but lately abandoned, and luxuriously hutted on the terraced hillside at Éclusier.

Two days' rest was allowed here, and spare time was spent in fishing for eels in the Somme Canal and eating them. Lieut.-Colonel O. S. Davies, D.S.O., promoted from the command of a field company in the 61st Division, joined the 66th Division as C.R.E. while resting here, in relief of Lieut.-Colonel Goodwin, who had left during the summer, as stated earlier. Lieut.-Colonel Davies had only a few hours in which to make the acquaintance of his companies when orders came for the whole of the divisional engineers to move east at once for work under the C.E. of the Corps.

The march up to the scene of operations took two days. The first day was a long trek and climb, and ended in huts and shelters in what was once Combles, but was now a desert with an occasional brick wall. The next day a long but interesting trek brought the column to Epéhy, where after some delay bivouacs were made amongst the ruins, and under a few sheets of corrugated iron, to the accompaniment of a 6-inch Howitzer Battery, also concealed among the ruins. The day following, work was commenced on the Epéhy–Basse Boulogne Road, only to be stopped that night. On the 5th October the companies marched to Villers-Faucon, where 480 Field Company billeted in the ruins of the village and 431 and 432 Field Companies in the ruined huts of a transport camp to the west of the village. The reason for this move was that the battle needed the whole Division as much as it needed sappers, and so companies were once more placed under their brigade groups. On October 6th and 7th, details from each field company were employed on reconnaissance work. The 430 Field Company repaired a dry weather track between Ronssoy and Guillemont Farm which was used for the advance of the Division. By the night of the 7th, each field company had moved up with its brigade group and bivouacked, some in dug-outs in the Hindenburg Line, others amongst the ruined houses in and about Bony, Gouy and Le Catelet.

The night of the 7th/8th was a busy one for those whose duty it was to issue orders. Before dawn on the 8th the Division had been launched to the attack. It was a new experience for many of the sappers.

First in the darkness to the north the guns of the Third Army flashed out, and then came those near at hand—a continuous line of flashes as far as one could see to north and south, and then the long line advanced towards the rising sun. The enemy reply was feeble, and the attack was a great success. The Division advanced past Beaurevoir to Serain, and captured many prisoners and guns. Towards evening some of the Division were lucky enough to witness the attack of a cavalry division, but unluckily the machine-gun fire was too heavy, and after a very pretty and unusual sight for us, they had to retire. Next day before dawn the attack was pushed on and reached a line east of Maretz. More prisoners and guns were taken. That evening, the 9th October, the 3rd Cavalry Division went through, and late on in the night we learnt that they had reached Reumont. At 3 a.m. on the 10th, the Division was up and moving on again, and took over the attack at Reumont from the cavalry. The infantry now deployed, and advanced against a fairly heavy fire from the enemy guns to the banks of the River Selle and the outskirts of Le Cateau.

During this great attack, which lasted five days, each field company had parties told off to follow up the attacking infantry closely, for the purpose of consolidating each successive position captured, but owing to the rapidity of the advance, and the almost complete breakdown of the enemy resistance, little consolidation work was necessary. The remainder of each field company followed up as closely as they were able, and found plenty of work to do, in filling mine craters, removing unexploded mine charges, and laying out tracks to avoid dangerous and impassable places. At Avelu and Maurois the roads were very badly cratered indeed, and all hands were called upon to take part in the work of rebuilding the roads and constructing deviations, without which further advance would have been impossible. The 480 Field Company found good billets with the 431 Field Company at Maurois, where they were comfortable except for the high velocity shells and the distance from the line; the 432 Field Company erected their bivouac sheets on a hill outside Reumont and the C.R.E. found a lucky cottage at the western end of Reumont—it was lucky in not being hit.

The next question was the crossing of the Selle—a fair-sized stream rapidly getting into flood, as rain had fallen in fair quantities during the last couple of days. The 480 Field Company had the first try, and unluckily believing the enemy not to be on the other bank, made a very gallant attempt to build by night a medium bridge near Montay. They were quickly disillusioned and had to give up the attempt. The next night the 432 Field Company made good with four foot-bridges near the same site. Several nights were now spent in reconnaissance of the Selle in and around Le Cateau : it is recorded that on one night the C.R.E. and one company commander carried a duckboard of large size down the main street and duly laid it in the gap in the centre of the town. The difficulties of reconnaissance were enhanced by placing too much confidence in certain optimistic reports regarding the exact position of the enemy, but any doubt that may have existed was finally cleared away in a minor attack carried out on the 16th. On the night of 17th/18th, the 431 and 432 Field Companies, assisted by parties of the 9th Gloucesters, placed eight foot-bridges across the Selle. These bridges consisted each of two petrol-tin rafts and three ten-foot trussed duck-walks, which were constructed in the companies' advanced billets and taken up on trestle wagons as near as possible to the river on the previous night. Having placed the bridges in position about midnight, the enemy wire on the far bank of the river was cut so as to clear the way for an attack timed to take place at dawn.

At dawn the South Africans attacked, protected by smoke and shell, and swept across the river up the steep slope the other side and into the railway cutting. Here, after a bloody fight, they climbed the other side and drove the enemy down the slope towards the River Richemont. Meanwhile another brigade of the Division had cleared Le Cateau itself and established a line on the eastern outskirts, linking up with the South African Brigade. After this action the 430 and 432 Field Companies erected trestle bridges in Le Cateau. The enemy before leaving had managed to drop the brick railway arch with its abutments and two steel girder bridges into the road to Bazuel. This completely blocked the eastern exit from Le Cateau, which was now a few hundred yards behind our line. Working parties from the three field companies and the 9th Gloucesters were immediately organized, and by dint of working through the night in four-hour reliefs and using explosives freely, the road was cleared for double traffic by the afternoon of the following day.

On the 20th the 66th Division went back to rest at Serain, but the R.E. remained at Le Cateau under the orders of the Corps. On the 21st the 430 Field Company and 9th Gloucesters moved into Le Cateau, in which, although damaged badly, they succeeded in finding some quite good and complete houses as billets. They were quite comfortable here, except for the high velocity shelling which continued at intervals every day for some time. The 431 Field Company built a bridge to carry lorries in Le Cateau, and completed it on the 22nd. On the 23rd the 18th Division continued the attack and swept forward over the River Richemont. The 431 and 432 Field Companies were detailed to follow up the field companies of the 18th Division and replace the light bridges that the latter had made over the Richemont river by bridges to take motor transport. This work was put in hand as soon as the situation was sufficiently clear on the 23rd and completed during the following days, three heavy trestle and crib-pier bridges in all being erected, over average spans of forty-five feet. On the 23rd the 431 and 432 Field Companies moved their wagons and horses into Le Cateau, and were very comfortably quartered in the damaged and ransacked, but waterproof, houses there. General Rawlinson, commanding the Fourth Army, came up to view the battlefield round Le Cateau, and congratulated the field companies on their work in bridging the Selle. Unfortunately these last battles had caused gaps in our ranks—notably, Lieutenant H. M. Davies, D.C.M., of the 430 Field Company, and Lieutenant K. Sinclair of the 432 Field Company were killed. Both officers had seen much service with the 42nd Division in the 428 and 429 Field Companies. Captain Panet of the 430 Company had also been wounded, and each company had lost several of their sappers and N.C.O.s. As soon as the bridging, etc., had been done the work slackened a little and became a matter of patching roads, improving billets and baths and erecting notice-boards (always an important matter in an advance). The rest was short, for on the 2nd of November the Division returned to Le Cateau, and preparations for another battle kept every one busy. On November 5 it opened, and, after much marching in rain and over bad roads through the edge of the Forêt de Mormal, the Division entered Landrécies on the heels of the infantry of the 25th Division, who had led the attack. The inhabitants—the first normal ones we had met—were overjoyed to see British soldiers. Their town was burning, but nevertheless they remembered the Corps of Sir Douglas Haig in 1914, and told us of the battle there then. Late that night—after saving the Boche prisoners from the fury of the inhabitants who came in a mob to get their blood—the companies turned in, in some cases into real beds, but at any rate in decent buildings. Many of the men were in the old barracks, and the rest in various houses in the old-fashioned streets. The next morning was spent in overhauling transport and readjusting loads. The 431 Field Company had two sections employed with an Army Troops Company repairing the old swing-bridge across the lock, the new girder-bridge having been dropped by the enemy. The afternoon saw the Division on the move again. Maroilles was reached that night in pitch darkness and drizzling rain.

The R.E. advance parties had done pretty well here, and companies soon got settled down to pretty good billets and sleep. The next day the companies left their brigade groups and went to Dompierres, Taisnières and Marbaix. At Marbaix that night Lieutenant Gotobed, in charge of the combined bridging equipment of the three field companies, which had been lent to the 25th Division for the battle, rejoined his company in an exhausted condition, after nearly seventy-two hours continuously in the saddle. He was restored to life with hot food and a sleep in the straw of the lofts at the farm in which the field company had found a billet. The next day the 432 Field Company left Marbaix and went to Le Petit Fuchay, there making two approaches to a pontoon-bridge erected by the 25th Division. That day the 66th Division had taken over the attack from the 25th Division, and on the 9th of November approached Avesnes. The enemy about midday having vanished, the South African Brigade was ordered up, and the 430 Field Company following them, reached Solre-le-Château late that night. Meanwhile the 431 Field Company had done excellent work on a dry weather diversion north of Avesnes, rendered necessary by the very good road demolition of the enemy, whilst the 432 Field Company, having completed additions and other work on the pontoon bridge at Le Petit Fuchay, had started a lorry bridge at the western entrance to Avesnes. This company also completed a bridge and its approaches on the Maubeuge–Avesnes Road. On the evening of the 9th both companies (431 and 432) were ordered forward, but, on account of work in hand, the order was countermanded until the next morning.

On the 10th, the works being completed, the 431 and 432 Field Companies marched to Solre-le-Chateau. The roads were in a fearful condition, cratered nearly every quarter of a mile, but nevertheless the horses pulled the vehicles over or round as no M.T. could. Invaluable work on the roads was done by the villagers, who were quickly available in large numbers. Arrived at Solre-le-Château on the evening of the 10th were two brigades of infantry, one of cavalry, one of R.F.A., three field companies of sappers, and certain other units. The whole field was under the command of Major-General H. K. Bethell—G.O.C. 66th Division—and became known as " Bethell's Force." As such these units formed an advanced guard to the Fourth Army, and were detached ready to move east in pursuit of the enemy with three days' supply of hard rations, carried by a specially organized Supply and Transport column.

On the morning of the 11th the march was resumed. The 430 and 432 moved with their brigade groups and reached Hestrud and Sivry respectively. The 431 Field Company remained at Solre-le-Château, where they had had a very lively evening on the 10th, due to the enemy shelling the railway station and blowing up an ammunition train.

Very much to every one's surprise came the armistice at 11 a.m. on the morning of the 11th. Rumour told of delegates crossing the line, but this was such an old story that hardly any one believed a word of it. Slowly it dawned on every one that this really was a cessation of hostilities. The air became electric. The habitually dull countenances blossomed out in beaming smiles. Nothing like it had been seen since 1914. The inhabitants of the country turned out and pressed the men into their houses. They gave bits of ribbon, turned out their best linen and their plate. They gave us what scanty food remained in their possession, and did everything in their power to make the atmosphere one of general rejoicing. This was, however, in Belgium, and therefore unlike their conduct in France, the enemy had left some cattle and fowls behind. So we were able to get eggs—a luxury we had not seen for a long time.

But all this did not stop work. The R.E. that day and the next built four bridges, removed many road mines and, being in a wooded area, cleared many miles of road across which trees had been felled by the Boche. The 430 Field Company had moved again on the 11th to Beaurieux. The 432 remained at Sivry in Belgium. On the 14th all three companies were concentrated in Solre-le-Château, and worked hard cleaning up for the march forward. The billets in this small market town were quite good, but not as nice as the farms at Sivry and Beaurieux. On the 16th the 432 marched to Montbliart and joined its infantry brigade group, marching forward on the 18th to Cerfontaine. The 430 moved to Montbliart, and thence on the 19th to Villers-deux-Eglises; meanwhile the 431 Field Company, remaining with its brigade group, moved to Philippeville. The weather here grew extremely cold and frosty, but otherwise delightful. The inhabitants were very obliging and the villages fairly comfortable, so all ranks quite enjoyed a rest.

The next moves commencing on the 23rd brought the companies as follows: 430 to Agimont, 431 to Waulsort, 432 to Miavoye. Waulsort is in the most beautiful part of the Meuse Valley, as is also Agimont, whilst Miavoye, a tiny village, lies in the hills some miles to the west. The billets were quite good, and the places, in spite of some wet weather, perfect. The work was little, though quite a number of small services were done. Several train-loads of material that the enemy had abandoned on the railway lines through the Meuse Valley were collected. After three pleasant weeks the companies were glad to cross the Meuse and march, 430 Field Company to Marche, 431 to Ciney, 432 to Huy. Marche and Ciney were small country market towns, but the field companies nevertheless had pretty good billets. Huy was a larger manufacturing town on the Meuse between Namur and Liège. In it the 432 Field Company had very fine billets in an abandoned draper's shop facing the river, with stoves and electric light, using the shop itself as a dining-room. The mounted section and N.C.O.s had an excellent empty house facing the river. At Ciney the 431 Field Company had a large old château, which made excellent billets and had nice grounds behind. At Marche the 430 Field Company was equally well off. As the Division was now in practically permanent billets, the field companies had a very busy time indeed until the end of January. Large supplies of timber, etc., were found, mostly in barges at or near Huy, and, together with supplies from Agimont, these were more than sufficient. At Christmas each company had a great feast, a general holiday and a visit from the C.R.E. It was their first peace Christmas, and they were very happy. As January wore on news came in about the scheme for demobilization. It turned our thoughts towards home. In the second week in February the 430 and 432 Companies, being reduced in numbers, marched in cold and snowy weather to Achêne and Taviet, and after three weeks, keeping warm by means of games in lack of fuel, all three companies

66TH DIVL. R.E.

gathered together at Ciney, less a section of the 432 Field Company still engaged on work at Andenne-Seilles.

The weather now grew warmer. Leave locally was freely given, and the men who had not been to Liège and other places, now got a turn. Many went to Namur and Brussels, but the lucky ones got demobilized. Time passed slowly but pleasantly, and on the 21st of May the cadre of the 430 Field Company left for home. It was afterwards decided to break up the other two field companies' cadres at Ciney. This was completed, and officers and men were sent to Marchienne-au-Pont, near Charleroi, on June 13 for demobilization.

By this time the greater part of the 66th Division had been broken up. Our pioneer battalion—the 9th Gloucesters—was an exception. This battalion was made up to strength with men who had time to serve, and in April left to join the 29th Division on the Rhine.

COMMANDING OFFICERS 66TH DIVISIONAL R.E.

C.R.E.:
    Lieut.-Colonel H. A. Fielding.
    „ „ F. G. Guggisberg, C.M.G., D.S.O., R.E.
    „ „ G. S. Knox, C.M.G., R.E.
    „ „ G. C. Williams, C.M.G., D.S.O., R.E.
    „ „ G. J. P. Goodwin, D.S.O., R.E.
    „ „ O. S. Davies, D.S.O.

Adjutant:
    Captain S. H. Morgan, M.C.
    „ C. A. West, M.C., R.E.
    „ S. Shaddock.
    „ F. J. Osborne, M.C.

430 Field Company, R.E.:
    Major E. C. Q. Henriques.
    „ W. M. Butler.
    „ W. Garforth, D.S.O., M.C., R.E.
    „ S. H. Morgan, M.C.

431 Field Company, R.E.:
    Major R. Carlyle.
    „ E. Davenport.
    „ P. H. Sharpe, M.C., R.E.

432 Field Company, R.E.:
    Major R. H. Joseph, D.S.O.
    „ E. C. Graves.
    „ R. L. Gracey, D.S.O.

66th Divisional Signal Company:
    Major J. S. Parsons, D.S.O.
    „ E. N. Eveleigh, D.S.O., R.E.
    „ A. L. McIntosh, M.C., R.E.

Pioneer Battalions.
    10th Battalion, D.C.L.I., March 1917 to November 1917.
        Lieut.-Colonel Ionides, D.S.O.
    1/5th Battalion, Border Regt., February 25, 1918 to April 1918.
        Lieut.-Colonel W. B. Little, D.S.O., M.C.
    9th Battalion, Gloucester Regt., September 21, 1918, to April 1919.
        Lieut.-Colonel E. P. Nares, M.C.

SUMMARY OF BRIDGING BY 66TH DIVISIONAL R.E.—
Oct.-Nov. 1918.

430 *Field Company, R.E.*

18. 10. 18.	Field Artillery Bridge. Le Cateau.
19. 10. 18.	Assisted 144 A. T. Company, R.E. with M.T. Bridge to replace above.
10. 11. 18.	M.T. Bridge. R. Thure—Hestrud (axle loads 9 tons dead).

431 *Field Company, R.E.*

17. 10. 18.	Four Floating Footbridges. R. Selle—north of Le Cateau.
22. 10. 18.	M.T. Bridge in Le Cateau (axle loads 9 tons dead).
25. 10. 18.	Two Bridges to carry 6" Howitzers. R. Richemont—east of Le Cateau.
12. 11. 18.	M.T. Bridge over road crater west of Solre-le-Chateau (axle loads 9 tons dead).

432 *Field Company, R.E.*

13. 10. 18.	Four Footbridges. R. Selle—south of Montay.
17. 10. 18.	Four Floating Footbridges. R. Selle—north of Le Cateau.
18. 10. 18.	Field Artillery Bridge. Le Cateau (45' 0" total span).
24. 10. 18.	Heavy Bridge to carry axle loads 20 tons (dead). R. Richemont—east of Le Cateau.
9/10. 11. 18.	M.T. Bridge at western entrance to Avesnes (axle loads 9 tons dead) (55' 0" total span).
9. 11. 18.	Field Artillery Bridge. Maubeuge–Avesnes Road.
11. 11. 18.	M.T. Bridge—eastern entrance to Solre-le-Château.
11. 11. 18.	Field Artillery Bridge on Clairfayts–Eppé Sauvage Road.

PART IX

A BRIEF NOTE ON THE THIRD LINE EAST LANCASHIRE ROYAL ENGINEERS

TOWARDS the middle of the year 1915, it was decided that, instead of sending drafts of reinforcements from the 66th Division to the 42nd Division, a third line should be formed which would train and provide drafts for the first and second lines, and which would also serve as a depot to which convalescent officers and men from overseas could return. The Third-line Depot, East Lancs. R.E. was therefore formed at the old Headquarters at Old Trafford in August of that year, Major R. Carlyle being appointed to the command. During the following month a move was made to Southport, the total strength at that time being about 1200, organized in three field companies and a signal company.

As a result of the decision to allow three field companies to a division instead of two, the 1/3rd East Lancs. Field Company had to be supplied by the Third-line Depot for the 42nd Division, and the 2/3rd Field Company for the 66th Division. The latter was sent to Crowborough to join its own division towards the end of 1915, and in January, 1916, the 1/3rd Field Company also went to Crowborough, and another field company, viz., the 3/3rd, was formed to keep the depot up to three field companies. Immediately after this, the Third-line Depot was moved from Southport to Carnarvon, where it joined, and became part of, the Western Command Reserve Training Centre, R.E., T.F., under the command of Colonel T. A. Cregan, R.E. This training centre subsequently consisted of nine field companies and three signal companies, comprising the third-line units of the West Lancs., East Lancs., and Welsh Divisional R.E. Later in 1916, the signal companies left and went to a Signal Service Training Centre; and later still, the organization of the field companies was altered, all three East Lancs. companies being combined, becoming the 435th (East Lancs.) Reserve Field Company, R.E., T.F. At the same time the title of the training centre was changed, and became the Western Group, Reserve Field Companies, R.E., T.F. Carnarvon proved to be an excellent centre for R.E. training; grounds for almost all forms of training were found conveniently near the town and camp. The earthworks ground, a field of forty-five acres, was rather farther away than one would have wished; and for firing the General Musketry Course it was necessary to go by train to either Aber or Pant Glas, although miniature ranges were available on the spot. With these two exceptions, everything was conveniently situated.

At first training was carried out separately by the various companies, but later the direction of training was centralized in three schools: the School of Military Training, the School of Military Engineering, and the School of Instruction in Mounted Duties. There is no question but that this arrangement brought about a great improvement in efficiency, and the reports of inspecting Generals were always commendatory. One report stated that the R.E. training being given at Carnarvon was superior to that in any other training centre in Great Britain at that time.

During the summer months the units were under canvas at Coed Helen, just outside the town, and were billeted during the winter. For the second winter the Schools of Military Training and Mounted Duties were moved to Bangor, as there was not sufficient billeting accommodation in Carnarvon. This meant that men were detached from their units during this portion of their training; but although one could have wished for a more compact arrangement, this worked quite well.

A great number of returned overseas officers and men came to Carnarvon from hospital in various stages of convalescence, and many of them were used on the administrative and instructional staffs. Thus, Captain D. E. Gough became Adjutant to the Commandant, and Sergt.-Major Thomas rendered invaluable service in the training of recruits, and became the mainstay of the Military Training School. Many other East Lancs. N.C.O.s were of great assistance, more especially in bridging, and in practically every branch of training we had some N.C.O.s acting as instructors. Although the majority of these men were far from fit, they all entered into their tasks with the greatest energy, and never tired of helping to devise new schemes to make the training more varied and more useful.

There were, of course, among the overseas men, many whose health was really badly broken down, and most of these were billeted separately in some schools, remaining there during the summer also instead of going into camp. In this way it was possible to give them a special diet, and to arrange light progressive training, so as to make them gradually fit to undertake ordinary training.

Carnarvon does not in itself provide much opportunity for amusement, and the units themselves had to organize entertainments of various kinds as a variation from that provided at the two picture houses of the town. While the signal companies were there, they could always be relied on to provide some very good talent for concerts, and one of the most successful concerts was that organized entirely by Corporal Nolan, who later became one of the star performers of the " Blue Birds " in the 42nd Division. Concerts were generally held in the Guildhall, and there was never any difficulty in borrowing this for such purposes. The people of the town were very good in that way, and always did all they could to help in making entertainments a success. During the summer it was of course possible to arrange sports, and this was done.

Although it was agreed that the work done at Carnarvon was of the highest order, with other Territorial R.E. Training Centres the

3RD LINE EAST LANCS. R.E.

Group was disbanded on the 31st December, 1917. By that date, the number of officers and men who had been trained there was greater than the total strength of the Royal Engineers at the outbreak of war. On disbandment of the Carnarvon Group, some of the officers and men under training went to the training centre at Monmouth, but the greater number went to Christchurch. Small parties were employed at Carnarvon for about three months, filling in earthworks and removing stores.

ROLL OF HONOUR

427TH FIELD COY. R.E.

Lieut. Eastwood, R. A.
,, Mackenzie, L. A.
,, Taunton, O. H., M.C.
2nd Lieut. Ainley, K. E. D.
,, Hunter, J. K.
,, Malcolm, W. N.
Sergt. Garstang, J. E.
,, Later, J. O.
,, Moss, H.
,, Nolan, J. W.
Corp. Sprosson, G.
2nd Corp. Abrahams, E.
,, Horne, W.
,, Tolson, H.
L.-Corp. Henderson, J. F.
,, Perkins, F.
,, Smith, E.
Sapper Bailey, E.
,, Bancroft, A.
,, Barlow, E.
,, Bettley, J. H.

Sapper Birkenshaw, F.
,, Bishop, T.
,, Bowker, A.
,, Broady, G. H.
,, Burke, F.
,, Burton, L.
,, Catterall, J.
,, Cawley, H.
,, Coglan, T.
,, Conway, T.
,, Dixon, R.
,, Dwyer, A.
,, Eastwood, H.
,, Farnworth, J.
,, Francis, F.
,, Giles, W. D.
,, Gloyne, P.
,, Greenhalgh, E. A.
,, Halliwell, G. N.
,, Hopkins, H. B. J.

Sapper Hulme, J.
,, Hurring, W.
,, Jennings, A.
,, Lee, H. A.
,, Leppard, P.
,, Loxley, E.
,, Maher, R.
,, Melville, H.
,, Mottram, W.
,, Owen, H.
,, Penny, A.
,, Probyn, H. A.
,, Ritchie, C.
,, Smith, H.
,, Wilkinson, W.
Driver Bird, C.
,, Bowker, T.
,, Lees, F. B.
,, Smith, J.
,, Wright, W.

428TH FIELD COY. R.E.

Capt. Carver, O. A.
Lieut. Bull, G. J. O.
2nd Lieut. Angus, R. B.
,, Saint, J. H.
,, Woods, B. H.
Sergt. Mellor, W.
Corp. Kerridge, W.
,, McLeavy, G.
,, Naylor, W.
,, Shaw, H.
2nd Corp. Goldstraw, R.
,, Wielding, T.
L.-Corp. Butterworth, J.
,, Brocklesby, E.
,, McQuinn, O.
,, Pickston, H. V.
,, Shaw, T. E.
,, Swift, H.
Sapper Atkinson, M.

Sapper Barlow, W.
,, Bradshaw, A.
,, Cooper, A.
,, Dunn, J.
,, Elliott, C. K.
,, Greenhalgh, H.
,, Gore, A.
,, Grimshaw, G. H.
,, Greenwood, W.
,, Hodge, W. R.
,, Harwood, J.
,, Hinsley, T.
,, Hampson, G.
,, Jackson, H.
,, Kelsall, J. H.
,, Knott, W.
,, McLeod, W.
,, Moor, H.
,, Moscrop, J. A.

Sapper Mountfield, H.
,, Nugent, J.
,, O'Donnell, F.
,, Palmer, J. E.
,, Potts, J.
,, Robinson, G.
,, Saunders, J.
,, Scott, J.
,, Staresmere, W.
,, Stephenson, F.
,, Warburton, H.
,, Ward, T. H.
,, Waterhouse, T.
Driver Bold, C. H.
,, Farmer, H.
,, Magee, J.
,, Taylor, J.
Trumpeter Brookes, W.

429TH FIELD COY. R.E.

Lieut. Chapman, D. C.
Sergt. Newton, J. L.
Corp. Hynes, W.
,, Mort, S. C.
L.-Corp. Machin, J.
,, Walker, G. H.
,, Wright, D.
Sapper Ashton, J.
,, Barraclough, F.
,, Baker, W. F.
,, Bates, S.
,, Carter, J. W.

Sapper Cooke, F.
,, Deedman, S. F.
,, Evans, J. T.
,, Flynn, J.
,, Galpine, H.
,, Hallon, J. W.
,, Holland, J.
,, Kershaw, G. R.
,, Mansfield, A.
,, McCannah, S.
,, Rooney, J.
,, Royles, J. H.

Sapper Scott, W.
,, Shaw, T. J.
,, Staveley, H.
,, Tomlinson, J.
,, Thompson, J. C.
,, Watson, H. H.
,, Wilkinson, W.
,, Williams, C.
,, Williams, R. C.
,, Yates, S.
Driver Jones, B.
,, Walker, A. W.

EAST LANCS. R.E. HISTORY

42ND DIVISIONAL SIGNAL COY. R.E.

Capt. Williamson, C. H., M.C.
Lieut. Moore, H. T. P., M.C.
Sergt. Fielding, J., M.M. (with Bar).
Corp. Ardis, J.
„ Kennedy, J.
L.-Corp. Couch, H., M.M.
„ Cox, R. S.
Shoeing-Smith Edwards, T.
Sapper Aitchison, E.
„ Broderick, J., D.C.M. (Serb. Silver Medal).
„ Dowd, H. W.
Sapper Garside, F.
„ Heap, C.
„ Heywood, A.
„ Higginbottom, G.
„ Humphreys, C. Y.
„ Jackson, F.
„ Latter, S.
„ Ling, A.
„ Lorimer, W. E.
„ Naylor, E. C.
„ Penson, C. W.
„ Poole, A.
„ Sheppard, F. W.
Sapper Sinclair, J.
„ Smith, J. W.
„ Walsh, J.
Pioneer Findlay, R.
„ Hall, E.
„ Law, J. W.
„ Richardson, J.
„ Sutcliffe, N.
Driver Bayley, T.
„ Hartley, W.
„ Lowe, J.
„ Maguire, J.

430TH FIELD COY. R.E.

Major Butler, W. M.
2nd Lieut. Cook, H. H.
„ Davies, H. M., D.C.M.
„ Shorto, H. M.
„ Smart, D. L.
Sergt. Hitchmough, R.
„ Lord, S. G.
„ Smith, W. S.
2nd Corp. Boardman, H.
„ Sturrock, G.
2nd Corp. Coackley, J.
„ Heath, E.
L.-Corp. Armstrong, J.
Sapper Axon, W.
„ Bevan, T.
„ Barker, T.
„ Crossley, S.
„ Hannah, A.
„ Houlden, A. E.
„ Keogh, F.
„ Kinsman, E.
Sapper McKinley, J.
„ Mitchell, S. J.
„ Nelson, E.
„ Nichols, F. C.
„ Paterson, T.
„ Reed, W.
„ Simpson, S. W.
„ Slater, A.
„ Taylor, H.
„ Townson, F.
Driver Hayes, H.

431ST FIELD COY. R.E.

Farr.-Sergt. Lloyd, H.
Sergt. Hibbard, R.
„ Yates, E. J.
2nd Corp. Davey, J.
„ Savage, P.
„ Wallwork, W. H.
L.-Corp. Neal, H. S.
„ Millhouse, A. R.
Sapper Adamson, L.
„ Armstrong, B.
„ Aspin, H.
„ Booth, J. E., M.M.
Sapper Blackburn, F.
„ Clarkson, E. H.
„ Coupe, H. W.
„ Coupe, J.
„ Darlington, W.
„ Dobson, E.
„ Duffy, T.
„ Ellis, A. L.
„ Gilbert, G.
„ Hill, H.
„ Jones, I. M.
„ Miller, J. P.
Sapper Oldham, H.
„ Palmer, G. F.
„ Peach, H.
„ Ray, J. A.
„ Rawcliffe, F.
„ Reeve, C.
„ Sixsmith, A.
„ Stevenson, H. H.
„ Webster, W. R.
Driver Lawton, J. G.
„ Pearson, A. J.
„ Taylor, W.

432ND FIELD COY. R.E.

Lieut. Sinclair, W.
Sergt. Aldcroft, E.
Corp. Shaw, T.
2nd Corp. Morrell, S.
„ Waterworth, H.
L.-Corp. Evans, J.
„ Harvey, F.
„ Hitchin, J.
„ Small, J.
Sapper Andrews, H.
„ Bailey, H. B.
„ Bramley, W.
„ Cheetham, S.
„ Dascombe, C. W.
Sapper Davis, C.
„ Draper, H.
„ East, H.
„ Field, G. (Ital. Bronze Medal).
„ Fletcher, H.
„ Gillett, J.
„ Hocking, J.
„ Hook, P.
„ Huddart, W.
„ Hughes, A., (Serb. Gold Medal).
„ Ingham, C. H.
„ Johnson, J. C.
Sapper Lord, H.
„ Marsden, S.
„ Meara, M.
„ Paylor, J.
„ Pride, F. N.
„ Read, A.
„ Rumsey, S. F.
„ Spivey, C.
„ Stearn, W. W.
„ Swanston, W.
„ Townsend, F.
„ Wilson, F.
Driver Hutchinson.

66TH DIVISIONAL SIGNAL COY. R.E.

2nd Lieut. Smith, F. R.
2nd Corp. Heywood, W.
„ Smith, A. H.
L.-Corp. Ludbrook, P. A., M.M.
„ Platt, R. C.
„ Roe, T. V.
Sapper Campbell, J.
„ Chantry, W.
„ Dunlop, A.
„ Hurley, G.
„ Kerr, R.
„ Luck, A. H.
Sapper Nutbrown, M. V.
„ Regan, E.
„ Trueblood, N.
Driver Burgess, J.
„ McNuff, H.
„ Simpson, E.

EAST LANCS. R.E. SERVING WITH OTHER UNITS

Sergt. Shaw, R.
L.-Corp. Beckett, F.
,, Henshaw, S.
Sapper Alker, L.
,, Armstrong, H.
,, Ashcroft, E.
,, Ashton, J.
,, Barrett, E.
,, Bishop, A.
,, Bradley, J.

Sapper Dickman, G. H.
,, Foster, J.
,, Frost, A.
,, Gee, B. J.
,, Hitchen, J
,, Holden, H.
,, Jackson, F.
,, Jones, W.
,, Kear, W.
,, King, E.

Sapper McCullough, G. H.
,, McQueen, J. W.
,, Pearson, H.
,, Robinson, H.
,, Scott, J. H.
,, Turton, H.
,, Wilson, W.
,, Wolstencroft.
,, Wroe, J.

HONOURS AND AWARDS
GRANTED TO OFFICERS AND MEN OF THE 42ND DIVISIONAL ROYAL ENGINEERS

Officers

D.S.O.
Lt.-Col. Mousley, J. H.
  ,,   Riddick, J. G.

Lt.-Col. Wells, L. F.

Major Johnson, S. G., M.C.

Brevet Lieut.-Colonel.
Lt.-Col. Wells, L. F., D.S.O.

O.B.E.
Capt. Broad, G. L.

M.C.
Major Entwistle, J.
Capt. Bateman, W. H.
  ,, Broad, G. L.
  ,, Horner, H.
  ,, Jones, C. E. T.
  ,, Newton, R. S.
  ,, Roberts, A. (with Bar).

Capt. Williamson, C. H.
Lieut. Brown, H. G.
  ,, Bogle, J. M. L.
  ,, Cameron, A.
  ,, Echlin, J. P.
  ,, Ellis, A. J.

Lieut. Fletcher, P.
  ,, Mellor, W. L.
  ,, Moore, H. T. P.
  ,, Osmaston, G. H.
  ,, Taunton, O. H.
2nd Lieut. Nicolson, J. F. H.

M.B.E.
Lieut. Morrey, P.

Foreign Decorations.
Capt. Allard, W. . . Croix-de-Guerre. (French.)
  ,, Echlin, J. P. . . Order of Crown of Italy.
  ,, Gracey, R. L. . . White Eagle 5th Class with Swords. (Serbian.)
Lt.-Col. Lawford, A. N. . Croix-de-Guerre. (Belgian.)
Major Riddick, J. G. . . Legion d'Honneur. (Croix de Chevalier.)
Capt. Roberts, A. . . Serbian Order. (White Eagle.)
Major Wells, L. F. . . Order of Karageorge 4th Class. (Serbian.)

Mentioned in Dispatches.
Lt.-Col. Tennant, S. L.
Major Forsyth, J. S.
  ,, Lawford, A. N.
  ,, Mousley, J. H.
  ,, Wells, L. F.

Capt. Riddick, J. G.
  ,, Jones, C. E. T.
  ,, Walker, A. N.
Lieut. Arkieson, J. E.
  ,, Eastwood, J. E.

Lieut. Sinclair, K.
  ,, Watkinson, A. S.
2nd Lieut. Angus, R. B.
  ,, Eastwood, R.
  ,, Entwistle, J.

Other Ranks

D.C.M.
R.S.M. Sowray, F. J.
C.S.M. Gray, W.
  ,, Davies, H. M.
  ,, Waterworth, W.
  ,, Wilcock, H.
C.Q.M.S. Williams, C.
Sergt. Hahn, A.
  ,, Needham, A.

Sergt. Mallalieu, J.
  ,, Pinder, H.
Corp. Cliff, L.
  ,, Kirkpatrick, D.
  ,, Moores, H. J.
2nd Corp. Williams, W.
Sapper Broderick, J.

Sapper Eachus, W.
  ,, Gourlay, A.
  ,, Jones, A.
  ,, Pollitt, G.
  ,, Smith, H.
  ,, Vick, E. H.
Pioneer Gray, A. S.

HONOURS AND AWARDS

M.M.

Sergt. Kinley, J.
,, Pinder, H.
,, Templeton, B.
Corp. Baldwin, A. L. (with Bar).
,, Brightmore, R.
,, Fielding, J.
,, Flaws, L. R.
,, Gregson, W.
,, Rhodes, T.
,, Roscoe, E.
,, Riding, T. E.

Corp. Pike, W.
,, Taylor, T. E.
2nd Corp. Duffy, J.
,, Hart, M.
,, Jones, J.
,, Thompson, J.
L.-Corp. Ashworth, R.
,, Butler, W. H.
,, Collins, W.
,, Jenkinson, W.
,, Mullaney, J.

L.-Corp. McEwan, F.
Sapper Bennett, J.
,, Johnson, F. E.
,, Jackson, R. C.
,, Rylance, J.
,, Tudor, W. G.
,, Walsh, J.
,, Williamson, J.
Pioneer Kirkham, J.
,, Phillips, H. H.
,, Reeder, R. H.

M.S.M.

R.S.M. Sowray, F. J.
C.S.M. Garnett, J. H.
C.Q.M.S. Gilt, H.
,, Young, A. J.

Sergt. Higgins, W.
,, Shimmin, W. H.
Corp. Eccles, S.
,, Whitehead, R. B.

2nd Corp. Folwell, A. T.
Sapper McGrath, J.
,, Rowlands, A.
,, Taylor, W. V.

Foreign Decorations.

Corp. Boyes, B. . . . Croix-de-Guerre. (Belgian.)
Sapper Broderick, J. . . Silver Medal. (Serbian.)
Driver Buckle, H. N. . Medaille d'Honneur. (French.)
Sapper Cottriall, J. . . Croix-de-Guerre. (Belgian.)
C.S.M. Cowsill, J. H. . ,, ,, ,,
Sergt. Ellwood, J. . . Medaille Militaire. (French.)
,, Garnett, J. H. . . Cross of Karageorge 1st Class. (Serbian.)
Sapper Hall, E. V. . . Silver Medal. (Serbian.)
L.-Corp. Hardman, W. H. . Croix-de-Guerre. (Belgian.)
Sergt. Harrison, R. . ,, ,, ,,
Sapper Hughes, A. . . Gold Medal. (Serbian.)
Sergt. Johnson, G. H. . Silver Star 2nd Class. (Serbian.)
Corp. Mills, J. . . . Croix-de-Guerre. (Belgian.)
Sapper Redfern, G. . . ,, ,, ,,
L.-Corp. Robinson, J. . ,, ,, ,,
Sergt. Robinson, W. O. . Silver Star. (Serbian.)
Sapper Rowlands, L . . Gold Medal. (Serbian.)
L.-Corp. Scanlon, G. . ,, ,, ,,
Corp. Scott, J. M. . . Croix-de-Guerre. (French.)
Sergt.-Instr. Sowray, F. J. . ,, ,, ,,
Sapper Spaven, R. J. . . ,, ,, (Belgian.)
Sergt. Waterworth, W. . ,, ,, (French.)
,, Watters, W. . . ,, ,, (Belgian.)
2nd Corp. West, F. . . ,, ,, ,,
Sergt. Woods, T. . . ,, ,, ,,

Mentioned in Dispatches.

C.S.M. Davies, H. M.
C.Q.M.S. Walker, P.
Sergt. Edge, T.
,, Law, D.
,, Lee.

Sergt. Johnson, G. F.
,, Waterworth, W.
Corp. Craig.
,, Kinley.
,, Nicol.

Corp. Patrick.
2nd Corp. Jervis.
L.-Corp. Lomax, S.
Sapper Broadbent, J. D.
,, Clayton, E.
,, Thompson, W.

66TH DIVISIONAL R.E.

Officers

D.S.O.

Major Garforth, W.

Major Gracey, R. L.

M.C.

Major Morgan, S. H.
,, Sharpe, P. H.
Capt. Hanton, W. A.
,, Kendall, J. F. H.

Lieut. Beaumont, W. S.
,, Brewerton, F. A.
,, Hovey, E. L.
,, Wilkie, J.

2nd Lieut. Dowdall, H.
,, Osborne, F. J.
,, Prosser, R. M.
,, Struthers, R. A.

Foreign Decoration.

Major Sharpe, P. H. . . Croix-de-Guerre. (Belgian.)

Mentioned in Dispatches.

Major Garforth, W.
,, Gracey, R. L.

Major Morgan, S. H.
Lieut. Beaumont, W. S.

Lieut. Hovey, E. L.
,, Price, J. L.

Other Ranks

D.C.M.

C.S.M. Williams, F.
Sergt. Bramwell.

Sergt. Hardesty, B.

Sergt. Hulme, B.

M.M.

Sergt. Aldridge, R.
," Apsden, J. R.
," Barker, S.
," Evans, D. L. (with Bar).
," Fotheringham, F. (with 2 Bars).
," Hulme, B.
," Hulse, G.
," Mageehan, H.
," Walton, B.
," Woulds, H.
Corp. Ashworth, J.
," Cooper, W. H.
," Corson, J.
," Daggett, W.
," Owens, F.
," Robinson, P. (with Bar).

Corp. Siddall, W.
," Wolstenholme.
," Waller, P.
2nd Corp. Bell, T.
," Collier, J. C.
," Chapman, F.
," Dignam, A.
," Fairhurst, W.
," Marriott.
," Price, J. A.
," Schofield, A.
," Schofield, F.
L.-Corp. Clough, R. C.
," Ludbrook, P. A.
," McLean, J. G.
," McMillan, W.

L.-Corp. Wilson, W.
Sapper Booth, E.
," Booth, J. E.
," Childs, M. G.
," Cleary, J.
," Conolly, J. E.
," Crowley, P.
," Holthan, W.
," Jones, E.
," Kennerley, J.
," Moody, B. R.
," Phythian, A. V.
," Robb, W. M.
," Shaw, H.
," Smith, C.
," Turner, E.

M.S.M.

C.S.M. Armstrong, W.
C.Q.M.S. Gardener, F. W.
Farr.-Sergt. Pickstock, S.
Sergt. Byron, A.

Sergt. Malone, P. J.
," Tootell, R. C.
," Williams, F.

Sapper Brideson, J.
," Conolly, J. E.
Driver Bradley, J.

Foreign Decorations.

Sapper Feild, G. . . . Bronze Medal for Military Valour. (Italian.)
Sergt. Hankinson, W. H. . Medaille Militaire. (French.)
," Harrison, J. . . . Croix-de-Guerre. (Belgian.)
C.S.M. Leak, C. E. . .
2nd Corp. Marriott . . Croix-de-Virtute Militara. (Roumanian.)
Sapper Turner, E. . . Croix-de-Guerre. (Belgian.)

Mentioned in Dispatches.

C.Q.M.S. Kay, A.
Sergt. Fawcett, E.
," Hankinson, W. H.

Corp. Baron, T. L.
," Hammond, J. C.
," Wolstenholme.

2nd Corp. Price, J. A.
Sapper Lee, B.
," Maclagan, N. T.

www.ingramcontent.com/pod-product-compliance
Lightning Source LLC
Chambersburg PA
CBHW022002160426
43197CB00007B/228